THE POTENTIAL FOR REFORM
OF
CRIMINAL JUSTICE

Other books in this series:

Volume III. Sage Criminal Justice System Annuals

THE POTENTIAL FOR REFORM
OF
CRIMINAL JUSTICE

HERBERT JACOB, *Editor*

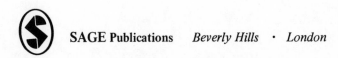

SAGE Publications   *Beverly Hills   ·   London*

For information address:

SAGE PUBLICATIONS, INC.
275 South Beverly Drive
Beverly Hills, California 90212

SAGE PUBLICATIONS LTD
St George's House / 44 Hatton Garden
London EC1N 8ER

Printed in the United States of America

International Standard Book Number 0-8039-0219-0

Library of Congress Catalog Card No. 73-77871

FIRST PRINTING

CONTENTS

ABOUT THE AUTHORS

CARL BAAR has taught at Cornell University and the University of Michigan. He received his Ph.D. from the University of Chicago and is a graduate of the Institute for Court Management. He is editor of *The Justice System Journal*, and is currently completing a book on state judicial budgetary processes and the separation of powers.

EGON BITTNER is the Harry Coplan Professor in the Social Sciences at Brandeis University. He is the author of *The Function of the Police in Modern Society*, and several articles about the police which have appeared in various scholarly publications.

HERBERT JACOB is Professor of Political Science at Northwestern University. He has also taught at Tulane University and the University of Wisconsin at Madison, and has been a Fellow at the Center for Advanced Study in the Behavioral Sciences. His publications include *Justice in America* and *Urban Justice*. He is presently completing a co-authored study of plea bargaining and the felony disposition process in three large American cities entitled *Felonious Justice* (forthcoming, 1976).

LUCINDA LONG is Assistant Professor of Political Science at Montclair State College, and a Ph.D. candidate at Johns Hopkins University. She has published in various journals, including *The New Republic* and *Court*. Her special interests are judicial process, public administration, and urban politics.

JOHN VAN MAANEN is Assistant Professor at the Sloan School of Management of the Massachusetts Institute of Technology, and Organizational Behavior Consultant for National Training and Development Service, Washington, D.C. He received his Ph.D. from the Graduate School of Administration at the University of California at Irvine in 1972. He is the author of *The Process of Program Evaluation* (1973), and a contributor to various books and journals. His research interests include adaptation of individuals to organizations, work and motivation, and organizational ethnography.

LYNN M. MATHER is Instructor of Government at Dartmouth College, and Director of the Dartmouth-MIT Urban Studies Program. She is currently completing her Ph.D. in political science at the University of California at Irvine. Her major interests are in legal processes, the administration of criminal justice, women and law, and urban politics.

FRANK L. MORRIS is Associate Professor of Political Science and Urban Affairs at Northwestern University. He received his Ph.D. from Massachusetts Institute of Technology, and has held various government positions in the Department of State, Agency for International Development, and Department of Housing and Urban Development. He has written extensively on Blacks and urban bureaucracy and prison reform. His current research involves a study of Black voting participation in the United States.

RAYMOND T. NIMMER is a Research Attorney for the American Bar Association, and Project Director for various American Bar Foundation studies, including public drunkenness and the criminal law, federal criminal courts omnibus hearing, and delay in the courts. He received his J.D. from Valparaiso University School of Law in 1968. His publications include *2,000,000 Unnecessary Arrests* (1971), *The Omnibus Hearing: An Experiment in Relieving Inefficiency, Unfairness and Judicial Delay* (1972), *Alternative Forms of Prosecution* (forthcoming), *Court Delay and the Process of Reform* (forthcoming), and several articles in various law journals.

ELINOR OSTROM is Associate Professor of Political Science and a participant in the Workshop for Political Theory and Policy Analysis at Indiana University. She has published numerous articles in various journals and books on metropolitan organization, the delivery of public services, and social research methodology.

ANTHONY PLATT is Assistant Professor of Criminology at the University of California at Berkeley, and a member of the Union of Radical Criminologists. He is the author of *The Child Savers, The Politics of Riot Commissions,* and *Policing America.*

RANDI POLLOCK received her Bachelor of Arts degree in Criminology with honors from the University of California at Berkeley in 1971. She is graduating in 1974 from Hastings College of Law, and will pursue a career in the area of criminal defense.

WESLEY G. SKOGAN is Assistant Professor of Political Science at Northwestern University where he received his Ph.D. in 1971. He has contributed articles to various books and journals, including *Social Science Quarterly* and *Urban Affairs Quarterly.* He is currently working on a book on the impact of the growth of the city upon the development of the local justice system in Chicago from 1840-1970. During 1974-75 he will be a Visiting Scholar at the National Institute of Law Enforcement and Criminal Justice in Washington, D.C.

DENNIS C. SMITH is Assistant Professor of Public Administration at the Graduate School of Public Administration of New York University. He was co-director with Elinor Ostrom and Roger B. Parks of the study of institutional arrangements and the St. Louis police which supplied the basis for the study reported in this volume. His research interests include urban politics and administration, public policy analysis, and public administration and organization theory.

Chapter 1

INTRODUCTION

HERBERT JACOB

The "war on crime" has captured enormous public attention in recent years. Just as the Johnson Administration sought to end poverty with massive infusions of public moneys into welfare programs, so the Nixon Administration has sought to conquer crime with novel programs and huge expenditures. The OEO was the symbol of the Johnson policy thrust; LEAA has been the symbol of the Nixon Administration's domestic policy. Both administrations attacked the short-comings they saw in American society with naive enthusiams. The Johnson Administration promised an end to poverty within a decade; the Nixon Administration promised dramatic declines in crime rates and a return to safe streets and homes.

It did not take long for detached observers and political critics to discover the absurdity of the Johnsonian promise. The large, new programs did little to reduce poverty and were accompanied by increased unrest in large cities where many of the poor lived. Before the decade was out, the new programs were being dismembered and their funds diverted to other causes. The same fate is likely to ensnare the crime control programs of LEAA. Little progress has been made in reducing crime. The boldest claim for the new programs is that they have slowed the growth of crime, although there is little evidence that the administration's programs caused the flattening in the crime rate curve. Just as with poverty, we possess no sure knowledge about the genesis of crime or about the effects of social intervention, in this case by police, judicial, and penal institutions.

One of the byproducts of the popular and governmental concern with crime has been a substantial increase in scholarly attention to crime and crime control agencies. This volume presents some of that work, much of it by a new generation of scholars. It illustrates how little we know and suggests how seriously awry is the direction of many new programs.

Three of the papers deal with the police, the agency to which most of the LEAA dollars have gone. Much of the drift of the new police reforms has been in the direction of requiring more formal training for policemen, recruiting only among college graduates, equipping them with fancier weapons and more sophisticated technology, and simply increasing their numbers. Egon Bittner's paper implies that most of these reforms are misdirected because they misunderstand what the police function is. It is not to be a social worker or ambulance attendant or superclerk, although much of a policeman's time is spent in doing things which resemble these other functionaries. Bittner argues that the real police function is to take emergency action when no one else can save the situation. In those cases the policeman alone has the authority to act, with force if necessary. No one may question his actions. His authority is certainly awesome, but it is not the sort that can be improved with technology or with college courses in criminology or police science.

Dennis Smith and Elinor Ostrom show that this is in fact the case. Examining a large number of police departments in the metropolitan St. Louis area, they find that the amount of training and college schooling is not related to more firm adherence to legal principles, nor is it related to public perceptions of the quality of their police. Requiring a college degree may simplify the screening process for police departments by disqualifying some applicants, but it is unlikely to improve police performance.

The reasons for the failure to improve police performance become clear in John Van Manem's picturesque description of the training and socialization process of the police in a large city. Formal training in the police academy is generally assessed as useless by policemen. The real training occurs on the streets and it often promotes norms which the formal training ignored or repudiated. For instance, while the formal training in the police academy emphasized legal norms, on-the-street experiences quickly taught recruits that they had to lie about factual descriptions of events in order to protect themselves against outside criticism. As Westley (1967) and Rubenstein (1973) had shown earlier, policemen work in such an incredible web of rules that all of them must sometimes violate some of the regulations and therefore are subject to disciplinary action. To protect themselves against such a contingency, policemen engage in a gigantic conspiracy against the outside world and cover up for each other. That conspiracy is deeply imbedded in the norms and work routines of policemen. It cannot be significantly altered by police science courses or by recruiting college graduates. That also means that civilian review of police activities is bound to arouse frantic opposition by the police; even in-house investigatory agencies will usually fail to penetrate the protective wall that patrolmen have built around themselves. Exceptional efforts to punish unusual instances of police brutality may bring the removal of a handful of men from one department or another, but the general tenor of policing is likely to remain unaffected by such activities. At the same time, Van Manem's description of police work, when added to Westley's and Rubenstein's, shows how fruitless the better equipment and technology are likely to be. Most crime occurs in private places out of the sight of policemen. They may catch the burglar if they stumble across him as he is making his escape. But except for the lucky encounter, arrests are unlikely. Even criminals who pursue their crimes at more predictable sites—such as drug traffickers—are infrequently apprehended except by actions which often violate legal norms, such as warrants based on unconfirmed information, or illegal searches, or evidence planted on people whom the police believe to be guilty but who are not engaged in crime at the moment. As Rubenstein puts it: "The police have been given an impossible responsibility. They cannot prevent crime altogether, and whatever amount of crime they actually do prevent by their presence on the street cannot be demonstrated" (Rubenstein, 1973: 368).

The courts to which the police bring suspects are perhaps even less well understood. As Wesley Skogan's paper makes clear, congestion and the various organizational responses to it are not new phenomena. The diffusion patterns of innovation which are the subject of Lucinda Long's paper show that there is no simple recipe for reform. But even when a reform is adopted and implemented, its consequences are often quite different than anticipated. The American Bar Association's Omnibus Hearing Plan was supposed to reduce court delay; instead it increased it, as Raymond Nimmer shows. That reform simply added another occasion for everyone to appear in court, but it did not increase the incentive for expeditious handling of cases. A simple edict to hurry up is unlikely to be heeded as long as delay is caused by defendants' unwillingness to speed their possible incarceration (if they are on bail), or by defendants' delay in paying their attorneys (who in turn are reluctant to proceed until they have received their fees), or witnesses' neglect to come to court on the day of the trial, or the failure of the prosecutor to be prepared on the trial day because he had other cases to attend to. The adjudicatory process is far more complex than many reformers assume.

Indeed, we need to stop thinking about trial courts as if they were institutions reflecting the will of a single individual, the judge. Trial courts are small organizations; the decisions which flow from them reflect their organizational structure, their goals, the incentives which govern the participants, the communication patterns that are established, and their work routines. Trial courts vary along these dimensions within a single city and even more so between cities. The relationships between judges, prosecutors, and defense counsel determine to a considerable degree the outcome of cases. A plea bargain may be accepted in one courtroom because the prosecutor and defense attorney know and trust each other and understand the preferences of their judge. In another courtroom, a plea bargain cannot be worked out because the prosecutor and defense attorney are strangers to each other or because they must work before a judge whom they do not know. Furthermore, cases are settled in the context of a busy docket. In one courtroom, a plea may be promoted because the judge and prosecutor are in the midst of a jury trial on another case or because it is the end of the month and time to boost disposition statistics. In another courtroom or on another day, no one will press for a plea because there is time to hold a trial or because disposition statistics look all right for the moment.

The conditions surrounding plea bargains are analyzed by Lynn Mather; the effect of the process on public defenders is examined by Anthony Platt and Randi Pollock. The results of their investigations, and those by Greenwood et al. (1973) and Taylor et al. (1972), show that the consequences of using public defenders to represent the poor are complex and unclear. On the one hand, public defenders are an integral part of the court system. When they are perceived as uncooperative they are subject to more day-to-day discipline by judges than private attorneys might be. However, many criminal defendants are represented by attorneys with a high volume of cases who are in a somewhat similar position as the public defender vis-á-vis the judge. Nevertheless, public defenders have been accused of using plea bargains more frequently than private attorneys. But Platt and Pollock show that lawyers come to a public defender office like that in Oakland in order to improve their trial skills. Many also have an ideological commitment to defend the underdog. That commitment is quickly turned to cynicism as the young public defender confronts a court system that demands a high guilty plea rate.

Mather indicates that public defenders and private attorneys weigh the same elements of a case to determine whether to go to trial. But she suggests that unique situational factors are added for private attorneys. The fee may affect the private attorney's propensity to plea bargain. On the one hand, it provides an incentive for him to avoid trial as his collectable fee is often no greater for a bench or jury trial than for a negotiated plea. On the other hand, the defendant may be more willing to listen to his attorney when he is paying for the advice than when it is free (Casper, 1972).

The statistical studies of dispositions reflect this unclear situation. Greenwood et al. (1973: 48, 53) show that in Los Angeles robbery and burglary cases, private attorneys and public defenders went to trial in the same proportion of cases.[1] Taylor et al. (1972: 18-20) come to the same conclusions from their analysis of the disposition of felony cases in San Diego and Denver. Thus we are confronted with somewhat different conclusions from micro and macro analyses. The micro analysis suggests that somewhat different incentives and constraints operate on private attorneys than on public defenders, but the macro analysis of case disposition demonstrates that those differences do not persist over a large number of cases when prior record, bail/jail status, and offense charged are held constant.

The activity of the police and the courts may be thought of as a screening process through which recruits for the state's penal institutions are selected. That screening process is supposed to differentiate between the innocent and the guilty, and among the guilty should make those distinctions which will optimize the deterrent effect of the sanctions imposed and maximize the rehabilitation potential of the convicted defendants. Much has been written recently about variations in sentences given by judges, but there is little understanding of the relationship between the sentence, the court participants, and the defendant's fate. In most jurisdictions, the actual number of years a defendant must serve depends on the standard discount rate applied to all sentences by the parole board and on the man's record in prison. The sentence handed down by the judge sets only the maximum period of incarceration; very few prisoners serve the whole period. When several separate sentences are imposed on a prisoner for distinct crimes, they usually are served concurrently. Prison authorities are concerned with the size of their inmate population, and releases are in part the consequence of admissions.

My own research suggests that sentences serve important symbolic functions for the prosecuting attorney and defense attorney that have nothing to do with the fate of the defendant. For both prosecutor and defense attorney it indicates an authoritative affirmation or denial of their evaluation of the case and their handling of it. A long sentence is regarded as a significant victory by the prosecution team regardless of how long the *actual* sentence will be; it is something to be talked about back in the office. A relatively lenient sentence provides positive support to the defense attorney because it implies approval of his handling of the case by the judge and because it can also be used to persuade his clients of the attorney's effectiveness in pressing their cause.

We know little about what makes prison experience rehabilitative except that rehabilitation does not occur frequently. Nor do we know much about its deterrent effect. One clue as to why both are true is contained in Greenwood's study. It shows that severe prison sentences are reserved for prisoners with substantial prior records. Such prisoners are the defendants most likely to be committed to a career of crime; they are the hardest to resocialize. Moreover, severe sentences to such prisoners do not even have a general deterrent effect, because the ordinary public easily differentiates itself from these most deviant cases.

Frank Morris examines another element of prison life that may be related to rehabilitation; the manner in which Black prisoners are discriminated against behind prison walls. He shows that those prisoners who maintain links to the outside world through membership in organizations that the prison authorities perceive as militant are systematically treated worse than those prisoners who keep their noses clean and keep themselves clear of such associations. There is much to suggest that such outside organizations may be substantial aids in rehabilitating criminals who are just embarking on a career of crime. The systematic suppression of such links undermines that role. It is nevertheless pursued because prison authorities fear these organizations as rivals to their own authority.

Observers of American justice have increasingly viewed the police, courts, and prison institutions as interrelated elements of a single justice system. They are not independent structures; they do not operate in isolation from each other. Change in one part of the system produces responses elsewhere; often those responses have been unanticipated and undesired. However, Carl Baar warns that there is a significant difference between conceptualizing these institutions as a single system and treating them as one when considering policy changes. Focusing on the unique contribution that courts may make in legitimizing the application of sanctions through independent and impartial application of law, Baar suggests that trial courts must not simply respond to the pressures of police and prison authorities. On the contrary, to persist as courts, trial courts must impose their own standards on the other elements of the criminal justice system.

Each of the papers in this volume makes a substantial and provocative contribution to our understanding of American criminal justice. Nevertheless, they represent only a small beginning to a very large and long task. I hope our endeavors can survive the war on crime.

NOTE

1. Their findings apply only to defendants with no prior record and defendants with one or two prior convictions and 90 days in jail.

REFERENCES

CASPER, J. (1972) American Criminal Justice. Englewood Cliffs, N.J.: Prentice-Hall.
GREENWOOD, P., S. WILDHORN, E. POGGIO, M. STRUMWASSER, and P. deLEON (1973) Prosecution of Adult Felony Defendants in Los Angeles: A Policy Prospective. Santa Monica, Calif.: Rand Corp.
RUBENSTEIN, J. (1973) City Police. New York: Farrar, Straus, Giroux.
TAYLOR, J., T. STANLEY, B. de FLORIO, and L. SEEKAMP (1972) A Comparison of Counsel for Felony Defendants. Arlington, Va.: Institute for Defense Analysis. (Available from National Technical Information Service, Springfield, Va. as PB 209626 and PB 209627.)
WESTLEY, W. A. (1967) Violence and the Police. Cambridge, Mass.: MIT Press.

Chapter 2

FLORENCE NIGHTINGALE IN PURSUIT OF WILLIE SUTTON: A THEORY OF THE POLICE

EGON BITTNER

Among the institutions of modern government the police occupies a position of special interest: it is at once the best known and the least understood. Best known, because even minimally competent members of society are aware of its existence, are able to invoke the services it provides with remarkable competence, and know how to conduct themselves in its presence. How and how well the police is known, and the ways it matters in the lives of people, vary considerably over the spectrum of social inequality. But to imagine people who are not at all touched by the police one must conjure images of virtually complete isolation or of enormous wealth and power. Least understood, because when people are called upon to explain on what terms and to what ends police service is furnished they are unable to go beyond the most superficial and misleading commonplace which, moreover, is totally unrelated to the inter- actional skill that manifestly informs their dealings with policemen. What is true of people generally is true of the police as well. Policemen have not succeeded in

AUTHOR'S NOTE: A shorter version of this paper was delivered as the August Backus Memorial Address at the University of Wisconsin Law School in 1971. I am deeply indebted to Professor Herman Goldstein for his mentorship in all matters concerning the police. But he is, of course, in no way responsible for my errors.

Florence Nightingale is the heroic protagonist of modern nursing; Willie Sutton, for those who are too young to remember, was in his days a notorious thief.

formulating a justification of their existence that would recognizably relate to what they actually do (not counting those activities the doing of which they disavow or condemn). The situation is not unlike that of a person who, asked to explain how he speaks, offers an account which, while itself linguistically in perfect order, does not even come close to doing justice to the skill involved in producing the utterance.

In this paper I propose to explain the function of the police by drawing attention to what their existence makes available in society that, all things being equal, would not be otherwise available, and by showing how all that policemen are called upon to do falls into place when considered in relationship to it. My thesis is that police are empowered and required to impose or, as the case may be, coerce a provisional solution upon emergent problems without having to brook or defer to opposition of any kind, and that further, their competence to intervene extends to every kind of emergency, without any exceptions whatever. This and this alone is what the existence of the police uniquely provides, and it is on this basis that they may be required to do the work of thief-catchers and of nurses, depending on the occasion. And while the *chances* that a policeman will recognize any problem as properly his business depend on some external regulation, on certain structured social interest, and on historically established patterns of responsiveness and responsibility, every stricture arising out of these factors is defeasible in every *specific case* of police work. This means that the appropriateness of police action is primarily determined with regard to the particular and actual nature of the case at hand, and only secondarily by general norms. The assessment whether the service the police are uniquely competent to provide is on balance desirable or not, in terms of, let us say, the aspirations of a democratic polity, is beyond the scope of the argument. But in reviewing practice and organization I will weigh what is against what ought to be, by certain criteria internal to the enterprise.

The paper is frankly argumentative and intended to furnish grist for the mills of debate. Hence, I shall not attempt to view all questions from all sides, and I will especially avoid giving consideration to mere administrative expediency or yielding to those demands of reasonableness that are connected with taking a live-and-let-live attitude. All this counts, to be sure, but I will try not to let it count in what I will have to say; and in arguing as strongly as I know how, I do not aim to dismiss polemic opponents but to pay tribute to them. My plan is to begin with a cursory review of some preliminaries—dealing mainly with the police idea—in ways I consider indispensible for what will follow. Next I shall sketch a rather ordinary and common event in police work, and use it to explain what a policeman is required to do in this situation, in such situations, and by extension, in any situation whatever. Finally, I will attempt to characterize the problems that appear to summon police intervention and to define the role force plays in these interventions. In wrapping things up I will comment about the practical significance of police work in society and about the skills that come into play, or should come into play, in this regard.

THE OFFICIAL BASIS OF
LAW ENFORCEMENT MANDATES

While we use the term Police to refer to specific corps of public officials, it bears mentioning that original usage embraced the entire field of internal government, as distinct from the conduct of foreign affairs. Sir Francis Bacon, for example, asserted that in being "civil or policied," a nation acquired the right to subdue others that were "altogether unable or indign to govern" (Bacon, 1859: 29). In time this usage gave way to one restricted to the exercise of proscriptive control in matters affecting the public interest. Blackstone stated that "public police and economy . . . mean the due regulation and domestic order of the Kingdom, whereby the individuals of the state, like members of a well governed family, are bound to conform their general behavior to the rules of propriety, good neighborhood and good manners, and to be decent, industrious and inoffensive in their respective stations" (Blackstone, n.d.: 161). This definition is located in the volume dealing with Public Wrongs, in relation to a specific class of delicts, called Offences against the Public Police and Economy. By the end of the nineteenth century this class of delicts is treated by Sir James Fitzjames Stephen as lying outside of the scope of criminal law, but is, nevertheless, explicitly related to the existence of the then existing police forces in England (Stephen, 1883: 246). Though both Blackstone and Stephen treat the category of police offenses cursorily, they do furnish *legal authority* for each item discussed. The intent at scrupulous legalization of proscriptive control also inheres in the "idiom of apologetics which belongs to the vocabulary of constitutional law," in the United States: Police Power (Hamilton and Rodee, 1937: 192), commonly invoked to justify abridgements of civil liberties in the interest of "public health, morals, and safety" (Mugler v. Kansas, 1887). Indeed, in keeping with American concepts of legality, Mr. Justice Harlan, speaking for the majority in Mugler, reserved the right of judicial review of statutes enacted in the exercise of police power.

Most of the offenses against the Public Police mentioned by Blackstone are no longer regarded as culpable. But the domain of legally sanctioned proscriptive control he discussed has expanded enormously since the Commentaries appeared, as have the provisions of criminal law. There are scarcely any human activities, any interpersonal relations, any social arrangements left that do not stand under some form of governmental regulation, to the violation of which penalties are attached. To say that modern life is thus controlled does not mean saying that it is more controlled than earlier life. Tribesmen, peasants, or citizens of colonial townships most assuredly did not live in a paradise of freedom. In fact, the most widely accepted explanation of the proliferation of formal control, which associates it with the growth of a market-oriented, industrial, and urban order, implies primarily a shift from reliance on informal mechanisms of traditional authority to reliance on legal rational means (Weber, 1947: 324).

Urbanism brought with it the need for explicitly formal regulation because the lives of the people living in cities are replete with opportunities of infringing upon one another and virtually devoid of incentives to avoid it. The former is due to the sheer congestion of very large numbers of people, the latter to the social distance between them. More importantly, perhaps, urban strangers cannot entrust their fate to the hope of somehow muddling through because of the manner in which they attend to the business of making a living, and because of the paramount significance of this interest in their lives.

Two conditions must be met to satisfy the need for formal governmental control that would bind effectively the behavior of individuals to rules of propriety. The first, already recognized in the treatment Blackstone accorded to the matter, is that all controls rest on specific authorization set forth in highly specific legal norms. The second, explicitly acknowledged by Stephen, is that the implementation of the authorizing norm must be entrusted to impersonal enforcement bureaucracies. In sum, "the due regulation and domestic order" in our times is the task of a host of law enforcement bureaucracies, each using procedures legitimized by, and incidental to, the attainment of explicitly formulated legal objectives.

Naturally, the actual interests and practices of enforcement officials are rarely as specific or explicit as the verbal formulations of their respective mandates. Hence, for example, while the formal authorization of the work of a health inspector may be clear and specific, things are apt to become a bit sticky when he undertakes to match factual realities with provisions of statutes. The amount of discretionary freedom it takes to fill the interstices of the legal formulation of law enforcement competence probably varies from one bureaucracy to the next. Agents concerned with weights and measures are probably less free than building inspectors. On the whole, however, it is safe to assume that none will busy himself, nor be permitted to busy himself, outside of the sphere of his mandate. More importantly, there is no mystery about the proper business of such law enforcement agents, and citizens are generally quite able to hold them to their limits. For example, though a truant officer's enforcement activities could be rich and varied, especially if he happens to be dedicated to his tasks, he can claim legitimate interest in the child's health, the conditions of his home, or some such matter, only insofar as they can be linked with school attendance. In practice it can be debated whether the connection he sees is defensible or not, but there is not debate about the terms on which the question must be decided. Because it is known what a truant officer is supposed to do, therefore he can be held to account for doing more or doing less than his mandate authorizes or requires him to do, and by the same token, the officer can reject demands he deems *ultra vires*.

It would seem reasonable to expect that the proper business of the police—that is, of the corps of officials who inherited the name once used to refer to the entire domain of internal, proscriptive regulation—should be determined in the manner in which the business of all other law enforcement bureaucracies is determined. That is, one would expect that their service and powers be derivative from some substantive authorizing norm. And, indeed, it is commonly assumed that the penal code contains this authorization, in addition to which the police are required to enforce other laws, in particular laws regulating vehicular traffic, and beyond that may have some responsibilities concerning such matters as the licensing of the possession of firearms or the operation of certain business enterprises, which vary greatly from place to place. All in all, however, activities relating to crime control are generally considered basic to the mandate of the police by both citizens and police officials, at least in the sense that its needs are regarded as having priority over other needs (Gorman et al., 1973; Leonard and More, 1971).[1] Though I will argue that this presumption is misguided and misleading, and that one could not possibly understand or control what policemen actually do by assuming it, it must be said that it is not without some carefully laid foundations, the import of which is difficult to overcome.

The following considerations appear to justify the presumption that the police are a law enforcement agency whose mandate is basically derivative of the provisions of penal codes. First, the police, together with many others, cultivate and propagate the image of the policeman as the vanguard fighter in the war on crime. Americans from the members of Congress to readers of tabloids are convinced that what the police do about crime is the main part of the struggle against it and that, therefore, doing something about it is the policeman's main care. Second the formal bureaucratic organization of policework stringently reinforces the view that the police are primarily dedicated to criminal law enforcement. Police training, such as it is, heavily emphasizes criminalistics, criminal law, and related matters; the internal administrative differentiation of departments tends to reflect primarily formal criminal enforcement special-izations and units are designated by names of species of offenses; and police record keeping is almost wholly dedicated to the recording of law enforcement activity as a result of which crime control is the only *documentable* output of police work. Most importantly perhaps, career advancement in departments is heavily determined by an officer's show of initiative and ability in criminal law enforcement or, at least, an officer who has some so-called good pinches to his credit can always count that this will weigh more heavily in his favor when it comes to assessing his overall performance than any other factor. Third, the criminal process is virtually always set into motion by the police, and prosecutors, judges, and correctional personnel are heavily dependent on the police to remain occupied. Moreover, the part the police play in the administration of justice is very specific and indispensable. They are charged with the responsibility of conducting investigations leading to the identification of suspects and with securing the evidence required for successful prosecution. And they are obliged to apprehend and detain identified suspects, in the course of which they are empowered to use force if force is necessary. Fourth, the work of a certain number of policemen—the number is probably not very large but large enough to be significant—is in fact quite plainly determined by the provisions of the penal code in more or less the same manner in which the work of building inspectors is determined by building codes. These are officers assigned to various detective bureaus, whose daily routines consist of investigating crimes, arresting offenders, and of otherwise being engaged with matters related to efforts to obtain convictions.

In sum, the exercise of internal, proscriptive control by modern governments has been highly legalized, at least since the end of the eighteenth century. The exercise of this control is assigned to specifically authorized bureaucracies, each of which has a substantively limited field of enforcement competence. Even though it is allowed that officials retain a measure of discretionary freedom, the terms on which substantive decisions can be made are not in dispute. In accordance with this view the police often are viewed as one of several enforcement bureaucracies whose domain of competence is determined by penal codes and certain other statutory delegations.

THE POLICE AND CRIMINAL LAW ENFORCEMENT

With all this admitted as true, why can the police mandate not be conceived as embodying the law enforcement mandate inhering in criminal law enforcement? The answer is quite simple. Regardless of how strenuously criminal law enforcement is emphasized in the image of the policeman and in police administration, and regardless of how important police work might actually be for keeping the administration of criminal justice in business, the activity of criminal law enforcement is not at all characteristic of day-to-day, ordinary occupational practices of the vastly preponderant majority of policemen. In other words, when one looks at what policemen actually do, one finds that criminal law enforcement is something that most of them do with the frequency located somewhere between virtually never and very rarely.

Later in this paper I will address this paradox directly and try to assign to criminal law enforcement its proper place within police work. Before moving on to this, however, I must touch on some matters connected with manpower allocation, opportunity for crime control, and routine work orientation. Unfortunately the data base on which the first two observations rely is poor, partly because the information available on these matters is not as good as it could be, but in larger measure because the actuarial ratios and frequencies I shall mention are drawn from data produced to meet requirements of accountability rather than strictly factual reporting. A word of caution is in order here; it is all too easy to fall into an attitude of supercilious critique concerning the poverty of data. The fact is that neither the police nor functionaries in other practical endeavors should be expected to keep records that would make it convenient for scholars to study them. Indeed, they usually have good reasons for keeping what in the scholar's view appear to be poor records (Garfinkel and Bittner, 1967: 186-207).

According to a survey of municipal police departments of cities in the 300,000 to 1,000,000 population range which is, alas, neither exhaustive nor complete, 86.5% of all police line personnel—that is, excluding officers occupying supervisory positions from sergeant up—are assigned to uniformed patrol (Kansas City Police Department, 1971; Wilson, 1963: 293).[2] Though this figure excludes persons holding the civil service rank of patrolman while assigned to detectives' bureaus, it probably overestimates the relative size of the force of patrolmen actually working on the streets. But it would certainly seem safe to assume that four out of five members of the line personnel do the work of patrolmen, especially since patrol-sergeants, whose work is essentially of the same nature as the work of those they supervise, are not included in the 86.5%. But the importance of the uniformed patrol in the police is not altogether derivative from the preponderance of their number. They represent, in even greater measure than their numbers indicate, the police presence in society. In fact, I will argue that all the other members of the police—in particular, the various special plainclothes details—represent special refinements of police-patrol work that are best understod as derivative of the mandate of the patrol, even though their activities sometimes take on forms that are quite unlike the activities of the patrol. But I should like to make clear now that in subordinating the work of the detectives to the work of the patrol *conceptually,* I do not intend to cast doubts on the special importance the work of the former has for the prosecutors and judges. Indeed, I hope to make clear by dint of what circumstance prosecutors and judges come to be the beneficiaries of a service they ordinarily take for granted but for which—in rather rare moments of candor—they profess to lack understanding.

For the reasons I indicated, and because of reasons I hope to add as I go along, the following remarks will concern primarily the work of the uniformed patrol. But I do intend to make references to other parts of the police wherever such references are called for. In fact, the first observation about criminal law enforcement pertains equally to the work of detectives and patrolmen.

It is well known that the penal codes the police are presumed to enforce contain thousands of titles. While many of these titles are obscure, unknown, or irrelevant to existing conditions, and the administration of criminal justice is concentrated around a relatively small fraction of all proscribed acts, the police select only some, even from that sample, for enforcement. Relying mainly on my observations, I believe the police tend to avoid involvement with offenses in which it is assumed that the accused or suspected culprits will not try to evade the criminal process by flight. Characteristically, for example, they refer citizens who complain about being defrauded by businesses or landlords directly to the prosecutor. The response is also often given in cases involving other types of allegations of property crimes involving persons, real or fictional, who own substantial property. To be sure, in some of these instances it is possible that the wrong is of a civil rather than a criminal nature, and it also should be taken into account that a principle of economy is at work here, and that the police disavow responsibility for some delicts simply because of lack of resources to deal with them. It is at least reasonable to suggest, however, that police interest in criminal law enforcement is limited to those offenses in which the perpetrator needs to be *caught* and where catching him *may* involve the use of physical force. The point in all this is not that the police are simply ignorant of, and uninterested in, the majority of the provisions of the penal code, but that their selectivity follows a specific principle, namely, that they feel called upon to act only when *their* special competence is required, and that special competence is related to the possibility that force *may* have to be used to secure the appearance of a defendant in court. This restriction is certainly not impermeable, and it happens often enough that policemen are for a variety of circumstantial reasons required to proceed in cases in which the voluntary appearance of a defendant in court is not in doubt. Interestingly, however, in many of these cases the police are likely to put on a symbolic show of force by gratuitously handcuffing the arrested person.

It has become commonplace to say that patrolmen do not invoke the law often. But this is not a very good way of putting things because it could also be said that neurosurgeons do not operate often, at least not when compared with the frequency with which taxi drivers transport their fares. So it might pay to try to be a bit more specific about it. According to estimates issued by the research division of the International Association of Chiefs of Police, "the percentage of the police effort devoted to the traditional criminal law matters probably does not exceed ten per cent" (Niederhoffer, 1969: 75). Reiss, who studied the practices of the patrol in a number of American metropolitan centers, in trying to characterize a typical day's work, stated that it defies all efforts of typification "except in the sense that *the modal tour of duty does not involve an arrest* of any person" (Reiss, 1971: 19). Observations about arrest frequency are, of course, not a very good source of information about law enforcement concerns. Yet, while they must be viewed skeptically, they deserve mention. According to the Uniform Crime Reports, 97,000 detectives and patrolmen made 2,597,000 arrests, including 548,000 for Index Crimes.[3] This means that the average member of the line staff makes 26 arrests annually, of which slightly more than five involve serious crimes. Though it is admittedly no more than a rough guess, it would seem reasonable to say, allowing for the fact that detectives presumably do nothing else, that patrolmen make about one arrest per man per month, and certainly no more than three Index Crime arrests per man per year. In any case, these figures are of the same order of magnitude as reported in the draft of a report on police productivity, where it was said that patrolmen assigned to New York City's Anti-Crime Squad average about 15 felony arrests per man per year, while "a typical uniformed patrolman makes only about three felony arrests per year." In Detroit members of the Special Crime Attack Team make ten felony arrests per man per year, "considerably more than the average patrolman" (National Commission on Productivity, 1973: 39f). And the figures are also in good accord with estimates reported by the President's Commission on Law Enforcement and Administration of Justice, where it was calculated on the basis of data drawn from the operations of the Los Angeles Police Department that "an individual patrol officer can expect an opportunity to detect a burglary no more than once every three months and a robbery no more than once every 14 years" (Institute for Defense Analysis, 1967: 12).

It could be said, and should be considered, that the mere frequency of arrest does not reflect police work in the area of criminal law enforcement adequately. Two points deserve attention in this regard: first, that clearing crimes and locating suspects takes time; and second, that policemen frequently do not invoke the law where the law could be invoked and thus *are* involved in law enforcement, albeit in an unauthorized way.

In regard to the first point, it is certainly true that there are some cases that are subject to dogged and protracted investigation. It is even not unheard of that uniformed patrolmen work on some crime for long periods while attending to other duties. This, however, is not characteristic of the work of either detectives or patrolmen generally. For instance, in the majority of reported burglaries, a patrolman or a team of patrolmen are dispatched to survey the scene; this is followed by investigations done by detectives, who, after writing up a report of their investigation, in the majority of cases simply move on to the next case (Conklin and Bittner, 1973: 206-23).[4] Along these lines, Conklin reports that criminal *investigations* of robberies produce clearances only in one out of fifty cases (Conklin, 1972: 148f). And even if it were to be assumed that detectives engage in five investigations for every one they conclude successfully—no doubt a gross exaggeration—it would still remain that in the run-of-the-mill crime the kind of investigation common lore associates with detective work is not characteristic of the police, and could not be, if only because the press of new business pushes old cases into the dead file. I must add that the whole matter of crime investigation is complicated, involving activities that I did not mention. But I only intended to show that the spacing of arrests is not due to the fact that the policemen need time to work out a solution. All this means is that cases are solved, when they are solved, either at the time the offense takes place or shortly thereafter or, by and large, not at all. The information required for such solution must be mobilizable in short order, or the quest will be abandoned. In other words, either a detective knows quite clearly in the case where to turn or he will not try to pursue the matter. That he often knows where to turn is part of his craft (Bittner, 1970: 65ff).[5]

The other point, that policemen make law enforcement decisions of "low visibility," is the topic of a fairly substantial body of literature.[6] According to the prevailing view expressed in this literature, patrolmen usurp the rights of judges in a host of minor offenses and, by not invoking the law, exculpate the offender. While most authors find such practices reasonable and for the most part desirable, they also recommend that the exercise of such discretion should be placed under administrative, if not statutory, regulation (Davis, 1971). They urge that, though it appears to make good sense that policemen do not enforce statutes pertaining to gambling literally and in every applicable case, it is not right that the decision when to proceed and when to desist should be left entirely to the lights of the individual officers. Provided with more detailed instructions officers would be, presumably, on firmer grounds and, hopefully, less arbitrary. Unfortunately, underlying the approach is a presumption that begs the principal question; namely, whether in making the arrests they make, and not making the arrests they do not make, policemen are acting as the *functionaries of the law* they invoke or fail to invoke, as the case may be. All available information about the practices of patrolmen place this presumption in grave doubt, especially in regard to laws pertaining to minor offenses. I am not aware of any descriptions of police work on the streets that support the view that patrolmen walk around, respond to service demands, or intervene in situations, with the provisions of the penal code in mind, matching what they see with some title or another, and deciding whether any particular apparent infraction is serious enough to warrant being referred for further process. While it does happen occasionally that patrolmen arrest some person merely because they have probable cause to believe that he has committed crimes, this is not the way all but a small fraction of arrests come about. In the typical case the formal charge *justifies* the arrest a patrolman makes but is *not* the *reason* for it. The actual reason is located in a domain of considerations to which Professor Wilson referred as the need "to handle the situation," [7] and invoking the law is merely a device whereby this is sometimes accomplished. Since the persons who are arrested at a backyard game of craps are not arrested because they are gambling but because of a complex of situational factors of which no mention is made in the formally filed charge, it would seem specious to try to refine the law pertaining to the charge, since any policeman worth his salt is virtually always in a position to find a *bona fide* charge of some kind when he believes the situation calls for an arrest. In sum, if criminal law enforcement means acting on the basis of, and in accordance with, the law's provisions, then this is something policemen do occasionally, but in their routine work they merely avail themselves of the provisions as a means for attaining other objectives.

In sum, the vastly preponderant number of policemen are assigned to activities in which they have virtually no opportunities for criminal law enforcement, and the available data indicate that they are engaged in it with a frequency that surely casts doubts upon the belief that this is the substance, or even the core, of their mandate. Moreover, criminal law enforcement by the police is limited to those offenses in which it is assumed that force may have to be used to bring the offender to justice. Finally, in the majority of cases in which the law is invoked, the decision to invoke it is not based on considerations of legality. Instead, policemen use the provisions of the law as a resource for handling problems of all sorts, of which *no mention* is made in the formal charge.

THE ELEMENTS OF ROUTINE POLICE PRACTICE

To explain by what conception of duty policemen feel summoned into action, and what objectives they seek to attain, I should like to use an example of ordinary practice. One of the most common experiences of urban life is the sight of a patrolman directing traffic at a busy street intersection. This service is quite expensive and the assignment is generally disliked among policemen. Nevertheless it is provided on a regular basis. The reason for this is not too difficult to divine. Aside from the private interests of citizens in maintaining safe and otherwise suitable conditions for the use of their automobiles, there is the consideration that the viability of urban life as we know it depends heavily on the mobility of vehicular traffice. No one knows, of course, how helpful police traffic control is in general, much less in the special case of a single patrolman directing traffic at a particular place and time. However uncertain the value of traffic control, the uncertainty is resolved in favor of having it simply because of the anticipated gravity of the consequences its absence might engender. In sum, traffic control is a matter of utmost seriousness. Despite its seriousness and presumed necessity, despite the fact that assignments are planned ahead and specifically funded, no assignment to a traffic control post is ever presumed to be absolutely fixed. The assigned officer is expected to be there, all things being equal, but he is also expected to have an independent grasp of the necessity of his presence. The point is not that this opens the possibility of a somewhat more casual attitude towards traffic control than the police care to admit, but rather that there exists a tacit understanding that no matter how important the post might be, it is always possible for something else to come up that can distract the patrolman's attention from it and cause him to suspend attending to the assigned task.

This understanding is not confined to traffic control assignments, but functions in all prior assigned tasks without any exceptions whatever, regardless whether the assignment involves investigating a heinous crime or feeding ice cream to a lost child, and regardless whether the prior assignment derives from the most solemn dictates of the law or whether it is based on mundane commands of immediate superiors. I am saying more than merely that patrolmen, like everybody else, will suspend the performance of an assigned task to turn to some extraordinary exigency. While everybody might respond to the call of an emergency, the policeman's vocational ear is *permanently and specifically attuned* to such calls, and his work attitude throughout is permeated by preparedness to respond to it, whatever he might happen to be doing. In the case at hand, it is virtually certain that any normally competent patrolman would abandon the traffic post to which he was assigned without a moment's hesitation and without regard for the state of the traffic he was supposed to monitor, if it came to his attention that a crime was being committed somewhere at a distance not too far for him to reach in time either to arrest the crime in its course, or to arrest its perpetrator. And it is virtually certain that all patrolmen would abandon their posts even when the probability of arresting the crime or its perpetrator was not very high, and even when the crime was of the sort which when reported to the police in the ordinary manner—that is, some time after it happened—would receive only the most cursory attention and would tend to remain unsolved in nine out of every ten reported cases. Finally, there is no doubt that the patrolman who would not respond in this manner, would thereby expose himself to the risk of an official reprimand, and to expressions of scorn from his co-workers, and from the public.

Yet there exists no law, no regulation, no formal requirement of any kind that determines that practice. Quite the contrary, it is commonly accepted that crime control cannot be total, must be selective, and that policemen cannot be expected to rush to the scene of every crime and arrest every offender. Why then should all concerned, inside and outside the police, consider it entirely proper and desirable that a patrolman abandon his post, exposing many people to serious inconvenience and the whole city to grave hazards, to pursue the dubious quest of catching a two-bit thief?

At the level of reason the patrolman himself might advance, the action merely follows the impulse to drop everything and catch a crook. And it seems perfectly reasonable that policemen should follow this impulse more readily than others, since they presumably are being paid for it. Thus considered, the action draws its justification from the public sentiment that a crime must not be allowed to pass without at least an attempt to oppose it, and from the policeman's special obligation in this regard. This sentiment is certainly a very important aspect of the policeman's frame of mind; it directs his interests, establishes priorities, furnishes justification for action, governs the expectations of reward and honor, and ultimately supplies the rhetoric with which his ready aggressiveness is explained.

But I have argued earlier that, the strength of this sentiment notwithstanding, criminal law enforcement could not possibly be the fulcrum on which the police mandate rests. How then do I explain the alacrity of the patrolman's response? Let me begin with an aside which is in its own way important but not central to the argument. For the patrolman, rushing to the scene of a crime is an opportunity to do something remarkable that will bring him to the attention of his superiors in a way that might advance his career. This aspect of his vocational interest is not rooted in the work he does but in the administrative setting within which it is done. Skolnick (1966: 231) has furnished extensive documentation for the importance of this factor in police work. Still, however important the explanation is, it fails in explaining police routines generally.

When I stated in the vignette that the patrolman will abandon his assignment to rush to the scene of a crime, I assumed without saying that the crime would be something like an act of vandalism, an assault, or a burglary. But if the crime that came to the attention of the officer had been something like a conspiracy by a board of directors of a commercial concern to issue stock with the intention of defrauding investors, or a landlord criminally extorting payments from a tenant, or a used-car dealer culpably turning back an odometer on an automobile he was preparing for sale, the patrolman would scarcely life his gaze, let alone move into action. The real reason why the patrolman moved was not the fact that what was taking place was a crime in general terms, but because the particular crime was a member of a class of problems *the treatment of which will not abide.* In fact, the patrolman who unhesitatingly left his post to pursue an assailant would have left his post with just a little hesitation to pull a drowning person out of the water, to prevent someone from jumping off the roof of a building, to protect a severely disoriented person from harm, to save people in a burning structure, to disperse a crowd hampering the rescue mission of an ambulance, to take steps to prevent a possible disaster that might result from broken gas lines or water mains, and so on almost endlessly, and entirely without regard to the substantive nature of the problem, as long as it could be said that it involved *something-that-ought-not-to-be-happening-and-about-which-someone-had-better-do-something-now!* These extraordinary events, and the directly intuited needs for control that issue from them, are what the vocational interests of patrolmen are attuned to. And in the circumstances of such events citizens feel entitled and obliged to summon the help of the police. Naturally, in retrospect it is always possible to question whether this or that problem should or should not have become the target of police attention, but most people will agree that urban life is replete with situations in which the need for such service is not in doubt, and in which, accordingly, the service of the police is indispensible.

It is scarcely possible not to notice that the definition of the police mandate escaped Ockham's Rasor. It cannot be helped; I have seen policemen helping a tenant in arrears gain access to medication which a landlord held together with other possessions in apparently legal bailment, I have seen policemen settling disputes between parents as to whether an ill child should receive medical treatment, I have seen a patrolman adjudicating a quarrel between a priest and an organist concerning the latter's access to the church. All this suggests more than the obvious point that the duties of patrolmen are of a mind-boggling variety, it compels the stronger inference that no human problem exists, or is imaginable, about which it could be said with finality that this certainly could not become the proper business of the police.

It is fair to say that this is well-known even though police work is not thought of in these terms. It must be assumed to be well-known because in almost all instances the police service is a response to citizen demands, which must be taken as reflecting public knowledge of what is expected of the police. But evidently it is not thought of in these terms when it comes to writing books about the police, to making up budgets for the police, and to training policemen, administering departments, and rewarding performance. And even though the fact that policemen are "good" at helping people in trouble and dealing with troublesome people has received some measure of public recognition recently,[8] the plaudits are stated in ways reminiscent of "human interest stories" one finds in the back pages of the daily papers. More importantly, when it is asked on what terms this police service is made available in every conceivable kind of emergency, the usual answer is that it happens by default because policemen are the only functionaries, professionals, officials—call them what you will—who are available around the clock and who can be counted on to make house-calls. Further, it is often said that it would be altogether better if policemen were not so often called upon to do chores lying within the spheres of vocational competence of physicians, nurses, and social workers, and did not have to be all things to all men. I believe that these views are based on a profound misconception of what policemen do, and I propose to show that no matter how much police activity seems like what physicians and social workers might do, and even though what they actually have to do often could be done by physicians and social workers, the service they perform involves the exercise of a unique competence they do not share with anyone else in society. Even if physicians and social workers were to work around the clock and make house-calls, the need for the police service in their areas would remain substantial, though it certainly would decline in volume. Though policemen often do what psychologists, physicians, or social workers might be expected to do, their involvement in cases is never that of surrogate psychologists, physicians, or social workers. They are in all these cases, from the beginning, throughout, and in the last analysis, policemen, and their interest and objectives are of a radically distinct nature. Hence, saying that policemen are "good at" dealing with people in trouble and troublesome people does not mean that they are good at playing the role of other specialists. Indeed, only by assuming a distinct kind of police competence can one understand why psychologists, physicians, and social workers run into problems in *their* work for which they seek police assistance. In other words, when a social worker "calls the cops" to help him with his work, he mobilizes the kind of intervention that is characteristic of police work even when it looks like social work.

   To make clear what the special and unique competence of the police consists of I should like to characterize the events containing "something-that-ought-not-to-be-happening-and-about-which-somebody-had-better-do-something-now," and the ways the police respond to them. A word of caution: I do not intend to imply that everything policemen attend to can be thus characterized. That is, the special and unique police competence comes into play about as often as practicing medicine, doing engineering, or teaching—in the narrow meanings of these terms—come into play in what physicians, engineers, and teachers do.

First, and foremost, *the need to do something* is assessed with regard for actually existing combinations of circumstances. Even though circumstances of need do become stereotyped, so that some problems appear to importune greater urgency than others, the rule *it depends* takes precedence over typification, and attention is directed to what is singular and particular to the here-and-now. Policemen often say that their work is almost entirely unpredictable; it might be more correct to say that anything unpredictable that cannot be dismissed or assimilated to the usual is *pro tanto* a proper target of police attention. That experience plays an important part in the decision-making goes without saying, but it is not the kind of experience that lends itself easily to the systematization one associates with a body of technical knowledge. Most often the knowledge upon which patrolmen draw is the acquaintance with particular persons, places, and past events. Patrolmen appear to have amazingly prodigious memories and are able to specify names, addresses, and other factual details of past experiences with remarkable precision. Indeed, it is sometimes difficult to believe that all this information could be correct. However this may be, the fact that they report their activities in this manner, and that they appear to think in such terms, may be taken as indicative of the type of knowledge they depend on in their work. It could be said that while anything at all could become properly the business of the police, the patrolman can only decide whether anything in particular is properly his business after he "gets there" and examines it.

Second, the question whether some situational need justifiably requires police attention is very often answered by persons who solicit the service. Citizen demand is a factor of extraordinary importance for the distribution of police service, and the fact that someone did "call the cops" is, in and of itself, cause for concern. To be sure, there are some false alarms in almost every tour of duty, and one reason why police departments insist on employing seasoned policemen as dispatchers is because they presumably are skilled in detecting calls which lack merit. Generally, however, the determination that some development has reached a critical stage, ripe for police interest, is related to the attitudes of persons involved, and depends on common sense reasoning. For example, in a case involving a complaint about excessive noise, it is not the volume of the noise that creates hazards for life, limb, property, and the public order, but that the people involved say and otherwise show that the problem has reached a critical stage in which something-had-better be-done-about-it. Closely connected with the feature of critical emergency is the expectation that policemen will handle the problem "then-and-there." Though it may seem obvious, it deserves stressing that police work involves no continuances and no appointments, but that its temporal structure is throughout of the "as soon as I can get to it" norm, and that its scheduling derives from the natural fall of events, and not from any externally imposed order, as is the case for almost all other kinds of occupations. Firemen too are permanently on call, but the things they are called upon to do are limited to a few technical services. A policeman is always poised to move on any contingency whatever, not knowing what it might be, but knowing that far more often than not he will be expected to *do something.* The expectation to do something is projected upon the scene, the patrolman's diagnostic instinct is heavily colored by it, and he literally sees things in the light of the expectation that he somehow *has* to handle the situation. The quick-witted and decisive activism of the police is connected with the fact that they are attuned to dealing with emergencies; and in many instances the response-readiness of the policeman rounds out the emergency character of the need to which the response was directed.

Third, though police departments are highly bureaucratized and patrolmen are enmeshed in a scheme of strict internal regulation, they are, paradoxically, quite alone and independent in their dealings with citizens. Accordingly, the obligation to do something when a patrolman confronts problems—that is, when he does police work—is something he does not share with anyone. He may call for help when there is a risk that he might be overwhelmed, and will receive it; short of such risks, however, he is on his own. He receives very little guidance and almost no supervision; he gets advice when he asks for it, but since policemen do not share information, asking for and giving advice is not built into their relations; his decisions are reviewed only when there are special reasons for review, and records are kept of what he does only when he makes arrests. Thus, in most cases, problems and needs are seen in relationship to the response capacity of an individual patrolman or teams of two patrolmen, and not of the police as an organized enterprise. Connected with the expectation that he will do what needs to be done by himself is the expectation that he will limit himself to imposing provisional solutions upon problems. Though they often express frustration at never solving anything—especially when they arrest persons and find them quickly back on the street—they do what they do with an abandon characteristic of all specialists who disregard the side-effects of their activities. As they see it, it is none of their concern that many provisional solutions have lasting consequences. In fact, it would be quite well put to say that they are totally absorbed with making arrests, in the literal sense of the term. That is, they are always trying to snatch things from the brink of disaster, to nip untoward development in the bud, and generally to arrest whatever must not be permitted to continue; and to accomplish this they sometimes arrest persons, if circumstances appear to demand it.

Fourth and finally, like everybody else, patrolmen want to succeed in what they undertake. But unlike everybody else, they never retreat. Once a policeman has defined a situation as properly his business and undertakes to do something about it, he will not desist till he prevails. That the policemen are uniquely empowered and required to carry out their decisions in the "then-and-there" of emergent problems is the structurally central feature of police work. There can be no doubt that the decisive and unremitting character of police intervention is uppermost in the minds of people who solicit it, and that persons against whom the police proceed are mindful of this feature and conduct themselves accordingly. The police duty not to retreat in the face of resistance is matched by the duty of citizens not to oppose them. While under Common Law citizens had the right to resist illegal police action, at least in principle, the recommendations contained in the Uniform Arrest Act, the adoption of which is either complete or pending before most state legislatures, provides that they must submit. To be sure, the act pertains only to arrest powers, but it takes little imagination to see that this is sufficient to back up any coercive option a policeman might elect.[9]

The observation that policemen prevail in what they undertake must be understood as a *capacity* but not a necessarily invariant practice. When, for example, a citizen is ordered to move or to refrain from what he is doing, he may actually succeed in persuading the policeman to reverse himself. But contrary to judges, policemen are not required to entertain motions, nor are they required to stay their orders while the motion receives reasoned consideration. Indeed, *even* if the citizen's objection should receive favorable consideration in *subsequent* review, it would still be said that "under the circumstances" he should have obeyed. And even if it could be proved that the policeman's action was injudicious or in violation of civil liberties, he would be held to account only if it could also be proved that he acted with malice or with wanton frivolity.[10]

In sum, what policemen do appears to consist of rushing to the scene of any crisis whatever, judging its needs in accordance with canons of common sense reasoning, and imposing solutions upon it without regard to resistance or opposition. In all this they act largely as individual practitioners of a craft.

THE SPECIFIC NATURE OF POLICE COMPETENCE

The foregoing considerations suggest the conclusion that what the existence of the police makes available in society is a unique and powerful capacity to cope with all kinds of emergencies: unique, because they are far more than anyone else permanently poised to deal with matters brooking no delay; powerful, because their capacity for dealing with them appears to be wholly unimpeded. But the notion of emergency brings a certain circularity into the definition of the mandate. This is so because, as I have indicated, the discernment of the facts of emergency relies on common sense criteria of judgment, and this makes it altogether too easy to move from saying that the police deal with emergencies, to saying that anything the police deal with is, *ipso facto,* an emergency. And so, while invoking the notion of emergency was useful to bring up certain observations, it now can be dispensed with entirely.

Situations like those involving a criminal on the lam, a person trapped in a burning building, a child in desperate need of medical care, a broken gas line, and so on, made it convenient to show why policemen move decisively in imposing constraints upon them. Having exploited this approach as far as it can take us, I now wish to suggest that the specific competence of the police is wholly contained in their capacity for decisive action. More specifically, that the feature of decisiveness derives from the authority to overpower opposition in the "then-and-there" of the situation of action. *The policeman, and the policeman alone, is equipped, entitled, and required to deal with every exigency in which force may have to be used, to meet it.* Moreover, the authorization to use force is conferred upon the policeman with the mere proviso that force will be used in amounts measured not to exceed the necessary minimum, as determined by an intuitive grasp of the situation. And only the use of deadly force is regulated somewhat more stringently.[11]

Three points must be added in explanation of the foregoing. First, I am *not* saying the police work consists of using force to solve problems, but only that police work consists of coping with problems in which force *may have to be used.* This is a distinction of extraordinary importance. Second, it could not possibly be maintained that everything policemen are actually required to do reflects this feature. For a variety of reasons—especially because of the ways in which police departments are administered—officers are often ordered to do chores that have nothing to do with police work. Interestingly, however, the fact that a policeman is quite at the beck and call of his superior and can be called upon to do menial work does not attenuate his powers vis-a-vis citizens in the least. Third, the proposed definition of police competence *fully embraces* those forms of criminal law enforcement policemen engage in. I have mentioned earlier that the special role the police play in the administration of criminal justice has to do with the circumstance that "criminals"—as distinct from respectable and propertied persons who violate the provisions of penal codes in the course of doing business—can be counted on to try to evade or oppose arrest. Because this is so, and to enable the police to deal effectively with criminals, they are said to be empowered to use force. They also engage in criminal investigations whenever such investigations might be reasonably expected to be instrumental in making arrests. But the conception of the police role in all this is upside down. It is *not* that policemen are entitled to use force because they must deal with nasty criminals. Instead, the duty of handling nasty criminals devolves on them *because* they have the more general authority to use force *as needed* to bring about desired objectives. It is, after all, no more than a matter of simple expediency that it should be so; and that is is so becomes readily apparent upon consideration that policemen show little or no interest in all those kinds of offenders about whom it is not assumed that they need to be caught, and that force may have to be used to bring them to the bar of justice.

CONCLUSIONS

There is a threefold paradox in the awesome power of the policeman to make citizens obey his command, both legitimately and effectively. First, how come such a power exists at all? Second, why has the existence of this power not received the consideration it deserves? Third, why is the exercise of this power entrusted to persons recruited from a cohort from which all those with talent and ambitions must be assumed to have gone on to college and then to other occupations? I shall attempt to answer these questions in the stated order.

The hallmark of the period of history comprising the past century and a half is a succession of vast outbreaks of internal and international violence, *incongruously combined* with an unprecedently sustained aspiration to install peace as a stable condition of social life.[12] There can be no doubt that during this period the awareness of the moral and practical necessity of peace took hold of the minds of almost all the people of our world, and while the advocacy of warfare and of violent revolution has not disappeared, it has grown progressively less frank and arguments in their favor seem to be losing ground to arguments condemning violence. The sentiments in favor of peace draw in part on humane motives, but they derive more basically from a profound shift of values, away from virtues associated with masculine prowess and combativeness, and towards virtues associated with assiduous enterprise and material progress. There is still some glamor left in being an adventurer or warrior, but true success belongs to the businessman and to the professional.[13] Resorting to violence—outside of its restricted occasions, notably warfare and recreation—is seen as a sign of immaturity or lower-class culture (Miller, 1958: 5-19; Adorno et al., 1950). The banishment of violence from the domain of private life—as compared, for instance, with its deliberate cultivation in Medieval Chivalry—is the lesser part of the story. More important is the shift in the methods of government to an almost complete civil and pacific form of administration. Physical force has either vanished or is carefully concealed in the administration of criminal justice, and the use of armed retainers to collect taxes and to recruit into the military are forgotten. Paper, not the sword, is the instrument of coercion of our day. But no matter how faithfully and how methodically the dictates of this civil culture and of the rule of law are followed, and no matter how penetrating and far-reaching the system of peaceful control and regulation might be, there must remain some mechanism for dealing with problems on a catch-as-catch-can basis. In fact, it would seem that the only practical way for banishing the use of force from life generally is to assign its residual exercise—where according to circumstances it appears unavoidable—to a specially deputized corps of officials, that is, to the police as we know it. Very simply, as long as there will be fools who can insist that their comfort and pleasure take precedence over the needs of firemen for space in fighting a fire, and who will not move to make room, so long will there be a need for policemen.

I must leave out one possible explanation for the neglect of the capacity to use force as the basis of the police mandate; namely, that I am wrong in my assessment of its fundamental importance. I have no idea why the authors of many superb studies of various aspects of police work have not reached this conclusion. Perhaps they were either too close to, or too far from, what they were researching. But I believe I know why this feature of police work has escaped general notice. Until recently the people against whom the police had cause to proceed, especially to proceed forcefully, came almost exclusively from among the blacks, the poor, the young, the Spanish speaking, and the rest of the urban proletariat, and they still come preponderantly from these segments of society. This is well-known, much talked about, and I have nothing to add to what has already been said about expressions of class- and race-bias. Instead, I should like to draw attention to a peculiar consequence of this concentration. The lives of the people I mentioned are often considered the locus of problems in which force may have to be used. Not only do most of the criminals with whom the police deal hail from among them, but they, more often than other members of society, get into all sorts of troubles, and they are less resourceful in handling their problems. And so it could be said that the police merely follow troubles into trouble's native habitat and that no further inferences can be drawn from it, except, perhaps, that policemen are somewhat too quick in resorting to force and too often resort to it for what seem to be inadequate reasons, at least in retrospect. Of course, the rise of the counter-culture, the penetration of drug use into the middle classes, the civil rights movements of the 1960s, and the student movement have proven that the police do not hesitate to act coercively against members of the rest of society. But that too has been mainly the target of critique, rather than efforts to interpret it. And the expressions of indignation we hear have approximately the effect "gesundheit" has on whatever causes a person to sneeze. The police are naturally baffled by the response; as far as they can see they did what they always did whenever they were called upon to intervene. In point of fact policemen did, *mutatis mutandis,* what physicians do under similar circumstances. Physicians are supposed to cure the sick through the practice of medicine, as everyone knows. But when they are consulted about some problem of an ambiguous nature, they define it as an illness and try to cure it. And teachers do not hesitate in treating everything as an educational problem. It is certainly possible to say that physicians and teachers are just as likely to go overboard as policemen. This does not mean, however, that one cannot find in these instances the true nature of their respective bags of tricks more clearly revealed than in the instances of more standard practice. In the case of the police, it merely obscures matters to say that they resort to force only against powerless people, either because it is more often necessary or because it is easier—even though these *are* important factors in determining frequency—for in fact, they define every summons to action as containing the possibility of the use of force.

The reasons why immense powers over the lives of citizens are assigned to men recruited with a view that they will be engaged in a low-grade occupation are extraordinarily complicated, and I can only touch on some of them briefly. Perhaps the most important factor is that the police were created as a mechanism for coping with the so-called dangerous classes (Silver, 1967: 1-24). In the struggle to contain the internal enemy and in the efforts to control violence, depredation, and evil, police work took on some of the features of its targets and became a tainted occupation. Though it may seem perverse, it is not beyond comprehension that in a society which seeks to banish the use of force, those who take it upon themselves to exercise its remaining indispensible residue should be deprecated. Moreover, in the United States the police were used blatantly as in instrument of urban machine-politics, which magnified opportunities for corrupt practices enormously. Thus, the Americam urban policeman came to be generally perceived as the dumb, brutal, and crooked cop. This image was laced by occasional human interest stories in which effective and humane police work was portrayed as the exception to the rule. The efforts of some reformers to purge the police of brutality and corruption have inadvertently strengthened the view that police work consists of doing what one is told and keeping one's nose clean. To gain the upper hand over sloth, indolence, brutality, and corruption, officials like the late Chief William Parker of Los Angeles militarized the departments under their command. But the development of stringent internal regulation only obscured the true nature of police work.

The new image of the policeman as a snappy, low-level, soldier-bureaucrat created no inducement for people who thought they could do better to elect police work as their vocation. Furthermore, the definition of police work remained associated with the least task that could be assigned to an officer. Finally, the most recent attempts to upgrade the selection of policemen have been resisted and produced disappointing results. The resistance is in large measure due to the employee interests of present personnel. It seems quite understandable that the chiefs, captains, and even veteran patrolmen would not be happy with the prospect of having to work with recruits who outrank them educationally. Furthermore, few people who have worked for college degrees would want to elect an occupation that calls only for a high school diploma. And those few will most likely be the least competent among the graduates, thereby showing that higher education is more likely to be harmful than helpful. And it is true, of course, that nothing one learns in college is particularly helpful for police work. In fact, because most college graduates come from middle-class backgrounds, while most of police work is directed towards members of the lower classes, there is a risk of a cultural gap between those who do the policing and the policed.

But if it is correct to say that the police are here to stay, at least for the foreseeable future, and that the mandate of policemen consists of dealing with all those problems in which force may have to be used, and if we further recognize that meeting this task in a socially useful way calls for the most consummate skill, then it would seem reasonable that only the most gifted, the most aspiring, and the most equipoised among us are eligible for it. It takes only three short steps to arrive at this realization. First, when policemen do those things only policemen can do, they invariably deal with matters of absolutely critical importance, at least to the people with whom they deal. True, these are generally not the people whose welfare is carefully considered. But even if democratic ideals cannot be trusted to insure that they will be treated with the same consideration accorded to the powerful, practicality should advise that those who never had a voice in the past now have spoken and succeeded in being heard. In sum, police work, at its core, involves matters of extraordinary seriousness, importance, and necessity. Second, while lawyers, physicians, teachers, social workers, and clergymen also deal with critical problems, they have bodies of technical knowledge or elaborate schemes of norms to guide them in their respective tasks. But in police work there exists little more than an inchoate lore, and most of what a policeman needs to know to do his work he has to learn on his own. Thus, what ultimately gets done depends primarily on the individual officer's perspicacity, judiciousness, and initiative. Third, the mandate to deal with problems in which force may have to be used implies the special trust that force will be used only *in extremis.* The skill involved in police work, therefore, consists of retaining recourse to force while seeking to avoid its use, and using it only in minimal amounts.

It is almost unnecessary to mention that the three points are not realized in police work. Far too many policemen are contemptuous towards the people with whom they deal and oblivious to the seriousness of their tasks. Few policemen possess the perspicacity and judiciousness their work calls for. And force is not only used often where it need not be used, but gratuitous rudeness and bullying is a widely prevalent vice in policing. While all this is true, I did not arrive at those points by speculating about what police work could be. Instead I have heard about it from policemen, and I saw it in police work. I say this not to make the obvious point that there exist, in many departments, officers whose work already embodies the ideals I mentioned. More important is that there are officers who know what police work calls for far better than I can say, and from whom I have learned what I said. As far as I could see they are practical men who have learned to do police work because they had to. No doubt they were motivated by respect for human dignity, but their foremost concern was effectiveness and craftsmanship. Perhaps I can best describe them by saying that they have in their own practices placed police work on a fully reasoned basis, moving from case to case as individual practitioners of a highly complex vocation.

Though I cannot be sure of it, I believe I have written as a spokesman of these officers because I believe one must look to them to make police work what it should be. But the chances that they will prevail are not very good. The principal obstacle to their success is the presently existing organization of police departments. I cannot go into details to show how the way police work is administratively regulated constitutes a positive impediment in the path of a responsible policeman, quite aside from the fact that most of his work is unrecognized and unrewarded.[14] But I would like to conclude by saying that, far from providing adequate disciplinary control over patent misconduct, the existing organizational structures encourage bad police work. Behind this is the ordinary dose of venality and vanity, and the inertia of the way-things-are. But the principal cause is an illusion. Believing that the real ground for his existence is the perennial pursuit of the likes of Willie Sutton—for which he lacks both opportunity and resources—the policeman feels compelled to minimize the significance of those instances of his performance in which he seems to follow the footsteps of Florence Nightingale. Fearing the role of the nurse or, worse yet, the role of the social worker, the policeman combines resentment against what he has to do day-in-day-out with the necessity of doing it. And in the course of it he misses his true vocation.

One more point remains to be touched upon. I began with a statement concerning the exercise of proscriptive control by government, commonly referred to as Law Enforcement. In all instances, except for the police, law enforcement is entrusted to special bureaucracies whose competence is limited by specific substantive authorization. There exists an understandable tendency to interpret the mandate of the police in accordance with this model. The search for a proper authorizing norm for the police led to the assumption that the criminal code provided it. I have argued that this was a mistake. Criminal law enforcement is merely an incidental and derivative part of police work. They do it simply because it falls within the scope of their larger duties—that is, it becomes part of police work exactly to the same extent as anything else in which force may have to be used, and only to that extent. Whether the police should still be considered a law enforcement agency is a purely taxonomic question of slight interest. All I intended to argue is that their mandate cannot be interpreted as resting on the substantive authorizations contained in the penal codes or any other codes. I realize that putting things this way must raise all sorts of questions in the minds of people beholden to the ideal of the Rule of Law. And I also realize that the Rule of Law has always drawn part of its strength from pretense; but I don't think pretense is entitled to immunity.

NOTES

1. Most textbooks on the police emphasize this point and enumerate the additional law enforcement obligations; see for example, A. C. Gorman, F. D. Jay and R.R.J. Gallati (1973); V. A. Leonard and H. W. More (1971).

2. Kansas City Police Department (1971). The survey contains information on 41 cities of 300,000 to 1,000,000 population. But the percentage cited in the text was computed only for Atlanta, Boston, Buffalo, Dallas, Denver, El Paso, Fort Worth, Honolulu, Kansas City, Memphis, Minneapolis, Oklahoma City, Pittsburgh, Portland, Ore., St. Paul, and San Antonio, because the data for the other cities were not detailed enough. The estimate that detectives make up 13.5 percent of line personnel comports with the estimate of O. W. Wilson (1963: 293), who stated that they make up approximately 10 percent of "sworn personnel."

3. Federal Bureau of Investigations, Uniform Crime Reports (1971). The data are for 57 cities of over 250,000 population, to make the figures correspond, at least roughly, to the data about manpower drawn from sources cited in note 2, supra. I might add that the average arrest rate in all the remaining cities is approximately of the same order as the figures I use in the argument. The so-called Index Crimes comprise homicide, forcible rape, robbery, aggravated assault, burglary, larceny, and auto theft. It should also be mentioned that arrests on Index Crime charges are not tantamount to conviction and it is far from unusual for a person to be charged, e.g., with aggravated assault, to induce him to plead guilty to simple assault, quite aside from failure to prosecute, dismissal, or exculpation by trial.

4. I have accompanied patrolmen and detectives investigating burglaries in two cities and should like to add on the basis of my observation and on the basis of interviews with officers that, in almost all of these cases, there is virtually no promise of clearance, that in most of them the cost of even a routine follow-up investigation would exceed the loss many times over, and that, in any case, the detectives always have a backlog of reported burglaries for which the reporting victims expect prompt consideration. I might also add that it seemed to me that this largely fruitless busy-work demoralizes detectives and causes them to do less work than I thought possible. See J. E. Conklin and E. Bittner (1973).

5. I have reference to the ramified information systems individual detectives cultivate, involving informants and informers, which they do not share with one another. I have touched on this topic in E. Bittner (1970).

6. The work that brought this observation into prominence is J. Goldstein (1960); a comprehensive review of the problem is contained in W. LaFave (1965).

7. J. Q. Wilson (1968: 31, and Chapter II). The observation that policemen make misdemeanor arrests most often on practical rather than legal considerations has been reported by many authors; cf., e.g., J. D. Lohman and G. E. Misner (1966: 168ff.). I have discussed this matter extensively in E. Bittner (1967a). Wistfully illuminating discussions of the topic are to be found, among others, in J. Hall (1953); J. V. Henry (1966); C. D. Robinson (1965).

8. The first expression of recognition is contained in E. Cumming, I. Cumming and L. Edell (1965); cf. also E. Bittner (1967b).

9. S. B. Warner (1942); Corpus Juris Secundum (Vol. 6: 613ff.); M. Hochnagel and H. W. Stege (1966).

10. There exists legal doctrine supporting the contention that resisting or opposing the police in an emergency situation is unlawful, see H. Kelsen (1961: 278ff.), and H.L.A. Hart (1961: 20 ff.). I cite these references to show that the police are legally authorized to do whatever is necessary, according to the nature of the circumstances.

11. "Several modern cases have imposed [a] standard of strict liability . . . upon the officer by conditioning justification of deadly force on the victim's actually having committed a felony, and a number of states have enacted statutes which appear to adopt this strict liability. However, many jurisdictions, such as California, have homicide statutes which permit the police officer to use deadly force for the arrest of a person 'charged' with a felony. It has been suggested that this requirement only indicates the necessity for reasonable belief by the officer that the victim has committed a felony." Note, Stanford Law Review (1961: 566-609).

12. The aspiration has received a brilliant formulation in one of the most influential documents of modern political philosophy, Immanuel Kant (1913); a review of the growth of the ideal of peace is contained in P. Reiwald (1944).

13. Literary glorification of violence has never disappeared entirely, as the works of authors like Nietzsche and Sorel attest. In the most recent past these views have again received eloquent expression in connection with revolutionary movements in Third World nations. The most remarkable statement along these lines is contained in the works of Franz Fanon.

14. But I have given this matter extensive consideration in E. Bittner (1970), note 5, supra.

REFERENCES

ADORNO, T. W. et al. (1950) The Authoritarian Personality. New York: Harper & Row.
BACON, F. (1859) "An Advertizement Touching an Holy War," in Collected Works. Volume 7. London: Spottiswood.
BITTNER, E. (1967a) "Police on skid row: a study of peace keeping." American Sociological Review 32: 600-715.
——— (1967b) "Police discretion in emergency apprehension of mentally ill persons." Social Problems 14: 278-292.
——— (1970) The Functions of the Police in Modern Society. Washington, D. C.: U.S. Government Printing Office.
BLACKSTONE, W. (n.d.) Commentaries on the Laws of England. Volume 4. Oxford, England: Clarendon.
CONKLIN, J. E. (1972) Robbery and the Criminal Justice System. Philadelphia: J. B. Lippincott.
——— and E. BITTNER (1973) "Burglary in a suburb." Criminology 11: 206-232.
Corpus Juris Secundum. "Arrest." Volume 6.
CUMMING, E., I. CUMMING, and L. EDELL (1965) "Policeman as philosopher, guide and friend." Social Problems 12: 276-286.
DAVIS, K. C. (1971) Discretionary Justice: A Preliminary Inquiry. Urbana, Ill.: University of Illinois Press.
Federal Bureau of Investigations (1971) Uniform Crime Reports. Washington, D. C.: U.S. Government Printing Office.
GARFINKEL, H. and E. BITTNER (1967) "Good organizational reasons for 'bad' clinic records," pp. 186-207 in H. Garfinkel, Studies in Ethnomethodology. Englewood Cliffs, N.J.: Prentice-Hall.
GOLDSTEIN, J. (1960) "Police discretion not to invoke the criminal process." Yale Law Journal 69: 543-594.
GORMAN, A. C., F. D. JAY, and R.R.J. GALLATI (1973) Introduction to Law Enforcement and Criminal Justice. Rev. 19th printing. Springfield, Ill.: C. C. Thomas.
HALL, J. (1953) "Police and the law in a democratic society." Indiana Law Journal 23: 133-177.
HAMILTON, W. H. and C. C. RODEE (1937) "Police power," in Encyclopedia of the Social Sciences. Volume 12. New York: Macmillan.
HART, H.L.A. (1961) The Concept of Law. Oxford, England: Clarendon Press.
HENRY, J. V. (1966) "Breach of peace and disorderly conduct laws: void for vagueness?" Howard Law Journal 12: 318-331.
HOCHNAGEL, M. and H. W. STEGE (1966) "The right to resist unlawful arrest: an outdated concept?" Tulsa Law Journal 3: 40-46.
Institute for Defense Analysis (1967) Task Force Report: Science and Technology. The President's Commission on Law Enforcement and Administration of Justice. Washington, D. C.: U.S. Government Printing Office.
Kansas City Police Department (1971) Survey of Municipal Police Departments. Kansas City, Mo.
KANT, I. (1913) "Zum Ewigen Frieden: Ein Philosophischer Entwurf," in Kleinere Schriften zur Geschichtsphilosophie, Ethik und Politik. Leipzig: Felix Meiner. (Originally printed in 1795.)

KELSEN, H. (1961) General Theory of Law and State. New York: Russel & Russel.

LaFAVE, W. (1965) Arrest: The Decision to Take a Suspect into Custody. Boston: Little, Brown.

LEONARD, V. A. and H. W. MORE (1971) Police Organization and Management. 3rd ed. Mineola, N. Y.: Foundation Press.

LOHMAN, J. D. and G. E. MISNER (1966) The Police and the Community. Report prepared for the President's Commission on Law Enforcement and Administration of Justice. Volume 2. Washington, D. C.: U.S. Government Printing Office.

MILLER, W. B. (1958) "Lower-class culture as a generating milieu of gang delinquency." Journal of Social Issues 14: 5-19.

National Commission on Productivity (1973) "Report of the Task Force to Study Police Productivity." Mimeo. Draft.

NIEDERHOFFER, A. (1969) Behind the Shield: The Police in Urban Society. Garden City, N. Y.: Anchor Books.

REISS, A. J., Jr. (1971) The Police and the Public. New Haven, Conn.: Yale University Press.

REIWALD, P. (1944) Eroberung des Friedens. Zurich: Europa Verlag.

ROBINSON, C. D. (1965) "Alternatives to arrest of lesser offenders." Crime and Delinquency 11: 8-21.

SILVER, A. (1967) "The demand for order in civil society: a review of some themes in the history of urban crime, police, and riot," pp. 1-24 in D. J. Bordua (ed.) The Police: Six Sociological Essays. New York: John Wiley.

SKOLNICK, J. H. (1966) Justice Without Trial: Law Enforcement in a Democratic Society. New York: John Wiley.

Stanford Law Review (1961) "Justification for the Use of Force in the Criminal Law." Volume 13: 566-609.

STEPHEN, J. F. (1883) A History of Criminal Law in England. Volume 3. London: Macmillan.

WARNER, S. B. (1942) "Uniform arrest act." Vanderbilt Law Review 28: 315-347.

WEBER, M. (1947) The Theory of Social and Economic Organization. Translation edited by T. Parsons. Glencoe, Ill.: Free Press.

WILSON, J. Q. (1968) Varieties of Police Behavior: The Management of Law and Order in Eight Communities. Cambridge, Mass.: Harvard University Press.

WILSON, O. W. (1963) Police Administration. 2nd ed. New York: McGraw-Hill.

Chapter 3

THE EFFECTS OF TRAINING AND EDUCATION ON POLICE ATTITUDES AND PERFORMANCE: A PRELIMINARY ANALYSIS

DENNIS C. SMITH and ELINOR OSTROM

Increasing the educational levels and the amount of training provided police are two reforms which have long been recommended as keys to the improvement of police services in America. A Task Force of the President's Commission on Law Enforcement and the Administration of Justice in 1967 and the Wickersham Commission, in its report on police more than three decades earlier, expressed "the need for highly educated personnel" (Task Force on the Police, 1967: 126; National Commission of Law Observance and Enforcement [Wickersham Commission], Report on Police, 1931). Charles Saunders, Jr., in his recent book, *Upgrading the Police: Education and Training for Better Law Enforcement*, builds his case for increased police education and training on a proposition, stated by Raymond Fosdick in one of the first major studies of police in this century, that "the heart of the police problem is one of personnel" (Saunders,

AUTHORS' NOTE: The authors wish to acknowledge their indebtedness to the many people and several organizations who made vital contributions to the two-year study of police services in the St. Louis Metropolitan area on which this paper is based. We cannot mention each individually, but we would be remiss if we failed to thank the

1970: 4). According to Jerome Skolnick the notion that the solution to police problems is to "upgrade" the police pervades the tradition of police reform in the United States (Skolnick, 1966: 4).[1] While few have claimed that education or training are panaceas for police problems, substantial claims have been made for the salutory consequences which are expected to flow from "improving the quality of law enforcement personnel."

Despite the long history of proposals to mandate higher education and training requirements for police personnel, minimal public action has occurred until the last five years. With the advent of urban riots and increased fear of crime, the previously local issue of law enforcement became an item on the national policy agenda. A series of national commissions have studied the police and proposed reforms (President's Commission on Law Enforcement and the Administration of Justice, 1967; National Advisory Commission on Civil Disorders, 1968; National Commission on the Causes and Prevention of Violence, 1970). The need for additional training and education for police has been a common theme in the commission reports. The President's Commission on Law Enforcement and the Administration of Justice developed the most detailed brief for this reform policy. The Report of the Task Force on the Police of that commission assembled data on education and training levels of police departments throughout the United States. It concluded that current levels "remain minimal in most departments." It asserted, "The quality of police service will not significantly improve until higher educational requirements are established for its personnel" (Task Force on the Police, 1967: 126). "Cities and counties which fail to recognize the vital necessity of upgrading the educational levels of their departments are," according to the Task Force on the Police (1967: 126), "guilty of perpetuating ineffective police service and are not providing their citizens with adequate police service and protection." The Task Force also states that training "is one of the most important means of upgrading the service of a police department" (Task Force on the Police, 1967: 137).

participating chiefs of police and other St. Louis area law enforcement officials, scholars at the University of Missouri, St. Louis, the graduate and undergraduate students at Indiana University who did most of the interviews, members of the Workshop in Political Theory and Policy Analysis office staff, and especially our colleague throughout the study, Roger B. Parks.

We appreciate the critical scrutiny an earlier version of this paper received from Charles Kuhlman, Elliot Liebow, Jim McDavid, Nancy Neubert, Roger Parks, and Michael Vlaisavljevich.

The St. Louis area police study was made possible through Grant Number 5 R01 MH 19911 from the Center for the Studies of Metropolitan Problems of the National Institute of Mental Health to Dr. Elinor Ostrom, supplemented with support from the Center for Urban Affairs, Indiana University.

An earlier draft of this paper was presented at the 1973 Annual Meetings of the Society for the Study of Social Problems, August 24-27, New York.

The Commission's final recommendations include the following:

The ultimate aim of all police departments should be that all personnel with general enforcement powers have baccalaureate degrees. (p. 109)

Police departments should take immediate steps to establish a minimum requirement of a baccalaureate degree for all supervisory and executive positions. (p. 110)

All training programs should provide instruction on subjects that prepare recruits to exercise discretion properly, and to understand the community, the role of the police, and what the criminal justice system can and cannot do . . . (p. 112)

Formal police training programs for recruits in all departments, large and small, should consist of an absolute minimum of 400 hours of classroom work spread over a 4- to 6-month period so that it can be combined with carefully selected and supervised field training. (p. 112)

Every general enforcement officer should have at least one week of intensive inservice training a year. Every officer should be given incentives to continue his general education or acquire special skills outside his department. (p. 113)

In 1968, in response to the recommendations of the President's Commission, Congress for the first time authorized and appropriated significant amounts of money to support police education and training programs (Law Enforcement Assistance Administration, 1971: 81-87). Congress has continued to allocate monies for this purpose. State and local governments have also taken a variety of steps to bring education and training levels of police within the purview of public policy. Commissions have been established to set requirements. Training academies have been created. Incentive programs for educational attainment have been funded. In some cases, requirements for specific amounts of training have been mandated by state legislation (Law Enforcement Assistance Administration, 1971: 81-87; Section 66.250 R.S. Mo. Supp. 1972). In short, these reform proposals have been the subject of a significant amount of public policy-making over the last five years.

One might assume that the considerable emphasis on education and training as a police reform is based on a solid body of research on the relationship between those factors and police performance. However, there is a notable paucity of such research. Instead, as Saunders (1970: 81-82) conceded in stating his case for the reform:

The reasons advanced for college education for police are essentially the same as those used to justify higher education as preparation for any other career. They rest more on faith than fact.

The case for increasing the education and training of policemen rests, in part, on an analogy. Advocates of these reforms contend that police work is or should be (the distinction is not always made clear) a profession. The police are called upon to provide a vital service to the community. The structure of their present organization results in the individual police officer exercising extensive discretionary power which can have a profound effect on the lives of individuals. In the case of urban disorders, the entire community may feel the effects of police discretion. The Task Force on Police of the President's Commission on Law Enforcement and the Administration of Justice (1967: 125-126) stated: "Few professionals are so peculiarly charged with individual responsibility." The Task Force also maintained that "the complexity of the police task is as great as any other profession." After stressing the points of similarity between the tasks of policemen and those of the "learned" professions, the advocates of these police reforms typically emphasize the absence of advanced formal education (Task Force on the Police, 1967: 126-127; Clark, 1970: 146-148; Harvie, 1971: 59-61). Thus, they advocate "professionalizing" the police. When the President's Commission recommended that, due to "the nature of the police task and its effect on our society, all personnel with general enforcement powers have baccalaureate degrees," their recommendation corresponds to Wilbert Moore's (1970: 11) contention that for professional status "the minimum educational requirement be placed at the equivalent of the college baccalaureate degree."

Making brief what could be a lengthy discussion, it may suffice to note here that the status of professions is viewed by most advocates of increasing the levels of education or training for police through lenses shaped by the sociology of work literature (Moore, 1970: 245-301). In this literature a profession is taken to be an abstract model of occupational organization and practice characterized by certain key elements. Oversimplified, the model refers to an occupation whose members use formally acquired technical skills to provide service to "clients" in accordance with publicly proclaimed standards of practice. Discussions of this model frequently refer to the way in which the technical skills or competence are acquired (prolonged education and training) and the role of a written code of ethics in guaranteeing a service orientation on the part of practitioners. According to the model, professions are typically granted authority to regulate their own practice in reward for their expertise and service orientation (Wilensky, 1964; Eulau, 1973; Haug and Sussman, 1969: 153-155). Professions in this conceptualization know what is best (competence) and can be relied upon to do what is best (service orientation) if allowed to exercise their own judgment (autonomy). The role of education and training is regarded as critical in professions both for imparting the necessary skills and for inculcating the appropriate values. Applied to police the contention is this: if urban communities want their police to be competent and dutiful servants, they must be trained and educated, they must be professionalized.

The policy of professionalizing the police has many advocates and some critics. Advocates of the reform place primary emphasis on the competence and service orientation elements of the model of professions, while giving slight mention to the element of autonomy.[2] Critics of the policy typically focus on the element of autonomy (Milner, 1971 and Westley, 1970). They question whether the introduction of greater autonomy into the governance of police is consistent with the maintenance of a democratic rule of law. However, one advocate of professionalization, Albert J. Reiss, Jr., bases his case for the reform largely on the hope that the self-regulation implied by professional organization will be more successful in constraining the use and abuse of police power than is the current practice of relying on bureaucratic organization (Reiss, 1971: 202). These issues set the stage for a much larger discussion than is possible here.[3]

Questions could be raised about (1) the appropriateness of the analogy between police and such occupations as law and medicine, (2) the adequacy of the "model" of professions as an explanatory tool or a prescriptive guide, and (3) the degree of fit between the model of profession and the actual practice of law and medicine from which the model was abstracted. However, the approach in this paper will be to set aside those questions for the present.

An Empirical Analysis

We will undertake an empirical analysis of some of the claims of particular relationships between each of these reforms and the attitudes and performance of police. An empirical study of the relationships between training and/or education of police and their attitudes is a relatively noncontroversial method of examining propositions derived from the work of those proposing increased reliance on both of these strategies. As will be discussed in the next section, advocates of reform make specific references to the changes in police attitudes which increases in training or education will produce. Thus, examining the relationship between an officer's level of training and/or his level of education and his attitudes with regard to key aspects of his job is a very obvious method for examining these propositions.

However, it is almost impossible to find a non-controversial method for examining the relationships between training or education and police *performance*. The measurement of police performance, like the measurement of the output of most public goods and services, is exceedingly complex. Reliance on F.B.I. crime statistics as a measure of performance is subject to severe methodological criticism (Biderman, 1966; E. Ostrom, 1971). In this study, as in a series of previous studies on the organization of police in metropolitan areas

(E. Ostrom et al., 1973; IsHak, 1972; E. Ostrom and Parks, 1973), surveys of citizens' experiences with and evaluation of the police serving them have been used as an instrument to measure the performance of police agencies. The use of citizen surveys as a measure of the consequences of police professionalization is likely to be especially controversial. According to classical statements of the professional model, a professional must be judged by his peers; the lay community is presumed incapable. In Ernest Greenwood's (1966: 12-13) widely cited article on "Attributes of a Profession," he states:

> In a professional relationship, however, the professional dictates what is good or evil for the client, who has no choice but to accede to professional judgment. Here the premise is that, because he lacks the requisite theoretical background, the client cannot diagnose his own needs or discriminate among the range of possibilities for meeting them. *Nor is the client considered able to evaluate the caliber of the professional service he receives. (emphasis added)*

As part of their claim to professional status, some police have asserted that citizens are inappropriate judges of their performance. Neiderhoffer notes the use of the professional model as an argument against civilian review boards (Neiderhoffer, 1967: 4, also 178-190). Louis Radelet (1966: 89), in discussing the nature of "professional police-community relations," stresses the idea that professionals determine and respond to the "needs" and not the "wants" of clients. Viewed in this way, the use of citizen evaluations of police as a measure of police performance may be challenged. The disqualification of laymen as judges of performance is a paradoxical element in the professional model when considered alongside another component of the same model. As Haug and Sussman note, professional autonomy is granted as a result of public acceptance of an occupation's dual claim of expertise and service orientation (Haug and Sussman, 1969: 53). The dependence of professional status on community sanction, on public acceptance, clearly implies public evaluation. Hence the paradox.

Several premises underlie the prominent place of citizen evaluations in our study of police performance. First, as Reiss (1971: 65-88) stresses, citizens play a critical role in the provision of police services and the law enforcement process. Police depend upon citizens to call when events arouse their suspicion, to supply information, and to testify as witnesses. Citizen willingness to participate depends, it is assumed, on their perception of the likely consequences of that participation (Riker and Ordeshook, 1973). That depends, in turn, on their perception of the competence, reliability, and responsibility of the police. Thus, as a practical matter citizen evaluations of police performance are important indicators of police performance.[4]

Second, some of the effects which are predicted to flow from increasing the levels of training or education of police should be felt directly by citizens. Thus, a citizen survey is a major method of ascertaining if citizens' perceptions reflect any difference in the performance of better trained or better educated police compared with the performance of police having lower levels of training or education.

Third, few of the records routinely maintained by police departments or other agencies provide adequate indicators of police performance. The most frequently collected data—reported crimes listed in the F.B.I. crime index—normally account for only 10 to 20 percent of the total activities of a police department. Arrest rates and clearance rates provide some interesting insights into the activity patterns of a department but may heavily reflect the incentive system established by a police chief.

Education and training are expected by proponents of these reforms to produce a variety of specific benefits. One category of predicted effects relates to changes in the outlook, attitudes, and orientation of police officers. Both education and vocational training are expected to increase the officer's capacity to cope with the complex tasks which his job may entail. These effects will lead, according to the justification of the reform, to a second category of effects: improved police performance resulting in higher regard for police in the communities they serve.

In our analysis, the effects of training and education are considered separately. Training and education are frequently grouped together under the rubric of professionalization or "upgrading police personnel." The impact of training and education are not however, expected to be equal in impact but frequently to have the same type of effect. For example, college education is considered more important than training in shaping attitudes toward due process and other democratic values, but a unit on this subject is normally included in proposed training curricula (Saunders, 1970: 122-123). Training is expected to play a greater role in the acquisition of skills for handling specific police assignments, but college is expected to have a general, positive impact on the competence and self-assurance of the officer in facing complex tasks.

Hypotheses

The following hypotheses are among those which follow from the case presented for policies requiring increased training and education for police.[5] Police officers with higher levels (as compared with lower levels) of training (T) and education (E) will:

H_{1T} and H_{1E} have a lower estimation of the efficacy of force in solving crime problems;

H_{2T} and H_{2E} have a view of the goals of law enforcement which includes the protection of civil liberties even of persons suspected of criminal acts;

H_{3T} and H_{3E} be less critical of Supreme Court decisions;[6]

H_{4T} and H_{4E} be more tolerant of public protest and dissent;

H_{5T} and H_{5E} have greater willingness to accept innovation in the structure of police departments;

H_{6T} and H_{6E} be less approving of a military model of organization for police departments;

H_{7T} and H_{7E} have greater confidence in their competence and preparedness for coping with police assignments.

In addition to the above hypotheses relating training and education to specific attitudes of the individual police officer, a second series of hypotheses can be posited which examine the relationship between the amount of training or the amount of education present in a police department and the performance of that department. When performance is evaluated by citizens, citizens served by departments whose officers have higher levels of training or education (compared with citizens served by departments having lower levels) will:

H_{8T} and H_{8E} tend to give their police services a higher rating;

H_{9T} and H_{9E} tend to give a higher rating to police-community relations in their neighborhood;

H_{10T} and H_{10E} be more likely to believe that police respond quickly when called;

H_{11T} and H_{11E} be more likely to report that police treat all citizens equally; and

H_{12T} and H_{12E} be less likely to report that crime is increasing in their neighborhood.

When performance is measured by the success with which a police department is able to obtain warrants from a Prosecuting Attorney, departments whose officers have higher levels of training or education (compared with departments having lower levels) will:

H_{13T} and H_{13E} be more successful in obtaining warrants from the Prosecuting Attorney's office.

Data Base

In order to examine the above hypotheses we rely upon data collected during the spring and summer of 1972 in a major study of police performance conducted in the St. Louis metropolitan area. For the first series of hypotheses we will examine data obtained from interviews with 712 police officers employed in 29 different police departments. The departments varied in size from those employing only part-time officers (no full-time officers) to one employing over 2,200 officers. For the second series of hypotheses we will examine data obtained from approximately 4,000 citizens, distributed across jurisdictions served by 29 police departments. To each citizen case we added the aggregate characteristics of the department or district of a department serving his neighborhood. There were 45 neighborhoods included in the survey. The research design underlying the choice of neighborhoods and communities within the St. Louis metropolitan area has been discussed elsewhere (E. Ostrom, Parks and Smith, 1973). The Appendix provides a brief overview of the sample frame employed and the methods of data collection utilized.

RELATIONSHIPS BETWEEN TRAINING AND EDUCATION OF POLICE AND ATTITUDES TOWARD WORK

The proponents of increased education and training regard the reform to be important not only because they are expected to increase the skills available to the officer, but also because both education and training are thought to have an important impact on the orientation of policemen toward their work.

In order to examine the effects of training and education on the attitudes of officers toward work, our survey included the following items:

A. If a patrolman in tough neighborhoods had fewer restrictions on his use of force, many of the serious crime problems in those neighborhoods would be greatly reduced.
Strongly Agree___ Agree___ Disagree___ Strongly Disagree___

B. Police here would be more effective if they didn't have to worry about "probable cause" requirements in questioning or searching citizens.
Strongly Agree___ Agree___ Disagree___ Strongly Disagree___

C. What effects have Supreme Court decisions over the last ten years had on law enforcement here?

D. In this country there is no real justification for protest and dissent.
Strongly Agree___ Agree___ Disagree___ Strongly Disagree___

E. Is the command and discipline found in a military organization a good model for a police department?
Yes___ No___

F. The following have been suggested as ways of improving law enforcement in this country. Would you favor or oppose:
[list, including the following:]
Seeking chiefs and other top officers from outside of the department.
Favor___ Oppose___ Strongly___

The two measures of police training used at this stage in the analysis are (1) total weeks of training (including "basic training" at recruit schools or academies, F.B.I. courses on specialized subjects, training offered by other agencies such as the Department of the Army or the Federal Bureau of Narcotics and Dangerous Drugs, and short courses such as the ones held at Michigan State University on police-community relations); and (2) length of basic or recruit training.[7] Recruit training is now the exclusive province of a single Greater St. Louis Metropolitan Police Academy, which has a sixteen-week program. Until several years ago, only officers in the City of St. Louis had the sixteen-week training. Officers in the municipalities typically attended an intensive two-week course sponsored by the Missouri Highway Patrol. Some, however, attended the twelve-week County Police Department Academy prior to its merger in the Greater St. Louis Metropolitan Police Academy.

Thus, even though all new officers are now required to take sixteen weeks of training at a single academy, the vast majority of officers in our sample joined their respective departments when length of training was highly variable. This variation is reflected in our sample.

Findings: The Relationship Between Police Training and Attitudes Toward Work

We begin by examining the simple association of training and attitudinal variables. The relationships between these variables and the background or contextual variables of officer age, tenure in a particular department, total years as a police officer, rank, assignment (uniform or plainclothes), and size of the officer's department was also examined. Where these provide additional insight, those results are also presented.

Use of Force (H_{1T}). Approximately 40 percent of all officers agreed with the statement (A, above) attributing effectiveness to force as an instrument of crime control. Total weeks of training does not discriminate between those who agree or disagree on the use of force ($tau_c = -.03$).[8] Controlling for age, race, or length of service did not change the lack of relationships between total amount of police training and orientation toward the use of force.

Length of recruit training does make some difference. The direction of the relationship, however, is *opposite* the prediction derived from the reform literature (tau$_c$ = −.12). When we compare the extreme cases (those who attended the sixteen-week course)[9] the overall character of the relationship prevails in most of the categories of the control variables. The relationship is somewhat stronger (tau$_c$ = −.18) in smaller departments (less than or equal to 11 men). Officers in the largest department, all of whom have had the longer recruit training, are the ones most likely to strongly agree (20 percent) and agree (30 percent). While these results provide quite insufficient warrant for asserting the existence of a relationship which is the reverse of reform expectations, the data do not support reform claims.

Probable Cause (H$_{2T}$). If police officers have a view of the goals of law broad enough to include the protection of citizens' civil liberties, they will be unlikely to concur with the assertion that "probable cause" requirements reduce police effectiveness. Those officers who consider suppression of crime as an overriding objective might well agree with the assertion (Skolnick, 1966: 196-199). Just under half of the officers surveyed (48.8 percent) did agree with the statement (B above), and of that group, 17 percent indicated "strong agreement." Only 10 percent strongly disagreed. Amount of police training does not appear to be related to attitudes toward probable cause limits on searches and interrogation of citizens (tau$_c$ = .08), nor does length of recruit training makes a difference (tau$_c$ = −.02).

Effects of Supreme Court Decisions (H$_{3T}$). In the last decade, actions by the United States Supreme Court pertaining to police behavior have been a source of bitter controversy in law enforcement circles (Neiderhoffer, 1967: 161-174). Decisions such as Mapp v. Ohio, Escobedo v. Illinois, Miranda v. Arizona and others have been criticized for "handcuffing" the police. Neiderhoffer (1967: 173), recognizing the demands resulting from the decisions, stated an alternative interpretation: "Any department worthy of being called professional will meet this challenge successfully and emerge the stronger for it." The contention is made that through education and training police officers will learn what the law requires of them and gain an understanding of the American system of constitutional government in which Supreme Court protection of civil liberties is accepted as legitimate.

We asked each respondent to assess the effects of Supreme Court decisions on law enforcement (C above). Answers were coded into categories which included "very harmful," "somewhat harmful," "ambivalent," "somewhat helpful," and "very helpful." A statement such as "We do much better, more professional police work because of them" was coded "very helpful." "They ruined us; tied our hands completely" was coded "very harmful." The statement "They made our job harder, but I guess it should be that way" was placed in the middle or ambivalent category.

About half of all policemen surveyed regarded the decisions as harmful or very harmful. In contrast to the 20 percent who said the decisions were very harmful, only 5 percent said they were very helpful. Total amount of training shows no simple relationship to attitudes toward the Court (tau$_c$ = $-.03$). When a control for size of department is introduced, the negligible relationships prevail, except for a weak relationship (tau$_c$ of $-.12$) for officers serving in the smallest departments. This relationship, however, is not in the direction which the reform advocates suggest. Whereas 63 percent of those in the lowest training category found the decision of the court harmful in some degree, and 31 percent said they were somewhat helpful, 72 percent of those in the highest training category characterized the decisions as harmful and no officer in that category gave an answer that could be placed in "decisions are helpful" categories. Controlling for rank did not affect the lack of a relationship.

Protest and Dissent (H$_{4T}$). Only 20 percent of all officers surveyed expressed any degree of agreement with the statement "In this country, there is no real justification for protest and dissent." Total amount of training is not related (tau$_c$ = .07) with attitudes toward protest and dissent. Controlling for age and length of service, however, results in the appearance of a weak relationship between total training and favorable attitudes (that is, disagreement with the statement) toward protest (tau$_c$ = .15) in the highest age and length of service categories.

Length of recruit training (whether two or sixteen weeks) and attitudes toward protest appear not to be related.

Lateral Entry (H$_{5T}$). The President's Commission on Law Enforcement and the Administration of Justice noted that "Most departments today do not permit 'lateral entry' into command or staff position by officers from other departments or by civilians" (President's Commission on Law Enforcement and the Administration of Justice, 1967: 111). The Commission states that America's police personnel are "virtually frozen into the departments in which they started" in part "because of a traditional police resistance to 'outsiders' " (President's Commission on Law Enforcement and the Administration of Justice, 1967: 111). Since barriers to lateral movement are characterized as "stifling the professional development of the police service," it seems useful to ask (F above) whether the more highly trained police in our survey were less inclined to oppose lateral entry than their less "professionalized" fellow officers.

Total weeks of police training is not related to an officer's attitudes toward lateral entry (tau$_c$ = .00). Controlling for size of department, age of officer, or length of recruit training does not alter the finding of no relationship. Training, thus, does not help discriminate between the officers who favor (31 percent) and the officers who oppose (69 percent) opening top positions to lateral entry.

Military Model (H$_{6T}$). The status of a military model of organization for police departments (or "quasi-military" model as police tend to say) is extremely ambiguous. It is included in this discussion not because the literature on police reform has provided a clear hypothesis. It has not.[10] There is one reform tradition that views the infusion of police organization with military discipline and bearing as "professionalization" (Bittner, 1970: 53; Bordua and Reiss, 1966: 68-76). In that tradition, the role of training is largely the inculcation of discipline, with the curriculum patterned after and named after its military counterpart, "basic training" (Neiderhoffer, 1967: 45). Officers so trained might prefer a military organizational style. Another tradition expects training and education to produce competence and capacity for responsible exercise of discretion (Task Force on the Police, 1967: 136; Bittner, 1970: 86). One would expect, on the basis of this second tradition, high levels of training to be associated with rejection of the military model of police organization. While our hypotheses derives from the second tradition, the findings are relevant to both.

Most police officers (64 percent) answered in the affirmative our question about whether the command and discipline found in a military organization is a good model for a police department. Total amount of police training was not simply related to acceptance or rejection of the military model (tau$_c$ = −.01). The percent of officers approving the model in the three categories of total training were 64 percent, 65 percent, 65 percent. Introducing controls did not change the finding of no relationship.

Feelings of Preparedness (H$_{7T}$). Included within the set of tasks assigned to police are some which are quite complex. Advocates of "upgrading police personnel" frequently contrast the present need in police work for brains with the requirement in times past for brawn. Their belief is that training can better prepare police officers to cope effectively with the demands of their office (Clark, 1970: 132-150; Task Force on the Police, 1967: 125-137; Bittner, 1970: 83-85). Quite a different perspective is offered by James Q. Wilson, who contends (1968: 283) that competence in police work is derived not through formalized training but through apprenticeship. He is not merely recounting the current practice in law enforcement but making a more substantial assertion that police competence, at the present time, *cannot* be based on classroom learning (whether at the academy or college) because, he maintains, police work lacks a "proven technology" (Wilson, 1968: 63).

We asked each to indicate how well his training and experience had prepared him for handling family disturbances, civil disorders, traffic accidents, narcotics cases, court appearances, and problem juveniles.

Police officers do not feel equally prepared for all six types of assignments. Whereas almost 80 percent of all officers in the survey felt "very well prepared" for traffic accidents, and almost as frequently felt that they were very well prepared for family disturbances and court appearances, only 26 percent indicated that they were very well prepared for narcotics cases and less than 40 percent stated that they were very well prepared for civil disorders and problem juveniles. The distribution of answers on the other extreme ("not very well" prepared) was similarly varied, ranking in the opposite order from preparedness. All of the associations between total weeks training of officers and reported feelings of preparedness are negligible. The length of time spent in basic training is weakly associated with feeling of preparedness in dealing with problem juveniles (tau$_c$ = $-.14$). However, increased training is weakly related to reported feelings of *un*preparedness.

Findings: The Relationship Between Education and Attitudes Toward Work

At this stage of preliminary analysis of data we will follow the precedent of the few studies which have undertaken an empirical examination of the effects of education on police (Neiderhoffer, 1967; Walsh, 1970; Milner, 1971; Smith, Locke, and Walker, 1967; Cohen and Chaiken, 1973). That is, we will ignore the obviously important refinements which are possible and appropriate in the use of college education as a variable.[11] Number of college credits, grouped into categories representing years of college education (30 credit hours equals one year), is used as our measure of college education. While many of the discussions recommending college education requirements for police refer specifically to a need for "college graduates," they typically indicate that some college is preferable to no college where degree holders are not available. Thus, for policy purposes, college credit is treated as at least an ordinal measure. We follow that practice in our analysis.

Use of Force (H$_{1E}$). The advocacy of college education for those who engage in police work rests, in a large measure, on the conclusion that intelligence and knowledge rather than physical force are the keys to successful law enforcement. There is the assumption, more or less explicitly stated, that intelligent, well-adjusted men today go to college and that college has a capability to impart knowledge which surpasses other learning situations. Finally, there is an assumption that the college milieu has a broadening, a humanizing effect (Task Force on the Police, 1967: 126; Clark, 1970: 146-147; Smith, Locke, and Walker, 1967; Saunders, 1970: 81-92). As a consequence, the college educated policeman is expected to understand the inadequacy of force as an instrument of crime control and to accept limits of the use of force by police on humanitarian and constitutional grounds. Restraint in the use of force is a characteristic attributed to "professional police" (see Skolnick, 1969: 248-149; Clark, 1970: 132-150).

Our question on the use of force by police simultaneously probed acceptance of limits on the use of force and perceptions of the efficacy of force as a solution to problems of crime. Approximately 40 percent of the respondents agreed or strongly agreed that limits on the use of force in tough neighborhoods reduced success in controlling crime. To what extent is amount of college education associated with rejection of freer use of force as a solution to crime? The preliminary answer is: To some small extent.

Years of college and disagreement with the use of force statement are weakly associated (tau_c = .11). Controlling for the effects of other variables produces in most cases only small changes.

Probable Cause Reduces Police Effectiveness (H$_{2E}$). A study (Smith, Locke, and Walker, 1967: 132) cited by advocates of college education for police concludes that:

> There are certain personality characteristics of police who attend college that make it likely that they will be able to function more effectively with respect to the problems stemming from civil rights demonstrations and more effectively in accordance with the guidelines set down by the Supreme Court with respect to arrests and search and seizure.

It is clear that reform advocates expect college educated officers to include the protection of civil liberties as part of their responsibility to uphold the law. Saunders (1970: 89), citing the 1967 study mentioned above and several others as support for the reform proposal, states: "Such findings are not conclusive but they suggest that large scale recruitment of college graduates would significantly affect police performance."

While 49 percent of all respondents agreed or strongly agreed with the assertion that probable cause requirements reduce police effectiveness, those with any college at all were somewhat less likely to agree than those with none (tau_c = .15). Years of college work is also weakly related (tau_c = .12). These preliminary findings provide some weak support for the hypotheses derived for reform proposals. However, controlling for size of department complicates the picture. Only in the middle-size departments does the weak relationship exist in the reform-predicted direction. The largest and smallest departments show only a negligible relationship between years of education and attitudes toward probable cause.

Effects of Supreme Court Decisions (H$_{3E}$). One goal of educating policemen, according to the Task Force on Police, is to increase their appreciation of our constitutional system of government in which, as Skolnick (1969: 249) says, the police "are not supposed to adjudicate and punish; they are supposed to apprehend and take into custody." Milner (1971: 197) concludes, "Most advocates of police reform would expect a positive relationship between education and the degree of approval of a decision like Miranda." And, as noted earlier, a 1967 study of police suggested that the inclination to attend college by itself augured a capacity to function more effectively in accordance with Supreme Court guidelines (Smith, Locke, and Walker, 1967).

In the realm of attitudes, we find some support for reform expectations about effects of college. Slightly more than 60 percent of the officers interviewed assessed the effects of Court decisions to be harmful or very harmful to law enforcement. Those with college were less inclined to perceive the decisions as harmful. Years of college is weakly related to characterizing the decisions as helpful ($tau_c = .19$). The relationship is slightly weaker for patrolmen ($tau_c = .17$) and slightly stronger among command rank personnel ($tau_c = .22$). Rank itself is weakly related to acceptance of the Court as helpful ($tau_c = .13$).

The relationship between college and regarding the Court decision as helpful is not the same for officers in departments of all sizes. The relationship is negligible in departments of 11 men or less, is strongest in the middle-sized municipal departments ($tau_c = .20$) and the county department ($tau_c = .18$), and is reduced to a tau_c of .12 among officers in the largest department in the study. In this connection, the actual percentages of agreement and disagreement are worth reporting (Table 1). One might expect to explain the Court's low score among officers in the largest (though certainly not the "mini") departments with the fact that the largest department also has the largest proportion of officers who are older and have significantly longer tenure. There is a tendency in the literature to contrast the "old breed" of cop with the new policeman (Wilson, 1968a: 173-195). Overall, there is no relationship between an officer's age and his attitudes toward the Court. But a weak relationship does appear when we control for size of department with age being related negatively to considering

Table 1. POLICE OFFICERS' ATTITUDES TOWARD EFFECTS OF SUPREME COURT
DECISIONS IN DIFFERENT SIZED DEPARTMENTS

Department Size	Percent Very Harmful or Somewhat Harmful	Percent Very Helpful or Somewhat Helpful	N
Mini (0-11)	64	28	(47)
Muni (12-70)	58	28	(342)
County (422)	55	36	(81)
St. Louis City (2,200)	83	13	(95)
TOTAL	62	27	(565)

the Court helpful in the largest department (tau_c = −.15). For middle-sized departments the relationship either remains negligible (muni's) or becomes weakly positive (county, tau_c = .17). Thus, if the "old breed" explanation serves at all, it does not pertain to all sizes of departments.

Protest and Dissent (H_{4E}). Ramsey Clark and others have held that college educated officers will feel less threatened by and more easily accept the legitimacy of public protest and dissent in America (Clark, 1970: 144-145). Our findings provide some confirmation for their expectations.

Years of college work is weakly related to acceptance of protest and dissent overall (tau_c = .14), and for both patrolmen (tau_c = .12) and command rank personnel (tau_c = .16). When a control for age is introduced, however, the relationship disappears for the middle age categories (including officers who are between 30 and 50 years old).[12]

Lateral Entry (H_{5E}). There is a weakly negative relationship between college work done and opposition to lateral entry (tau_c = −.16) which holds for patrolmen (tau_c = −.14) and grows slightly stronger for command personnel (tau_c = −.21). The relationship also remains in categories of age and length of police service. However, the effects of college are different in different sized departments. The relationship is negligible in the smallest departments, is very weak in the largest department (−.11). but is slightly stronger than the overall relationship in the middle-sized departments (tau_c = −.17) for both muni and county police. The reaction to lateral entry varies by size of department. If we compare the extreme answers we obtain the percentage distribution in Table 2.

Military Model of Police Organization (H_{6E}). The traditional reliance of police departments on a military model of organization has been identified by some reformers as a barrier to recruiting and retaining college educated policemen. For Bittner, the resistance college educated men will pose to perpetuation of the military style of organization is a major reason for having educated policemen (Bittner, 1970: 86-87). However, is education level related to an officer's view of the appropriateness of military command and discipline in police work? At this point, we cannot conclude that it is.

Table 2. RELATIONSHIP BETWEEN SIZE OF DEPARTMENT AND ATTITUDE
TOWARD LATERAL ENTRY (in percentage)

Number of Full-Time Officers	Mini (0-11)	Muni (12-70)	County (422)	St. Louis City (2,200)
Strongly Oppose	32	37	40	66
Strongly Favor	19	13	12	5
Grand N = (686)	(68)	(409)	(94)	(115)
tau_b = .17				

In our survey 64 percent of all officers expressed acceptance of military organization as a model for police. Years of college was negligibly related to acceptance or rejection (tau—.04). When controls are introduced the relationship remains negligible.

Feelings of Preparedness (H$_{7E}$). The levels of association between amount of college education and reported feelings of preparedness are mixed. Although in four of the six preparedness items the relationship is negligible, family disturbances and civil disorders show a tau of .13 and .12, respectively. However, the direction of the relationships is the opposite of the reformers' expectations. In each case, the more college work an officer had done, the less likely he was to choose "very well" prepared and the more likely "not very well" appears as his answer.

In addition to the specific preparedness questions, officers were asked a general question related to Wilson's contention that police work lacks a body of knowledge, a "proven technology." A large majority of the respondents in our survey (84 percent) agree or strongly agree with the statement: "There is available today the knowledge to enable policemen to handle almost any of the situations they face." Agreement with this statement does not vary appreciably with length of training or amount of college education, nor does it vary with the officer's age, length of service as a policeman, or the size of the department in which he works.

While it seems clear that the police surveyed agree on the existence of the knowledge necessary to cope with the demands of their jobs, it is less clear how this knowledge is to be obtained. Only 25 percent of all respondents would set the formal education requirement for new police officers at higher than high school. Most of that group specified only "some college." Less than 5 percent would require a degree of any kind and only 0.6 percent would require a baccalaureate as recommended by the Task Force. On this question, college education of the respondent is positively related to requiring college of recruits.

SUMMARY

In summary, as Table 3 shows, the simple relationship between training of officers and their attitudes rank from negligible to weak. The direction of some of the relationships is opposite that which reform advocates would predict. While education generally shows relationships which have the sign predicted by the advocates of these reforms, all relationships are weak except one, which is negligible. Furthermore, as noted in the preceding discussion, these weak relationships are altered by the introduction of controls. In particular, controlling for size of department often resulted in the finding that the

Table 3. SUMMARY OF SIMPLE RELATIONSHIPS BETWEEN TRAINING AND
EDUCATION LEVELS OF POLICE AND THEIR ATTITUDES TOWARD WORK

	Amount of Training (tau_c)	Length of Basic Training (tau_c)	College Credits (tau_c)
H_1 Use of force effective	−.03	−.12**	.11*
H_2 Probable cause reduces effectiveness	.08	−.02	.12*
H_3 Supreme Court decisions harmful	−.03	−.03	.19*
H_4 No justification for protest or dissent	.07	.05	.14*
H_5 Lateral entry	.01	.05	−.16*
H_6 Military model of police organization	−.01	−.10**	.04

 * A weak relationship (tau ⩾.10 and <.25) in the reform-predicted direction
** A weak relationship (tau ⩾.10 and <.25) in the opposite direction of reform prediction

relationship obtains only in the middle-sized departments; it is reduced to a negligible level for the largest and the smaller departments. This preliminary finding points to a conclusion tentatively asserted previously, that relationships between police-relevant variables may not be the same in different sized jurisdictions (Ostrom and Parks, 1973: 385).

Findings Regarding the Relationship Between Training and Police Performance Evaluated by Citizens (H_{8T}-H_{12T})

Each officer interviewed was asked about each of his training experiences; where they occurred, the type of training, and the length of each training experience. From these responses a score was computed for each officer for the amount of training (in weeks) he had received. From these individual scores, a departmental average was computed (or, for districts in the City of St. Louis or St. Louis County, a district average was computed). The average weeks of training for a department (or district) was then collapsed into three categories:

(1) Departments (or districts) whose average weeks of training was less than or equal to 12 weeks.

(2) Departments (or districts) whose average weeks of training was 13 through 16 weeks.

(3) Departments (or districts) whose average weeks of training was more than 16 weeks.

Each citizen respondent was then assigned the appropriate score for the police department (or district of a department in the City of St. Louis or St. Louis County) serving his neighborhood. All police officers hired after September 28, 1971, must have a minimum of 16 weeks training. But at the time of our survey, approximately equal numbers of citizens interviewed were served by police departments (or districts of departments) which were distributed across the three categories of training level.

The citizen survey included the following five questions:

(1) What rating would you give police services in your neighborhood (Outstanding, Good, Adequate, Inadequate, or Very Poor)?

(2) When the police are called in your neighborhood, in your opinion, how fast do they come (Very Rapidly, Quickly Enough, Slowly, Very Slowly, and Not At All)?

(3) Do you think crime in your neighborhood is increasing, about the same, or decreasing?

(4) What rating would you give police-community relations in your neighborhood (Outstanding, Good, Adequate, Inadequate, or Very Poor)?

(5) The police in your neighborhood treat all citizens equally according to the law (Strongly Agree, Agree, Disagree, Strongly Disagree)?

If the average level of training of police officers serving a neighborhood affects citizen evaluation of police performance, one would expect that those respondents served by departments (or districts of departments) with the highest levels of training would be more likely to:

(1) Rate police services in their neighborhood as outstanding.

(2) Rate police as responding very rapidly in their neighborhood.

(3) Evaluate crime trend as not increasing.

(4) Rate police-community relations in their neighborhood as outstanding.

(5) Agree that police in their neighborhood treat all citizens equally according to the law.

However, as shown on Table 4, three of the relationships are very weak and opposite of that predicted. The other two relationships are negligible.

The possibility of a stronger relationship between race, length of residence, and the educational level of a respondent with these five evaluations has also been examined. A respondent's race is weakly related to his rating of police services (tau = .13), his rating of police-community relations (tau = .13), and to whether he agrees that police treat all equally (tau = .11). In each of the above three cases, black respondents are more likely to give negative evaluations of

Table 4. RELATIONSHIP BETWEEN AVERAGE WEEKS OF TRAINING OF OFFICERS
SERVING A NEIGHBORHOOD AND CITIZEN EVALUATIONS OF POLICE
PERFORMANCE (Citizen Evaluations of Police Performance)

Average Weeks of Training of Officers in Department Serving Neighborhood	Rate Police Service Outstanding	Rate Police Response as Very Rapid	Rate Crime as Increasing in Their Neighborhood	Rate Police-Community Relations as Outstanding	Agree or Strongly Agree Police Treat All Citizens Equally
Less than or Equal to 12	34% (376)	59% (601)	24% (229)	24% (234)	79% (735)
13 to 16	27% (429)	52% (779)	29% (409)	15% (198)	84% (1069)
Over 16	22% (256)	41% (447)	39% (418)	14% (134)	82% (1790)
N for full table	(3903)	(3634)	(3414)	(3193)	(3164)
Predicted sign of relationship	+	+	−	+	+
Tau	−.10	−.12	.10	−.05	−.01

police services received. The educational level of a respondent is not related to
responses on any of the five evaluation questions, while the length of residence is
weakly related only to one; rating of police-community relations (tau = .11).

In order to examine the differential effect of training on significant
sub-populations of the sample frame, each of the cross tabulations between
levels of training and evaluations of police services were run controlling for race,
length of residence, and educational levels. Introducing length of residence and
educational levels as controls had minimal effect on the signs or strength of
coefficients. The signs of all but a few coefficients remained opposite to those
predicted and all remained extremely weak. When race of respondent is used as a
control, the sign changes for each relationship except for that between the
average level of training of the police serving a neighborhood and respondent's
evaluation of the crime trend. All relationships are negligible except for the weak
relationship between black respondents agreeing to the statement that police
treat all equally and the average level of training of the department (or district)
serving a neighborhood (tau = .12).

From these findings one would have to conclude that, in general, only weak
or negligible relationships exist between the level of training of police serving a

neighborhood and any of the evaluations given by residents of that neighborhood.

On the basis of this data, one could not find support for the hypotheses posited above concerning the relationship between the average levels of training provided police and police performance as evaluated by citizens.

Findings Regarding the Relationship Between College Education and Police Performance Evaluated by Citizens (H_{8E}-H_{12E})

Each officer interviewed was asked about the number of college credits he had obtained. From these individual responses, a departmental (or district) average was computed. The average number of college credits for the officers interviewed within a department (or district) was then collapsed into three categories:

(1) Departments (or districts) whose average number of college credits was 15 credits or less.

(2) Departments (or districts) whose average number of college credits was 16 to 30 credits.

(3) Departments (or districts) whose average number of college credits exceeded 30 credits.

Each citizen respondent was then assigned the appropriate score for the police department or district of a department in the City of St. Louis or St. Louis County serving his neighborhood.

We then examined the relationship between the average level of college work completed of police serving a neighborhood and the ratings citizens gave their police on the same five questions examined in the preceding section on training. The expected direction of all relationships for average level of college work completed would be the same as that expected for average level of formal police training.

As shown in Table 5, all five relationships are negligible. Controlling for length of residence or level of respondent's education did not change the direction of the relationships nor, in general, increase their strength. Controlling for race produced two slightly stronger relationships for black respondents: (1) the relationship between the level of college work completed for police serving a neighborhood and the respondent's general evaluation of police services (tau = .11), and (2) the relationship between the level of college work completed by police serving a neighborhood and the respondent's rating of police response rate (tau = .13).

In general, these preliminary findings provide little support for the hypotheses on the effects of college education derived from the literature on police reform.

Table 5. RELATIONSHIP BETWEEN AVERAGE COLLEGE CREDITS OF OFFICERS
SERVING A NEIGHBORHOOD AND CITIZEN EVALUATIONS OF POLICE
PERFORMANCE (Citizen Evaluations of Police Performance)

Average College Credits of Officers in Department Serving Neighborhood	Rate Police Service Outstanding	Rate Police Response as Very Rapid	Rate Crime as Increasing in Their Neighborhood	Rate Police-Community Relations as Outstanding	Agree or Strongly Agree Police Treat All Citizens Equally
Less than or Equal to 15	26% (359)	46% (582)	37% (454)	18% (198)	83% (915)
16 to 30	24% (386)	52% (758)	31% (437)	14% (182)	79% (1022)
Over 30	34% (316)	55% (487)	21% (165)	24% (186)	86% (657)
N for full table	(3903)	(3634)	(3414)	(3193)	(3164)
Predicted sign of relationship	+	+	−	+	+
Tau	.04	.07	−.09	.003	.02

The Relationship Between Education and Training Levels of Police Departments and Success at the Warrant Office

One of the frequently cited negative effects of "inadequate" training and "insufficient" education of police is the loss of convictions as a result of mishandling of cases by police. Clark (1970: 139) states:

> If police are not familiar with the law, there is no law—there is only arbitrary force. Police ignorant of the law risk destroying important prosecutions in a number of ways, as when evidence is obtained illegally or wrongful arrests are made. . . . If government is to be more than arbitrary and capricious power, police must be thoroughly familiar with the laws they enforce. This is a difficult intellectual undertaking. It must rest on a solid educational base. It requires continuing and sophisticated education to keep current.

Saunders (1970: 118) stresses the need for better trained police. He quotes approvingly J. Edgar Hoover's statement that:

> The efficiency of law enforcement today is commensurate with the degree of training of its officers. Only through modern police training can we

keep abreast of the times in the unceasing fight against lawlessness . . . Police work by untrained men . . . is as obsolete as the practice of
medicine by sorcery.

In light of such statements it seemed appropriate to find a means to measure
the degree of police effectiveness in their role as legal agents. To do this, we
measured police success in obtaining warrants from the prosecuting attorney for
their jurisdiction. This measure is the number of warrants issued by the Warrant
Office expressed as a percent of the total number of warrants for which
application was made (excluding checks, nonsupport, and traffic cases).[13]
This measure pertains to an entire department (or district of larger departments),
not to individual officers. It is, of course, a summary measure. We assumed that
prosecutors allocate their scarce resources to cases they believe will have a high
probability of success before judge and jury. The items that comprise the score
reflect the judgment of lawyers in the prosecuting attorney's office that the
applying department:

(1) has accurately identified a violation;

(2) has presented sufficient evidence;

(3) has obtained the evidence properly, that is, it will be admissable;

(4) is capable of bringing forth appropriate witnesses; or

(5) has officers who perform capably in court appearances.

Obviously, different prosecuting attorneys' offices operate or may operate under
somewhat different criteria, for a variety of reasons. Fortunately for compara-
bility, 28 of the 29 departments included in our study work with the same
Warrant Office of the Prosecuting Attorney of St. Louis County. The districts of
the St. Louis Metropolitan Police Department included in our study take their
applications to the Circuit Attorney for the City of St. Louis. We found (by
examining the data including and excluding the City Districts) that the
relationships were not affected by this factor.

Although success in obtaining warrants is obviously a crude measure (a
"batting average" of sorts), there is no single precise and convincing measure of
police performance. Consequently, we suggest warrant success as a measure,
among others (Ostrom, 1971; Parks, 1973). Furthermore, we recognize the
appropriateness of considering other factors (such as volume of work load, types
of criminal activity occurring, as so on). Since reform propositions have not
countenanced the complexity of the relationships involved. we feel justified in
presenting simple correlations at this stage of the analysis. We will, however, in
future analysis introduce other relevant variables.

The Findings (H_{13T} and H_{13E})

We calculated Warrant Success Scores for each department for 1970, 1971, and 1972. For the City of St. Louis, we calculated scores for each of the three districts of the St. Louis Metropolitan Police Department serving the neighborhoods included in our citizen survey. For the three-year period considered the average score ranged from a high of 88 percent to a low of 33 percent (both earned by very small departments). Most (90 percent) had a three-year average score falling within a 40 to 70 percent range.

For the years 1970, 1971, and 1972 the mean level of college education of officers in a department was weakly and negatively related to success in obtaining warrants.[14] For 1970, the correlation coefficient (r) is −.38; for 1971, −.30; and 1972, −.31. An average success score for the three years shows a similar negative correlation coefficient (r = −.25). The strength and direction of the relationship remained relatively constant for the three-year period. Despite the fact that relationships are weak, the finding that they are opposite the direction predicted by those who call for increased education as a police reform means our findings do not support the hypothesis derived from reform literature.

Mean total weeks of training, which ranges from 5 to 22, show a weak correlation with success scores and for each of the three years (.29, .14, −.07, for 1970-1972, respectively). Note that over the three years, the tendency is in the direction of a weaker and, ultimately, negative relationship. Given the small size of the correlation coefficient, we cannot provide much support for the hypothesized relationships between levels of training and education of department and success in obtaining warrants. Our hesitation is reinforced by the perplexing fact that, while levels of training and education of police in St. Louis County have presumably been rising from 1970 through 1972, the percent of total applications issued (for felonies and misdemeanors) has decreased from 60 percent in 1970, to 55 percent in 1971, to 50 percent in 1972 (McNary, 1970: 19; McNary, 1971: 27; McNary, 1972: 6).

CONCLUSION

The point of departure for this discussion was an observation of the prevalence of proposals calling for increased training and education for American policemen. The notion that higher levels of training and more college educated policemen will improve the quality of police services approaches the status of "conventional wisdom." The limited extent and substantive findings of the reported research on the effects of training and education suggested to us the need to pursue this topic at an early stage in our analysis of data collected in a sizeable survey of police services in a major metropolitan area. The preliminary character of the analyses require us to emphasize the tentativeness of our conclusions.

We found little evidence to support the claims which have been made for the beneficial effects of longer periods of training for police. We found little basis to conclude that an officer's total weeks of training or length of training as a recruit had an important impact on his feelings of preparedness for specific assignments or his attitudes towards selected law enforcement controversies. We did not find that departments with higher levels of training got appreciably higher evaluations from the citizens they serve, nor were they particularly more successful in obtaining warrants when they applied for them from the Prosecuting Attorney.

The relationships between college education levels and the dependent variables included in our analysis were weakly consistent with predictions of those advocating education as an important reform in the police field with a few exceptions. Although college educated officers did tend somewhat to manifest the reform predicted attitudes toward use of force, probable cause requirements, the Supreme Court, and lateral entry, they did not differ from less educated officers in the assessment of the appropriateness of a military model of organization for police departments. On questions about their feeling prepared for specific police assignments, college educated officers tended to be less confident. Departments whose officers had higher levels of college education were not given higher ratings by the citizens they serve. Nor were they more successful than less educated departments in obtaining warrants.

While considerably more analysis is obviously required, the results from our study thus far provide slight confirmation for hypotheses derived from police reform literature calling for higher levels of training and education.

APPENDIX

Given that the type of neighborhood served is a major factor affecting many aspects of police performance, we utilized a "most similar systems" research design in the selection of neighborhoods within the St. Louis area (Przeworski and Teune, 1970). A neighborhood is defined for this study as consisting of either:

(1) an independently incorporated community in St. Louis County with a population in 1970 less than or equal to 28,900;

(2) a census tract *within* an independently incorporated community in St. Louis County with a population in 1970 of greater than 28,900;

(3) an urban place as designated by the 1970 census within the unincorporated portion of St. Louis County; or

(4) a Planning Neighborhood (as designated by the St. Louis City Planning Commission) within the City of St. Louis.[15]

Using these criteria, over 170 neighborhoods existed in the City of St. Louis or St. Louis County at the time of our study.

The selection of sample neighborhoods first focused on the elimination of neighborhoods in which:

(1) the percentage of population over 65 years of age exceeded 20 percent;

(2) the percentage of population under 21 years of age exceeded 45 percent;

(3) the median value of owner-occupied housing was greater than or equal to $25,000;

(4) less than 60 percent of the dwelling units were owner occupied (this criterion was relaxed slightly in two cases to allow inclusion of two predominantly black communities).

The remaining relatively homogeneous neighborhoods were then stratified along dimensions of neighborhood wealth on the one hand and community size (or form of police provision) on the other. Along the community size and form of police provision dimension were seven strata:

(1) independently incorporated communities containing between 500 and 4,999 population;

(2) independently incorporated communities containing between 5,000 and 15,999 population;

(3) independently incorporated communities containing between 16,000 and 28,900 population;

(4) neighborhoods within communities ranging in size from 28,901 to 66,000;

(5) neighborhoods within the City of St. Louis;

(6) neighborhoods within the unincorporated sections of St. Louis County served by St. Louis County Police;

(7) independently incorporated communities which contract with other police departments for service.

In the first six categories above, police services are provided to citizens by the jurisdiction in which they live. In the seventh category, a separate jurisdiction provides police services to the community under contract arrangements.

Our wealth dimension contained three strata:

(1) those communities and neighborhoods in which median value of owner-occupied housing units is less than $10,000;

(2) those communities and neighborhoods in which median value of housing is between $10,000 and $14,999, plus those communities and neighborhoods in which median value of housing is between $15,000 and $19,999 *and* median contract rent per month is less than $120;

(3) those communities and neighborhoods in which median value of housing is between $15,000 and $19,999 *and* median rental per month is greater than or equal to $120, plus those communities and neighborhoods in which median value of housing is between $20,000 and $24,999.

Stratification utilizing these factors in combination produces a seven by three matrix with 21 cells. For seven of these logically possible cells there were no existing cases. From the fourteen remaining cells, we chose 45 sample areas for examination as illustrated in Table A-1. In choosing from the potential neighborhoods for each cell, we first dichotomized these into neighborhoods with greater than 30 percent black population in 1970 and those with less than or equal to 30 percent. Sensitivity to this dichotomy in selecting neighborhoods for inclusion ensured that—to the extent allowed by the existence of appropriate neighborhoods—we would include a significant black sample.

Having determined through use of the criteria described above those neighborhoods which were of interest, we proceeded to choose among them on the basis of contiguity into cluster neighborhoods. These considerations allowed us to choose our 45 sample areas in such a way that meaningful variations along the dimensions of size and organization for provision of police service, individual wealth within the community, and presence or absence of a sizeable black population could be obtained while maintaining the "most similar systems" research design.

Data Collection

For each of the neighborhoods in our sample frame we obtained data from five types of sources: (1) interviews with citizens residing in the neighborhoods; (2) interviews with police officers serving the neighborhoods; (3) internal and published police and other local agency records pertaining to the neighborhoods; (4) published and unpublished data relating to the neighborhoods from agencies external to the communities studied; and (5) unobtrusive observation of neighborhood conditions. Wherever possible we attempted to obtain overlapping information from two or more sources, a procedure which can often provide additional credence in the data as well as additional insight (Webb et al., 1966). Data analysis in this paper relies primarily on surveys of citizens and police, supplemented to some degree by agency records (Sources 1, 2, and 3 above).

In obtaining interviews from citizens residing in the neighborhoods, we used a combination of in-person, mail, and telephone interviews. In the neighborhoods of relatively higher SES (socio-economic status) rank in our sample frame, we utilized exclusively mail questionnaires for initial contact, following with a second wave of mail questionnaires to non-respondents and an attempt to contact second wave non-respondents by telephone (Hochstim, 1967). In the neighborhoods of middle SES rank, and in a few of the higher ranked neighborhoods (to provide a control group), we utilized mail questionnaires for initial contact with one-half of the neighborhood respondents and in-person interviews for the initial contact with the other one-half. The follow-up on the mail questionnaires was the same as described above. Several call-backs were attempted for respondents who were not at home for the initial in-person contact. Telephone interviews were attempted with potential respondents who were not at home after several in-person attempts or with those who had refused an in-person interview. In the lowest SES rank neighborhoods in our sample frame, and in some in the middle rank, we relied entirely on in-person interviews for initial contacts with return attempts and telephone follow-up where needed.

For the mail sample, a random sample of addresses was drawn from land-use files maintained at the University of Missouri-St. Louis. In-person interview respondents were chosen by selecting census blocks at random from a list of all

Table A-1. DISTRIBUTION OF CITIZEN INTERVIEWS

Median Housing Value	Independently Incorporated Communities				St. Louis Neighborhood Planning Areas	St. Louis County	
	500-4,999	5,000-15,999	16,000-28,900	28,901-66,000		Unincorporated Neighborhoods	Communities with Contract Police
$20,900 to $24,999 and $15,000 to $19,999 with rent ≥$120	1.1 N*=275 SA**=3	1.2 N=594 SA=6	1.3 N=192 SA=2	1.4 N=378 SA=4	1.5 None in this cell	1.6 N=79 SA=1	1.7 N=81 SA=1
$10,000 to $14,999 and $15,000 to $19,999 with rent <$120	2.1 N=178 SA=2	2.2 N=276 SA=3	2.3 N=409 SA=4	2.4 N=333 SA=4	2.5 N=589 SA=7	2.6 N=108 SA=2	2.7 N=309 SA=4
Less than $10,000	3.1 None in this cell	3.2 N=115 SA=2	3.3 None in this cell	3.4 None in this cell	3.5 None in this cell	3.6 None in this cell	3.7 None in this cell

*N = number of respondents interviewed.
**SA = number of sample areas included.

blocks in the neighborhood. All households on the chosen blocks were included in the sample.

The mail questionnaire utilized essentially a shortened version of the in-person questionnaire. Telephone follow-up interviews for both the in-person sample and the mail sample were a very short version of the in-person interview. The primary purposes of the telephone follow-up included:

(1) obtaining data on a limited set of major questions;

(2) using the data so obtained to evaluate the potential differences in the patterns of response which might have occurred had the "not-at-home" respondents and those respondents who refused to be interviewed all been included;

(3) gaining a validity check on interviewer remarks concerning refusals and not-at-homes.

The differences found so far among the three methods of data collection (in-person, mail, and telephone) are not so great that we are hesitant to combine data collected by these different methods. We did find respondents returning the mail questionnaire to have slightly higher educational levels than respondents to the in-person or telephone interviews. We plan to introduce controls for educational levels in all our analysis of the citizen survey data.

In departments with 25 full-time officers or less the goal was to interview all police officers. In those departments with more than 25 full-time officers, a sample was drawn by first stratifying the department roster into command and non-command groups, and then drawing a combined sample of 25 men at random from these two strata, choosing from each strata in proportion to its percent of the department. For the St. Louis City and St. Louis County departments this sampling method was employed at departmental headquarters and in each of the districts serving neighborhoods in our sample frame. All interviews with police officers were conducted in-person during working hours.[16]

Officers were interviewed in every department serving the neighborhoods in the sample frame. These interviews are distributed by department size as shown in Table A-2.

In addition to survey data, a variety of records including crime statistics, calls for service, and budgets were obtained from departments. Additional data from related agencies such as the prosecuting attorney's office were collected. Census data and other materials descriptive of the communities studied were obtained.

Table A-2. DISTRIBUTION OF POLICE INTERVIEWS

Number of Full-Time Officers	Number of Departments	Number of Interviews
1-5	5	15
6-10	4	33
11-25	8	135
26-50	8	215
51-100	2	100
Over 100	2	214
TOTAL	29	712

NOTES

1. Skolnick, however, notes (1966: 4-5): "It is rarely recognized that the conduct of police may be related in a fundamental way to the character and goals of the institution itself—the duties police are called upon to perform, associated with the assumptions of the system of legal justice—and that it may not be men who are good or bad, so much as the premises and design of the system in which they find themselves."

2. As noted by Bordua and Reiss (1967: 288-293), some police reformers use the label "professionalization" to refer to organizational changes involving tightening of internal discipline and centralization of control which, for the patrolman at least, are at variance with a model of professional work in which practitioner autonomy derives from personal competence.

3. For a more extensive discussion of these issues, see Smith (forthcoming).

4. The extent to which different measures of police performance are associated is the subject of a paper by Roger B. Parks (1973).

5. The fact that some of the propositions are not logically consistent with the model of profession summarized earlier reflects the noted tendency of advocates of professionalization to ignore the issue of autonomy. The consistency of the propositions derives instead from a tendency which Goldstein (1967) observed: "It is now commonplace to refer to practically any effort that is aimed at improving law enforcement as a contribution to the professionalization of the police." There is a corollary tendency to attribute all preferred changes in police to professionalization.

6. This proposition, which reflects the stated expectation of advocates of increased education and training, is indicative of the tendency of proponents of these reforms to overlook the element of autonomy in the professional model. If the element of autonomy is considered salient, one *could* hypothesize the reverse of the reformers expectations. Professionalized police might see court "interference" as an affront to their expertise.

7. The designation of categories is arbitrary and exploratory at this point in the analysis. In some instances there appear to be quantitative breaks in the array of data. Size of department exemplifies this: a number of departments cluster in a range from 0-11 full-time sworn officers. There are no departments from 12 to 19, 15 fall in the 20 to 70 officer range, one has 440 officers and another has 2,200. These clusters correspond to our

mini, muni, county, St. Louis City categories. Included in each of the two largest size categories are districts in single departments.

For other variables, different criteria were used. The aggregate high, middle, and low levels of training and education categories were selected to distribute citizen respondents into approximately equal-sized clusters. For the individual officer data analysis, years of education was selected because it corresponds to university practices for designating class standing. There appeared to us too few police respondents holding a baccalaureate degree to consider that a separate category to contrast with all other officers. Age was arbitrarily broken into decades, tenure into five-year units, which had the practical effect of giving each variable four values.

None of the above categorizations are completely satisfactory. As the analysis proceeds, we will continue to explore the effects of different categorization schemes and report the consequences of using different categories.

8. In this paper we have chosen to measure the degree of association among variables by Kendall's tau. The larger the magnitude of that measure, the higher the association between variables and vice versa. Our use of the entire sets of police and citizen respondents, which do not constitute a random sample (we sampled within neighborhoods and within departments), precluded the use of tests of significance. To guarantee a modicum of consistency in our verbal interpretation, we follow the advise of Davis in specifying arbitrary rules for interpretations of strength of relationships. Our decision to consider tau between .10 and −.10 as negligible was intended to make it relatively easy for slight associations to be acknowledged. Associations between ..11 and .29 are considered to be weak; .30 to .49 to be moderate; .50 to .69 to be substantial, and over .70 to be very strong. A recent article in the American Political Science Review illustrates the need for the general adoption of conventions noted by Davis (1971: 49). In that article, authors who express a desire similar to our to make it easy for the existence of relationships to be conceded "adopt .20 as a marginal but perhaps acceptable relationship" and consider tau scores under .30 to be weak (Searing, Schwartz, and Lind, 1973: 424).

9. We decided to use the extreme cases, the shortest and longest recruit training programs, to examine the effects of length of recruit training programs because of the invidious comparisons between short and long programs found in the literature, because a sizeable number of officers have attended one or the other of the two programs over similar periods of time, and those attending the two programs are distributed across a number of departments. There are, however, no members of the largest department who attended the shorter program. We must eventually decide the proper way to treat those officers who have attended both programs.

10. McNamara noted a choice between strategies, "whether to emphasize training strategies aimed at the development of self-directed and autonomous personnel or to emphasize strategies aimed at developing personnel over whom the organization can readily exercise control." He concluded (1967: 251): "It appears that the second strategy is the one most often emphasized."

11. Literature on police reform tends to treat college education as a simple concept when, in fact, it is quite complex. Many highly diverse institutions grant "college" credits and programs within institutions vary remarkably. It also seems reasonable to hypothesize that the impact of a college education (whatever it is, wherever it is obtained) varies with the age and prior experience of the student and the degree of concentration of his college attendance (part-time v. full-time). Further refinements are conceivable, but the point is that reform recommendations calling for college educated police usually do not include the

degree of refinement suggested above. One reason for this is, as Charles B. Saunders, Jr., states (1970: 192): "There is no common agreement among police officials or educators as to what is meant by 'higher education for police.' " The Task Force, citing a lack of analysis, recommends (1967: 128): "Until the educational needs of field officers are more fully evaluated . . . undergraduate programs should emphasize the social sciences and liberal arts." In addition to problems of gauging the content, setting, and pace of college, college education as a variable poses other measurement problems which are ignored at this point. A slight exception to the above and a step in the right direction is found in a very recent study of New York police officers' personnel files in which education prior to recruitment was treated as a variable separate from total education [regardless when obtained] (Cohen and Chaiken, 1973).

Most of the officers included in our sample who have college credits have acquired them recently. Most began college work on a part-time basis after entering police work and have been only part-time students. Most have attended only the junior colleges in the area which now offer a two-year program awarding an Associates of Arts degree in Law Enforcement.

12. Age is categorized by decade (under 30, 30 through 39, 40 through 49, 50 and above). When the analysis is refined further, considerable attention must be paid to possible confounding influences resulting from the inverse relationship which exists between age and college education (tau$_c$ = .25).

13. The use of "warrant success scores" as a measure of police performance has implications for police relations with the warrant office. For a variety of reasons, police-prosecutor relations have manifested strain (Skolnick, 1966; Reiss, 1971). Refusals of police applications for warrants do not endear the prosecutor's office to the police. In our survey, 45 percent of the officers (N = 684) rated the cooperation of the prosecuting attorney's office as "outstanding" or "good," 27 percent rated prosecutor cooperation as adequate, and 28 percent rated the level of cooperation as "inadequate," "very poor," or "worse than very poor." The most common complaint was that the prosecutor was only willing to accept "sure thing" cases. They typically attribute his unwillingness to take on "hard" cases to the fact that his performance is measured by a "conviction success score." If warrant success scores were institutionalized as a measure of department performance, pressure to improve the score could (1) improve the quality of policing or (2) result in fewer applications for warrants. We can see potential advantages and disadvantages to the second prospect. Bittner (1970: 29), for example, acknowledges the possibility that the Supreme Court decision restricting the admissability of evidence may have had the effect of encouraging harrassment arrests. In any case, we would expect general use of warrant success scores to increase police-prosecutor tensions.

14. The availability of ostensibly interval measures of both variables in the relationship seemed to justify the use of the more widely and easily interpreted Pearson's r. Variables explaining less than 10 percent of the variance were designated as "weak."

For districts in the City of St. Louis, warrant data were obtained only for 1971 and 1972.

The correlations were calculated excluding one case. In that case (a very small department), one officer, majoring in music education, reported having an excess of 170 hours of college credits. The effect of this number on the small department's average college credits seemed to justify its exclusion.

15. The St. Louis City Planning Commission has divided the city geographically into 70 Planning Areas or Planning Neighborhoods. This division was designed to take account of natural boundaries such as highways or industrial concentrations, natural focii such as parks

or community centers, and existing neighborhood organizations. We are indebted to Mr. James Schoonover of the Planning Commission Staff for a pre-publication copy of the document describing these Planning Areas.

16. Departments to be included were chosen indirectly. We automatically included departments serving neighborhoods selected. In contrast to the legendary "code of secrecy" under which, according to Bittner (1970: 64), "no members of the department talk about anything remotely connected with police work with any outsiders," we received outstanding cooperation from the departments included in our survey. That is not to say that all chiefs were equally enthusiastic about us privately interviewing them and all those members of the department *whom we chose*. Ultimately, every single department agreed to be interviewed and provide such other requested data as were available. There was only *one* refusal among all officers selected to be interviewed (he maintained that his aversion to interviews had also led him to refuse to be interviewed by representatives of the U.S. Census Bureau).

We owe a large debt of gratitude to the law enforcement officials of the St. Louis Metropolitan area.

REFERENCES

BIDERMAN, A. D. (1966) "Social Indicators and Goals," pp. 68-153 in R. A. Bauer (ed.) Social Indicators. Cambridge, Mass.: M.I.T. Press.
BITTNER, E. (1970) "The Functions of the Police in Modern Society: A Review of Background Factors, Current Practices, and Possible Role Models." Department of Health, Education and Welfare Publication No. (HSM) 72-9103.
BORDUA, D. J. and A. J. REISS, Jr. (1966) "Command, control, and charisma: reflections on police bureaucracy." American Journal of Sociology 72 (July): 68-76.
CLARK, R. (1970) Crime in America, Observations on Its Nature, Causes, Prevention and Control. New York: Simon & Schuster.
COHEN, B. and J. M. CHAIKEN (1973) Police Background Characteristics and Perform- ance. Lexington, Mass.: D. C. Heath.
DAVIS, J. A. (1971) Elementary Survey Analysis. Englewood Cliffs, N.J.: Prentice-Hall.
ENNIS, P. H. (1967) Criminal Victimization in the United States: A Report of a National Survey. Report submitted to the President's Commission on Law Enforcement and Administration of Justice. Washington, D.C.: Government Printing Office.
EULAU, H. (1973) "Skill revolution and consultative commonwealth." American Political Science Review 17 (March): 169-191.
GOLDSTEIN, H. (1967) "Police policy formulation: proposals for improving police performance." Michigan Law Review (April): 1123-1146.
GREENWOOD, E. (1966) "Attributes of a Profession," pp. 10-19 in H. M. Vollmer and D. L. Mills (eds.) Professionalization. Englewood Cliffs, N.J.: Prentice-Hall.
HARVIE, R. (1972) "The myth of police professionalism." Police (December): 59-61.
HAUG, M. R. and M. B. SUSSMAN (1969) "Professional autonomy and the revolt of the client." Social Problems 17 (Fall).
HOCHSTIM, J. R. (1967) "A critical comparison of three strategies of collecting data from households." Journal of American Statistical Society 62: 976-989.
Law Enforcement Assistance Administration (1971) Third Annual Report—Fiscal Year 1971. Washington, D.C.: U.S. Government Printing Office.
LIEBERSON, S. and A. R. SILVERMAN (1965) "The precipitants and underlying conditions of race riots." American Sociological Review 30, 6 (December): 887-898.

McNAMARA, J. H. (1967) "Uncertainties in police work: recruits' backgrounds and training," pp. 163-252 in D. J. Bordua (ed.) The Police: Six Sociological Essays. New York: John Wiley.

McNARY, G. (1970) Annual Report: A Year of New Ideas and Programs to Improve the System and Quality of Justice. St. Louis County, Mo.: Office of the Prosecuting Attorney.

——— (1971) Annual Report: A Year of Continued Growth and Achievement. St. Louis County, Mo.: Office of the Prosecuting Attorney.

——— (1972) Annual Report: Fulfilling the Needs of the Community. St. Louis County, Mo.: Office of the Prosecuting Attorney.

MILNER, N. (1971) "The biases of police reform," pp. 159-174 in E. S. Greenberg, N, Milner, and D. J. Olson (eds.) Black Politics: The Inevitability of Conflict. New York: Holt, Rinehart & Winston.

——— (1971) The Court and Local Law Enforcement: The Impact of Miranda. Beverly Hills: Sage Publications.

Missouri Law Enforcement Assistance Council, Region V (1973) Criminal Justice System Description. St. Louis, Missouri.

MOORE, W. E. (1970) The Professions: Roles and Rules. New York: Russell Sage Foundation.

National Advisory Commission on Civil Disorder (1968) Final Report. New York: Bantam Books.

National Commission of Law Observance and Enforcement [Wilkersham Commission] (1931) Report on Police. Washington, D.C.: U.S. Government Printing Office.

National Commission on the Causes and Prevention of Violence (1970) Final Report: To Establish Justice, To Insure Domestic Tranquility. New York: Bantam Books.

NEIDERHOFFER, A. (1967) Behind the Shield. Garden City, N.Y.: Doubleday.

OSTROM, E. (1971) "Institutional arrangements and the measurement of policy consequences," Urban Affairs Quarterly 6 (June): 447-476.

——— W. BAUGH, R. GAURASCI, R. PARKS, and G. WHITAKER (1973) "Community Organization and the Provision of Police Services." Sage Professional Papers in Administrative and Policy Studies No. 03-001. Beverly Hills: Sage Publications.

OSTROM, E. and R. B. PARKS (1973) "Suburban police departments: too many and too small?" Urban Affairs Annual Review. Beverly Hills: Sage Publications.

——— and D. C. SMITH (1973) "A Multi-Strata, Similar Systems Design for Measuring Police Performance." Paper presented at the Midwest Political Science Association Meetings (May), Chicago.

OSTROM, E., R. B. PARKS, and G. P. WHITAKER (1973) "Do we really want to consolidate urban police forces? A reappraisal of some old assumptions." Public Administration Review 5 (September/October): 415-432.

OSTROM, E. and G. P. WHITAKER (1973) "Does local community control of police make a difference? Some preliminary findings." American Journal of Political Science 17 (February): 48-76.

PARKS, R. B. (1973) "Complementary Measures of Police Performance: Citizen Appraisal and Police-Generated Data." Paper presented at the American Political Science Association Meetings (September), New Orleans.

——— (forthcoming) "Production of Police Services in the St. Louis Metropolitan Area." Ph.D. dissertation. Bloomington: Indiana University.

President's Commission on Law Enforcement and Administration of Justice (1967) The Challenge of Crime in a Free Society. New York: Avon Books.

PRZEWORSKI, A. and H. TEUNE (1970) The Logic of Comparative Social Inquiry. New York: John Wiley.

RADELET, L. (1966) "Implications of professionalism in law enforcement for police community relations." Police (July/August): 82-86.

REISS, A. J., Jr. (1971) The Police and the Public. New Haven, Conn.: Yale University Press.

REITH, C. (1952) The Blind Eye of History: A Study of the Origins of the Present Police Era. London: Faber & Faber.

RIKER, W. H. and P. C. ORDESHOOK (1973) An Introduction to Positive Political Theory. Englewood Cliffs, N.J.: Prentice-Hall.

SAUNDERS, C. B., Jr. (1970) Upgrading the American Police. Washington, D.C.: Brookings Institute.

SEARING, D. D., J. J. SCHWARTZ, and A. E. LIND (1973) "The structuring principle: political socialization and belief systems." American Political Science Review LXVII (June): 415-432.

SKOLNICK, J. H. (1966) Justice Without Trial: Law Enforcement in Democratic Society. New York: John Wiley.

——— (1969) The Politics of Protest. New York: Ballantine Books.

SMITH, A. B., B. LOCKE, and W. F. WALKER (1967) "Authoritarianism in college and non-college oriented police." Journal of Criminal Law, Criminology and Police Science 58: 128-132.

SMITH, D. C. (forthcoming) "Police Professionalization and Performance: An Analysis of Public Policy from the Perspective of Police as Producers and Citizens as Consumers of Police Services." Ph.D. dissertation. Bloomington: Indiana University.

St. Louis Planning Commission (1971) Description of Program Areas. St. Louis, Mo.: St. Louis Planning Commission.

Task Force on the Police (1967) Task Force Report: The Police. The President's Commission on Law Enforcement and Administration of Justice. Washington, D.C.: U.S. Government Printing Office.

VOLLMER, H. M. and D. L. MILLS (1966) Professionalization. Englewood Cliffs, N.J.: Prentice-Hall.

WALSH, J. L. (1970) "Professionalism and the police, the cop as medical student." American Behavioral Scientist 13 (May-August).

WEBB, E. J., D. T. CAMPBELL, R. D. SCHWARTZ, and L. SECHREST (1966) Unobtrusive Measures. Chicago: Rand McNally.

WESTLEY, W. A. (1970) Violence and the Police: A Sociological Study of Law, Custom and Morality. Cambridge, Mass.: M.I.T. Press.

WILENSKY, H. (1964) "The professionalization of everyone." American Journal of Sociology LXX (September).

WILSON, J. Q. (1968) Varieties of Police Behavior. Cambridge, Mass.: Harvard University Press.

——— (1968a) "The police and the delinquent in two cities," pp. 173-195 in J. Q. Wilson (ed.) City Politics and Public Policy. New York: John Wiley.

Chapter 4

WORKING THE STREET:
A DEVELOPMENTAL VIEW OF POLICE BEHAVIOR

JOHN VAN MAANEN

The people on the street would miss us if we weren't there. I mean they expect us out there and we're part of the whole scene too. That's what everybody seems to miss. We've got a say in what goes on in the streets. You just can't give an honest picture of what happens in society without talking about what the cop on the street does.

A patrolman

In the midst of derogatory epithets, laudatory salutations, and apathetic silent-American acquiescence, the "man" acts out a curious societal role. To some, a policeman is a "fucking pig," a mindless brute working for a morally bankrupt institution. To others, a policeman is a courageous public servant, a defender of life and property, regulating city life along democratic lines. To most, a policeman is merely an everyday cultural stimulus, tolerated, avoided, and ignored unless non-routine situational circumstances deem otherwise. Yet,

AUTHOR'S NOTE: I would like to express my appreciation for the generous cooperation of souls like Dave, MC, Doug, Jim and Bill who, like myself, learned what it means to live in the emotionally hazardous police culture. They shared with me the ugliness and humor, tedium and wonder that exist in the sometimes bizarre and paralyzing world of city streets. I would also like to gratefully acknowledge a Ford Foundation grant (administered through M.I.T.) and the Organizational Behavior Research Center at the University of California, Irvine for patrial support and full encouragement throughout this research effort.

virtually all persons in this society can recognize a policeman, have some conception of what it is he does, and, if asked, can share a few "cop stories" with an interested listener.

Fundamentally, a police officer represents the most visible aspect of the body politic and is that aspect most likely to intervene directly in the daily lives of the citizenry. If one considers the President to be the "head" of the political system, then the patrolman on the street must be considered the "tail." The critical and symbolic nature of the police role in society is perhaps best illustrated by a number of child socialization studies indicating that it is the head *and* tail of a political system which are its most salient aspects, the features most likely to be learned first as a child develops an awareness of his surrounding environment (Hyman, 1959; Almond and Verba, 1963; Easton and Dennis, 1969, 1967; Brown, 1971).

Given this rather dramatic position in society, it is somewhat surprising that social scientists have, until recently, largely ignored the police. In particular, little research has been devoted to the everyday standards of police behavior. The few studies we do have tend to confirm an occupational stereotype of the police as a conservative, defiled, isolated, and homogenous grouping of men bound together perceptually through a common mission (Rubenstein, 1973; Reiss, 1971; Wilson, 1969; Neiderhoffer, 1967; Skolnick, 1966). Indeed, this stereotype seems to run deeply through all societies regardless of social, economic, or political orientations. It may be, in the discerning words of Trotsky, "There is but one international and that is the police." And whether or not one views the police as a good or evil force in society does not detract from the prevailing sentiment subscribing to this peculiar form of occupational determinism.

Occupational characterization is, of course, not unknown. Professors, doctors, hangmen, insurance salesmen, corporate executives all have their counterparts in the popular culture. Yet, what is of interest here is the recognition by the police themselves of the implied differences. According to one knowledgeable observer, a former chief of police:

> The day the new recruit walks through the doors of the police academy he leaves society behind to enter a profession that does more than give him a job, it defines who he is. For all the years he remains, closed into the sphere of its rituals . . . he will be a cop (Ahern, 1972: 3).

Policemen generally view themselves as performing society's dirty work. Consequently, a gap is created between the police and the public. Today's patrolman feels cut off from the mainstream culture and stigmatized unfairly. In the percussive words of one young patrolman:

I'll tell ya, as long as we're the only sonfabitches that have to handle ripe bodies that have been dead for nine days in a ninety degree room or handle skid row drunks who've been crapping in their pants for 24 hours or try to stop some prick from jumpin' off the Liberty Bridge or have to grease some societal misfit who's trying to blow you goddam head off, then we'll never be like anyone else . . . as far as I can see, no one else is ever gonna want to do that shit. But somebody's gotta do it and I guess it'll always be the police. But hell, this is the only profession where ya gotta wash your hands before you take a piss![1]

In short, when a policeman dons his uniform, he enters a distinct subculture governed by norms and values designed to manage the strains created by his unique role in the community. From the public point of view, a policeman is usually treated as a faceless, nameless "Rorschach-in-blue" with persons responding either favorably or unfavorably according to ideological predisposition or situational imperative. Yet, a policeman's response to the cornucopia of civilian manners and mores follows a somewhat more orderly and acquired pattern. Thus, policemen learn—in a manner quite similar to the way in which all occupations are learned—characteristic ways of conducting themselves on the street, devices for organizing work routines about their perceived areas of responsibility, and methods of managing their own careers vis-a-vis the police department. The learned guidelines and rules police officers (in particular, patrolmen) develop to handle these problematic areas define the everyday meaning of policing and, as such, are the subject of this paper.

Contextual Issues

If one takes seriously research findings regarding esoteric subcultures, social scientists interested in police behavior are somewhat limited in their choice of methodological strategy. The direct approach will not work because the police, like other stigmatized groupings, have invented sophisticated coping mechanisms designed to present a certain front to the non-police world (for example, special interface divisions like Community Relations or Public Information, special events such as Officer Friendly programs in the public schools or citizen ride-along programs, extreme bureaucratic red-tape, and, of course, the open hostility displayed by police in general to the critical questioner). Therefore, if we are to gain insight into the police environment, researchers must penetrate the official smokescreen and observe directly the social actions in social situations which, in the final analysis, represent the reality of police work.

While observation of the police in naturally occurring situations is difficult, lengthy, and often threatening, it is imperative. Unfortunately, most research to date relies almost exclusively upon interview-questionnaire data (for example,

Bayley and Mendelsohn, 1969; Wilson, 1968), official statistics (for example, Webster, 1970; President's Commission on Law Enforcement and the Administration of Justice, 1967), or broad-ranging attitude surveys (for example, Sterling, 1973; McNamara, 1967). The very few sustained observational studies have been concerned with specific aspects of police behavior patterns (for example, Skolnick, 1966: vice activities; Reiss, 1971: police-citizen contacts; Bittner, 1967; Cicourel, 1967—police encounters with "skid row alcoholics" and juveniles, respectively). This is not to say that these diverse investigations are without merit. Indeed, without such studies we would not have even begun to see beneath the occupational shield. Yet, the paucity of in-depth police-related research—especially from an "insider's" perspective—represents a serious gap in our knowledge of a critical social establishment.[2]

The data for the following analysis are drawn from a participant-observation study I conducted in Union City.[3] In July of 1970, I entered the Union City Police Academy and, upon graduation thirteen weeks later, joined the patrol division as an armed backseat observer with many training teams, each comprised of a veteran and a rookie policeman. For approximately the following six months I worked a regular departmental schedule, alternating my observational excursions among all work shifts and precincts. During this period my academy classmates concluded their field training and were assigned to a specific district with a permanent patrol partner.[4]

In January of 1973, I returned to Union City for a follow-up study. During this period (lasting approximately two months) I interviewed both formally and informally the members of my Academy class and again spent a good deal of time as an observer in various patrol units. The purpose of this part of the study was to check the accuracy of my original analysis as well as to discover what changes, if any, had occurred in my Academy cohorts two and one-half years down their respective career paths.[5]

In essence, what follows is an account of the organizational socialization process associated with the patrolman's role in an urban police department. Such a process provides, when efficacious, the new member with a set of rules, perspectives, prescriptions, techniques, and/or tools necessary for him to continue as a participant in the organization. In Bakke's (1950, 1955) seminal terms, the fully socialized actor is "fused" to the organization by the structural and interpersonal bonds growing from task, status, communication, and reward networks in which the individual is located.

Somewhat arbitrarily, I will treat this fusion process from three distinct perspectives. The first part describes briefly the sequence, pace, and associated organizational features of the socialization process. The second part sketches out the critical occupational perspectives developed as the new member passes through his initiation rituals. These career perspectives are not concerned directly with the everyday behavior of patrolmen, but rather deal with certain long-range, occupationally-relevant orientations. In a sense, they provide a sort of occupational ideology or credo which serves to assist the patrolman in developing a conception of who he is and what he is to do. Finally, the third part delineates a few of what I will call patrolmen meta-prescriptions. These are the work-related rules or operating axioms which define the boundaries of the patrolman's activity space. To be sure, like occupational perspectives, they are learned and consensually validated by most officers, but these meta-prescriptions are more specific and provide the patrolman with established conceptions as to the "how" of his work.[6]

THROUGH THE LOOKING GLASS:
THE POLICE SOCIALIZATION PROCESS

The development of a community of purpose and action among police officers is characterized as a four-phase socialization process. While these stages are only analytically distinct, they serve as useful markers for describing the route traversed by a recruit. The sequence is related to the pre-entry, admittance, change, and continuance phases of the organizational socialization process and are labeled choice, introduction, encounter, and metamorphosis, respectively.[7]

Choice

What sort of man gravitates toward and is selected for a police career? The literature notes that police work seems to attract local, family-oriented, military-experienced, high-school educated, and working-class whites (Neiderhoffer, 1967; President's Commission, 1967; Watson and Sterling, 1969). Importantly, the authoritarian syndrome which has popularly been ascribed to persons selecting police careers has not been verified by empirical study (McNamara, 1967; Sterling, 1972). Generally, the available literature supports the contention that the police occupation is viewed as simply one job among many and considered roughly along the same dimensions as any job choice.

While my research can add little to the above picture, several qualifications are in order which provide a greater understanding of the particular occupational choice process. First, the security and salary aspects have probably been overrated. In police work, a pervasive cultural stereotype involving adventure, romance, and societal value (that is, performing a function that has point, weight, interest, and consequence to the community) exists and is shared by virtually all who join the police ranks. Relatedly, the out-of-door, non-routine, and masculine (that is, "machismo") task aspects of the work—as portrayed by the media—are undeniably strong inducements for young men selecting a police career. All recruits stressed these features as the primary virtues of the occupation. Certainly the choice is buttressed by the security and salary properties—as a sort of necessary but not sufficient precondition—but the occupational choice rests on the more glamorous concerns. Perhaps this pre-entry consensus among police aspirants can best be called a "meaningful work" expectation.

Second, the stretched-out screening factor associated with police selection is a critical aspect of the socialization process. From the filing of the application blank to the telephone call which finally informs the recruit of his acceptance into the department, the individual passes through a series of events which serve to impress him with the sense of being admitted into an "elite," "top-notch," or "tough-to-make" organization.[8] The written and physical examinations, the oral board, the psychiatric interview, and, in particular, the background investigation (in which an applicant's friends and relatives are questioned about the most delicate of matters) demonstrate to the would-be officer the department's serious interest in him—i.e., they are willing to spend a great deal of time and money before he is allowed to pass through the organizational portals.[9] Few men move through all sequential stages of the process—often taking up to a year or more—without becoming committed earnestly to a police career. As such, the various selection devices, if successfully surmounted, increase the person's self-esteem and cement the neophyte's evaluation of the police organization as an important and difficult place to work.

Finally, as in most organizations, the department is depicted to individuals who have yet to take the oath of office in its most favorable light. A potential recruit is made to feel as if he were important and valued by the organization. Furthermore, virtually all recruitment occurs via generational or friendship networks involving on-line police officers and potential recruits. Hence the individual receives personalized encouragement and support which help sustain his interest during the formidable screening procedure. Such links begin to attach the would-be policeman to the organization long before he actually joins.

Introduction

Once the individual has "made it," the department quickly and somewhat rudely informs him that he is now a "probie" or a "greenpea," and until he has served his six-month probationary period he can be severed from the department's membership rolls at any time without warning, explanation, or appeal.[10] This sort of "lowest-of-the-low" position reserved for incoming participants is common to many organizations, but in the paramilitary environment of the police department, the ironic shift from "successful aspirant" to a position something akin to a wartime draftee is particularly illuminating to the new member.

As he stands in long lines with other recruits waiting to receive his departmental issues (rulebook, badge, Smith and Wesson thirty-eight calibre revolver, ticket book, mace, rosewood nightstick, and other symbols of police status) or spends several hundred dollars in a designated department store buying uniforms (some of which he will never wear again following his academy training period), the recruit begins to acclimatize himself to the formal, mechanical, and arbitrary bureaucratic features which will characterize his career. Instead, even the swearing-in ceremony is carried out en masse, with the words of the civil service official barely audible above the din of a busy public building. Thus, the sheath of uncritical attitudes toward the department—which served the recruit well during the arduous screening process—begins to show wear as he gradually develops notions of his role in the organization from personal experience rather than from aggrandizing accounts told him by others.

For most recruits, their first sustained contact with the police subculture occurs at the Academy. Surrounded by forty to fifty contemporaries, the novice is introduced to the austere and sometimes imperious discipline of the organization. Absolute obedience to departmental rules, rigorous physical training, dull lectures devoted to various technical and organizational aspects of police work, and a ritualistic concern for detail characterize the Academy. A recruit soon discovers that to be one minute late to a class, to utter a careless word in formation, or to be caught walking when he should be running may result in a "gig" or "demerit," costing a man an extra day of work or the time it may take to write a long essay on, say, "the importance of keeping a neat appearance."[11]

Wearing a uniform which distinguishes the novice from "real" policemen, recruits are expected to demonstrate group cohesion in all aspects of Academy life. The training staff actively promotes solidarity through the use of group rewards and punishments, identifying garments for each recruit class, interclass competition, aggregate chastisement for the errors of one or a few, and cajoling the newcomers—at every conceivable opportunity—to "show some unity." It is no exaggeration to state that the "in-the-same-boat" collective consciousness which arises when groups are processed serially through a harsh set of experiences was as refined in the Union City Police Department as in other institutions such as military academies, fraternities, or medical schools.

The formal content of the training Academy is almost exclusively weighted in favor of the more technically oriented side of police work. A few outside speakers are invited to the Academy, but the majority of class time is filled by departmental personnel describing the more mundane features of the occupation. To a large degree, the Academy may be viewed as a didactic sort of instrumentally oriented ritual passage. Yet, the novices' overwhelming eagerness to hear what police work is "really like" results in considerable time devoted to "war stories" (alternatively called "sea stories" by some officers) told at the discretion of the many instructors. Such "war stories" provide the recruit with an opportunity to begin learning, or, more properly, absorbing the tradition which typifies the occupation.

By observing and listening closely to police stories and style, the individual is exposed to a partial "organizational history" which details certain personalities, past events, places, and implied relationships which the recruit is expected eventually to learn. The social psychological correlates of this history are mutually held perspectives toward certain types of persons, places, and things which compromise the "objective reality" of police work. Critically, when "war stories" are presented, discipline within the recruit class is relaxed and a general atmosphere of comaraderie is maintained. The near lascivious enjoyment accompanying these informal respites from routine serve to establish congeniality and solidarity with the experienced officers in what is normally a rather uncomfortable environment. Clearly, this is the material of which memories are made.[12]

Despite these important breaks in formality, the recruit's early perceptions of policing are formed in the shadow of the submissive and often degrading role he is expected to play. Long, monotonous hours of static class time are required; a seemingly endless set of examinations on, for example, the organization of the administrative services bureau or the fundamentals of fingerprinting are daily features of Academy life. Out-of-date, greyish-white documentary films on such topics as childbirth, riot control, or the judicial system are shown with borish regularity. Meaningless assignments such as recopying class lecture notes consume valuable off-duty time. Various mortifying events are institutionalized throughout the training program (for example, each week a class "asshole" was selected and presented with a trophy depicting a gorilla dressed as a policeman). And, of course, relatively sharp punishments are enacted for any breach of Academy regulations.

The net result of such "stress" training is that the recruit begins to alter his high but unrealistic attitudes about the department. Although he learns little about policing per se, he learns a great deal about the formal and informal operations of the department. Importantly, he learns that the formal rules and regulations are applied inconsistently. As in other highly regulated social systems, behavior that is punished in one case is ignored in another. To the recruits, Academy rules become normative behavioral prescriptions which are to be coped with formally but informally dismissed. The newcomer learns that when the department notices his behavior it is usually to administer a punishment, not a reward.

Encounter

Following Academy training, a recruit is introduced to the realities and complexities of policing through his Field Training Officer (hereafter referred to as the FTO).[13] Representing the first partner assigned to a rookie policeman, the FTO is a veteran officer who has been working patrol for at least several years and is the single most important person shaping the behavior of the novice. For it is through the eyes of his experienced FTO that the newcomer begins to learn the subtle nuances of the police function and develop notions about the kinds of behavior which are appropriate and expected of him within his new social setting.

His other instructors in this phase are almost exclusively his fellow patrolmen working the same precinct, shift, and district; his squad. While his sergeant may occasionally offer tips on how to handle himself on the "street," the supervisor is more notable for his absence than for his presence. When the sergeant does seek out the recruit it is probably to inquire as to how many hazardous traffic violations the "probie" has written or to remind him to keep his hat on while out of the patrol car. As a matter of formal policy in Union City, the department expected the FTO to handle all recruit uncertainties. Informally, the other members of the squad strictly adhere to the code which delegates training responsibility to the FTO. Certainly among members of the squad there is intense interest in the progress, skill, and inclinations of the rookie, but few experienced officers will give specific advice to the newcomer unless requested explicitly to do so by the FTO. Of course, most recruits are bombarded with general advice from "street-wise" officers (for example, "Now that you're done with that verbal strangulation that passes for training, you can buy a dose of Preparation H and sit back and relax for awhile." Or, "We don't eat in this district 'cause the poison factories will kill ya faster than your tin badge will rust."), but no veteran officer would consider telling a rookie who was not under his direct charge how to handle a particular call or what to do in a specific instance. To do so would violate the trust and guarded independence existing among experienced officers in the squad.

During the protracted hours spent on patrol with his FTO, the recruit is instructed as to the "real nature" of police work. He is first instructed by word and deed as to the worth of his Academy preparation. As one persuasive FTO told me:

> I hope that academy didn't get to you. It's a bunch of bullshit as far as I can tell. . . . Most of those guys they've got working there haven't been on the street for ten years. They can't teach ya nothing 'cause they don't know what it's like anymore. Only a working cop can teach you that the laws and procedures don't translate very easily to the action on the street.

And, as if behavioral confirmation were required, the rookie discovers on his first tour of duty that he does not have the slightest idea of his district's physical and social terrain, or how to handle an unruly drunk, or even how to quickly spot a traffic violator. His Academy training soon represents merely something that all policemen endure and has little, if anything, to do with "real" police work. Consequently, the Academy experience for the recruits stands symbolically as their rites de passage, permitting them access to the occupation. That the experienced officers confirm their negative evaluation of the Academy heightens the assumed similarity among the recruits and the veterans and serves to facilitate the rookies' absorption into the squad.

For the novice policeman, the first few months on patrol are an extremely trying period. He is slightly fearful, ill at ease, and woefully unprepared for both the routines and eccentricities of police work. While he may know the rudimentaries of arrest or search and seizure, the fledgling patrolman is perplexed and uncomfortable in his application. Encounters with the hostile public leave him cold and apprehensive. At first, the squawk of the police radio transmits only meaningless static. The streets of his sector appear to be a maze through which only an expert could maneuver. The use of report forms seems inconsistent and confusing. As so on. It is commonplace, indeed expected, for the rookie to never make a move without first checking with his FTO. By watching, listening, and mimicking, the neophyte gradually learns characteristic ways to deal with the objects of his occupation: the rowdy bar, the "brass" in the department, the centrally located park, the hippie, the family squabble, the patrol unit in an adjacent district, and the criminal justice complex itself.

Critical to the practical, on-the-street learning process is the recruit's own developing repertoire of experiences. These events are normally interpreted to him by his FTO and other veteran squad members. Thus the "reality shock" of being "in-on-the-action" is absorbed and defined by the recruit's fellow officers. As a somewhat typical example, one newcomer, at the prodding of his patrol partner, "discovered" that to explain police actions to a civilian invited disrespect. He explained:

> Keith was always telling me to be forceful, to not back down and to never try and explain the law or what we are doing to a civilian. I didn't really know what he was talking about until I tried to tell some kid why we have laws about speeding. Well, the more I tried to tell him about traffic safety,

the angrier he got. I was lucky to just get his John Hancock on the citation. When I came back to the patrol car, Keith explained to me just where I'd gone wrong. You really can't talk to those people out there, they just won't listen to reason.

To a determining degree, these experiences are dependent upon the recruit's FTO assignment. If, for instance, he is assigned to an "active" central precinct, his learning will occur at a considerably faster pace than an Academy cohort assigned to a "slow" suburban (sometimes called "cow") precinct. Not only will his learning proceed at a quicker tempo, but the content will be vastly different. In large measure, the patrolman is tied inextricably to the territory he patrols. His world and related occupational identity therefore rarely extend beyond his assigned police jurisdiction (see the third section entitled "Meta-prescriptions: Street Codes").

Yet, patrolmen do have a common set of experiences which thread their way through the fabric of their early police career. These experiences occur, to some degree, independently of the city geometry which determines the boundaries and cadence of police work. And it is from these early "core" experiences that the highly valued subcultural norms are carved.

In general, the first few months on the "street" is a stimulating, exciting, and rewarding period for the recruit. He is busy learning a district and working out solutions for the everyday problems of his field. As one young officer noted:

God, those first couple of months are amazing. You need to learn everything . . . like how to walk and how to talk and how to think and what to say and see.

While the recruit is busy absorbing a myriad of novel experiences, his partner is appraising his colleague's responses to certain situations. Aside from assisting the recruit with the routines of patrol work, the training officer's main concern is in how the rookie will handle the "hot" calls (or in the vernacular of the seventies, the "heavy" calls). In general, such calls represent those situations the experienced officer knows may result in bodily harm to himself or his partner. They may be dispatched calls such as "man-with-gun," "tavern brawl," "domestic disturbance," or "in-progress robbery." They may involve a hair-raising automobile pursuit of a fleeing suspect across the length of the city, or they may be those rare "on-view" situations in which the partnership must take ready action. But regardless of their origin, "hot" calls symbolize everything a policeman feels he has been prepared for. In short, they call for "police work," and such work is anticipated by patrolmen with both pleasure and anxiety. Clearly, a recruit's performance in such situations is in a very real sense the measure of the man. An articulate patrolman put it in the following manner:

The heavy ones are ultimately our only rationale for being. You could give most of what we do around here to any idiot who could put up with the insanity that passes for civilized conduct. But you know that old John Q. Citizen isn't gonna put his ass on the line just to stop a couple of strung-out motherfuckers from tearing each other up. But we're expected to be willing to do it everytime we go out there. . . . Now I don't necessarily enjoy going around putting guys in the hospital and laying my family jewels out for any jerk to kick around. But I'll tell you that any street cop who's worth the taxpayer's money just better be willing to mix it up anytime there's action coming down or that sonfabitch is gonna get walked on by the assholes out there, as well as the assholes inside this department. When I'm jumping outta that goddamn patrol car with my stick ready, any partner of mine better be right behind me or his ass will be in a sling when the whole thing's over.

While hot calls are relatively rare on a day-to-day basis, their occurrence signals a behavior test for the recruit. To pass, he must be willing to use his body as a weapon, to fight if necessary. Or more generally, he must be willing to share the risks of police work as perceived by the experienced officers. Furthermore, he must demonstrate this willingness by placing himself in a vulnerable position and pluckily "backing-up" his FTO and/or other patrolmen. Through such events, a newcomer quickly makes a departmental reputation that will follow him throughout his career.[14]

At another level, testing the recruit's propensity to partake in the risks which accompany police work goes on continuously within the department. For example, several FTO's were departmental celebrities in Union City for their training techniques. One officer made it a daily ritual to have his recruit write parking citations in the front of the local Black Panther Party headquarters. Another was prominent for requiring his recruit to "shake-out" certain "trouble" bars in the rougher sections of town (that is, check identifications, make cursory body searches, and possibly roust out customers ala *The French Connection*). Less dramatic but nonetheless as important, recruits are judged by their FTO's as to their speed in getting out of the patrol car, their hesitation (or lack of it) when approaching a "suspicious character," their composure during a high-speed chase, or their willingness to lead the way up a darkened stairwell. The required behaviors vary from event to event. However, based on an ex-post-facto evaluation of the situation (for example, Was a weapon involved? Did the officers have to fight the suspect? How many other patrolmen were on the spot? In what particular part of the district did the event occur? and so on), a novice determines his acceptance into the cadre of his fellow officers. While some FTO's actively promote these climactic events, most wait quietly for such situations to occur. Such behaviorally demonstrated commitment to one's colleagues is a particularly important stage in the socialization process. To the FTO, he has watched his man in action and now knows a great deal more about his occupational companion.

Aside from what I will call (for lack of a better term) this "back-up" test applied to all recruits, the other most powerful experience in a recruit's early days on patrol is his first arrest ("breaking-the-ice"). Virtually all policemen can recall the individual, location, and situation surrounding their first arrest. Although unexpected contingencies sometimes interrupt an otherwise orderly progression, a rookie's first arrest is usually based upon his FTO's evaluation of his learned police skills. If progress is normal, the FTO will allow the recruit after a month or so of partnership to take charge of an entire arrest procedure. From the particulars at the scene (for example, the decision to arrest, the gathering of incriminating evidence, the interviewing of witnesses, the pro forma issuance of the arrestee's rights, and so on), to the booking and jailing procedures (for example, fingerprinting, report writing, strip searching, and so on), the FTO will remain in silent repose, neither suggesting shortcuts nor insuring that all the technicalities are covered. The FTO and even the squad sergeant are almost ceremonial in their conspicuous silence. The recruit is not evaluated during this trial-like process as to his boldness or reticence but is judged on his appreciation for thoroughness and detail, avoiding any "mistake" which might cast a disparaging light on himself, on his FTO, or his sergeant.

It is such occurrences that determine the recruit's success in the squad and, by implication, in the department. To a large extent, both the "back-up" test and the first arrest are beyond the control of the newcomer. The fact that both occur somewhat at the discretion of the FTO underscores the regularity of the socialization process. In effect, these knife-edge experiences demonstrate to the recruit his new status and role within the department and denote to his immediate colleagues that he is a member of the working police. For, after passing through this regulated sequence of events, the recruit can say, "I am a cop!"

Metamorphosis

The FTO period in Union City lasts approximately three months. At the end of that time, each recruit is assigned to a permanent squad in the same precinct but generally not in the same district as he worked with his training colleague. As near as my experience can tell, most of these reassignments are based (like the assignments out of the Academy) on the peculiar manpower requirements existing in the department at any particular time. Thus, some men receive permanent assignments immediately following the three-month period, while others wait from several weeks to several months before leaving their FTO. Yet as long as the recruit remains with his FTO, his metamorphosis, both socially vis-a-vis other officers and psychologically vis-a-vis his own identity, will be incomplete. For the new officer to break the stigma of "trainee" or "rookie," he must be first assigned a role in which dependency ties are not institutionalized and his position in a patrol partnership is more or less equalized in terms of responsibility.[15] As one officer suggested:

> In this job, the first time it really hits you that this job ain't so easy is when your working a car with some joker and there's no distinction between just who is senior man and who is junior man. Boy, you realize pretty quick that if something happens it is totally up to you and your partner. No more are you waiting to be told what to do. You're on your own. That's the real stuff 'cause you've got to take responsibility for what happens.

A few officers may be assigned a permanent district car directly following their FTO period (notably those with departmental connections), but most receive what are called relief assignments.[16] A relief assignment means that the officer will work shifting sectors with a variety of partners until his sergeant sees fit to assign him a permanent district car. For most, this assignment comes within the first year on the job. In a way, each time the man receives a new assignment with a different squad he must start the encounter cycle anew. However, he has a departmental reputation which precedes him and now has some experience to smooth over such transitions.

With the reality shock of entry well behind him, the newly assigned squad member has at least six-months invested in his police career. Furthermore, others are beginning to enter the patrol division with the "rookie" label and no longer is he on the bottom rung of the experience ladder. Thus the man begins gradually to settle into the relatively slow-moving, steady, repetitious monotony that is a special characteristic of police work. He begins to realize that his work consists primarily of performing routine services and administrative tasks—the proverbial clerk in the patrol car.[17] Indeed, he discovers that he is predominantly an order-taker, a reactive member of a service organization. For example, most officers never realized the extent to which they would be "married to the radio" until being on the receiving end of a stern lecture or a formal reprimand for failing to respond to the dispatcher. During the FTO period, the burden of such a blunder would of course fall on one's experienced trainer, with the recruit escaping with only a mild warning. But once on the "street" as an equal in a squad car, no such allowances are made for inexperience.

It is important to note, however, that the distinction between working relief and working a regular district car is critical and real to the patrolman. Moving to a permanent car is a significant career step for all officers for it implies a degree of acceptance and stability within one's own squad. Furthermore, it is only with a permanent car that an officer can ever hope to properly begin learning the territory in his sector. The critical nooks, trouble spots, and social peculiarities that are of manifest importance to policemen cannot be grasped when one spends his time rotating among various locales in the city or even in a district. Such territorial knowledge is critical for the patrolman's sense of safety as well as his perceived comfort. Indeed, he can never be at ease unless he has a clear idea of place, and this takes time to acquire.

Despite the relative peaceful and routine nature of much policing, the unpredictable elements of working a regular patrol shift provide self-esteem and stimulation for the officers. To classify the police task as bureaucratically routine and tiresome ignores the psychological omnipresence of the "good pinch" (felony arrest) or "hot call." In fact, it is precisely the opportunity to exercise his perceived police role (that is, "real" police work) that gives meaning to the occupational identity of patrolmen. Operationally, this does not imply that patrolmen are always alert and working hard to make the "good pinch." Rather, it simply suggests that the unexpected is the primary aspect of the job that helps maintain the patrolman's self-image of performing a worthwhile, exciting, and dangerous task. To some degree, the anticipation of the "hot call" allows for the crystallization of his personal identity as a policeman.

Still, one of the ironies of police work is that the recruits were attracted to the organization by and large through the unrealistic expectation that the work role would be exciting and dramatic. Yet, the experienced officer knows that such activities are few and far between. Once the man has mastered the various technical and social skills of policing (for example, learning the district, developing a set of mutual understandings with his partner, knowing how and when to fill out the plethora of various report forms, and so on), there is little left to learn about his occupation which can be transmitted by formal or informal instruction. Consequently, the patrolman must then sit back and wait, absorb the subjective side of police work and let his experiences accumulate.[18]

Patrolling the street on a regular basis can be regarded from several perspectives. But, for the purposes of this section, it is perhaps best to describe this learned skill first in the words of the police themselves. One officer, a hardened, three-year veteran, responded to my query about how he presently patrols his district in the following manner:

> That's a rough question. I guess what I've picked up is a certain toughness on the street. I never ask anybody twice to do something. Either they do it the first time or I knock 'em down. I would say that I'm much less

inclined to talk somebody in now than I was when I first came on. . . . Not that I still don't do that though. In fact, I talked a guy in just last night. But it's more like I know now the kind of guys you can and can't talk to. I guess when it comes right down to it, the only thing I'm really conscious of and care about is the safety of me and my partner. After a while you don't give a fuck what your sergeant or the department thinks. You just want them to leave you alone and let you get your work done.

Another patrolman, a ten-year veteran, answered the same question in this fashion:

Hell, I just put in my time and hope to get home in one piece each night. I could care less about what the mayor or some sociologist might say about my street manners. If I see some asshole fooling around the district or looking suspicious, I'll either run the bastard out of my sector or take him in. You learn that you can't take any shit on the street and stay healthy. I'd much rather hassle with IID [Internal Investigation Division] than take the risk over my safety. After you've been out there for a while, you realize that it's easy to die and it's awfully final. I'd much rather get another goddamn greenie than have some animal break me in two.

Finally, one twenty-two-year street veteran summarized his learned adjustment as follows:

I look at it as war, it's us versus them. Sure I know all about that goody-goody crap people are trying to cram down our throats about us having to help the poor and oppressed. But, I'll tell ya, the assholes that are laying on that shit don't have to go out there and work eight hours a day, six days a week. They don't have to see the mutilated bodies, the junkies, the whores, the homos or smell the stink of a skid row john. The niggers don't call them pigs cause they never see 'em. But I do. And tomorrow and the next day and the day after that it'll be the same. The only way you survive on this job is to grow callouses. You put on a shell the beginning of every shift and take it off when you get home. When I'm working, I'm as hard as stone 'cause I gotta be, it's my only defense. . . . You figure your only friends are gonna be other cops cause they're the only ones who have been there and know the score. Even the department don't help ya much. The desk jockeys inside are so damn chickenshit that they figure they got to appease every jerk who's got a beef. And you know who gets it everytime? It's us, the lousy patrolman. Shit, I've just learned to let it roll off my back. I got my time in now and there ain't a goddamn thing anybody can do about it. I can draw my pension in prison if I had to.

These quotations suggest pointedly that disenchantment has two edges. One, the police with the general public—the "cynical" cop; and two, the disenchantment with the police system itself—"abandoned" cop. Both develop rather quickly as a recruit passes along the path of structured socialization. First through proverb, then by example, and finally through his own experiences, the patrolman comes to the realization that it is his relationship with his immediate street companions—his squad—which protects his interests and allows him to continue on the job; without their support he would be lost.

In most ways, the patrolmen—particularly those in a squad—represent what Goffman (1959: 104) calls a team. In Goffmanesque, a "team" is:

> A set of individuals whose intimate co-operation is required if a given projected definition of a situation is to be maintained.

The fundamental situational definition to be maintained in the patrol setting is simply that "all-is-under-control." Yet the setting is multifaceted and hence the definition must be partialled into several more explicit counterparts. For example, to the so-called law-abiding public, the situational definition is translated roughly into "don't-worry-we-can-take-care-of-everything." To persons with whom the patrolman encounters in what can only be termed adversary relationships—the "street" people—the definition becomes "watch-your-step-because-we-can-do-whatever-we-want-to-you." To the department, the patrol situation is defined as "all-is-going-well-and-there-are-no-problems." Without question, each newcomer comes to fully accept and project these situational definitions if he is to be a "team" member. Indeed, as he discovers the importance and value of his squad, he also learns the corresponding "team" definitions of his patrol situation.

An example of the manner in which the "team" works is given below. It is concerned with an incident which occurred to a recruit during his third month on the "street." The material is quoted from my field notes.

> Approximately 2:30 a.m. we were requested by another unit to meet in the parking lot behind the Crazy Horse [a local nightclub]. The other unit was working an adjacent sector in Charlie Three. We parked and waited. After a brief delay, the requesting officer, apparently working a solo shift, approached our vehicle on foot carrying a clipboard. Talking to Marty, Dick's FTO, he stated that there had been some trouble and he'd coldcocked" some "obnoxious little nigger." . . . This officer also stated that he'd "sluffed" a knife into the other party's coat after the ambulance had "taken him away." The officer said he expected some shit from the department unless we'd sign a report essentially stating that we'd seen the man causing a disturbance earlier in the night. This other officer then handed a blank report form to Marty and asked him to sign. Marty signed first, then handed the clipboard to Dick and Dick signed. . . . At no time did we observe the reputed offender. The solo officer told us he'd type in the report and explain the details to us later (October 23, 1970).

While this is only one of many similar incidents I observed (that is, falsification of information), it was one of the more serious. While the specific recruit involved expressed certain misgivings to me at a later time, it was apparent that if he wished to remain a squad member of good standing, he had little choice but to sign the report form. It would seem therefore that by increasing one's vulnerability to sanction, the sine qua non of the "team" is made quite conspicuous to the newcomer.

In a similar vein, others have observed that the rules and regulations which typify police departments are so numerous and patently unenforceable that no one will (or could) obey all the cannons of "professional" conduct (Reiss, 1971; Radano, 1968; Skolnick, 1966). This situation was evidenced in Union City where, for example, patrolmen were supposedly prohibited from smoking in public, borrowing money from another police officer, criticizing orders from superior officers, seeking notoriety, excessive drinking off-duty, carrying their weapons beyond the city limits, accepting any gratuity including the symbolic free cup of coffee, and so on. The result of such departmental prescriptions —which delve deep into a patrolman's private life—is to place the individual in great need of colleague support. The existence of such regulations—alongside their widespread violation—makes most officers extremely susceptible to departmental discipline. Ergo, the value of the "team" is again reified by its members.

To summarize briefly, the adjustment of a neophyte in police organizations is one which follows the line of least resistance. By becoming similar in word and deed, sentiment and behavior to his peers, a recruit can avoid censor from most of his audiences and continue more or less successfully in his chosen field. Although the timetrack may vary according to assignment, the process itself represents the *deformation professionale* which occurs to virtually all upon entrance into the police occupation.

OCCUPATIONAL PERSPECTIVES: KINSMEN IN REPOSE

Workers in all occupations develop ways and means by which they manage certain structural strains, contradictions, and anomolies of their prescribed role and task. In police work, with danger, drudgery, and dogma as prime occupational characteristics, these tensions are extreme. Correspondingly, the pressure on new members to bow to group standards is intense. Few, if any, pass through the socialization cycle without being persuaded—through their own experiences and the sage-like wisdom passed from generation to generation of policemen—to accept the occupational accepted frame of reference. This frame of reference includes, of course, both broad axioms related to police work in general (role) and the more specific corollaries which provide the ground rules of the work-a-day world (operations). In this section, the label "occupational perspectives" is affixed to the former. It is intended merely to imply that my concern is with the wider, institutional view of policing shared by patrolmen rather than the explicit "how-to" work prescriptions which are considered in the next section.

Although occupational perspectives are connected intimately to the stages of recruit socialization described (albeit tersely) in the preceding section, interest here is tied primarily to what Becker et al. (1960) called the final perspective. As such, the focus is upon the characteristic view patrolmen eventually come to hold regarding their organizational and occupational milieu—to use a dramaturgic metaphor, the "backstage" views of police. Occupational perspectives represent the solution to what Schein (1961) has suggested is the critical problem of organizational socialization, namely, "coping with the emotional reality of the job." In the police world, these perspectives provide the perceptual filter through which a patrolman views his work life. In a sense, they provide him with something akin to an occupational ideology. Such an ideology—rooted in common experience and knowledge—serves to support and maintain the codes, agreements, and habits existing in the work place.

Two distinct occupational perspectives are crucial for our understanding of patrolmen. Together they form a definitive credo which shapes the personal identity of policemen and regulates the pace, style, and direction of "on-the-street" police behavior. The first perspective grows from the patrolman's unique role in the social world and concerns his "outsider" position in the community. The second perspective develops from the nature of the patrolman's task requirements and deals with the survival dictums of his occupation.

The Outsider: Separate and Apart

A young patrolman soon learns that in uniform he is a very special sort of person. Not only does he have a low visibility vis-a-vis his superiors, but he has a monopolistic grip on the legal application of force. Amplifying this societal trust is the awesome responsibility of deciding virtually on his own and in sometimes terrible situations when to and when not to exercise this force. This feature alone places him in a solitary and somber position compared to the rest of society. Certainly there are legal and administrative guidelines set up which presumably govern his actions. Yet, in by far the majority of cases in which his right to force and violence may be utilized, the decision must be made in the emotional fever of fear or anger, the immediacy of danger, and in the flicker of an instant. In these powerful and dark moments there is not time to ponder the alternatives. Such is the ultimate responsibility of a patrolman.[19]

Of course, situations of the extreme are rare. Some officers progress through their entire career without once having to draw their weapons or physically subdue an obstinate suspect. But among those who spend their days on the street, they are few. Uncommon indeed are those officers who have not come within a hairbreadth of "squeezing-off-a-round" or who have not been through the bruising give-and-take of street battle. For most, these experiences are the defining characteristics of their occupation and it distinguishes them from other gentler ways of life.

While it would be a mistake to view police work from this danger aspect only, the symbolic importance of this feature cannot be underestimated. In large measure, these experiences (and their not infrequent retelling) set the tone for patrol work. As one young patrolman who had been on the street for several years explained:

> Most of the time this job is boring as can be. You just sit behind the wheel and go where they tell you. When you're not bullshitting with your partner, your mind kinda wanders and some nights it's a bitch to stay awake. . . . But somehow you never forget that the next call you get or car you stop might be your last. Mentally that's hard to accept but it's real. When I first came on I felt like I had a target painted on the back of my head. You know there's one hell of a lotta people out there who'd love to off a cop. I've gotten over that pretty much by now because you just gotta live with it. If anybody wants to kill you, there's no way you could ever stop 'em. . . . But what really gets you is that whoever it was probably wouldn't even know your name, he'd just be out to kill some cop. To the people out there we're just faceless blue suits. You sure begin to wonder what kind of crazy bastard you are for getting into this job in the first place.

The danger inherent in police work is part of the centripetal force pulling patrolmen together as well as contributing to their role as strangers to the general public.[20] Importantly, however, the risks of policing also provide real psychological satisfaction to men who spend most of their time performing activities of the more mundane or routine variety (for example, report taking, service calls, preventive patrolling, and so on). Without danger as an omnipresent quality of the work setting, patrolmen would have little of the visceral pleasures that contribute to their evaluation of performing difficult, important, and challenging (if unappreciated) tasks.

The "outsider" perspective arises as well from the unforgetably indifferent or antagonistic manner in which he is treated by the public. The rookie painfully discovers that wherever he is to go, his presence is bound to generate anxiety. People stare at him and scrutinize his movements. While driving through his sector, he finds that a major problem is avoiding accidents caused from the almost neurotic fashion in which other drivers react to his perceptually nefarious squad car. Soon he appreciates the relatively few places where he receives a warm and friendly welcome. All-night diners, hospitals, fire stations, certain niches in the courthouse, the precinct locker room, and even a private recess where a patrolman may park his squad car unnoticed become havens from his totem-like existence, providing him an opportunity to relax.

In general, there is little to link patrolmen to the private citizen in terms of establishing a socially satisfying relationship.[21] Small businessmen have perhaps something to gain in terms of the protection a rapid response might provide. However, businessmen know that there is little likelihood that the patrolman they are friendly with today will respond to a call for help tomorrow. Similarly, patrolmen recognize accurately that few civilians are likely to return favors. For mutual concern and friendship to develop, some sort of exchange relationship must be sustained—the quid pro quo of Homans (1950). In the police world, patrolmen rarely see the same people twice unless the contact is of the adversary variety. And such encounters are not apt to prove rewarding to the patrolman regarding the development of friendships.[22]

Thus, it is a lonely, largely friendless world the patrolman faces. The only assistance and understanding he can expect comes solely from his brother officers who, as the police enjoy saying, have "been there." In light of his public receptivity, it should not be surprising that policemen in general have assumed many of the characteristics of other stigmatized groupings.[23]

I suggested in the analysis of recruit socialization that the rules and regulations of police work are so numerous and immobilizing that, from the patrolman's point of view, no one could ever obey all of them. In effect, this implies that police officers, to be protected from their own infractions, must protect others. While rule violations run from the trivial to the serious, no officer is free from the knowledge that in his past (and no doubt in his future) are certain acts which, if reported, could cost him his job and perhaps even his freedom. From a failure to clear with his dispatcher for lunch to perjury on the witness stand, police must live each day with the knowledge that it is the support of their brother officers that insures their continuance on the job. Thus, it is his colleagues who represent the only group to whom the patrolman can relate. As one patrol veteran suggested:

> How the fuck can I tell anyone who ain't a cop that I lie a little in court or that sometimes I won't do shit on the street 'cause I'm tired or that I made some asshole 'cause he was just all out wrong. If I told people that they'd think that I'm nothing but a turd in uniform. The only people that can understand are people who've had to pull the same shit . . . and there just

ain't nobody in this department, from the Chief on down, who hasn't pulled some tricks in their time on the street.

When this officer speaks of "tricks" there are, of course, important matters of degree involved. Nevertheless, the point remains that all officers are indebted heavily to their patrol colleagues. In the last analysis, it is this two-way obligation which forms the basis of a relationship which can never be approximated with persons from the non-police world.

These features along with the more salient aspects of the occupation—the shift work, the uniform, the 24-hour nature of occupational responsibility, and so on—provide a perspective on the world which will last for as long as the patrolman remains with the department.[24] Behaviorally, all outsider groupings tend toward isolationism, secrecy, strong in-group loyalties, sacred symbols, common language, and a profound sense of estrangement from the larger society. It is these subcultural properties which underpin the common understanding among police that they are different.

The cynicism popularly attributed to police officers can, in part, be located in the unique and peculiar role police are required to play. Treated shabbily, hated, or feared by many of the contacts they have, police are asked frequently to arbitrate messy and uncertain citizen disputes. In such disputes, all concerned generally construct a particular account which exonerates them from blame. After a few years on the street, there are few accounts patrolmen have not heard. Hence, whether a claim is outrageous or plausible, police react by believing nothing and distrusting everything at the same time. Only one's colleagues can understand and appreciate such skepticism.[25]

The hardness commonly thought to be the mask of many policemen arises to fend off the perceived curse of doing society's dirty work. To be a sponge, absorbing the misery and degradation that pass daily through a patrolman's life, is an untenable position which would soon drive one from the police midst were it accepted. Therefore the proverbial "shell" is constructed, which protects the patrolman from the effects of nasty encounters which would leave most persons visibly shaken. But in the patrol world such coldness becomes almost a legendary personal property. To wit, one inexperienced patrolman related the following story:

> Man that Sergeant Kelly is something. . . . Remember the night that David Squad nailed that shithead coming out of Mission Liquor Store? Blew him up with a couple of rifle slugs and the guy's brains were splattered all over the sidewalk. You couldn't even tell if the dude was white or black 'cause of blood he was swimming in. Anyway we're standing there waiting for the coroner to show, when Sergeant Kelly decides it's time to eat. So what does he do? He goes back to his unit, grabs his brown bag and proceeds to

come back and start chowing down on an egg sandwich. Jesus! You shoulda seen the face on the kid working in the liquor store.

Only the police could understand the hardness implied in such stories. While many sordid tales are no doubt organizational fictions, they serve to denote the peculiar attributes of the police occupational code and also serve to detach patrolmen from the more polite social world of their origin.

In essence, the "outsider" perspective crystallizes the patrolman's occupational identity. It sets him off from others and provides an anchor to which he attaches his interpersonal relationships. Since the private interests and concerns of one are the interests and concerns of most others in the patrol setting (for example, avoiding injury and disciplinary action, displaying the proper amount of commitment and aggressiveness on the street, developing "pat" testimony for courtroom use, and so on), they form a common source of appeal and support. This can be summarized neatly by referring to a bond of sympathetic understanding existing among the police.[26] As one officer remarked succinctly:

To most people we seem to be inhuman, somehow separate and apart. Almost like another species. Maybe they're right but I'll tell you, I'd trust even my worst enemy in this department before I'd trust the people out there.

Survival: Lay Low and Avoid Trouble

Although police know that the unanticipated and nonroutine event may occur at any moment, they nonetheless have firm expectations about what work will consist of on any given shift.[27] An experienced officer establishes therefore his own tempo and style of work. Like any occupation, patrol work falls into set patterns: take a burglary report, meet complainant, interview victim, investigate open door, direct traffic, and so on. The discovery of certain organizing devices by which to categorize the myriad of work duties is a major task for young officers and—as with the perspective developed in response to their perceived declassé social position—follows the socialization paradigm as one learns what it is like to work the streets.

Importantly, the young officer learns that there is a subtle but critical difference between "real" police work and most of what he does on patrol. "Real" police work is, in essence, his raison d'être. It is that part of his job that comes closest to the romantic notions of police work he possessed before attending the Police Academy. In short, "real" police work calls for a patrolman to exercise his perceived occupational expertise: to make an arrest, save a life, quell a dispute, prevent a robbery, catch a felon, stop a suspicious person, disarm a suspect, and so on. In terms developed earlier in this essay, "real" police work involves the "hot" call, the unusual "on view" felony situation or the potentially dangerous "back-up" predicament in which an officer may have to assist a threatened colleague.[28] During such encounters all the contradictions and humiliations that accompany most of what the patrolman does evaporate as he, for example, pursues someone he believes to have committed a crime or defends his fellow-officers (and himself) in the chaos of a tavern brawl. Yet, because of this narrow definition of police work, little of his time on the street provides the opportunity to accomplish much of what he considers to be his primary function. Thus, "real" police work to the patrolman is paradoxical; a source of satisfaction and frustration.[29]

At another level, one can divide the patrolman's dispatched (radio) calls into a rush, non-rush dicotomy. Rush calls are those involving "real" police work. Statistically, however, non-rush calls are much more common.[30] The decision to rush is, of course, a learned one, developed as a patrolman learns his territory (see the third section entitled "Meta-prescriptions: Street Codes") and gains knowledge of the patrol lexicon. There is not a universal code for rush calls. They are dependent upon the dispatcher's choice of words, the time, the place, the particular unit receiving the call, and perhaps even the mood of the officer. For example, to some officers a 220 (in Union City, a so-called "dangerous mental case") represents a call demanding lightening speed; to others it is treated simply as a "normal" call and handled without undue rush or concern.[31] Only those situations calling for "real" police work are treated seriously by all officers.

The "back-up" responsibilities of patrolmen present an interesting amendment to the limited definition of "real" police work. Back-ups are those situations—dispatched or not—in which one patrol unit will proceed to a particular sector location to assist, if necessary, the patrol unit which has been assigned to the call. Certainly, most of the time back-ups amount to simply sitting in the squad car waiting to be waived off by the other unit; yet, the symbolic importance of back-ups cannot be dismissed.

There are several classes of dispatched calls which almost automatically guarantee the presence of a back-up, providing the sector work distribution at the moment is not overloaded. For example, the "help the officer" call is treated most seriously. Almost always such calls result in the rapid appearance of all officers in the district. In another class, less critical yet nonetheless sure to receive at least one back-up, are calls such as the felony-in-progress or man-with-gun. Other calls, such as the bar disturbance or the family fight in the ghetto neighborhood, also generate pro forma back-up units. To a large degree these back-up situations help young officers establish their street credentials as squad members in good standing. Patrolmen note the presence (or absence) of their peers as well as the speed with which they arrived. Such behavior demonstrates to all present the mutual concern and loyalty police feel they must have for one another. It is also the measure of one's commitment and motivation to share the risks involved in working the street. In the police world, such behavior is not overlooked. One officer suggested pointedly:

I'll put up with a hell of a lot from guys working this sector. I don't care if they're on the take, mean or just don't do anymore than they have to. . . . But if some sonfabitch isn't around on a help-the-officer call or shows up after everybody else in the city has already been there, I don't want him working around me. Those cops are dangerous.

In Union City, as in all large city departments, the work of patrolmen is difficult, if not impossible, to evaluate. There are the required annual patrolman performance ratings submitted by the sergeants, but these are essentially hollow paper exercises in which few men receive low marks.[32] The real task of evaluating patrolmen falls on the squad sergeant, and he is most concerned with the "activity" of his men.[33] However, activity is judged differently by sergeants. The same activity that is appreciated and perhaps demanded by one sergeant is treated indifferently by another sergeant. For example, one patrolman who had worked the same sector under several sergeants noted:

Now you take Sergeant Johnson. He was a drunk hunter. That guy wanted all the drunks off the street and you knew that if you brought in a couple of drunks in a week, you and he would get along just fine. Sergeant Moss now is a different cat. He don't give a rat's ass about drunks. What he wants are those vice pinches. Sergeant Gordon wanted tickets and he'd hound your ass for a ticket a night. So you see it all depends on who you're working for, each guy is a little different.

To patrolmen, such idiosyncratic policies, while sometimes difficult to understand, provide a margin of safety in what can be a very uncertain work environment. By satisfying the sergeant's rather unambiguous demands (tickets, drunks, vice, juveniles, field investigation reports, and so on) a man can insure a harmonious relationship with the department.[34] If he provides the activity his sergeant desires, he will be left alone to do his work. If not, he may find himself working his days off or transferred to another, less desirable sector. To the men, these activity guidelines are received with some grumbling. But, in the main, they are acknowledged as simply a fact of work life. Furthermore, they are, to some degree, valued as the lodestar of their day-to-day work activities. Patrolmen realize, of course, that these activity measures have little to do with "real" police work. Yet, when one's patrol log contains evidence of activity for the sergeant, a patrolman is provided with a certain degree of comfort as well as the gratification that follows a job completed successfully.

It is important to recognize, however, that providing one's sergeant with his required activity can be done with relative ease. Whether it is tickets, car stops, drunks, or vice, patrolmen have little trouble and spend little time accomplishing the required task. In fact, most officers in Union City would simply remark sometime during a shift something to the effect of, "well-let's-go-do-our-bit-for-the-sergeant," and proceed to casually make whatever the quota might be. One FTO explained his particular job requirement to his recruit partner in the following manner:

> Here's our little duck pond (a busy but poorly marked intersection in Union City). Just sit here for five minutes and you can write all the tickets Sergeant McCallion wants. Just bag five of those illegal left turners and you're done for the week. Keeps him off your back.

Aside from producing activity for the sergeant and the infrequent opportunities to perform "real" police work, most of the patrolman's work time is dominated by what the officers call "staying-out-of-trouble." Essentially, this means that the officer will do what is assigned to him and little more. The novice patrolman soon learns that there are few incentives to work hard. He also discovers that the most satisfactory solution to the labyrinth of hierarchy, the red tape, the myriad of rules and regulations, the risks of street work, and unpleasantness which characterize the occupation is to adopt the group standard, stressing a "lay-low-and-don't-make-waves" work ethic. And the best way in which he can stay out of trouble is to minimize the amount of work he pursues.[35] One veteran officer remarked caustically:

> The only way to survive on this job is to keep from breaking your ass . . . you just don't want to work hard on this job 'cause if ya do you're sure to get in trouble. Either some civic-minded creep is going to get outraged and you'll wind up with a complaint in your file; or the high and mighty in the department will come down on you for breaking some rules or something.

In particular, working hard implies that one will—without being cajoled either by radio or a sergeant—actively search for real police work. Thus, making street stops, checking for stolen cars, searching a neighborhood for a possible burglar, filling out a number of Field Investigations Reports, and performing cursory searches on suspicious persons and automobiles are examples of the behavioral meaning of working hard. It should be clear that working hard increases the number of citizen contacts an officer may have and, therefore, represents an opportunity to make both serious and banal mistakes. Citizen contacts are always delicate when an officer is on uncertain or merely suspicious grounds. Such encounters are strained interpersonally, troublesome legally, and almost always invite disrespect. In other words, aggressive patrol tactics are bothersome. Since working hard offers few occupational rewards, the logical solution for the patrolman is to organize his activities in such a fashion as to minimize the likelihood of being sanctioned by any of his audiences. The low visibility of the patrolman's role vis-a-vis the department (that is, his sergeant) allows for such a response. Thus the pervasive adjustment is epitomized in the "hang-loose-and-lie-low" advice frequently heard in the Union City department.[36]

Rookies were always accused of what was referred to as a "gung-ho" attitude (rushing to calls and pushing eagerly for action). They were quickly taught, however, the appropriate perspective toward their work.[37] For example, the aggressive patrolman who constantly was seeking out tasks to perform was the butt of community jokes. In fact, many police expressed the sentiment that it was wise to spend as much time off the street as possible for, as they claimed, "you-can-get-in-trouble-out-there." One experienced officer noted:

> Those goddamn rookies are dangerous. I worked with one guy who was so gung ho that every time I got in the car with him I figured I was gonna get killed. This ass used to drive like a bat outta hell just to go to lunch . . . he wanted to always be looking for stolens or stopping everybody on the street. He settled down eventually when he found out that he wasn't getting anything done except make the other cops in the squad laugh.

While staying out of trouble occupies a great deal of the patrolman's working hours, it is to be distinguished sharply from "loafing." While one may or may not work hard on any given shift, he is always to do his share by covering his district and answering his dispatched calls. Taking a call in another man's sector is occasionally acceptable. However, to do so consistently is personally insulting and considered by all policemen to be unjust. To the squad, answering a call for another indicates that the neglectful officer no longer cares or is committed to his "team," for he will not pull his fair share of the work. Relatedly, an officer who regularly fails to appear as a back-up on a call or arrives well after the potential danger has passed is considered to be either fearful or loafing and will, if possible, be expelled from the squad. The definition of loafing is therefore quite specific.

I have suggested earlier that during a newcomer's first few months on the street he is self-conscious and truly in need of guidelines as to his actions. A whole folklore of tales, myths, and legends surrounding the department is communicated to the novice by his fellow-officers, conspicuously by his FTO. Through these anecdotes—dealing largely with "mistakes" or "flubs" made by policemen—the recruit begins to adopt the perspectives of his more experienced colleagues. He becomes aware that "nobody's perfect," and the only way in which one can be protected from his own mistakes is to protect others. Among members of a particular squad, this "no rat" rule has deep and meaningful roots. Violations of the rule are met with swift (albeit informal) disapproval.[38] Since all officers have at sometime in their career broken a rule or regulation, the conspiracy-like network of support remains intact. The tacit norm is to never do something which might embarrass another officer. To draw critical attention to a colleague is strictly taboo in the police world. On the other hand, it is acceptable—and often demanded—that one cover for the mistake of another. While citizen complaints are felt to be unavoidable occupational hazards, fellow officers go to great lengths to insure such complaints against one of their squad members will be ruled unfounded.[39] The sergeant plays a critical role in this regard for he screens all reports written by his men. If an account on, for example, an arrest report contains an ambiguous phrase which could possible be interpreted negatively by the court, or the report fails to mention a detail (factual or otherwise) which might keep an officer (and, by implication, the squad and the sergeant) out of trouble, he will have the man rewrite the report until it is flawless in his eyes. Let me quote a passage from my field notes for illustrative purposes:

> When Blazier was placed under guard in the hospital (after a rather brutal encounter in which Blazier, a black homosexual, was severely beaten in the back of a patrol wagon), we returned to the precinct station to handle the paperwork. Officer Barns filled out the many reports involved in the incident and passed them to his sergeant for approval. The sergeant carefully read each report and then returned the "paper" to Barns saying that he better claim he was kicked in the face *before* he entered the patrol wagon or Barns would get a heavy brutality complaint for sure. He also told Barns to change the charge on Blazier to felony assault from refusal-to-obey and add drunk-in-public to the disturbing-the-peace charge Barns had originally thought appropriate. According to the sergeant, the heavier charges were necessary to protect Barns from IID (Internal Investigation Division). Finally, after some discussion and two re-writes, Barns finished a report which the sergeant said "covered their asses" (February 1973).

This "cover your ass" perspective pervades all of patrol work. In a sense, it represents a sort of bureaucratic paranoia which is all but rampant in police circles. Again, the best way for patrolmen to "cover their ass" is to watch carefully the kind of activities in which they engage. It is best therefore to not take the initiative on the street but rather react primarily to departmental direction. In this way, one seldom becomes involved in those potentially explosive situations which might result in disciplinary action for the patrolman.

The "lay low" occupational perspective also develops as officers gradually discover that the external rewards of a police career are more or less fixed. The patrolman knows for example that he will be at top salary within three years after joining the department. Advancement through the hierarchical network is a realistic expectation to only a few. In Union City, almost eighty percent of the men remain at the patrolman level for the extent of their careers.

At times, patrolmen feel as if the department goes out of its way to make things uncomfortable for them. For instance, Union City patrolmen are not provided parking spaces for their private automobiles and must spend considerable time locating spots on the busy and crowded city streets. Locker room facilities are dirty, cramped, and new officers often wait a year or so before they are assigned a space. The administrative detail in checking certain records or requesting information from one of the detective bureaus is almost prohibitive. An officer must also dig into his own pockets to cover many occupational expenses, such as having his uniforms cleaned or replaced after a duty-related accident. Critically, patrolmen discover that the department answers very few of their requests; for example, assignment shifts, new equipment, car repairs, expense reimbursements, and so on. And when the organization does act, it is usually after a long delay.[40]

In response to their situation, patrolmen assume a "don't-expect-much" stance. They begin to realize that it is the rewards of camaraderie and small favors granted to them by their sergeant that makes their daily task either pleasant or intolerable. A few extra days off, a good partner, enjoyable squad parties, an agreeable assignment, or an extra long lunch become important rewards offered by a police career. It would appear consequently that the following advice given me by an older street veteran in Union City represents a very astute analysis of the patrolman's work role. He suggested cryptically:

Being first don't mean crap around here. You gotta learn to take it easy. The department don't care about you and the public sure as hell ain't gonna cry over the fact that the patrolman always gets the shit end of the stick. The only people who do care are your brother officers. So just lay back and take it easy out here. Makes things a lot smoother for us as well as yourself.

The survival perspective is strengthened finally by the fact that patrol work prepares one for very few other occupations in this society. The knowledge and skill involved in working the street (and these are considerable) have meaning and value only in the police world. Thus, the only alternative a man has to his patrolman position is to return to the work he did before joining the department. To most this would be unthinkable, for patrol work remains, in the last analysis, far more interesting and stimulating than most occupations open to young men in the police environment. Even after an officer discovers that the work is much duller than he had imagined before his initiation into the occupation, the simple pleasures of warm fellowship and working in the heterogeneous, unpredictable world of city streets is enough to bind most men to their careers. As one officer remarked:

> If I ever quit, the only thing I guess I could do would be to go back to the market where I used to work. But the thought of stacking Del Monte tomato cans on aisle six at exactly ten o'clock every morning would drive me nuts. This job may be slow most of the time, but at least the routine doesn't get you down. Besides, once police work gets into your blood, that's it! You can never really go back out there again as a civilian.

META-PRESCRIPTIONS: STREET CODES

This section concerns the more specific ground rules of the police occupation; the explicit working codes adhered to by most patrolmen when on the street. In a real sense, the platitudinous police job description—to protect life and property, arrest law violators, prevent crime, regulate public conduct, preserve the peace—means little. What we need to know is how police actually decide to carry out their task.

The analysis is in part dependent upon the occupational perspectives discussed in the preceding section. Thus, some overlap is unavoidable. Yet one should keep in mind that, whereas occupational perspectives provide the work ideology followed by policemen, they do not provide the everyday guidelines needed in the situationally contingent world of the streets.

Two critical aspects of police work are used to organize this section. First, the meta-prescriptions that grow from the interrelated characteristics of territory and autonomy are considered. Second, meta-prescriptions arising from and in response to street work and public interaction are examined. Together, these work codes provide an individual with the experientially developed and consensually approved knowledge necessary to take action as a police officer.

Territory and Autonomy

Among the first lessons learned by a recruit after graduation from the Police Academy is how little he really knows about the geographical peculiarities of the city. Even if he has lived his entire life in the community, he will have little of the needed territorial grasp which typifies his more experienced colleagues. As one rookie, a native of Union City, was told by his FTO when preparing for his first night on the street:

> It don't matter whether or not you've lived here since year one, you don't know the city until you become a cop. Particularly you're gonna have to

learn your sector inside and out. You gotta know every street and alley, every building and vacant lot. You gotta know where the people are on a Friday night. Believe me, your life might depend on it someday. You learn not to take chances on this job and you'll start by memorizing every fucking driveway in this sector 'cause if you don't know where you are all the time, you're a lousy cop. And I don't train lousy cops.

Patrolmen are tied inextricably to their district and sectors, and a solid working knowledge of the terrain requires anywhere from six to twelve months to acquire. When a man receives a new assignment he normally only knows that area by reputation. Firsthand knowledge, however, is required. Thus, he will spend a great deal of time pushing his patrol car wherever it will go to learn his new territory.[41] The city does not represent a scatter of neighborhoods and civic symbols to police; it represents, as Rubenstein (1973) suggested, "a mosaic of linked districts."

Knowledge of each district includes the spatial geography as well as the social demographic patterns of place. The inexperienced officer soon begins labeling places good and bad. For example, the corner of First and Main is bad because of the "blood pit" bars located there; whereas Third and Main is good, the taverns are quiet and the clientele well-mannered. Thus the patrolman gradually learns his district, and such learning provides him with the behavioral guides he believes appropriate to each locale: to be rough and aggressive on Connecticut Avenue, cautious and stealthful on Broadway Street, or relaxed and easy-going on Park Boulevard.[42]

Associated closely to the patrolman's notion of place is his notion of time. He develops in essence a personalized watch which tells him whether the public use of a public place is proper or improper, suspicious or not suspicious, noteworthy or not noteworthy, according to the time of day. Thus, territorial learning involves space and time, and the interaction of the two coupled with observed behavior provide the symbolic calculus which determines police action.

After spending considerable time becoming familiar with one's territory, policemen develop some startling notions related to being "out-of-place." Once a patrolman crosses over certain boundaries into strange surroundings he feels uncomfortable, uneasy, and his actions are no longer grounded by the firm set of expectations he has developed in his "home" district. It is as if the ground has shifted so dramatically that the figure becomes distorted and unrecognizable. Thus, the patrolman has a vested interest in remaining within a district he knows well. That sergeants use this fact in maintaining a degree of managerial control is taken for granted by patrolmen. To be transferred to an unfamiliar district is by and large not a welcome prospect to most patrolmen, for they know they must begin anew to build the all-important map of their territory.

Tied to the geographical knowledge patrolmen possess is the accompanying knowledge of the people that frequent their district. Yet the understanding and labeling of the population proceeds at a much slower pace than the development of his territorial expertise. Aside from a few regulars in his sector whom he sees almost daily (for example, the so-called "habituals" whom he may have arrested numerous times such as the winos, prostitutes, addicts, gypsies, and various small-time hustlers, "uniform girls" such as waitresses and nurses, and a few "business" people such as bartenders, pool hall managers, ticket takers, and gas station employees), the patrolman has little contact with the people of his territory. Thus, in most encounters on the street, he must rely primarily upon his knowledge of place and time to guide his action. As one officer told me:

> If I see someone cruising around the waterfront between seventh and ninth street when the bars are closing, I'll stop him. I don't give a shit how well dressed he is or the fancy car he's driving. If he's down there late at night, he's either up to no good or is about to get himself taken. First, I'll stop him on some chippie thing like a faulty tail or license plate light and politely ask him what he's doing. If he ain't got a good reason for being there, I'll tell him, "Look mister, as far as I'm concerned you don't have any constitutional rights down here; maybe you do up on the north end, but not down here. So you get your ass outta here if you don't want trouble." That usually chases 'em right out.

A discussion of territory is, however, not complete unless the autonomy patrolmen demand in their sector is made salient. Essentially, the basic unit of analysis in police work is the sector, and within a sector it is a partnership (or a "solo" officer) who claim territorial rights on the sector during any particular eight-hour shift. Within their sector boundaries, patrolmen are fiercely independent and consider themselves to be their own boss over all action they may or may not take.[43] More often than not, sergeants will defer to their judgment, leaving them alone to do their work. Thus, during most working hours, the partnership is set apart, in some ways isolated, from the remainder of the department.

Such separateness is the preference of all patrolmen. In fact, great care is taken in guarding one's sector boundaries from the possible "poaching" of another patrol unit. One enraged officer told a colleague from an adjacent sector:

> Listen you prick, if you jump another one of my calls I'll personally see to it you get your teeth jammed down your throat. You and Mike stay on the west side of Spring unless we specifically invite you over. We don't fuck with your calls and we don't want you to fuck with ours!

Such a code holds for one's sergeant as well. Most patrolmen felt that the mark of a good sergeant was the fact that, unless requested, he would "leave-you-alone." An itchy sergeant who continually "jumped calls" was considered a menace to the squad's integrity. In such cases, the men may covertly agree to stop supplying the sergeant with his "activity" until he again leaves them alone. Of course, such a tactic could work only if all squad members acted together. Yet, such unison was relatively easy to obtain when a squad's autonomy was threatened. Sergeants finding themselves faced with such mutinous behavior on the part of their subordinates had little recourse other than to back down; since to bring this conflict to the attention of his superiors placed him in the awkward position of admitting that he was unable to properly control and direct his men.[44] Although patrolmen will, for example, accept quotas, special duty, or extra paperwork, to meddle in their perceived area of autonomy—the sector—resulted in a stiff and immediate reaction.

The autonomous code extends as well to people and information spheres. Among squads (and even between members of the same squad), patrolmen feel no necessity to exchange bits and pieces of information concerning informers or criminal activity in their district. Indeed, the men horde information as if it were their own personal property. For example, one officer explained:

> I'm not gonna tell anybody but my partner about where those guys are living now (two suspected burglars), not even the dicks. . . . Why should I? I weaseled it outta my crummy little informer so why should I pass it on for somebody else to get the credit? I want those guys myself even if it takes ten years.

Information, like territory, belongs to the patrolman who possesses it. It was standard practice in Union City for two patrol teams working the same sector, but different shifts, to never discuss with one another the various activity occurring in their sector. Furthermore, virtually no information of value was exchanged between patrolmen and detectives. From this perspective, the Union City police department resembled a feudal kingdom in which each patrolman was lord of his fief-sector.

The source of this secretive behavior lies in the territorial assumptions made by the patrolman, as well as the small rewards (primarily self-satisfaction) that resulted from an arrest. Yet, even the latter category is contingent upon the "turf" an officer works, for all patrolmen know that there are good sectors and bad sectors regarding arrests. If, for example, an officer works a "last-out" shift (12 p.m. to 8 a.m.) in a suburban, middle-class district, he will have little opportunity to ever arrest anyone other than perhaps an occasional clumsy burglar.

In short, one's territory and the autonomy that accompanies it provide a basic work code that is respected by all policemen. It has been said by other observers that patrolmen react most violently to a challenge of their authority. Yet, it is not so much their authority that patrolmen protect as it is their autonomy in a particular sector,[45] for it is the autonomy that gives meaning to their work role. Hence, to do one's work in one's sector and little more is among the most important operating maxims of the patrolman's job.[46]

Street Work and Public Interaction

Most policemen recognize the myth-like quality of their powerful image. While persons on the street may find him an omnipotent figure, the patrolman knows he is merely a city employee who can be pushed around and fired at the whim of his superiors. The patrolman realizes therefore that he must delicately manage his appearance on the street, maintaining as best he can the respect and fear he feels necessary for him to do his job. And he must accomplish this without overstepping what he considers to be the narrow limits on his public behavior. He must also satisfy those above him in the department by at least occasionally arresting someone, as well as performing his required tasks with proper diligence and speed. Finally, when working the street, he must guard against the careless mistake which, in the violent world he inhabits, might cost him his life.

The most basic ground rule for an officer on the street is, in the police vernacular, "maintain-the-edge." Fundamentally, this means one must be decisive in all situations. To many patrolmen, it is considered better to make a wrong decision rather than to make no decision at all. Hence, the officer learns to push when others would pale, and this hard-edged aggressiveness marks the patrolman's working behavior. In the words of one young officer:

> You've gotta be tough out here. If you're not they'll walk all over you and you may as well hand them over the keys to the city. . . . When I came on I figured you could be nice and still get your way. But I found out fast that if you don't look mean, talk mean and act like you know exactly what you're doing, nobody'll ever do what you say. Out there you gotta think fast and make decisions quick. Detectives maybe have the time to sit around and ponder their bellybuttons before they act, but we can't and the guy on patrol who can't handle the snap decision part of his job ought to get himself transferred inside to some nice jackoff desk job.

Many officers believe that one way in which one maintains his edge is to always have the first and last words in street confrontations. This everyday working theory is premised upon the assumption that to meet and leave a "civilian" abruptly, without opportunity to start, question, or terminate the encounter, gives one the upper hand and denotes the patrolman's right to initiate, direct, and close all conversation. On a proud note, one officer stated:

> I normally try to surprise them first and then leave them with their mouth hanging open. Like last night, we'd noticed this guy behind us kind of weaving around and driving in a reckless manner for a couple of miles. So we jerked him over, ran a check on him and talked to him for awhile. He seemed OK so just as we kicked him loose I told him: "Sir, we've written out a Field Investigation Report on you for suspicion of 'interfering' which, in plain language, means minding other people's business. I'd advise you to stay out of the police business from now on sir. . . . Good night." Then I turned around and split. God, I thought he was gonna have a heart attack.

Let us now examine another important street code of patrolmen. Reiss (1971) pointed out that the use of force is not a philosophical question to the police, rather it is a question of where, when, and how much. On the street, these decisions must be made quickly and, once made, are irrevocable. However, to the majority of patrolmen, the use of force is always a last resort, for it can get them in serious trouble. It comes only when the officer believes that there is no other route open to protect himself, safeguard his autonomy, or maintain his edge. In most threatening situations, the officer attempts to maintain his edge by managing his appearance such that others will believe he is ready, if not anxious, for action. The policeman's famous swagger, the loud barking tone of his voice, the unsnapped holster, or the hand clasped to his nightstick are all attitudes assumed to convey this impression. Decisiveness is readily apparent in such a posture, although the officer himself may have little, if any, idea of what he is about to do. For example:

> You can't look like a boy scout when you're on the street. You've gotta make them think you'd just as soon blow their head off as talk to them. . . . Not everybody of course, but it's not you're average creep you've got to worry about. It doesn't take long to figure out who the assholes are out there and they're the ones you gotta put on the I-chew-nails routine for.

Although all policemen develop somewhat idiosyncratic characteristics when working the street, most tend to first evaluate any person encountered in terms of whether or not they will be able, if necessary, to physically overpower them. As one officer suggested, "I always check out a guy to see if I can take him." Thus, one's age, height, weight, and muscular development are important clues to a patrolman's behavior. If it appears that he can "take" the man, then the patrolman may be more patient and reserved than would be the case otherwise.

To some degree, this represents a class of working habits which can be labeled "safety patterns." Others would include: sitting in a public place where one has a clear view of other patrons and both the exit and entrance; watching the hands of a suspicious person for telltale movements when approaching him; never leaving the patrol car without a nightstick; standing to the side of a door when knocking; requiring a suspect to lay spreadeagled on his stomach when searching him for weapons; approaching a suspicious vehicle with one's right hand around a small two-inch revolver (aimed at the driver) hidden inside the pocket of the officer's jacket; and so on. These safety patterns vary, of course, according to the personal style of the officer. But each and every patrolman develops a set of these habituated devices which he believes increase the probability of his avoiding injury.

Finally, it is important to at least briefly discuss the labeling of persons by patrolmen. For my purposes, three classes of people will be of interest: suspicious persons, assholes, and know-nothings.[47] The three classes are not mutually exclusive, but the categories do provide a useful way of examining the differential manner in which persons are accorded on the street. First, suspicious persons are those individuals who patrolmen have reason to believe may have committed a felony offense or serious misdemeanor. Depending on the severity of the particular crime, police treat such persons with great care in what is almost a parody of the "professional" manner. Thus, suspicious persons are approached and treated carefully. They are labeled for a specific past act and not for their immediate behavior. In those situations in which the suspicious person is not known but may be in the general vicinity (for example, the robber fleeing from the scene), the patrolman will slowly cruise through his sector looking for a person who, for reasons related to time and space, appears de trop or out of place. One officer suggested that in these situations:

> What I look for is someone who seems kinda jumpy and edgy. If he's walking, he'll usually look over his shoulder or stare straight ahead, walking either slower or faster than everybody else on the street. Mainly, what I look for is somebody who looks wrong, like he shouldn't be there. I guess it's just something that a policeman's sixth sense picks up. You gotta really work the street for a couple of good years before you start being able to make people.

On occasion, officers will stop a "suspicious person" for no other reason than the impression he made on them while passing. More often, however, the label arises in relation to a person's appearance in a particular location (for example, a person loitering on a corner known to be the approximate "drop point" for drug sellers; or a man aimlessly strolling through a garage from which a number of cars had recently been stolen). Thus it is some unique combination of time, place, and peculiar characteristics of a person's behavior or general appearance that result in the label "suspicious."[48]

On the other hand, the "asshole"—from the perspective of the patrolman—creates the label for himself while in the presence of the officer. The label is affixed to the person after a street stop has been made (usually the stop is for a petty misdemeanor such as a traffic violator, the corner lounger, the curfew offender, and so on). However, a "suspicious person" can also quite readily become an "asshole" as well. In essence, the "asshole" is one who refuses to accept (or, at least, remain silent for) the officer's definition of the situation (see Part 1). Hence, the person complains loudly, attempts to fight or flee, disagrees with the officer, does not listen, and generally, in the officer's eyes, makes a nuisance of himself. Clearly, the behavior of most student protestors, drunks, militants, foreign speaking, Jesus freaks, or those politically inclined would be perceived by policemen to fall into this category. Furthermore, the confused often are labeled assholes, as are those who claim to "know-their-rights." From the patrolman's view, the asshole is one who makes his job more difficult, and such actions are not looked upon kindly. In fact, if the asshole persists in his actions and pays no heed to an officer's repeated warnings to "shape-up," he may find himself charged with considerably more than he first thought. Or, in the extreme case, he may be severely "thumped" if the officer is so inclined. In the patrolman's world, such physical retaliation for the antics of an "asshole" is justified according to the doctrine of "street justice." While not reserved strictly for the asshole, this form of police action is designed to both punish the offender immediately and to reestablish the officer's control of the situation. As one ten-year street veteran put it:

> Shit, after you've been on this job for as long as I have, you get to know some of these assholes and realize that they're never gonna get what's coming to them. . . . Even if you haul them in, they'll get kicked loose with a warning. So you figure that teaching them a little respect on the street ain't gonna hurt things none.

Street justice is of course administered quite discreetly. Most patrolmen feel that they are sophisticated enough to effectively calculate just who will and who will not be in a position to charge them with "excess force," as well as being able to accurately decide just who is deserving. Furthermore, street justice is reserved for those settings in which it is unlikely that any nonpolice witnesses will be on hand. By and large, patrolmen make few mistakes in this regard.

It should be made clear that as the term implies, there is a notion of justice involved in such street "thumpings." Policemen rarely react physically without —in their eyes—good cause. Reiss' (1971) data indicate that there is something of the "golden rule" involved in an officer's street behavior. In other words, the more deferential the person, the more polite and restrained the patrolman. And, of course, the opposite holds as well. Hence, the more of an "asshole" the person, the more likely he will be the recipient of "street justice."

Finally, the "know-nothing" category (most certainly representing the largest number of people) is restricted to those contacts a patrolman may have with persons who cannot, by any stretch of the collective imagination, be labeled either "suspicious" or "assholes." The know-nothing distinction applies simply because they are not police officers and therefore cannot know what the police are about. The officer's behavior when dealing with know-nothings is rather detached and circumspect. Providing the person does not cross over into the "asshole" category (which is not as difficult as one may at first assume), the officer's air will be casual, perhaps somewhat bemused, and altogether polite.

This discussion indicates the range and type of street codes followed by patrolmen. While not inclusive, the point here was to delineate some of the everyday operating standards of police work. Only in this way can we hope to discover the parameters of criminal justice in this society for, in the last analysis, the police are the gatekeepers of the system. And, if one needs to be reminded, the task has just begun.

CODA: A NOTE ON REFORM

Three premises formed a kind of critical membrane inside which the considerations of this paper were confined. The first premise upon which my view of the behavioral system of patrolmen rested was simply that when individuals are introduced into any organization they are subject to a powerful process of internal (that is, within the organization) influence. In fact, it is during the "breaking in" period that an organization may be thought to be most persuasive, for the person has little if any organizationally based support for his "vulnerable selves" which may be the object of influence. Regardless whether or not this socialization is undertaken consciously or unconsciously, formally or informally, collectively or singularly, it represents an extremely prominent factor contributing to the organization's institutional stability, continuity of mission, social structure and climate, normative orientation and adaptive abilities. Thus, the institutional conservatism of police systems is preserved in part by the manner in which patrolmen pass to each generation of incoming recruits the conventional wisdom necessary to work the city streets.[49]

The second premise can be summarized adroitly by the open-system metaphor which emphasizes the external (that is, outside the organization) environment as a potent factor regulating the behavior of individuals within the formal boundaries of an organization. Indeed, in the police world, the primacy of this often neglected variable in organizational studies cannot be overlooked. Therefore, the unexpected, precarious, and territorially dependent realm of patrolmen represents another factor contributing to the character of the institution.

The third premise was of a more methodological nature. Essentially, this premise was based upon the need to outline the patrolman's frame of reference. Most police studies view the behavior of policemen as a "problem" for the department or society, not vice versa. I have tried, in a small way, to remedy this bias by describing the point of view of patrolmen themselves; in particular, the development of that point of view. This approach accentuates the situationally constrained character of the street officer's behavior as he works out solutions to his unique occupational problems. In short, we "looked out" at the network surrounding the patrolman rather than applying the usual perspective which, in the past, "looked in" on him. The elitist biases and distortions which result from a "looking in" approach have been demonstrated vividly through the failure of management-oriented change programs. Such programs have floundered precisely because they have not understood empathetically the more pragmatic and earthy characteristics of the patrolman's occupational problems.

The analysis resulting from the use of these three premises suggests that the intelligibility of social events requires that they always be viewed in a context which extends both spatially and in time. Relatedly, social actors must be granted rationality for their behavior. In the case of the urban police, is it any wonder that, faced with impossible demands and a pariah-like social position, they often lash out with bone-cracking urgency to defend their zone of self-esteem or seal themselves off interpersonally behind a blue curtain? Indeed, we seem to have reached what psychoanalyst R. D. Laing (1968) called the "theoretical limit of institutions." According to Laing, this paradoxical situation is characterized by a system which, when viewed as a collective, behaves irrationally, yet is populated by members whose everyday behavior is eminently rational. Perhaps this construct indicates the profound dilemma in which our police are indeed trapped.

The police response to this dilemma has been an attempt to infuse the occupation with a type of professionalism based on the paramilitary model. This conception of professionalism values efficiency, integrity and the impartial application of the law. On the surface, such goals are hardly questionable. But, in practice, this sort of professionalism has resulted in a technical emphasis ignoring the restraints presumably built into a democratic polity, providing patrolmen with more mobility and power without adequate restrictions. The concern for managerial effectiveness associates new cars, improved response time, better communication networks, improved internal reporting systems, and more firepower with professionalism. Yet there has been no evidence that these advances have resulted in any greater appreciation for the human dimensions of police work or, for that matter, have in any way reduced the level of urban crime. If anything, the professional edict has increased the polarity between watchers and watched.

On the other hand, the reform movement (located primarily outside the formal departmental boundaries) has promoted another sort of professionalism. Reformers tend to equate professionalism with an underlying humanistic attitudinal or value system. Such a value system is, as the writers of grant proposals are fond of saying, to be "inputed" into police officers. Thus, from this angle, education and training provide the solution to the arbitrary use of police orb and scepter. Furthermore, by concentrating upon the attitudes and values of individual officers it is believed that a greater understanding between the police and the community will grow. These reform tactics include: minority recruitment; encouraging officers to obtain a college degree; demilitarization (that is, organizational development programs aimed at reducing interpersonal distance among those within the police hierarchy); revising the reward systems within the department to recognize and compensate officers for acting more humanely; team policing concepts which build in formal police-community interactions; civilianization of managerial and clerical staff designed to bring new values into the police subculture; ad infinitum. Again, there is no evidence to date that any of these reform programs have been effective, at least in terms of "impacting" the on-the-street behavior of patrolmen.

What both approaches fail to recognize is the nature of the police function itself. As long as the prescriptions such as maintaining law 'n order, crime stopping, and crook catching remain the primary goals of police departments, little change is apt to come about within the system. What is required is a structural redefinition of the police task (for example, along the lines of creating a community-based, service-oriented, and internally democratic institution). Ways must be found to strengthen the external control principle so central to the rule of law. Of course, methods to make the patrolman's lot somewhat more tolerable—both to himself and to the general citizenry—must be explored. However, it is doubtful that, without deep alterations in the definition and structural arrangements surrounding the police task (and in the implied values such arrangements support), significant change is possible. It would seem, therefore, that only by concentrating less on the individual and more on the external configuration surrounding the patrolman can we ever begin to anticipate substantial alteration in the long-embedded patterns of police behavior.

NOTES

1. All police quotes unless otherwise stated are taken from my field study in Union City. Since I employed no recording device and took no notes during my Academy and street experiences, each quotation is as accurate as my memory and ear allow. I have not

eliminated any of the profanity in the police language because I believe it to be an important part of the occupational milieu. Furthermore, an empathetic understanding of the police perspective requires that we listen to patrolmen for, in many respects, talking is being. For a further discussion of my methods, see Van Maanen (1972).

2. There are two notable exceptions to the bibliographic report listed in the text. One is Rubenstein's (1973) brilliant report on the working life of patrolmen in the Philadelphia Police Department. In this work, Rubenstein provides a general ethology of the police world. The other exception is Wesley's (1951) insightful study of a midwestern police department. However, both studies are devoted mainly to the description of the more salient sociological features of the occupation and are concerned only peripherally with the "learning process" associated with the police career. My effort here is to locate individual action within the subcultural sea of the patrolman's surroundings and to demonstrate the developmental nature and source of such action.

3. Following a research agreement, Union City is a pseudonym for a sprawling metropolitan area populated by more than a million persons. The police department employs well over one thousand uniformed officers, has a traditional training program (following the guidelines suggested by the President's Commission on Law Enforcement and the Administration of Justice, 1967), provides a salary slightly above the national average, and is organized in the classic pyramidal fashion.

4. Union City's Police Department, like virtually all large departments in this country, divides up patrol responsibility among various precincts. Within each precinct are numerous districts which are further divided into sectors. For each of the three shifts in Union City, a particular district is patrolled by a squad, consisting of a sergeant and anywhere from ten to twenty-five patrolmen. Thus, a single sector covered by one patrol unit (comprised of either one or two officers) represents the basic territorial unit of analysis in the police world.

5. Certainly, the in situ method of naturalistic observation is unsystematic, biased, and to some, unscientific. Yet, as a partial defense, I know of no other method to explore and begin to describe the "backstage" orientation of actors to their work than to join with them and share both the objective and subjective "becoming" experience. As Goffman (1971) noted perceptively, variables which emerge from rigorous research designs tend to be creatures that have no existence beyond the room in which they were invented. My feeling is simply that in a study such as this, wherein understanding of ordinary behavior is crucial, the method of study must be one which reduces the distance between researcher and researched. In this manner, concepts are developed directly from observed social activity.

6. The use of the term meta-prescription comes from Brim (1966). He used the term to denote those rules individuals learn to apply to situations in which conflicting demands make choice difficult. Therefore, meta-prescriptions provide a person with a way to resolve potential conflict arising from situational and immediate pressure to take some type of action (that is, withdraw, avoid, compromise, and so on).

7. This discussion is based upon Van Maanen (1973) and is believed to be sufficiently general as to apply to most urban police departments. Of course, the training sequence may be shortened or extended from place to place, but the key experiences are virtually the same. My personal experience with three different departments bears this out. Furthermore, confidence in the ordering is increased via my personal communication with police administrators, interviews conducted with police personnel from a number of different departments, and, most importantly, critical readings of my work by experienced patrolmen. For a similar view noting the structural correspondence among training programs, see Westley (1951); President's Commission on Law Enforcement and the

Administration of Justice (1967); Berkeley (1969); Niederhoffer (1969); Ahern (1971); and Rubenstein (1973).

8. In Union City, the percentage of those applicants selected for service was roughly about ten percent over the past ten-year period. See Van Maanen (1972) for a further discussion of the police selection process.

9. No doubt the perception of this background investigation is dependent upon the eye of the beholder. To those officers in charge of the selection process, the investigation is barely adequate. However, to the entering recruits, the investigation is an awesome ordeal which penetrates deeply into their private spheres. It also demonstrates very effectively to potential recruits that there are a few facets of their lives (both work and non-work) not of pressing concern to the department.

10. Probationary periods apparently vary, according to department, from a minimum of six months to a maximum of two years. The importance of such marginal status to the recruits in Union City seemed, however, quite low. For example, most recruits I encountered were unaware of completing their probationary period unless explicitly reminded by another. Although the probationary status was important to the men upon joining the department, they quickly learned that few veteran officers (or, for that matter, few supervisors) attached much value to it and consequently they too became relatively unconcerned.

11. The following Union City Training Division "greenie" (that is, disciplinary memorandum which is placed in the man's permanent personnel file) illustrates the arbitrary nature of the dreaded "gigs" issued during the Academy phase of training:

> You were observed displaying un-officer like conduct in the academy class. You openly yawned (without making any effort to minimize or conceal the fact), (this happened twice), you were observed looking out of the window constantly, and spent time with your arms lying across your desk. You will report to Sergeant George in the Communications Division for an extra three hours of duty on August 15 (parentheses theirs).

The result of such "stress" training is that the recruit soon learns it is his peer group rather than the Academy "brass" which will support him and which he, in turn, must support. For example, the newcomers adopt "covering" tactics to shield the tardy colleague, develop "cribbing" techniques to pass exams, and become proficient at constructing consensual ad hoc explanations for a fellow recruit's mistake (for example, when a recruit accidentally blew a hole in the roof of a shed with his shotgun, it was because he had been "jostled" by those close to him, although no one was within ten feet of the blushing recruit). In short, such events impress upon the newcomer that he must now identify with a new group—his fellow officers.

12. Another aspect of Union City training should be mentioned in this regard—the two weeks recruits spent on the firing range learning to use a whole arsenal of police weapons (for example, revolvers, shotguns, mace, various gas hand grenades, fist loads, sap gloves, truncheons, and even a machine gun). To the recruit, this period was strikingly different than the typical drone of the Academy classroom. On the range, discipline was lax and the instructors were primarily old hands with a vast storehouse of war stories to entertain the recruits. Yet, the symbolic importance of this aspect of training was not lost on the recruits, as attested to by the many hours each man spent at home "dry-firing" (pointing his emptied service revolver at some imaginary spot and squeezing the trigger repeatedly to steady his aim and rid himself of the almost automatic quiver of the novice). For a similar view of the

differences between the "academic" and "applied" Academy staffs and routines, see McNamara (1967).

13. The term FTO is essentially an arbitrary one. It refers to the first officer a recruit works with following his Academy experience. However, most departments formalize this relationship by including an "on-the-street" period as part of a rookie's training program. In some ways, the FTO portion is similar to what Inkeles (1968: 152) referred to as a "second wave" of socialization. He describes this phenomenon in the following manner:

> The second wave in the socialization process occurs where and when the individual learns the detailed role contents which are socially necessary to behave in a previously acquired basic disposition and where new dispositions and social skills couldn't have been learned earlier.

14. Rubenstein (1973) points out that all policemen learn to keep quiet about their colleagues who are short-tempered, lazy, vicious, or dishonest. But they do not keep silent about a colleague who is considered dangerous. This "back-up" test represents, therefore, a real opportunity to discover if the newcomer has, as the police say, "balls."

15. Many young officers referred to this leave-taking as finally "climbing-from-the-womb." To most, the choice of words implied that they were soon to take their first breath as an autonomous police officer in a world still somewhat novel and strange.

16. As in all police departments, internal politics plays a powerful role in the distribution of the relatively few rewards available to patrolmen. Thus, rookies would talk of their "man" or their "hook" in the department; a well-placed departmental connection who would presumably aid the newcomer in receiving a desirous assignment. Such "hooks" were higher ranking officers linked to a recruit via kinship or friendship ties. In New York, this informal allocation system goes through one's "Rabbi" (Radano, 1968). However, in Union City, few connections seemed to have been made since only a few officers were pleased initially with their first permanent assignments. Further evidence for this rather uniform lack of "pull" can be found in a cursory survey of 124 rookies who reported that fewer than ten percent received their first choice of precinct and shift when leaving the Academy (Van Maanen, 1972).

17. By far, the majority of calls answered on patrol are of the service variety—estimates vary from around eighty to ninety percent. Furthermore, most of the time spent on patrol is of the routine preventative variety in which officers simply drive through their respective sectors presumably looking for evidence of criminal activity. The best statement on the task and time characteristics of the patrolman's role can be found in Reiss (1971) and Webster (1970).

18. Reiss (1971) noted perceptually the atypical routine enjoyed by patrolmen. After examining the police "straight-eight"—the tour of duty—he said "no tour of duty is typical except in the sense that the modal tour of duty does not involve the arrest of a person."

19. One of the standing jokes among police officers is that they were taught at the Academy—from the department's point of view—that they had little discretion on the street. According to their classroom instructors, hard and fast guidelines cover all police actions. Yet, as they discovered quickly on the street—indeed, knew instinctively at the Academy—police rules and regulations offer few solutions to the intricate, dynamic, and specific situations in which patrolmen become involved.

20. For another perspective emphasizing the danger inherent in police work, see Skolnick (1966).

21. It should be noted that the issue of police corruption is not covered here. Indeed, if

I were to include an analysis of "taking," the discussion would go well beyond the suggested length of this paper.

22. Whyte (1943) first noted the dilemma in which street officers are caught. If the officer takes a formal, no-discretion, duty-only position in his sector, he cuts himself off from the personal relationships necessary to receive information or settle disputes in the area. On the other hand, if he becomes close and involved in the personal affairs of his sector, he must necessarily utilize much discretion and is unable to act vigorously in situations which may demand such action. While the use of the automobile for patrol purposes has sealed-off most officers in a sort of urban spaceship (with few contacts in their sectors), it is still clear that discretion occupies a central place in the day-to-day environment of patrolmen and cannot be kept in the sub-rosa position of being a simple management control issue. For a most interesting discussion of social traps similar to those in which patrolmen are caught, see Platt (1973).

23. This argument is made forceably by Bayley and Mendlesohn (1969). See also Goffman (1963) for a sparkling theoretical treatment of stigmatization.

24. Police officers are legally bound to take action off-duty in the presence of a felony offense and can, in fact, be fired for a failure to do so. Few patrolmen go anywhere off-duty without first arming themselves; whether it be to the corner market, out "on-the-town," or to play golf. While the "off-duty gun" is more symbolic than functional, it is but another factor isolating patrolmen from the mainstream of social life.

25. An interesting analysis of the role patrolmen play as streetcorner politicians is provided by Muir (1971). Also, the quasi-fiction of Joseph Wambaugh [*The New Centurions* (1970), Boston: Little, Brown; *The Blue Knight* (1972), Boston: Little, Brown; and *The Onion Field* (1973), New York: Delacourt Press] provides an excellent, if sentimental, account of the patrolman's view of the street.

26. Certainly this bond is strongest among members of a particular squad. But it exists to some degree among all police officers. To wit, the unwritten code of never ticketing or arresting another police officer regardless of where he may be from unless the offense is very serious indeed.

27. Officers soon learn that there are quiet Sundays, busy Fridays and crazy Saturdays. There are those days when welfare or unemployment checks are distributed and certain sectors seem to be considerably faster than usual; drunk and disorderly calls, family fights, muggings, and so on. Of course, there are also those ubiquitous evenings of the full moon when, as one officer put it, "those demons wreck havoc until the sun rises." Whether or not such perceptions are backed by statistical evidence does not matter, for most officers nonetheless have firm expectations of public conduct fixed in their minds. And, to paraphrase W. I. Thomas' famous dictum, a man's actions are attributable to his perceptions of reality and not to reality per se.

28. In most ways the popular notion of "street crime" is a misnomer. The vast majority of crime takes place inside buildings, in entranceways, in alleys, in the dark and silent public parks, in living rooms of private homes, and so on. Policemen know this, and their expectations of catching a criminal "in-the-act" are consequently quite low. Thus, they wait patiently for the serendipitous "on-view" situation to arise if, in fact, it ever will.

29. It is interesting to note that I rode with many officers who claimed—when relaxing after a busy shift answering some ten calls or so, handling several traffic stops, assisting a few citizens, and driving fifty to seventy miles in and out of their respective sectors—that the night had been a "total waste" since they had not accomplished any "real" police work.

30. Again, see Webster (1970) and Reiss (1971).

31. For an analysis of the sociological meaning of "normal," see Sudnow (1965).

32. An example of just how pervasive such aggrandizing performance ratings are in Union City is provided by an analysis I conducted on the formal FTO progress reports. Of over three hundred report forms, only one contained an even slightly negative evaluation. Uniformly, all other forms were characterized by high praise for the recruit.

33. I am indebted to Rubenstein (1973) for coining the term "activity." However, in Philadelphia, where Rubenstein's work was done, activity had a specific referent in that it applied to the number of vice arrests a patrolman made. In Union City, no such department-wide focus existed. Each sergeant was more or less free to emphasize whatever activity he individually felt important; hence, activity is used here in a much broader fashion.

34. These demands are probably most important when a man is new to the squad. For the newcomer's behavior provides the sergeant with valuable information as to the ease or difficulty in which he will accept direction. If the man responds, the sergeant will slack-off, only occasionally suggesting activity to the man. Usually, a casual remark by the sergeant is enough to promote action.

35. An example of the disdain patrolmen feel toward the "rate-buster" is provided by Whittemore's (1973) romantic account of Batman and Robin, the so-called supercops in New York City. These officers met their biggest problem inside, not outside, the department. Most often, this pressure came from their fellow patrolmen who actively resented their aggressive approach. At various points in their early career, both officers were told point blank to "stop making waves and just do what you're supposed to do." Another similar account is found in Maas's (1973) superior biography of Serpico, a New York officer who—aside from his violation of the police code of secrecy in front of the Knapp Commission—was distrusted by his colleagues for his "working ways."

36. Verification for this ethic can be found among sergeants who in Union City spent an enormous amount of time simply attempting to locate various patrol units under their command. Humorously, the sergeants referred to this aspect of their job as the game called "finding your men."

37. This "gung-ho" attitude was a real source of irritation to most veteran officers in Union City. The "gung-ho" patrolmen were thought to be overly aggressive. In police argot, they wore "big-badges." It was felt that their presence in a squad created difficult situations in which other officers would have to assume needless risk untangling. Thus, most officers did not follow a "work-hard" rule. As noted, most learned to sit back and patiently answer their calls, rarely venturing from their squad car unless otherwise directed.

38. See Westley (1951) for a more extensive account of just how deep this code runs in police circles.

39. Complaints, as well as commendations in the police world, are viewed somewhat sardonically. To patrolmen, a complaint is more a sign of where an officer works than his particular policing style. For example, if an officer works a central city, black, lower class sector, complaints are felt to be simply a taken-for-granted feature of life in the area. Reciprocally, citizen letters of commendation will be extremely rare. On the other hand, if a man works a suburban, white, middle-class sector, commendations will be more frequent and complaints relatively few. Patrolmen know this and therefore assign little important to either of the two categories. Apparently, the only exception to this rule of unimportance are those extreme cases where an officer may be under investigation as a result of a serious complaint (for example, a shooting, extreme brutality, a felony, etc.). In such cases, patrolmen, if they are allowed to remain on the street, will act discreetly until the

department resolves the complaint. As patrolmen say, "they go hide because they have a big one hanging."

40. Police officers often mentioned that all precinct headquarters seemed to be encased by that "special grey air hanging over the ugliest building in town." The point here is simply that police sense a lack of concern for their role in the community. To most, the lack of facilities and their run-down nature is degrading and hard evidence of their collective neglect. And, if no one else seems to care about their occupation, why should they?

41. The patrolmen I observed took particular pride in knowing every accessible passageway in their sector. For example, I spent many hours on patrol driving across parks, down railroad easements, under bridges, along dirt roads, through storage yards and parking lots, traversing twisted hiking paths in the city's foothills, weaving through the backroads of the warehouse district, and so on. It would seem that anywhere a patrol car can conceivably be driven, pushed, or pulled will eventually be attempted by the officer as he explores his sector.

42. In many ways, the old policeman's adage about knowing his sector better than he knows the police headquarters is not an exaggeration. And many policemen feel far more comfortable among the transient population and decaying seaminess of skid row than they do in the functionally clean and well-lit corridors of their own headquarters.

43. The autonomy of a patrolman within his sector is for all intensive purposes an unwritten commandment among the police. For one officer to criticize the actions of another is virtually forbidden. As one veteran patrolman suggested bluntly:

> I never second guess another cop about what he did in a particular field situation. If there's one thing that's sacred it's that you're the boss over what happens out there. . . . You know what you shoulda or shouldn't a done at the time you do it. Only the guy that's there knows or could ever know.

44. It should be clear that sergeants generally attempt to play the role of "good guy" with their men. Since power is more or less equalized between superior and subordinate, a sergeant realizes that the maintenance of a synergetic relationship within the squad is his most important function. Thus, even the use of his power to transfer men is severely restricted by the necessity to maintain squad morale.

45. I have personally witnessed on several occasions officers absorbing verbal harangues or watching behavior in another sector that would be cause in their own sector for immediate action.

46. The notion of territorial perogatives as they relate to the analysis of police behavior suggests that the classical "chain-of-command" model used to describe police departments is woefully inadequate. On the street, patrolman ethics resemble more the "do-your-own-thing" youth philosophy than any "follow-orders" militaristic philosophy. For excellent discussions on the neglected sociological dimension of territoriality, see Goffman (1971) and Lyman and Scott (1970). A most extensive analysis of its role in the police world is provided by Rubenstein (1973).

47. These three classes are meant to be only suggestive. Their somewhat cavalier presentation here is not to be taken as a definitive statement on public labelling by police. Nor am I trying to make light of a serious concern. Rather, my purpose is simply to make salient an important factor of police behavior and to describe several relevant dimensions along which a complete typology eventually might fall.

48. Although the abstraction called "probable cause" does not concern us directly in this analysis, it is important to note that rarely do patrolmen stop a "suspicious person"

without some reason which they believe can be sustained in a court of law. Even though an automobile or pedestrian may appear highly suspicious (that is, to be a "good shake"), a patrolman knows that he may have difficulty in court articulating this suspicion. Hence, something more tangible must be found to support his claim to probable cause in the event an actual felony arrest is made. Such "tangibles" most often turn out to be relatively frivolous violations like "faulty tail light," "loitering," "jay-walking," or the tried and true "no rear plate illumination."

49. Support for this position comes from a wide variety of studies indicating that a person's early organizational learning is a major determinant of one's later work-relevant beliefs, attitudes, and behaviors. Essentially, the theory suggests that when a neophyte first enters an organization, that portion of his life-space corresponding to the specific role demands of the organization is blank. Depending on the persons's entering values and desires, he may feel a strong need to define the expectations of others (for example, the colleague groups, the supervisor, and so on) and develop constructs relating himself to these perceived expectations. In a sense, the individual, during his early days in the organization, builds a psychological map of his surroundings. For a deeper analysis of this topic, see Van Maanen (forthcoming).

REFERENCES

AHERN, F. (1972) Police in Trouble. New York: Hawthorn Books.

ALMOND, G. A. and S. VERBA (1963) The Civic Culture. Princeton: Princeton University Press.

BAKKE, E. W. (1950) Bonds of Organization. New York: Harper.

——— (1955) The Fusion Process. New Haven, Conn.: Yale University, Labor and Management Center.

BAYLEY, P. H. and H. MENDELSOHN (1969) Minorities and the Police. New York: Free Press.

BERKELEY, G. E. (1969) The Democratic Policeman. Boston: Beacon Press.

BITTNER, E. (1967) "The police on skid row." American Sociological Review 32: 699-715.

BRIM, O. G. (1966) "Socialization through the life cycle," in O. G. Brim and S. Wheeler (eds.) Socialization After Childhood. New York: John Wiley.

BROWN, M. E. (1971) "Alienation and Integration in the Political Attitudes of Suburban Adolescents." Unpublished Ph.D. dissertation. Los Angeles: University of Southern California.

CICOUREL, A. V. (1967) The Social Organization of Juvenile Justice. New York: John Wiley.

EASTON, D. and J. DENNIS (1967) "The child's acquisition of regional norms: political efficacy." American Political Science Review 61: 25-38.

——— (1969) Childen in the Political System: Origins of Political Legitimacy. New York: McGraw-Hill.

GOFFMAN, E. (1959) The Presentation of Self in Everyday Life. Garden City, N.Y.: Doubleday.

——— (1963) Stigma. Garden City, N.Y.: Doubleday.

——— (1971) Relations in Public. New York: Basic Books.

HOMANS, G. C. (1950) The Human Group. New York: Harcourt, Brace & World.

HYMAN, H. (1959) Political Socialization. New York: Free Press.

INKELES, A. (1968) "Society, social structure and child socialization," in J. A. Clansen (ed.) Socialization and Society. Boston: Little, Brown.

LAING, R. D. (1968) "The Obvious," in D. Cooper (ed.) Dialectics in Liberation. London: Institute of Phenomenological Studies.

LYMAN, S. M. and M. B. SCOTT (1970) A Sociology of the Absurd. New York: Appleton-Century-Crofts.

MAAS, P. (1973) Serpico. New York: Viking Press.

McNAMARA, J. (1967) "Uncertainties in police work: the relevance of police recruits' background and training," in D. J. Bordua (ed.) The Police: Six Sociological Essays. New York: John Wiley.

MUIR, W. K. (1971) "The Policeman as the Streetcorner Politician: Lord Acton Revisited." Unpublished paper. Berkeley: University of California.

NEIDERHOFFER, A. (1967) Behind the Shield. Garden City, N.Y.: Doubleday.

PLATT, J. (1973) "Social Traps." American Psychologists 28: 641-651.

President's Commission on Law Enforcement and the Administration of Justice (1967) Task Force Report: The Police. Washington, D.C.: U.S. Government Printing Office.

RADANO, G. (1968) Walking the Beat. New York: World.

REISS, A. J. (1971) The Police and the Public. New Haven, Conn.: Yale University Press.

RUBENSTEIN, J. (1973) City Police. New York: Farrar, Straus & Giroux.

SCHEIN (1961) "Management development as a process of influence." Industrial Management Review 2: 59-77.

SKOLNICK, J. (1966) Justice Without Trial: Law Enforcement in a Democratic Society. New York: John Wiley.

STERLING, J. W. (1972) Changes in Role Concepts of Police Officers. Washington, D.C.: International Association of Chiefs of Police.

SUDNOW, D. (1965) "Normal crimes: sociological features of the penal code in a public defender office." Social Problems 12: 255-276.

VAN MAANEN, J. (1972) "Pledging the Police: A Study of Selected Aspects of Recruit Socialization in a Large Urban Police Department." Unpublished Ph.D. dissertation. Irvine: University of California.

——— (1973) "Observations on the making of policemen." Human Organizations 32: 407-418.

——— (forthcoming) "Breaking-in: a consideration of organizational socialization," in R. Dubin (ed.) Handbook of Work, Organization and Society. Chicago: Rand McNally.

WATSON, A. and J. W. STERLING (1969) Police and Their Opinions. Washington, D.C.: International Association of Chiefs of Police.

WEBSTER, J. A. (1970) "Police task and time study." Journal of Criminal Law, Criminology and Police Science 61: 94-100.

WESTLEY, W. A. (1951) "The Police: A Sociological Study of Law, Custom and Morality." Ph.D. dissertation. Chicago: University of Chicago.

WHITTEMORE, L. H. (1973) The Super Cops. New York: Stein & Day.

WHYTE, W. H. (1943) Street Corner Society. Chicago: University of Chicago Press.

WILSON, J. Q. (1968) Varieties of Police Behavior. Cambridge, Mass.: Harvard University Press.

TRAFFIC AND THE COURTS:
SOCIAL CHANGE AND ORGANIZATIONAL RESPONSE

WESLEY G. SKOGAN

One of the consequences of urbanization for the legal system has been an enormous growth in the volume of cases it confronts each year. As a social and commercial system becomes larger, more heterogeneous, and more complex, more problems arise which require the intervention of the state for their solution. As society grows more interdependent, relationships between people who are otherwise strangers become more common and more complex, and more reliance is placed upon abstract and formal rules to govern those relationships. Utilitarian relationships between anonymous individuals are facilitated by the intervention of the law. In addition, the process of living together in urban communities generates problems requiring intervention. The regulation of land use, zoning and building code requirements, and many forms of waste disposal present serious problems only in the city. As more strangers rely more and more upon formal rules to regulate their relationships, and as there are more formal regulations to be followed, there is a continuous increase in the number of potential cases for the legal system, both in absolute numbers and per capita.

This increase in potential legal business has been paralleled in the United States by an expansion in the number of formal enforcement officials. There has been a steady increase over time in the number of policemen in cities, and a steady increase in the rate in which we invest public resources in formal social control. A consequence has been a vast proliferation in the number of cases generated for the legal system to process. An increase in potential enforcement situations, coupled with an increase in the number of authorities looking for violations, has produced a serious volume problem for the justice system.

This volume problem has been one of the forces shaping the evolution of urban court systems. The inexorable pressure generated by the increasing flood of cases entering the courts each year has goaded the development of a number of organizational innovations designed to alleviate "volume stress." In addition, we witness periodic waves of public discontent over the seeming inability of law enforcement officials to control many of the more undesirable consequences of social change. Sharp changes in social trends, episodic decreases in the apparent safety of city residents, produce demands for more effective law enforcement. These waves of public indignation spark rapid and often thoroughgoing reforms in the organization of the justice system, in contrast to the more gradual organizational reforms generated from within in response to volume stress. Together, these external and internal pressures help explain reform: the growth and specialization of urban court systems.

Court systems in Chicago and Illinois have reflected this trend. As the environment within which the legal system operates has grown more complex, the institutions of social control (the criminal courts) and dispute resolution (civil courts) have grown more numerous and more specialized.[1] The first judges to serve the people of Chicago were members of the state supreme court. So little legal business came to the courts during the early years of statehood that high court personnel spent several months each year riding the state's four judicial circuits. Traveling with a retinue of bailiffs, prosecutors, and defense attorneys, they set up court in this town and that, presiding over the disposition of cases which had accumulated since their previous visit. Before about 1830, none of the communities of Illinois were large or prosperous enough to demand more than part-time justice.

The growth of Chicago was so rapid that soon after its founding it became apparent that a more extensive local judiciary was required in the state's largest city. Under an early charter, the Chicago Common Council was empowered to name police magistrates to assist in the disposition of minor criminal cases, and the mayor of the city presided over a special "Mayor's Court," having jurisdiction over cases involving the violation of city ordinances. Over the years an extensive but haphazard collection of courts of limited and general jurisdiction developed to serve the needs of the growing metropolis. County, probate and juvenile judges, criminal, circuit, superior, recorder's and common pleas courts, justices of the police and police magistrates abounded. By 1900 the city and county were served by over 200 different courts and 300 judges.

However, the independence of these courts, and the "peculiar and arbitrary" division and overlap of jurisdiction among them, made it impossible to develop consistent and coordinated responses to caseload problems. The dockets of some courts were hopelessly jammed, while justices of the peace hotly contested for minor civil cases and the marriage trade. Corruption and partisan finagling were greatly facilitated in either circumstance. In an attempt to lend some order to the process of justice, the state legislature authorized the creation of a unified Municipal Court of Chicago in 1905. Staffed with full-time judges and an administrative clerk of the court, the municipal court enjoyed original jurisdiction over all minor civil and criminal cases arising within the city. In addition, the court held preliminary hearings in all felony cases brought from the city, sending those indicted to the countywide criminal court for final disposition.

But despite this minor reorganization of judicial personnel, the resources available to the justice system in Chicago lagged behind the requirements of the age. The city and its legislature are usually at loggerheads over either partisan or policy differences, and the general assembly has never appeared overly responsive to urban needs. The new municipal court was understaffed from birth, and pleas for the expansion of its staff of judges were only occasionally heeded. The criminal court drew its staff on temporary assignment from other county courts, and backlog problems were endemic. The result was the development of a number of institutional short-cuts which enabled the courts to function efficiently as organizations.

The most widely known contemporary process for coping with the volume problems which arise in the criminal courts is the plea bargain. In many courts, guilty pleas on the part of defendants are exchanged for lesser charges and lighter sentences on the part of prosecutors and judges. The process appears to stretch limited court resources while maintaining high conviction rates (Jacob, 1973). The practice of granting numerous continuances in major criminal cases, thus encouraging defendants, witnesses, complainants, or arresting police officers to cease pressing their claims, has been a common Chicago practice since the turn of the century.[2] Both of these practices have supplanted an earlier custom in the criminal courts of Chicago, the outright dismissal of a large number of cases. For example, the *Illinois Crime Survey,* a massive study of criminal justice in Chicago during the 1920s, reports that in 1926 over 70 percent of all felony defendants in Cook County were dismissed at preliminary hearings or grand jury sessions. Only 11 percent were found guilty of lesser charges on a guilty plea, now the common practice.[3] A *Chicago Daily News*

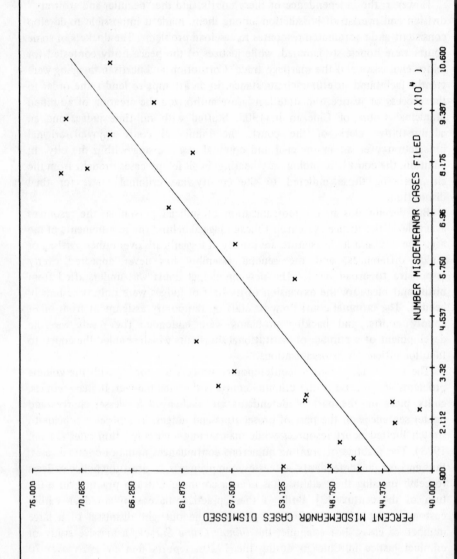

study of all arrests in the city of Chicago in 1924 revealed that 200,000 of 276,000 arrestees were dismissed in that year.[4]

A brief analysis of available court reports suggests that caseload volume serves as an excellent predictor of such procedures. If the dismissal of large numbers of cases proves an organizationally efficient way of coping with increasing caseloads in the face of limited resources, dismissal rates should closely parallel increases in the demand for court activity. The data to examine this relationship can be found in the *Annual Reports* of the Municipal Court of Chicago, 1908-1930. Figure 1 illustrates the relationship between one indicator of caseload volume in the court, the number of misdemeanor cases filed each year, and the proportion of the misdemeanor cases which were dismissed by the court in the same year. The correlation between input volume and this organizationally efficient form of output is .86. The line which best describes this relationship (the "line of best fit," or the "regression line") is also presented in Figure 1. Over the 1908-1930 period, each additional increment of 10,000 cases filed appears to have raised the dismissal rate 2.6 percent.[5]

That the dismissal rate was an "organizational maintenance" device, a procedure devised to enable the court to cope with volume problems, is suggested by a more complex analysis of the data. If we statistically control for the number of cases filed each year in the municipal court, the relationship between the misdemeanor dismissal rate and the number of judges serving on the court that year is negative; as judicial resources improve, organizational efficiency norms appear to have less impact upon disposition patterns.

But while courts, like other organizations, strive to do what they must to "get the job done," they are also expected to reflect less mundane values. Judicial decision-making is rule-bound, and perhaps more than most the official behavior of judges is legitimized by their adherence to formal decisional criteria. As we have seen, the courts face volume problems because of (1) the growth in scale of the social system within which they function, and (2) their limited ability to adapt their structure or resources in rapidly responsive ways. Pressures appear to exist for the invention of efficient procedures to circumvent this conflict, but somewhere there are limits upon the extent to which organizational norms can predominate in the legal system.

This essay examines the problems of caseload, volume stress, and organizational response in a particular legal arena. One of the major challenges to the ability of urban courts to effectively carry out their task has been the automobile. A most immediate social cost of the automobile, and one which produces legal problems which threaten to overwhelm local civil courts, is the personal and property carnage its use creates. Casualties on American highways outnumber those of all our wars. During both the Korean and Vietnam conflicts, highway deaths on the domestic front outran those on the battlefield.[6] By 1970, even minor automobile damage and the cost it entailed led to a political dispute of considerable magnitude over the cost and operation of automobile insurance schemes. At the same time, personal injury cases accumulating in the courts had created a serious backlog problem. In Chicago, delay averages three to five years, and no decrease is in sight.[7]

I then examine the regulatory response of the legal system. Regulation of the ownership and use of the automobile challenges the ability of the city to keep order. Controlling the flow of motor vehicles through the city demands the attention of numerous police officers and an armada of vehicles and specialized equipment. They enforce a host of formal rules governing the use of automobiles, rules which were created to facilitate the use of the automobile in the city and control its more undesirable consequences.

Finally, I examine the organizational response of the courts to the volume stress this enforcement effort created. At one point, traffic offenses made up 75 percent of the business of the municipal court of Chicago. "Crimes" such as double-parking and speeding, serious social problems only in the city, jammed already overloaded dockets, and the court was hardpressed to dispose of its business. The eventual response was the creation of specialized, autonomous branch courts which could process traffic cases with assembly-line efficiency. The compromises with traditional procedure which this organizational transformation demanded highlight the difficulty that the legal system has encountered in adjusting to the realities of urban life. Traffic, like many emerging urban problems, seriously challenges traditional conceptions of criminality, guilt, the personal responsibility of individuals for their behavior, and the deterrent impact of punishment upon unlawful behavior. In civil and criminal traffic cases we witness most clearly the clash between often inappropriate legal models for the settlement of disputes or the "treatment" of offenders and demands for organizational efficiency. Reflecting this, future reforms will probably focus not upon further increases in organizational efficiency, but upon the removal of traffic problems from the courts entirely.

THE AUTOMOBILE AS A REGULATORY PROBLEM

Figure 2 charts the rise in motor vehicle registration in Chicago over time.[8]

Early records of the number of automobiles and trucks in the city are not available. Before World War I motor vehicle use was not extensively regulated, and thus not well recorded. The first separate official accounting of the automobile as a legal problem appears in 1908—68 traffic arrests—and as late as 1912 there were two and one-half times as many buggys, wagons, and carriages in Chicago as there were motor vehicles.[9] The plot of available records documents the rapid increase in mechanized transport in the city after 1912. World War II, with gasoline rationing and severe restrictions upon the production of the motor car as a consumer good, accounts for the only substantial dip in the ever-increasing line. Even the Great Depression did not make serious inroads into our dependence upon the automobile.

Figure 2 also presents the distribution on a comparable scale of three major consequences of automobile use: accidents, injuries, and deaths.[10] The accident line, while rising with the number of automobiles, has a number of peculiar features, notably the enormous rise in the number of recorded accidents after World War II. This illustrates one of the difficulties of working with statistics of this kind: they are sensitive to reporting and recording contingencies which limit the inferences we can make from them. Accidents, first, are usually citizen-reported. Factors like the time of day, the condition of the parties involved, the "seriousness" of the affair, and whether drivers are insured or not, will have a major impact upon the tendency of people to report an accident to the authorities. Thus the expansion of the automobile insurance industry, and especially the requirement that drivers in Illinois carry liability insurance, may have had an enormous impact upon the apparent incidence of traffic accidents in the community. Further, even if they are reported, the capacity of the authorities to record accurately traffic statistics is problematic.[11]

This is nicely illustrated by the impact of automation upon accident statistics reported by the Chicago Police Department. In 1949, a mechanical tabulation system was installed to replace the old, cumbersome practice of filing multiple copies of often illegible carbons of police accident reports. A machine-readable computer card is now punched for each reported accident, and some accounting must be made for each accident report when statistical reports are generated from the accumulated data.[12] The impact of this change in recording procedures was dramatic. In 1947 the records unit of the department kept track of 17,424 motor vehicle accidents in the city of Chicago. In 1950, the first full year for the automated system, 78,153 accidents were recorded. At the same time, the State of Illinois' Division of Highways recorded an increase of only 14,837 accidents in Chicago on the basis of *their* record-keeping.[13]

It is not that one accounting is more accurate than another, but that every official statistic is shaped by the organization which collects, collates, and reports it. We will use these numbers, accordingly, not as indicators of the "actual" accident rate, injury rate, or other aspects of the legal environment; rather, we will use them as indicators of *potential inputs* into the legal system *which have come to the attention of the authorities*. An accident may have been reported or recorded because it was serious, or because one of the parties

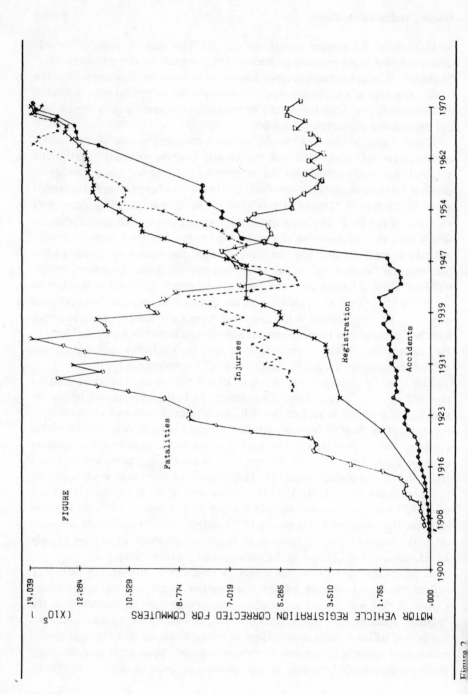

FIGURE

MOTOR VEHICLE REGISTRATION CORRECTED FOR COMMUTERS ($\times 10^5$)

Fatalities

Injuries

Registration

Accidents

Figure 2

involved insisted upon reporting it, or for a variety of other reasons. What is important is that these are the accidents (or injuries) which may become legal problems, and evoke the attention of the courts, the involvement of attorneys, and the authority of the state. And these potential inputs have increased enormously during the last two decades.

The number of injuries and motor vehicle fatalities recorded also rose steadily during the early years of the period for which we have systematic data. This steady rise was of some political importance, as we shall see. Deaths and injuries arising out of the introduction of large number of automobiles onto ill-prepared city streets spurred the definition of the automobile as a serious social problem. In 1921, the presiding judge of the traffic court lamented:

> Apparently life is held too cheaply in this community, and with the increase of the use of automobiles and the greater congestion of our streets, the toll of deaths, injury and misery will increase unless those public officials charged with the duty of enforcing the law stir up their consciences and give the masses the protection to which they are entitled.[14]

Deaths and reported injuries arising out of automobile accidents rose or remained at a high level until World War II. Again, wartime restrictions upon civilian automobile use and the greatly constricted supply of replacement units apparently curtailed their use and abuse, and both deaths and injuries appear to have dropped sharply during the war years.

But a curious pattern occurs following the war. While statistics on traffic injuries follow accidents, and the official figures skyrocket, the number of deaths arising from automobile accidents (probably as accurately reported a figure as we have) continued to decline. As a rate, computed as traffic fatalities per 10,000 motor vehicles, the decline is still more dramatic, for the number of cars on the road continued to increase. Increased reports of injuries, and even of the injury rate, probably reflects the same phenomenon we observed in the case of traffic accidents: the spread of insurance, improvements in police recording procedures, and the like. The fatality rate, on the other hand, is only partly a function of automobile use even when quite accurately reported and recorded. Advances in automobile design, the introduction of safety equipment, licensing and testing, improvements in highway construction, and the availability of increasingly sophisticated medical care in hospitals spread throughout the city, affect the death rate as well. The environment within which the automobile operates helps shape the consequences of its operation, and the nature and seriousness of the potential legal problems which it generates are influenced by a number of factors which interact in complex ways in the urban system.[15] But during the critical 1900-1930 period, during which the automobile became an integral part of the American economy and life style, speed and congestion seemed inevitably correlated with ever-increasing injury and death. During this period the automobile became a social problem of considerable proportions, and thus inevitably a legal and regulatory problem as well.

The control of the flow of traffic is a serious burden upon the authorities only in the city. It is there that formal rules of priority (who stops, who starts, and when) and the rules of position (where one goes in relation to others) assume a crucial role in promoting coordinated human behavior.[16] Even before the advent of the motor vehicle, city congestion led to the enactment of formal rules of the road backed by the police power of the state. In 1837 the city posted its first speed limit: the drivers of horses crossing the Chicago River Bridge were enjoined to hold their pace to a "walk."[17] "Driving immoderately" was forbidden in 1851, and by 1861 it was necessary to post regular traffic policemen at downtown intersections to regulate the flow of wagons and buggys.[18]

The speeder and the carnage he wrought became an object of major concern only after the advent of the motor car, however. In the "teens," Mayor Carter Henry Harrison II blasted the "scorchers" of his day (Lewis and Smith, 1929: 275):

> Something must be done about these fellows who run their machines ten to twenty miles an hour. I'm in favor of compelling the gears of all machines to be not above eight miles an hour.

Speeding, especially by "Young America," was defined as a serious menace to the social order.

> Speeding has become a menace far greater than that of carrying a concealed weapon. . . . The death and injury toll from this violation is far less than that caused by speeding. An auto driven by a careless or reckless speeder is as dangerous to the community as a revolver in the hands of a burglar. It spells injury and death.[19]

Injury and death, observable and apparently direct consequences of speed and congestion, rapidly led to the enactment of state legislation and city ordinances defining appropriate and forbidden behaviors on the roadway. The first comprehensive speeding code came in 1908. By 1910 the major rules of the road (stopping at intersections, staying to the right, and the like) were formalized. The first parking ordinances were drafted in 1917 after a complete breakdown in the flow of traffic through the central business district. The registration of automobiles with the city became a requirement in 1919 as part of a campaign to identify ownership and afix responsibility for the operation of individual motor vehicles. By 1920, laws prohibiting driving while intoxicated and age limits on the use of the motor car were found on the books. The environmental consequences of the motor car were also recognized by 1920: laws prohibiting glaring lights, excessive smoke, and the operation of a vehicle without a muffler were instituted. In that year, police department arrests and citation for these traffic-related offenses totaled 18,366.

The expansion of the regulatory power of the state in response to the social problem presented by the automobile in the city was inevitable. The nature of the behavior of man behind the wheel presents a particular problem in social control. Drivers are anonymous to one another. Their "interactions" are fleeting and narrowly defined. There is limited communication between parties, who are nevertheless attempting to coordinate their behaviors in a highly complex and interdependent environment. The formal rules of the road probably play a larger role in defining appropriate behavior behind the wheel than do laws for nearly any other public activity.[20] Moreover, most purposeful violations of driving rules result in positive short-run benefits for the violator (he gets there faster, makes a place to park his car, gets through the light) while having few negative consequences. Few pangs of conscience plague the traffic law violator, and a convicted offender does not appear disreputable to his neighbors, unfit for employment, or of questionable moral fiber. The kinds of informal sanctions and internalized norms which shape most of our behavior most of the time are not operative in this context.

The result is that responsibility for traffic law enforcement rests squarely upon the shoulders of the police. The nature of the activity is such that we must rely upon an abstract and often arbitrary set of laws to get along with one another, while at the same time the driver's decision to obey those rules is problematic. And, because of technology, individual citizens cannot play a major role in order maintenance. In the days of the horse-and-wagon, responsibility for enforcement lay partially in the hands of individuals. This was considerably encouraged by the practice of splitting fines for speeding and driving immoderately, one-half going to the city and one-half to the reporting citizen. But the anonymity of the city and the enclosed vehicle have conspired to foreclose this avenue for citizen participation in law enforcement, and the regulatory burden of the automobile must be born by law enforcement personnel.

One consequence of police traffic enforcement activity was a vast increase in the number of cases entering the local courts. More automobiles on the roadway, more policemen watching them, and advances in enforcement technology (most recently radar and the breathalyzer) conspired to produce an ever-increasing traffic arrest rate. This rate varied from year-to-year with fluctuations in police resources and changes in departmental leadership and organization, but the trend

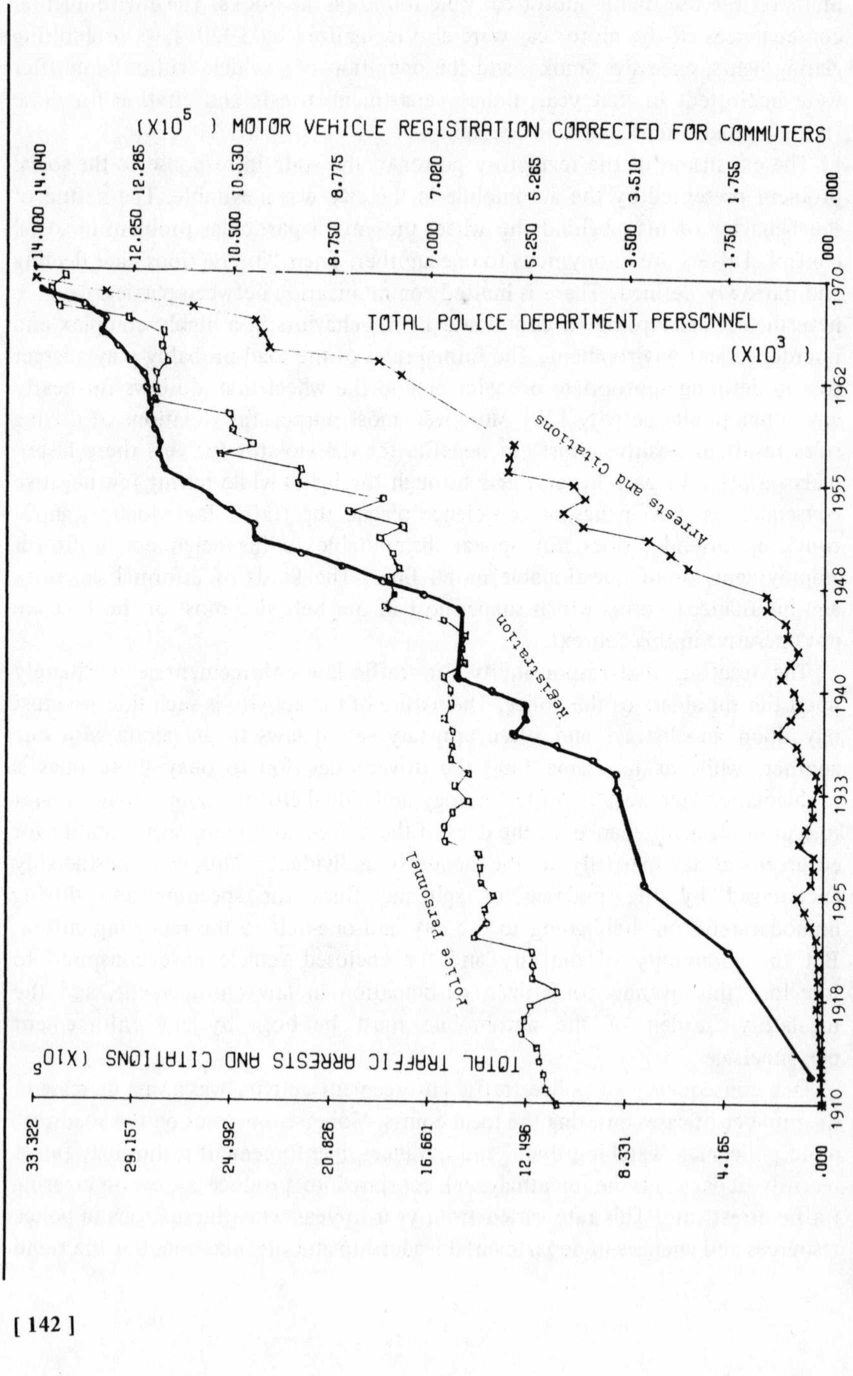

Figure 3

was inevitably upward. Figure 3 illustrates the rise in both motor vehicle registration and traffic arrests and citations over time.

The important fact about traffic crimes is that there are so many of them. Estimating the "true" or "underlying" crime rate for a population is difficult. All we can say with confidence is that much illegal behavior does not come to the formal attention of the authorities. Personal experience and observational studies of driver behavior suggest that most drivers violate most of the provisions of the traffic code quite frequently. The State of New York, for example, has estimated that at any given time about 36 percent of all drivers on the road are speeding.[21] Whatever the true figure, it is obvious that police enforcement activities merely sample a small proportion of all violations. The potential pool of offenders is enormous, and police squads simply dip into that pool to net violators. In this situation, the crucial determinant of the traffic arrest rate is the size of the scoop and the enthusiasm with which it is wielded. Assuming the widespread and relatively uniform tendency of motorists to violate at least some of the rules of the road some of the time, one indicator of the dimensions of this pool is the number of motor vehicles registered in the city, corrected to include the number of commuter automobiles entering the city each day. As Figure 3 illustrates, increases in this pool of enforcement situations is closely related to the number of traffic cases produced by the police.

The expansion of the pool of potential enforcement situations has been paralleled by an expansion in the size of the police department. Responding to increases in social scale—the size, density, and heterogeneity of the city—the department has grown over time. This widening span of formal social control, coupled with an increasingly dense traffic environment, generates an increasing number of traffic cases each year, cases which strain the processing capability of the local criminal courts.

SUMMARY: THE GENERATION OF INPUTS TO
THE LEGAL SYSTEM

Environmental changes inevitably lead to changes in the nature of the cases which confront the legal system. The impact of technological and economic change has been an increase in the size, density, heterogeneity, affluence, and interdependence of urban communities; together we will call these factors "social scale." Increasing social scale has in turn produced new problems (as well as more of many of the old ones) to which the community must respond. New laws, and larger and more sophisticated law enforcement agencies, have been created as governments have attempted to shape social change, to take advantage of its benefits, and reduce the impact of its less desirable consequences. This has led to an expansion in the scope of the criminal justic system, as new opportunities and technologies have demanded new regulatory responses. The complexity and anonymity of life in the city has also demanded the creation of new laws to facilitate the resolution of disputes among citizens who are essentially strangers to one another. The density, affluence, and interdependence of city life has guaranteed a lively business in the forums in which this resolution is achieved.

Figure 4 summarizes this argument and presents a set of correlations which estimate the strength of each of the conceptual linkages for the traffic problem. The Appendix reports the sources from which the indicators for each of the variables in this input model were derived.

Fundamental environmental changes are represented in Figure 4 by the Index of Social Scale, an indicator derived from nine measures of the conceptual components of the index: size, density, heterogeneity, affluence, and interdependence. The index is highly related to both the expansion of opportunities for law violation (motor vehicle registration, corrected for commuters) and the resources available to the community to apprehend law violators (police personnel). Vehicle use is further related to (1) the expansion of the legal code to regulate its abuse, and (2) a mounting toll of social consequences—injuries,

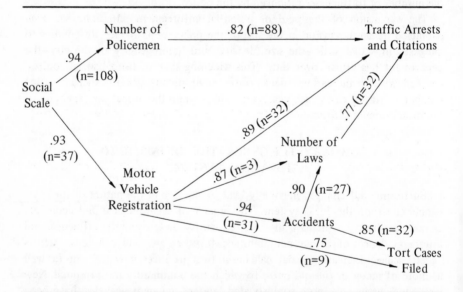

Figure 4: THE GENERATION OF INPUTS TO THE COURT SYSTEM: ZERO-ORDER
CORRELATIONS AND THE NUMBER OF CASES UPON WHICH THEY
ARE BASED

accidents, or fatalities. Together, the expansion of the legal code, the pool of potential law violators, and the resources of the formal agents of social control would appear to explain the growth of inputs into the criminal justice system over time. Likewise, expanded motor vehicle registration and the accident rate are highly correlated with the growth in the civil caseload in the Municipal Court of Chicago during the 1907-1938 period.

The strength of the relationship each linkage specifies is quite high, suggesting that the social-scale-and-legal-input model provides a useful explanation for the expansion of traffic-related legal business for the courts in Chicago over time. Due to the small number of observations (because of the limited motor vehicle registration data available before 1930), it is not possible to assess the predictive utility of the model's explanation of civil inputs. Correlations based upon the available data suggest that it is quite high.

The available data do enable us to estimate the relative impact of two crucial factors upon the expansion of inputs inot the criminal process: motor vehicle use and police resources. Again, in the broadest sense these measure crime opportunities and apprehension capability for this particular sub-set of illegal behaviors. As Table 1 suggests, variations in apprehension resources appear to be more important than variations in opportunities in the case of traffic. Table 1 estimates the impact of vehicle upon arrest and citation rates, all here expressed in per capita units to control for simple growth of the city over time.[22]

The simplest estimate of the relative contribution of each of our independent variables upon apprehension rates is the "elasticity" presented in Table 1. The

Table 1. THE DETERMINANTS OF INPUTS INTO THE CRIMINAL SYSTEM: TRAFFIC APPREHENSIONS PER CAPITA

Variable	Regression Coefficients*			
	b	B	Elasticity	F
Motor vehicles per capita	.75	.29	.65	18.36 (.01)
Police personnel per capita	301.85	.73	2.71	117.38 (.01)
R^2 = .96				
N = 32				

*"b" is the unstandardized regression coefficient—a measure of the direct effect of a variable upon the dependent variable.

"B" is the standardized regression coefficient—an indicator of the relative strength of each of the independent variables.

"Elasticity" is the percentage change in the dependent variable associated with a one-percent change in the value of the independent variable.

"F" is a measure of the statistical significance of the effects of each of the independent variables.

observed figures suggest that a one-percent increase in the relative size of the police department yields a 2.7 percent increase in the traffic arrest rate, while a similar increase in auto and truck registration yields only a .65 percent increase in the dependent variable. This estimate of these coefficients should be quite accurate, for the simple model explains 96 percent of the variance in the apprehension rate. The findings are also in line with our theoretical expectations: given the extremely large number of violations taking place at any given time on city streets, the major determinant of variations in formal sanctioning is police activity.

THE RESPONSE OF THE COURTS:
VOLUME STRESS AND ORGANIZATIONAL CHANGE

As a result of the ever-mounting level of inputs this police activity generated, "volume stress" rapidly became an organizational problem of major proportions in the courts of Chicago. Within the framework of the Municipal Court Act which governed them, it was difficult for the authorities to process this rising torrent of cases in an orderly fashion. Periodic breakdowns in the ability of the court to do so posed severe administrative and political problems for the city.

Volume stresses are problems which arise when an organism or an organization is unable to process satisfactorily the demands which are being made upon it (Meier, 1962: 69-71; Ashby, 1956; Haberstroh, 1960; Vickers, 1959). Factors in the environment which surrounds such an organization (called "stressors") are producing a greater volume of inputs than the agency can process (convert into acceptable outputs). Morale among members of such an organization typically suffers, they devise "short-cuts" which circumvent the agency rules, they lower performance standards, those who rely upon the organization to do its job properly complain, and outside investigations into the state of affairs begin (Meier, 1962: 73-78).

In the market economy, private organization, such as manufacturers or suppliers of services, have a ready response: they raise prices. By charging more, they reduce demand. Those who will not or cannot pay the price go elsewhere for satisfaction. Increased income from the remainder can be invested, enhancing the ability of the organization to meet demand through the expansion of its processing capacity. Public organizations, on the other hand, operate in a largely non-market context. Typically, they cannot impose severe limitations upon demands and they often cannot raise the prices charged those who demand their attention. Public organizations are rule-bound, and the rules are only partially responsive to market considerations. Courts, for example, are relatively open forums. If a problem meets certain criteria, which are historically and politically determined, it can get a hearing. The processing capacity of the courts (manpower, resource) is also a historical and political, rather than a market, concern. This institutional inflexibility has been a major target of court reformers, and courts are increasingly able to adjust to changes in demands for their services. But as they (1) remain responsible for settling all disputes brought to them, and they (2) cannot radically change their mode of operation, volume problems continue to plague urban courts.

The automobile in the city was a stressor which strained the capacity of the court system to cope with both criminal and civil matters. There are at least two general classes of organizational responses on the part of non-market agencies to volume stress: the organization and its members can lower performance standards and "do the best they can," or they can improve the system's through-put with organizational innovations which increase their processing capability (Meier, 1962: 71-72). The first response of the municipal court was to compromise traditional standards, provide less acceptable service, and informally circumvent the rules which bound its performance and defined the legitimacy of its outputs. Responses involving more thorough-going organizational reform only followed widespread dissatisfaction with these procedures.

In the municipal court, criminal cases generated by the police department were heard in the branch courts which serviced the geographical areas within which they arose. Each branch housed one judge and a minor retinue of bailiffs and clerks. A number of forces were at work which led these decentralized courts to respond to the traffic problem by dismissing traffic cases in wholesale lots. The vast majority of traffic cases were classified as "quasi-criminal acts," a legal category encompassing motorists' violations of city and state motor vehicle regulations. The 1908 total for such prosecutions was 56,795, and in that year municipal court judges dismissed 54.5 percent of those cases.[23] By 1911 the case total had risen to 72,189, and 57.7 percent were dismissed in court. In 1912, the dismissal rate rose to 61.7 percent.

One explanation advanced by participants for this tremendous dismissal rate was that careful police work, close judicial attention, and the studied application of sanctions was futile. Given a primitive record-keeping system and the decentralized disposition of cases, it was impossible to identify repeated offenders and it was difficult to observe any consequences of such individual investments in traffic enforcement. As one municipal court judge lamented:

> So long as a dozen or more judges were responsible for enforcing the laws concerning the use of motor vehicles, no one of them had the opportunity to pursue a constructive policy.[24]

In addition, traffic cases competed daily in these courts with equally pressing, and more important, criminal misdemeanors and preliminary hearings for felony

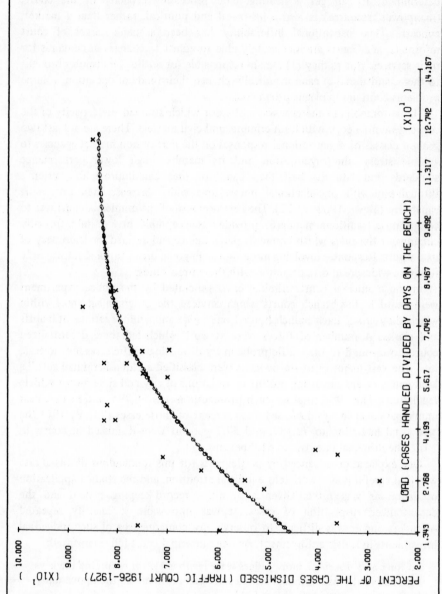

Figure 5.

cases. This competition facilitated the de-emphasis of traffic offenses in the court's list of priorities.

Perhaps the most important factor was the simple caseload problem. A standard organizational response to a growing queue of inputs awaiting processing is to summarily exclude low-priority items from consideration. The dismissal of difficult, or uncertain, or minor cases is one strategy by which courts can husband their resources. In general, we should find that, as caseloads increase, the proportion of them which are disposed of in organizationally efficient ways should increase as well. While prosecutors and the police do bring cases before the court which deserve rejection, the primary factor which is systematically related to the outright dismissal of large numbers of cases should be caseload. While the relationship between caseload and the dismissal rate reflects organizational processes, the hypothesis can be tested most adequately at the individual level. Data on the dispositional patterns of municipal court judges are presented in Figure 5.

The observations in Figure 5 illustrate the relationship between the traffic caseload facing individual judges (the cases they handled divided by the number of days they spent hearing traffic cases in 1926 and 1927), and the percentage of those cases they dismissed without punishment (fine, jail, or probation).[25] These were contested criminal and quasi-criminal cases, usually involving more serious charges to which the accused did not automatically plead guilty. Dismissed cases were "dismissed for want of prosecution," "non-suited," or a "nolle prose" was entered, dispositions which were variously selected for reasons of convenience rather than law. Judges on the municipal court heard these cases in rotation, serving various lengths of time and processing varying numbers of cases during each term of service.

While judges are scattered high and low, relatively low dismissal rates (below 50 percent) were found only when they handled less than about 40 cases per day. Above 50 cases per day, dismissal rates were uniformly high, averaging about 80 percent. The curved line in Figure 5 is the line which best represents the data statistically.[26] The curvilinear nature of the relationship between caseload and dismissal patterns suggests that caseload pressure affected individual judges only to certain limits. They continued to hear a few cases (the data suggest about 15 percent) which could not be dismissed regardless of load problems, and no additional increase in case volume (within the limits of the data available here) made serious inroads upon that core of legal disputes.

The curved line in Figure 5 explains 41 percent of the variance in dispositional patterns. It is interesting to note that there is substantial variation around that line (it fits the observed data points less accurately) at the lower end of the load continuum. There, it appears, individual variations in the policy perspectives and personalities of judges may have affected their dispositional tendencies. Casual inspection of court reports suggests, for example, that Democratic judges were more likely to dismiss traffic cases than Republican judges. Also, it was widely assumed at the time that experienced judges, who had heard many traffic cases and had developed uniform sentencing policies, were less likely to dismiss cases wholesale. Although there are not enough observations here to test those hypotheses systematically, differences between judges on these and other dimensions may account for the variation we observe among them when caseloads are low. But when caseloads climb, this variation vanishes, and it appears that individual differences among judges become less important than their common occupational problem. At the high end of the load continuum, the dismissal rate is much more closely tied to case volume.

Given their low priority, it was relatively easy to dismiss many traffic cases which came before the municipal court. Given their enormous number, pressures for organizational efficiency encouraged such a response on the part of local judges. They were able to cope with the rising volume of traffic-related criminal cases during the early years of the court only by sacrificing many traditional standards of appropriate conduct. The formal rationale for the existence of courts, the needs for the studied application of the law to concrete circumstances, was lost in the frantic atmosphere of the Roaring Twenties.

The operation of the automobile in the city generated an increasing number of civil cases as well, and this caseload posed similar, if less intense, problems during this period. Although many civil disputes which enter the courts never come to trial, those which do consume an enormous amount of judicial attention. Those which do not still engage clerks and judges when papers are filed and conferences held. By the mid-1920s, civil litigation strained the physical capacity of the municipal court. Reported the chief judge in 1924:

> The high pressure operation of the court has been coincident with a very unfortunate lack of court rooms. The expectation that the city government would provide needed space to enable the additional judges to work advantageously has been defeated after a number of projects. The difficulty has been met, so far as possible, by holding court in certain judges' chambers, in some instances for half of each working day. This is a very unsatisfactory condition. It means that two judges are endeavoring to function with the court room facilities designed for but one, that litigants and attorneys are put to some trouble and it is difficult, if not impossible, to preserve the order and decorum to which judicial work is entitled.[27]

Civil accident claims and insurance disputes entered the municipal court as "torts," technically defined as civil claims not involving a contract. Not long after it became a standard piece of household equipment, claims arising from automobile accidents made up the vast majority of all tort cases filed in the municipal court each year. Their numbers were constantly increasing. From the *Annual Report* of the court for 1921:

> More automobiles and more automobile accidents were reflected in the continued jump in tort cases of 800, or 21.5 percent to 4,523.

And in 1922:

> Increasing automobile accidents were doubtless responsible for the gain of 42 percent in tort cases filed, from 4,523 to 6,400.

Simple statistical analysis suggests that the relationship between the number of tort cases filed each year and motor vehicle statistics was indeed strong. Across the 1905-1938 time series, the correlation between torts and motor vehicle accidents was .85, and the correlation between torts filed and the number of registered motor vehicles was .75.

In the absence of any improvement in the processing capability of the court, the continued growth of the automobile industry and increasing congestion on the city's streets produced more legal claims each year which could not be settled. The mathematical function which describes the relationship between demands for service, or the number of cases entering the court system (the input rate), and the number of demands met, or the number of cases disposed of in one way or another (the output rate), is the "through-put" of an organization. When its through-put ratio is 1:1, an organization is processing inputs at an optimum rate, and no queue of unmet demands for service develops. When the through-put ratio drops, demands or cases build up on the input side, and the organization develops a "backlog." If the rules of the organization, or the norms of organization members, or the expectations of the public demand that backlogs do not grow, the through-put ratio is also a measure of volume stress. The greater the gap between the ideal input-output ratio and the actual performance of the organization, the greater the pressure for organizational innovations which improve the through-put ratio and limit the further expansion of the backlog.

The development of such a backlog of civil cases arising out of traffic accidents is presented graphically in Figure 6.

On the horizontal axis are charted the number of tort claims filed each year from 1908-1938. On the vertical axis are found the number of claims which were disposed of in the same year. This includes not only cases which were tried before a judge or jury, but all claims which were dropped earlier in the process after the negotiation of private settlements as well. As measures of backlog there is a certain amount of error in these figures: the cases which were filed late in a given year, for example, would not be decided until the next, and would appear

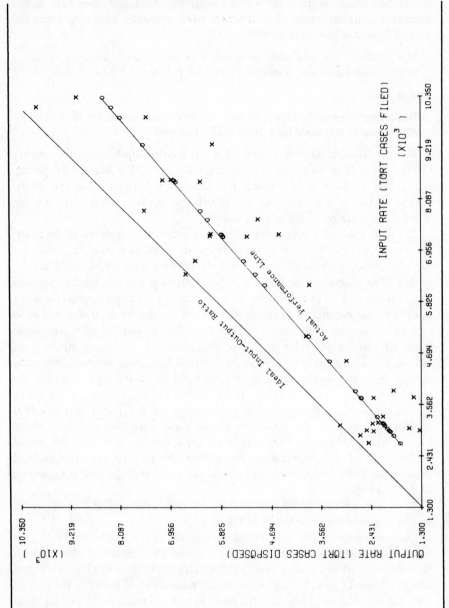

Figure 6.

to be "delayed." But the same spill-over occurred from the previous year, and such effects should at least partially cancel themselves out over the series.

Figure 6 compares the distribution of these inputs and outputs with the "ideal performance" ratio. The ideal performance line describes a 1:1 through-put ratio, while the "actual performance" line illustrates the general match of the through-put experience of the court to that optimal standard. The actual performance line explains 88 percent of the year-to-year variation in the municipal court.[28] Comparison of the two suggests that as the volume of inputs into the court increased, the gap between them—the backlog—increased at a fairly uniform rate. Even during the first three decades of the court, when automobile registration was still low and when the absolute volume of civil liability claims was quite small (a maximum of 10,340 cases filed per year), the municipal court was falling steadily behind in the processing of those claims. In the absence of any discernible innovation in the handling of automobile-related cases, the court's through-put rate deteriorated steadily.

The absence of innovation suggests that the influx of civil accident claims was not yet stressful. The mounting volume of criminal cases arising out of traffic forced the court to undertake a number of organizational reforms to increase through-put. However, neither internal nor external pressures upon the municipal court produced comparable responses to the civil claim backlog until after World War II.

First, the number of cases which was accumulating was relatively small. By 1964, the backlog of cases awaiting jury trial in Cook County as a whole totaled 50,000, and the average delay before trial was 62 months.[29] The magnitude of the problem was quite different before the post-war leap in recorded accidents and injuries described in Figure 2. Stress was also alleviated by the existence of alternative forums for dispute settlement. Many larger claims were taken to the circuit or superior courts, which had backlog problems of their own.

In addition, the formal norms of the court de-emphasized the civil delay problem. However more attractive civil litigation for judges and lawyers alike, practical considerations dictated that the court focus upon the reduction of its criminal backlog. As the court's *Annual Report* (1922: 13) stated:

> The Municipal Court Act expressly enjoins the prompt disposal of all criminal and quasi-criminal cases, only such time of judges being available for civil cases as is not required for criminal cases. This policy of the act is based not merely upon the importance of trying criminal cases promptly but also on the fact that in the City of Chicago there is no other court having concurrent jurisdiction in the trial of quasi-criminal and misdemeanor cases and the preliminary examination in felony cases.

Finally, we cannot overlook the positive functions of large civil backlogs for the court as an organization. In the absence of any outside concern, civil delay may be an organizationally efficient device by which the courts can pass on some of the costs of deciding cases to litigants, and force those who cannot or will not pay those costs to seek the resolution of their problems in other forums. In short, they can thus gain some of the flexibility of market organizations.

Civil delay may discourage suits in the first place. Many minor claims may not be filed because they are not worth the effort, given the backlog situation. More important, civil delay encourages the private negotiation and settlement of outstanding suits before they reach the trial stage (Ross, 1970). Faced with years of waiting, plaintiffs (largely individuals) and defendants (largely insurance companies) resolve their own disputes. Each of these passes on costs to litigants or potential litigants which would be borne by the state if trial delays were brief and through-put ratios low. Plaintiffs might receive more money, and more suits might be filed, but justice of this sort would be organizationally inefficient.

The absence of recorded complaints about the backlog problem before World War II may reflect the satisfaction of the primary participants in the process with these outcomes. The attorneys involved appear, in fact, to be at least partially responsible for the apparent magnitude of the problem. Lawyers specializing in personal injury litigation (who today in Cook County number only about 150) frequently schedule many more cases than they can possibly bring to trial, and then, through a series of delays (which keep the cases on the books), use their ability to bring particular cases to court if necessary as a bargaining tool in private negotiations (Rosenberg, 1965: 36-37). Insurance companies may profit from the negotiation of minor cases without trial, and their ability to invest their potential losses while major cases await trial often counterbalances these losses when delay is lengthy (Zeisel et al., 1959). Individual accident victims, on the other hand, are irregular, one-time users of the courts. While they suffer the consequences of civil delay, they do not have the kind of continuing stake in the process which generates loud and organized protest. In the absence of such protest, organizational efficiency norms predominate.

Organizational innovations in the processing of civil liability claims came after World War II, when caseloads mounted at an increasing rate. Compared with other cities, Chicago has an extremely high litigation rate; studies in the 1950s placed it third among major cities in the ratio of traffic accidents to court claims (Zeisel et al., 1959). It also has a high trial rate; in a recent year, 27 percent of all cases filed demanding juries eventually reached the trial stage. These factors have conspired to produce an enormous traffic-case backlog, recently pronounced the worst in the United States.[30] This caseload, combined with growing public and professional recognition of the dimensions of the problem, has produced a number of organizational reforms which only recently have begun to make inroads into the queue of cases awaiting disposition. These include a computerized system for assigning cases to judges, increased use of pre-trial conferences and impartial medical examiners, a specialized courtroom for the selection of jurors for civil panels, and other innovations. The ultimate goal is to reduce civil delay to "only" two years.[31]

One crucial element affecting the through-put problem in all civil and criminal cases was the court's manpower limitations. Dramatic improvement in the processing capability of the municipal court could be achieved only through organizational innovations which reduced the cost-per-case in judicial man-hours. Autonomous market organizations can increase their processing capability by adding personnel. Their willingness to do so will reflect the relative economies and diseconomies of scale this involves, and such expansion may not lower the total cost of processing additional units. The municipal court, on the other hand, was a creature of the state. The number of judges, the scarcest resource in the system, was determined by the Chicago City Council and the state legislature under the framework of the Municipal Court Act. In 1922, when the court received 287,438 cases, this number was fixed at 37. This figure remained unchanged until 1964. In 1963, the last full year of operation for the court, the 37 judges were faced with 1,500,000 new traffic cases alone. Given the unwillingness of the Republican-dominated state legislature to grant the city new Democratic judgeships, reforms which increased the efficiency of existing personnel were the only options open to the court.

The major organizational response to the criminal problem (there were others, as we shall see) was the creation of specialized courts and court-like agencies which could more effectively process inputs generated by the automobile. Differentiation and specialization are characteristic responses of organizations to stresses generated by volume overload. Such bodies are often able to reduce the cost-per-case ratio and alleviate volume problems without a tremendous increase in overall organizational resources. They can be delegated the power to schedule their own manpower allocations, direct the flow of inputs to appropriate offices, develop unique rules and procedures suited to the business at hand, focus administrative and supervisory attention on volume problems, and train a specialized staff organized to process a narrow range of inputs with maximal effectiveness. The difficulty in this case, of course, is that the resulting processing units no longer resemble courts.

The inevitability of specialization was recognized early by the municipal court. Its *Annual Report* in 1913 noted:

When the territory was the type of political development in this part of the United States the court ordinarily consisted of a single judge, clothed with the fullest judicial power. The judge under these primitive conditions heard and determined every sort of case, both civil and criminal. As population increased and judges became more numerous specialization came into being. With the growth of our large cities more and more specialization came into being. The economic advantage of specialization is so obvious that it necessarily comes into use in the judicial field as well as in the industrial field.[32]

Separate, specialized courts offered several advantages for the processing of traffic cases. Early centralized court record-keeping systems were inefficient, costly, and retrieved documents at a slow pace. Traffic cases, on the other hand, came before the court in great volume and demanded rapid disposition. Decentralized records specific to the branch court hearing traffic cases enabled municipal court judges to identify "repeaters" and keep useful court records. Judge Fry, an early judge of the new automobile court, remarked upon these advantages:

> The Automobile Branch of the Municipal Court was established to bring about uniformity in dealing with the automobile problem. By segregating these cases in one court it was possible to keep tab on the frequent and reckless offenders.[33]

The branch developed an index card system to keep track of the offenses of all those who appeared in it, and boosted fines levied on repeated offenders.

Specialization also enabled judges and prosecutors to develop uniform sentencing policies. This paid two dividends: it was more "just" in their eyes (the law was at last being equally applied), and it reduced decisional costs. Specialized judges could develop uniform sentences for "similar" cases, and the experience needed to arrive at those sentences and identify similar patterns of events could be more easily obtained in a specialized court.

The first specialized branch of the municipal court to attempt to reap these advantages was the automobile court, a branch established early in 1913. This was a period in which the city's 16,859 motorcars still jockeyed for the right-of-way with over 40,000 horse-drawn carriages and wagons, but careening automobiles had already become a major social problem. The formation of a specialized branch court focusing resources upon a single class of cases, speeding, enabled the judiciary to attack the growing dismissal problem.

> Judge Fry says that at the outset of the year's work he found the prosecuting officers frequently exercising the right to enter *nolle prosequis* and non-suits. . . . More than eighty speeding cases had been dismissed by

nolle from December 2, 1912, up to March 1913. An investigation showed that the prosecuting officials had not in a single case interviewed the police officer who made the arrest, before the dismissal.[34]

While Judge Fry reportedly discouraged the wholesale dismissal of cases in his court, the extremely limited nature of this investment in specialization limited its overall impact upon the municipal court's increasing use of such practices. Figure 7 illustrates municipal court dispositional patterns before World War II.

Figure 7 is an example of an "interrupted time series" analysis of the impact of an institutional reform upon the pattern of decision-making in an organization (Campbell and Stanley, 1963: 37-43; Caporaso and Roos 1973: 3-35). In such analyses, the variable of interest—here the disposition of quasi-criminal cases—is plotted over time. Comparison is made of the pattern of events before and after the change. This pattern is revealed by the extended time series, and is a more accurate gauge of the extent of any change than a simple "before and after" comparison when the events fluctuate from year-to-year due to other influences in the system. Visual inspection and statistical tests may reveal changes in the distribution of the variable of interest, jumps in the level of the line, or shifts in its slope, the direction in which events had been changing. In the absence of other relevant factors which may have occurred at the same time as the reform and may serve as an alternative explanation for any observed changes, these changes may be causally connected to the reform.

While there are not enough observations in this brief time series to support any elaborate statistical tests, the data suggest that the opening of the automobile branch did not greatly affect the distribution of dismissals for the court as a whole. The dismissal line illustrated in Figure 7 dropped slightly from 1912 to 1913, but its slope (long-run direction in which the court was going) was unchanged and rising. Its small apparent impact on the overall dismissal rate was quickly lost in this rise. This increase in the face of a rising caseload occurred within the speeding branch as well. By 1921, automobile court was hearing 250 speeding cases each day, and its own record-keeping system had broken down.[35]

The stress generated by increasing caseloads was unabated. By 1926, the flood of traffic cases reached crisis proportions. In 1921 the court received 15,576 city traffic ordinance violation cases alone. In 1922 the total rose to nearly 20,000; in 1923 to 38,000; in 1924 to 45,000; and in 1925 to 64,000. The year 1926 saw the creation of the city's first "cafeteria court."

The Traffic Bureau of Chicago was a major organizational response to the volume problem, an innovation copied by cities across the nation. Under the Municipal Court Act, the chief judge possessed the power to appoint up to six "assistant judges," non-elected hearing referees empowered to preside over

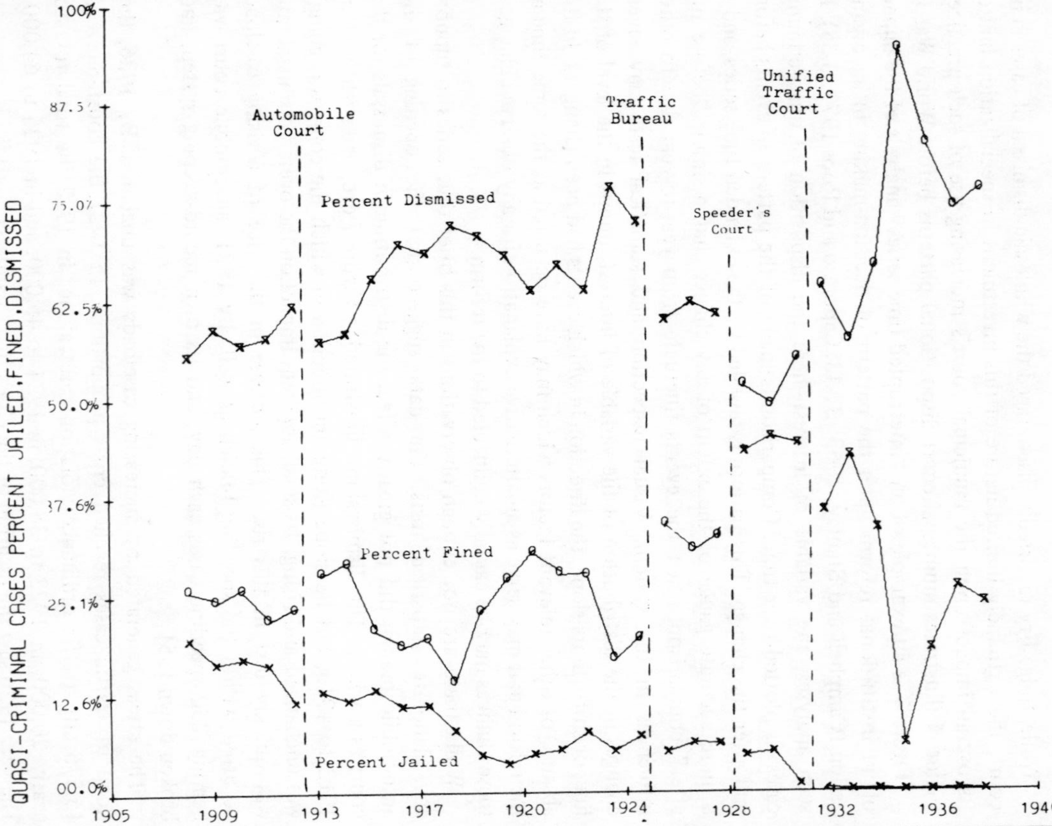

Figure 7

minor proceedings. They were assigned to the traffic bureau, housed in city hall, where many errant motorists filed past a counter and paid their fines, uncontested, to a cashier. Fines for various categories of offenses were uniform and were published in booklet form.[36] The "cafeteria" imagery was established in the newspapers even before the bureau officially opened for business.

> From now on minor offenders will be handled like luncheon "tray hounds," it is promised, and fines of $1 to $10 will be administered quickly and without legal gas.[37]

The traffic bureau was created following a study of the volume problems of the municipal court by the street traffic committee of the powerful Chicago Association of Commerce. The problem was one of balancing organizational efficiency and traditional legality. If the court was to successfully cope with the rising flood of traffic cases, new processing procedures had to be developed. But courts, more than other agencies of government, are rule-bound. Their rule-boundedness, the extent to which their decisions are made in traditional and procedurally appropriate ways, is in fact the unique characteristic which legitimizes the solitary and discretionary role of the judge as the settler of disputes.

The formal structure which emerged balanced these two sets of potentially conflicting standards. Production-line procedures processed the bulk of traffic cases, and fines were kept low to encourage "guilty pleas" in minor cases. Traffic bureau fines averaged less than $2.00 in 1926 and 1927.[38] The parking ticket which could be returned with the fine by mail was instituted, greatly decreasing the number of people who passed through the bureau's cashier line. The bureau was dubbed the "Help Yourself Court," and justice was speedy. As the presiding judge of the bureau described it, "if a person knows he is guilty . . . we can dispose of his case in three minutes."[39] These production-line procedures enabled the court to survive the enormous influx of minor traffic cases. By the 1950s, successors to the traffic bureau were processing over one million cases a year.

Organizational efficiency was balanced by traditional legality in the traffic court, an appendage to the traffic bureau to which contested cases could be transferred. There, any citizen, regardless of the charge, could "have his day in court." The availability of a forum where the accused, with or without counsel, could challenge the action of the arresting officer provided an air of legality which lent legitimacy to the traffic program of the municipal court.

The impact of the traffic bureau upon dispositional patterns in the court is apparent in Figure 7. The percentage of quasi-criminal cases dismissed, a figure which had been generally rising for a decade, dropped twelve percent during the first full year of the bureau's operation. The bulk of dismissals illustrated in Figure 7 came from the traffic court, where contested minor cases were mingled with major offenses (second offense speeding, drunk driving). During the 1926-1928 period the caseload in this court averaged over 54 per judge-day, a figure which, as we have seen, leads to high dismissal rates. In April 1929, a new speeder's court was opened with jurisdiction over all traffic misdemeanors (more serious charges). Their caseload considerably simplified, traffic court judges began convicting many more defendants in minor cases. During the years 1926-1927, traffic court judges dismissed over 70 percent of the contested cases transferred from the bureau, a figure which was encouraging such transfers at an increasing rate. After the opening of speeder's court, the figure dropped by 20 percent. The effect of this drop is reflected in the sharp increase in the percentage of defendants fined during the 1929-1931 period in Figure 7.

As before, organizational reform did not affect the rate at which defendants were jailed, as opposed to fined or dismissed. Throughout this period the size of the city's house of correction remained relatively constant, and as more persons came into the courts, a smaller proportion could be sent there regardless of the circumstances of their cases. The option of jailing offenders, unlike the others, was constrained by forces outside of the court organization, and remained unaffected by internal organizational processes.

While the internal operation of the court was now proceeding more smoothly, the environment which surrounded it was not. At the same time that the municipal court was learning to live with the problems of the automobile, the city was finding coexistence more and more difficult. The accident and death rate on the city's highways mounted throughout the late 1920s. In 1925, there were 11,319 reported accidents; by 1931 the total had risen to over 16,000, and over 18,000 were officially known to have been injured. The death toll mounted. In 1925, 649 traffic fatalities were recorded; in 1928, 918. In 1930, 886 were killed on the city's streets, and in 1931 a new unified traffic branch was created in the municipal court in order, as the headlines put it, to "Battle Rise in Auto Deaths." [40]

Formal plans for the unified traffic court were worked out by a task force representing several public and private agencies. Led by Mayor Cermak, representatives of the municipal court, the park commissions, the police, the Association of Commerce, and the Chicago Motor Club, planned a general attack upon the traffic problem through the courts. [41] Previous court reform efforts had come from within response to volume problems, and the innovations developed involved only court personnel. The involvement of outside parties led to a program coordinating the activities of other agencies and an increase in the resources allocated to court activity.

The new traffic court was to have jurisdiction over all quasi-criminal acts and misdemeanors defined in the State Motor Vehicle Act and the Municipal Traffic Ordinance. An improved record-keeping system was devised for the identification of repeated violators, and the bailiff of the court made assurances that warrants for the arrest of those who failed to appear in court would in fact be acted upon (a dramatic promise, given the fact that the "no show" rate often exceeded 50 percent).[42]

Municipal court officials assured that experienced traffic judges would be assigned to the new branch. While during the 1926-1927 period judges averaged 14 days of service on the court per year, the average rose to 80 days during the unified court's first year of operation.[43] Chief Judge Sonsteby demonstrated the new commitment to traffic law enforcement on the part of the court by personally presiding over the traffic bureau and taking his turn hearing contested traffic cases.

In operation, the court continued to encourage the automated disposal of cases. Fines paid "at the counter" remained low, averaging $1.78 in 1931. Fines were pegged higher for those found guilty in contested cases, and they averaged four times those imposed in contested cases in the old traffic court. Each year a smaller proportion of traffic cases were contested, and fewer of those contested were dismissed in favor of the defendant. While in 1926-1927 about 75 percent of the contested cases were dismissed, in 1935 only 17 percent were similarly disposed of, leading to the sharp increase in the fine rate illustrated in Figure 7. Welcomed in 1931 by headlines like "Judge Handles 400 Auto Cases in Five Hours," the unified traffic court efficiently handled the mounting traffic caseload, and increasingly dispensed justice in streamlined, assembly-line fashion.[44] The imposition of small, standardized fines replaced the wholesale dismissal of many offenses, but whether the larger purposes of the criminal law were better served is problematic.

THE ENVIRONMENT, THE LEGAL SYSTEM, AND MODELS OF HUMAN BEHAVIOR

The ever-mounting number of traffic cases which entered the Municipal Court of Chicago raises larger questions about the relationship between law enforcement activity and citizen behavior. Do the apparently endless apprehension and dispositional activities of the police and courts have any impact upon the incidence of traffic law violations? Did increasing police allocations of scarce resources to the traffic patrol, and the time and energy expended upon the processing of traffic cases in court have any consequences, or did this flurry of activity proceed without deterrent effect? In systems terms, is there any evidence of "negative feedback" processes for Figure 4, some indication that activity by the police and the court limits future enforcement opportunities and reduces the volume of cases entering the legal system, or at least inhibits the growth of those inputs?

This essay has documented the efficacy of *organizational* feedback processes, or the ability of the municipal court to adapt to stresses generated by the volume of cases entering the system. Figure 8 illustrates this, and the systemic consequences of deterrent feedback loops. Negative feedback processes are necessary for the continued existence of any system. Positive growth processes (arrow with positive signs) predict only endless, and eventually wildly impossible, growth, and such "positive growth systems" are inherently unstable. Stable systems develop mechanisms to suppress, or control, or cope with such expansion.[45]

As we have seen, organizations in the Chicago legal system responded to environmental change only slowly. These adaptations tended to be organizationally efficient, rather than legally appropriate, in the absence of external influence. Given society's ambivalence over the total enforcement of traffic regulations, there were few incentives for the courts to invest heavily in their processing. Only severe organizational stresses and periodic demands that they "do something" about the traffic problem stimulated the courts to reform their structures and increase their conviction rate. But these changes do not appear to have had much systemic, deterrent impact.

One explanation for the absence of negative deterrent feedback may be that the certainty and severity of punishment for traffic offenses in Chicago is low. It

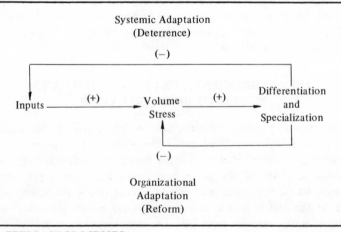

Figure 8: FEEDBACK PROCESSES

is the combination of the formal law and its vigorous enforcement which is presumed to maximize driver compliance with established norms. While the apprehension of numerous individual offenders by the police generates more business for the legal system, the general deterrence this produces—increased compliance with the law by those who would otherwise fail to do so—is assumed to reduce the overall incidence of illegal behavior in the community as a whole. The certainty with which offenders will be detected and the severity of their punishment are two general characteristics of a legal system which affect this process (Middendorff, 1968).

The best evidence available (which is not very good) indicates that more severe penalties, when combined with relatively high detection rates, will reduce the overall incidence of illegal behavior.[46] The nature of traffic offenses presents some limitations upon the severity of punishments available to sanction violations, however, and this may limit the deterrent effects of vigorous enforcement. First, apprehension and conviction for minor traffic offenses have very limited consequences. Not only are most penalties extremely low, but there are few of the collateral stigmas attached to traffic violations which come with the identification of many other forms of deviance. People rarely feel that pain of conscience when violating many of the provisions of the traffic code, and bringing them into court and labeling them as offenders does not bring the wrath of the community upon them. Typically, there is no victim pressing a claim and reminding others of the human costs of illegal behavior.[47]

Second, attempts to impose more severe penalties for traffic violations have been fraught with difficulty. Investigations indicate that such attempts are thwarted in practice by the informal reduction of charges and the unwillingness of judges and juries to convict their fellows of newly serious offenses.[48] This may be because traffic cases are more likely than others to involve middle-class and white defendants, or because most traffic laws are abstract and rational, and do not reflect ethical or religious tradition.[49] Given the widespread distribution of traffic law violations ("we all do it") and their normless character ("it's not so bad"), there appears to be considerable informal resistance to the imposition of severe penalties in traffic cases.

The problem is intensified by the low certainty of detection of traffic violations. Experts are in agreement that the severity of a penalty affects the regulated behavior only when the certainty of being apprehended is high (Goen, 1965: 21).

> The prevalence of traffic violations is usually attributed to lack of public support for severe enough penalties. Certainly, more severe penalties for violators, and removal of licenses of violators would increase compliance with traffic regulations, but the low probability of detection of traffic

violations must be an important factor in the lack of compliance. It is axiomatic in law enforcement that surety of punishment is a more important deterrent to crime than the severity of punishment. Thus an increase in the capabilities of detection of traffic violations is essential for adequate enforcement.

There is considerable experimental evidence that the physical presence of law enforcement personnel can reduce the incidence of traffic violations (and other public crimes as well); the difficulty is that the levels of enforcement required are simply too high for society to support on a general basis.[50] Increasing the resources allocated to traffic control activities three- or four-fold may reduce violations, but the social overhead cost (the amount of society's resources poured into administrative or control activities) of such policies would be tremendous. One consequence is that "realistic" levels of enforcement may well be below the level required to produce any general deterrence of traffic violations.

This may be the case in Chicago. While a specialized traffic division continually generates a large number of traffic cases, the ratio of motor vehicles to officers on the traffic detail is quite large. In 1946, the year before the traffic division was created, the ratio of motor vehicles to traffic officers was 1:1113. In 1970, the figure stood at 1:1433.

At the same time, severity levels remain low, and some have even dropped in response to the organizational needs of local courts. The cafeteria court and its variants have proven an effective bureaucratic device for coping with volume problems: they are an adaptive organizational response. But the need to make the agency work efficiently has affected the nature of the traffic law and the repertory of sanctions available to the court. The effectiveness of the traffic bureau and its successors depends upon the cooperation of the violators being processed. The court can be effective only to the extent to which it encourages guilty pleas. In order to maintain the guilty-plea rate, fines for traffic code violations have been kept low. If citizens appeared in court rather than mailing in most of their fines, the system would be clogged. If they contested moving violations, it would grind to a halt. Advocates of deterrence who would attempt to deal with traffic cases by escalating penalties are in a practical dilemma, for increased penalties have the effect of increasing trial demands. For example, when the legislature empowered the Illinois secretary of state to revoke or suspend the licenses of drivers convicted of multiple moving violations (a stiff penalty indeed), the number of cases transferred to the trial branch of the traffic court in Chicago rose 10 percent.[51] The minor traffic case thus raises the conflict between deterrence theories of crime control and organizational pressures to maximize the efficiency of the courts as organizations. Given our ambivalence about the imposition of severe penalties in traffic cases, organizational norms predominate. Before the organizational reforms of the 1920s and 1930s, the municipal court solved these problems by tolerating the non-appearance of large numbers of defendants and dismissing cases wholesale. After the reforms, the outcomes appear more legalistic—most are judged and sentenced—but the systemic impact of the process may be unchanged. Without a radical change in the way in which they are processed, the resource limitations and legal constraints which shape the disposition of minor traffic cases may preclude their deterrence.

We see currently in traffic code enforcement a halting, and at times controversial, attempt to find ways out of the bind we appear to be in. The first, and most limited, has been the introduction of new dispositional alternatives for traffic judges which enable them to escape the narrow and punitive range of sanctions to which they seemed in the past limited. The most important has been the traffic school. A number of states require attendance of a driver improvement program in place of, or in addition to, ordinary penalties for moving violations; in several states the program are directed at participants in accidents as well. There, individual counseling, group therapy sessions, and frightening movies are employed to reeducate and resocialize traffic offenders. Given the absence of good theory about the cases of such infractions, it is no surprise that systematic evaluations of the impact of such programs have not been hopeful.[52]

More radical have been programs designed to remove traffic problems from the courts entirely. For criminal offenses, the State of New York has led the way with the creation of administrative bodies to process traffic cases. Since 1970, moving violations in New York have been processed by hearing officers appointed by the New York Department of Motor Vehicles. They are the "court" in all cases which do not involve jail sentences. In New York City, attorneys appointed by the city's transportation administration hear all cases involving parking, stopping, standing, and jaywalking, and they too are the court, even in contested cases. The program has removed approximately 1,000,000 cases from the dockets of New York City courts yearly, freeing 18 judges for misdemeanor and felony hearings.[53]

This two-fold attack upon the traffic problem—expanding the organizational flexibility of the sanctioning system and expanding the range and severity of available sanctions—may prove to have deterrent effects. The best evidence suggests that court reforms will have such consequences only if the certainty with which violations are detected is increased as well. This is in part a technical problem (Goen, 1965). In principle, traffic law violations should be readily deterrable. The behavior is public and observable by routine police patrols, disobedience of the law can be objectively described and determined, and traffic offenses are utilitarian and minor. Their violation is not deeply seated in personality flaws or social roles: they are not career crimes, addictive, or particularly profitable.[54] But in the past, organizational processes have conspired to blunt whatever impact existing enforcement patterns may have had. The seemingly endless rise in the rate of detected violations may be one of the hidden costs we pay for our urban court system.

APPENDIX

DATE SOURCES

Variables and Indicators	Years Available	Sources
Index of Social Scale*		
Size		
population of Chicago	1840-1970	U.S. Census of Population
Density		
population over area	1840-1970	Area figures cited in B. Pierce, *A History of Chicago* (1940)
Heterogeneity		
number non-white	1840-1970	U.S. Census of Population
number foreign born	1850-1970	
number foreign stock	1890-1970	
Affluence		
number manufacturing establishments	1890-1967	U.S. Census of Manufacturing
number wage workers	1890-1967	and Statistical Abstract of the
value added by manufacturing	1899-1967	United States
Interdependence		
population suburban Cook County	1840-1970	U.S. Census
Size of police department		
total sworn and civilian personnel	1842, 1847, 1857-1970	Annual Reports and A. T. Andreas, *History of Chicago* (1885)
Motor vehicle registration	1912, 1921, 1926, 1933-1970	Annual Reports, Illinois Division of Highways and Chicago Police Department
Accidents	1905-1970	Annual Reports, Chicago Police Department
Laws regulating traffic	1900-1931	Traffic ordinance arrest categories, Annual Reports of the Chicago Police Department
Traffic arrests and citations	1900-1970	Annual Reports, Chicago Police Department
Tort cases filed	1907-1938	Annual Reports, Municipal Court of Chicago

*Nine components equally weighted, added, and averaged each year.

NOTES

1. This brief historical sketch relies upon Karlen (1958); Goodspeed (1896); Pierce (1937-1953); Lepawski (1932); Gilbert (1928).

2. Continuances during the 1920s are discussed in chapters 1, 3, and 6 of the Illinois Association for Criminal Justice (1968, reprint). For a discussion of the functions of continuances see Jacob (1973b).

3. Illinois Association for Criminal Justice (1968: 204).

4. *Chicago Daily News*, January 21, 1925.

5. That is, the regression equation which best describes the data is: y = 43 + (.00026 X CASES).

6. The social costs of the automobile are detailed in Buel (1972: chapter 3).

7. The three-year figure is that given by Cook County Circuit Court officials. A recent study by New York University's Institute for Judicial Administration sets the figure at 58 months for major civil cases and 43 months for minor cases (*Chicago Daily News*, August 26, 1972). The administrative office of the Illinois Courts charged in 1973 that Cook County delays statistics "amount to little more than an educated guess." See the *Chicago Tribune*, June 2, 1973.

8. Motor vehicle registration figures reported have been corrected to reflect the influx of automobiles from the suburban fringe into the central city. Census figures estimating the number of automobiles entering the city each day for employment purposes have been added to official city registration totals.

9. All arrest statistics are taken from the annual reports of the Chicago Police Department.

10. Accident and injury statistics are those reported in the annual reports of the Chicago Police Department. Police reports of fatalities have been supplemented with traffic fatality totals from *Accident Facts*, a yearly publication of the National Safety Council, when official figures are unavailable. The two sources report identical figures for years when both are available.

11. Accident and injury statistics for Chicago and Cook County are available from two independent sources: the Police Department, and the State Division of Highways. The latter records only more serious accidents. Across time, the correlation between accident totals from the two sources is .95, and the correlation for injuries is .88. The Chicago Police Department figures are considerably higher each year, but these independently measured figures co-vary quite closely. This suggests that accident and injury statistics reflect more than the organizational processes involved in their collection, and may serve as useful indicators of the "actual" distribution of these events over time.

12. *Annual Report of the Chicago Police Department* (1949: 17-18).

13. *Annual Report, Illinois Division of Highways* (1950).

14. *Annual Report of the Municipal Court of Chicago* (1921: 133).

15. This is also suggested by comparative statistics on the distribution of traffic fatalities in Illinois. Chicago, which in 1957 registered 30 percent of the state's motor vehicles, and recorded 40 percent of the state's traffic injuries, suffered only 17 percent of the state's traffic fatalities. While a number of factors may have contributed to this dramatic difference, the ready access of the city's citizens to modern medical facilities may have been a major one. See Illinois Traffic Study Commission of the American Bar Foundation (1958).

16. This terminology is used in Ross (1960-61).

17. Chicago Police Department (1966). A discussion of the problems in regulating horse-drawn vehicles in the city of London will be found in Reith (1952).

18. Chicago Police Department (1966).

19. *Annual Report of the Municipal Court of Chicago* (1921: 132).

20. Ross (1960-61: 231).

21. New York State Department of Public Works, Bureau of Highway Planning (1955).

22. This analysis is quite tentative, and should be taken only as simple description of the data. Time series data presents some complex statistical problems (such as autocorrelation of error terms) which have been glossed over in this presentation. Problems of trend, on the other hand, have been greatly alleviated by the per capita transformation of the variables. For a discussion see Quenouille (1952: chapter 11).

23. All dispositional figures were calculated from data presented in the yearly annual reports of the municipal court.

24. *Annual Report of the Municipal Court of Chicago* (1913: 86).

25. These data are from a special study of the operation of the Traffic Bureau conducted by the Street Traffic Committee of the Chicago Association of Commerce. They cover the first 14 months of the court's operation. They are reported in Table 2 of the *Annual Report of the Municipal Court of Chicago* (1928: 122). The figures here exclude three judges who sat in traffic court for only one day.

26. The equation generating this line is: $y = .36 + (.009 \times \text{CASES}) - (.00004 \times \text{CASES})^2$. The $R^2 = .41$ and $N = 22$.

27. *Annual Report of the Municipal Court of Chicago* (1924: 12).

28. The equation generating this line is $y = 605 - (.88 \times \text{INPUTS})$. The $R^2 = .88$ and $N = 31$. The data are from various annual reports of the municipal court.

29. *Chicago Tribune,* June 15, 1972.

30. In a study by the Institute for Judicial Administration of New York University, cited in the *Chicago Daily News,* August 26, 1972.

31. P. J. Johnen (1970: 291-295). There is evidence that not all of these tactics are successful. A recent investigation of the impact of pretrial discovery rules in the federal courts discovered that they served to (a) increase the proportion of cases coming to trial, (b) increase the length of trials and trial records, and (c) "unsettle" cases that might otherwise be settled out of court. See W. A. Glaser (1968).

32. *Annual Report of the Municipal Court of Chicago* (1913: 85).

33. Ibid., 100.

34. Ibid., 101.

35. *Annual Report of the Municipal Court of Chicago* (1921: 131-133). A. Wells and J. E. Parlee (1962: 116).

36. The operation of the cafeteria court is described in Traffic Court Committee of the American Bar Association (1959). See also the statewide report cited in note 8, supra.

37. *Chicago Daily News,* March 17, 1926.

38. All fines are calculated from figures released in various annual reports of the municipal court.

39. *Chicago Tribune,* March 18, 1926.

40. *Chicago Tribune,* September 5, 1931.

41. Ibid.

42. Ibid.

43. Calculated from breakdowns occasionally released in the annual reports of the municipal court.

44. *Chicago Tribune,* September 9, 1931.
45. See note 7, supra.
46. Barmack and Payne (1964). This and other evidence is reviewed by R. C. Cramton (1968). See also H. L. Ross, D. T. Campbell, and G. V. Glass (1970); J. Andenaes (1966).
47. The role of the victim is pointed out in J. A. Gardiner (1969), and Cramton (1968: 192).
48. W. Middendorff (1968: 73); D. T. Campbell and H. L. Ross (1968). The latter report that two consequences of Governor Ribicoff's crackdown on speeding in Connecticut during the mid-1950s were: (a) many fewer drivers were arrested for speeding, and (b) the conviction rate for those who were dropped considerably.
49. Ross (1960-61).
50. F. M. Council (1970); R. P. Shumate (1958); R. Michaels (1960). Enforcement studies are reviewed by Cramton (1968: 190-196).
51. Traffic Court Committee of the American Bar Association (1959: 30).
52. Middendorf (1968: 15-16). Studies are reviewed by Cramton (1968: 206-207).
53. Department of Motor Vehicles of the State of New York (1970).
54. These distinctions are elaborated by W. Chambliss (1969: 368-372).

REFERENCES

ANDENAES, J. (1966) "The General Preventive Effects of Punishment." University of Pennsylvania Law Review 114 (May): 176-193.
Annual Report of the Illinois Division of Highways (1950). Chicago.
Annual Report of the Chicago Police Department (1949). Chicago.
Annual Report of the Municipal Court of Chicago (1913). Chicago.
——— (1921-24). Chicago.
——— (1928). Chicago.
ASHBY, W. R. (1956) An Introduction to Cybernetics. London: Chapman & Hall.
BARMACK, J. E. and D. E. PAYNE (1964) "The Lackland Accident Countermeasure Experiment," in W. Haddon et al. (eds.) Accident Research. New York: Harper & Row.
BUEL, R. A. (1972) Dead End: the Automobile in Mass Transportation. Englewood Cliffs, N.J.: Prentice-Hall.
CAMPBELL, D. T. and J. C. STANLEY (1963) Experimental and Quasi-Experimental Designs for Research. Chicago: Rand McNally.
CAMPBELL, D. T. and H. L. ROSS (1968) "The Connecticut crackdown on speeding: time-series data on quasi-experimental analysis." Law and Society Review 3 (August): 33-53.
CAPORASO, J. A. (1973) "Quasi-experimental approaches to social science: perspectives and problems," pp. 3-35 in J. A. Caporaso and L. L. Roos, Jr. (eds.) Quasi-Experimental Approaches. Evanston, Ill.: Northwestern University Press.
CHAMBLISS, W. [ed.] (1969) Crime and the Legal Process. New York: McGraw-Hill.
Chicago Daily News (January 21, 1925).
——— (August 26, 1972).
Chicago Police Department (1966) "A haphazard history of the Chicago Police Department." Chicago Police Star (January).
Chicago Tribune (June 15, 1972).
——— (June 2, 1973).

COUNCIL, F. M. (1970) A Study of the Immediate Effects of Enforcement on Vehicular Speeds. Chapel Hill: University of North Carolina Highway Safety Research Center.

CRAMTON, R. C. (1968) "Driver behavior and legal sanctions: a study of deterrence," in J. O'Day (ed.) Driver Behavior: Cause and Effect. Washington, D.C.: Insurance Institute for Highway Safety.

Department of Motor Vehicles of the State of New York (1970) "Administrative Adjudication of Traffic Violations in New York City." Albany: New York Dept. of Motor Vehicles.

GARDINER, J. A. (1969) Traffic and Police: Variations in Law Enforcement Policy. Cambridge, Mass.: Harvard University Press.

GILBERT, H. T. (1928) The Municipal Court of Chicago. Chicago: privately published.

GLASER, W. A. (1968) Pretrial Discovery and the Adversary System. New York: Russell Sage Foundation.

GOEN, R. (1965) Drastic Measures for Reducing Traffic Casualties. Menlo Park, Calif.: Stanford Research Institute.

GOODSPEED, E. J. (1896) "The bench and the bar." Industrial Chicago. Volume 6. Chicago: Goodspeed Publishing.

HABERSTROH, C. W. (1960) "Control as an organizational process." Management Science 6: 165-171.

Illinois Association for Criminal Justice (1968) Illinois Crime Survey. Chicago: Illinois Association for Criminal Justice and the Chicago Crime Commission. (Originally published in 1929.)

Illinois Traffic Study Commission of the American Bar Foundation (1958) "The Changing State of the Unchanging Courts: A Report on Courts Trying Traffic Cases in Illinois."

––– (1973b) "Criminal Courts as Organizational Phenomena." Paper presented for the Conference on the Sociology of Judicial Proceedings (September), Zenturm fur Interdiszplinare Forschung, Universitat Bielefield, West Germany.

JACOB, H. (1973) Urban Justice. Englewood Cliffs, N.J.: Prentice-Hall.

JOHNEN, P. J. (1970) "Data processing in the circuit court of Cook County, Illinois." Judicature 53: 291-295.

KARLEN, H. M. (1958) The Governments of Chicago. Chicago: Courier Publishing.

LEPAWSKY, A. (1932) The Judicial Systems of Metropolitan Chicago. Chicago: University of Chicago Press.

LEWIS, L. and H. J. SMITH (1929) Chicago: The History of Its Reputation. New York: Harcourt, Brace.

MEIER, R. L. (1962) A Communication Theory of Urban Growth. Cambridge, Mass.: Joint Center for Urban Studies of Harvard and M.I.T.

MICHAELS, R. (1960) "Effects of enforcement on traffic behavior." Public Roads 31 (December).

MIDDENDORFF, W. (1968) The Effectiveness of Punishment, Especially in Relation to Traffic Cases. South Hackensack, N.J.: Fred B. Rotham.

New York State Department of Public Works, Bureau of Highway Planning (1955) "Driver Behavior Study: Speed Characteristics on Rural Highways." Albany, N.Y.

PIERCE, B. L. (1937-1953) A History of Chicago. 3 volumes. New York: Knopf.

QUENOUILLE, M. (1952) Associated Measurements. New York: Academic Press.

REITH, C. (1952) The Blind Eye of History: A Study of the Origins of the Present Police Era. London: Faber & Faber.

ROSENBERG, M. (1965) "Court congestion: status, causes and proposed remedies," in H. W. Jones (ed.) The Courts, the Public and Law Explosion. Englewood Cliffs, N.J.: Prentice-Hall.

ROSS, H. L. (1960-61) "Traffic violation: a folk crime." Social Problems 8: 231.

——— (1970) Settled Out of Court: The Social Process of Insurance Claims Adjustment. Chicago: Aldine.

——— D. T. CAMPBELL, and G. V. GLASS (1970) "Determining the social effects of a legal reform: the British breathalyzer crackdown of 1967." American Behavioral Scientist 13 (March/April): 499-504.

SHUMATE, R. P. (1958) Effects of Increased Patrol on Accidents, Diversion, and Speed. Evanston, Ill.: Northwestern University Traffic Institute.

Traffic Court Committee of the American Bar Association (1959) "Report to the Municipal Court of Chicago."

VICKERS, G. (1959) "Is adaptability enough?" Behavioral Science 4: 219-234.

WELLS, A. and J. E. PARLEE (1962) "The Chicago Traffic Court." Chicago Bar Record 44: 116.

ZEISEL, H., H. KALVEN, Jr., and B. BUCHOLZ (1959) Delay in the Court. Boston: Little, Brown.

Chapter 6

INNOVATION IN URBAN CRIMINAL
MISDEMEANOR COURTS

LUCINDA LONG

To most legal scholars, criminal misdemeanor courts are trivial. Perhaps this attitude is the result of both a negative value judgment about the seriousness of misdemeanor cases combined with the invisibility of these courts to most academicians.

This state of affairs is ironical because statistically misdemeanor courts are the most frequented type of criminal court and because many people assess the justness of the entire court system by their encounters with its "lowest" division. Preoccupied with the grandeur of the Supreme Court and the notoriety of felony courts, researchers forget the insight of the President's Commission on Law Enforcement and Administration of Justice that "most of the cases in the criminal courts consist of what are essentially violations of moral norms or instances of annoying behavior, rather than of serious crimes,"[1] and that "almost half of all arrests are on charges of drunkenness, disorderly conduct, vagrancy, gambling, and minor sex violations."[2]

This study focuses on the criminal misdemeanor courts in all American cities over 100,000 population. Three major questions are examined. First, what are the organizational characteristics of this universe of courts?[3] Second, what attempts have been made to innovate in these courts? Third, why have some courts innovated more than others?

METHODOLOGY

To answer the first and second questions, a questionnaire was sent in October 1971 to the chief judge of each court requesting factual information about the operations of the court.[4] Information about the introduction of different type of innovations was obtained through the same questionnaire by supplying a list of possible innovations and asking judges to indicate which items their court had adopted and when these innovations were initiated.[5]

Answering the third question involved several steps and methods. First it was necessary to construct some index of innovativeness for use as the primary dependent variable. A list of 36 potential innovations was sent to approximately 80 criminal justice experts who were asked how innovative they would consider the introduction of a particular item into a criminal misdemeanor court.[6] Alternative weighting schemes were constructed, but correlations between the resulting indexes were so high as not to warrant the selection of one form over another.[7] Thus, the least elaborate method was selected as being most appropriate.

Independent variables used to predict innovativeness were of five types: organizational variables; budgetary variables; city-type variables; variables related to the administration of the Law Enforcement Assistance Act; and attitudinal variables.[8] A total of 187 independent variables were considered.

A factor analysis of 45 independent variables was conducted and significant factors were identified. The factor scores for each court were used as the independent variables in a multiple regression program.[9]

URBAN CRIMINAL MISDEMEANOR COURT
ORGANIZATION: AN OVERVIEW

Many writers have stressed the relationship between organizational environment, or milieu, and innovation. For example, Tom Burns and G. M. Stalker (1961: 5), in their book *The Management of Innovation,* classify organizational management systems into two types, organic and mechanistic, and argue that the organic system is "required" if innovation is to occur. Robert K. Merton argues that "as organizations differ in the character of what they do, produce, and achieve, they get very different conditions for creativity."[10]

The characteristics of an organization affect innovative behavior at several points. For example, perceived organizational goals are often invoked to justify or to attack implementation of a particular innovation. The functions of an organization imply certain logical areas for innovation to occur. For instance, if a criminal misdemeanor court handles preliminary felony hearings as well as misdemeanors, that court is probably more interested in improved methods of record-keeping than a court which does not handle any felony cases for which detailed records must be maintained. The attributes of various personnel in the organization are also obviously important variables affecting the decision to be innovative. The resources of an organization can often determine the ability of an organization to implement an innovation once it has been deemed desirable. Finally, the structure and procedures of an organization can very definitely affect the impact of an innovation once introduced.

Although the characteristics of any organization are an important part of the attempt to innovate, they are especially important in the area of court reform. The primary source of their special significance to court reform is the belief of most reformers that the most effective way to improve the quality of justice is to improve the administration of justice. For example, most of the recommendations of the President's Commission on Law Enforcement and Administration of Justice are organizational in nature.[11] A more direct assertion of this philosophy is exemplified in U.S. Supreme Court Chief Justice Warren Berger's keynote address at the 1971 Williamsburg Conference on the Judiciary. He urged that reform "begin by giving priority to methods and machinery, to procedure and techniques, to management and administration of judicial resources even over the much needed re-examination of substantive legal institutions that are out-of-date."[12]

Given the importance of organizational setting to innovation, and the dearth of factual information about criminal misdemeanor courts, it seems appropriate to begin an analysis of innovation in these courts by describing their organizational characteristics.

Urban criminal misdemeanor court judges tend to be few in number, to have short terms of office, and to be relatively well-paid. About two-thirds (66.1 percent) of the courts have between one and four judges, while approximately 90 percent have fewer than nine judges. These judges usually work full-time (85.9 percent).

The average judicial term of office is between four and five years and over 90 percent of these judges have terms of less than seven years. About half (49.6 percent) of the judges are elected. Of those elected, 58.6 percent are chosen in non-partisan elections, while only 41.4 percent are chosen in partisan elections. Appointed judges usually are picked either by the mayor of the city or by the city council. The much-touted Missouri plan is almost ignored at the misdemeanor court level (only 3.4 percent).

Slightly over one-third (33.9 percent) of criminal misdemeanor court judges earn more than $25,000 per year, and over three-fourths (78.0 percent) earn at least $15,000 per year. The mean salary is about $20,000 per year. No judges in the study earned their salary through fees, a common practice in the past.

In about one-fourth (26.6 percent) of all criminal misdemeanor courts, the state is represented primarily by police officers. The remaining courts have either full-time or part-time prosecutors supplied by either city- or county-level governments and sometimes by both. In those courts with prosecutors, almost half (47.2 percent) have only full-time prosecutors. Even when full-time prosecutors are available, over half (59.1 percent) of the courts have fewer than five prosecutors. The breakdown between city- and county-supplied prosecutors is the following: 37.6 percent city-level; 23.8 percent county-level; 34.7 percent both city- and county-level.

Probation services are offered in about three-fourths (74.2 percent) of these courts. Of those courts with probation services, 54.8 percent have fewer than five probation officers available and the average probation caseload is 112 persons. Approximately one-tenth (9.5 percent) of the probation officers have a caseload over 300. Probation officers in criminal misdemeanor courts, however, provide minimal services, since almost two-thirds (61.8 percent) of them perform only one or two functions such as pre-sentencing investigations or post-sentencing monitoring of offenders with the latter being the most frequent activity. Most probation officers are supplied by either city- or county-level governments, although 18.3 percent of the probation officers are provided by state governments.

Contrary to past practices, most criminal misdemeanor courts (85 percent) are today not geographically decentralized in the sense that judges hear cases at separate courts spread throughout the city. When the court is decentralized, only one judge (94.1 percent) is assigned to each division. This type of misdemeanor court centralization is, however, not reflected in the actual workload of judges. Almost two-thirds (62.5 percent) of the judges in criminal misdemeanor courts rotate between civil and criminal cases. Thus, while the judges in criminal misdemeanor courts are, in fact, full-time judges, they do not allocate all of their judge-hours to criminal cases.

Budgets in criminal misdemeanor courts are usually formulated either by the judges (29 percent and usually the chief judge alone), by the non-judicial professionals (30.6 percent and either a chief clerk or court administrator), or by a combination of the former two (34.7 percent). When asked about their court's budgetary "track record," slightly over half (52.2 percent) of the judges believed they received about the same amount as requested, while almost one-third (29.2 percent) believed they generally received slightly less than requested. No judge stated his court usually obtained a great deal more money than requested despite increased interest in and funding of criminal justice activities in recent years.[13]

During the period 1967-1970, about one-fourth (26.2 percent) of these courts were affected by some kind of state-wide court reorganization plan. The most frequent changes introduced were the elimination of justice-of-the-peace courts (72.7 percent), reduction in the number of courts operating in the state (51.5 percent), transferral of control over misdemeanor courts from localities to the state (66.7 percent), and the raising of judicial salaries (57.6 percent). Nevertheless, it is interesting to note that almost three-fourths (73.8 percent) of the urbanized states carried out no reorganization of their courts.

Almost three-fourths (71.0 percent) of the courts surveyed replied that their jurisdiction did include the conducting of preliminary felony hearings in addition to the regular misdemeanor caseload. Only 13.8 percent of these courts have any type of organizational manual. The number of clerical staff ranges from none to well over 50, although the average court has approximately 20 workers.

THE UNIVERSE OF INNOVATIONS

Observers of the criminal misdemeanor courts have, in the past, usually been horrified by the sight. In its summary report, the Crime Commission stated that it "has been shocked by what it has seen in some lower courts. It has seen cramped and noisy courtrooms, undignified and perfunctory procedures, and badly trained personnel. It has seen dedicated people who are frustrated by huge caseloads, by the lack of opportunity to examine cases carefully, and by the impossibility of constructive solutions to the problems of offenders. It has seen assembly line justice."[14] An obvious question is whether the picture painted by the Crime Commission is still the reality of criminal misdemeanor courts.

One major goal in recent court reform movements has been increased "professionalization" of judges. Some of the most frequently cited suggestions are the following: requiring all judges to be lawyers; providing higher salaries and not allowing payment of judges by the fee method; establishing longer terms of office; and eliminating the practice of selecting judges in partisan elections.[15] Table 1 summarizes the number of courts who have adopted innovative procedures and programs relating to professionalization of judges.

The data in Table 1 generally indicate that the professionalization of misdemeanor court judges, as measured by the standard criteria, is by no means complete. For example, although no judges in the study are paid through a system of fees, 14.1 percent of these misdemeanor courts still do not require that judges be lawyers. Also, 49.6 percent of the judges are still elected. Advocates of professionalism might be comforted knowing that half of this group are at least selected in non-partisan elections. However, recent research about non-partisan elections has shown that partisan considerations are frequently only camouflaged, not eliminated (Wirt et al., 1972: 148-159).

Table 1. PERCENTAGE OF COURTS WHO ARE AND ARE NOT CHARACTERIZED BY
INNOVATIONS RELATING TO PROFESSIONALIZATION OF JUDGES

Innovation	Do You Have This Innovation?	
	Yes	No
(N=128)	N (%)	N (%)
1. Full-time judges	110 (85.9)	18 (14.1)
2. A requirement that judges be lawyers	110 (85.9)	18 (14.1)
3. Paying judges by salary rather than by fees	128 (100.0)	0 (0.0)
4. Orientation for new judges	55 (43.7)	71 (56.3)
5. Civil service status for clerical employees	65 (51.6)	61 (48.4)
6. Mandatory retirement age for judges	75 (58.6)	53 (41.4)
7. Within last five years, a commissioned management study by outsiders of the court system	46 (36.2)	81 (63.8)

Three other findings would tend to dim the optimism of reformers: 90
percent of the misdemeanor court judges studied have terms of less than seven
years (the Crime Commission recommended a minimum of ten-year terms for
"major trial courts");[16] less than half (43.7 percent) of these courts have any
kind of orientation program for new judges; and 41.4 percent of the courts have
no mandatory retirement age for judges (another specific recommendation of
the Crime Commission).[17]

The Crime Commission also concluded that "inadequate attention tends to be
given to the individual defendant, whether in protecting his rights, sifting the
facts at trial, deciding the social risk he presents, or determining how to deal
with him after conviction."[18] Table 2 summarizes the number of courts who
have adopted innovative techniques and programs relating to the treatment of
defendants.

It can be argued that the contents of Table 2 offer ample evidence that the

Table 2. PERCENTAGE OF COURTS WHO ARE AND ARE NOT CHARACTERIZED BY
INNOVATIONS RELATING TO TREATMENT OF DEFENDANTS

Innovation	Do You Have This Innovation?	
	Yes	No
(N=128)	N (%)	N (%)
1. Right to jury trial in misdemeanor cases	96 (75.0)	32 (25.0)
2. Public defender services	57 (44.5)	71 (55.5)
3. Full-time prosecutors	94 (73.4)	34 (26.6)
4. Using law students as assistant prosecutors or public defenders	38 (29.7)	90 (70.3)
5. New rules of criminal procedure in last five years	69 (54.3)	58 (45.7)

Table 3. PERCENTAGE OF COURTS WHO ARE AND ARE NOT CHARACTERIZED BY INNOVATIONS RELATING TO TREATMENT OF DEFENDANTS AT PRE-TRIAL STAGE

Innovation	*Do You Have This Innovation?*	
	Yes	*No*
(N=128)	*N (%)*	*N (%)*
1. Release on suspect's own recognizance as part of bail policy	114 (89.8)	13 (10.2)
2. Night sessions of court	36 (28.1)	92 (71.9)
3. Weekend sessions of court	38 (29.7)	90 (70.3)
4. Monitoring of jail lists	69 (57.5)	51 (42.5)
5. Statutory limit or judges' rule on length of time before trial	63 (49.6)	64 (50.4)

Commission's assessment is still accurate. Although three-fourths of the courts studied do give the defendant the right to a jury trial, this right is compromised, perhaps fatally, by the findings that only 44.5 percent of the courts provide public defenders and that police act as prosecutors in 26.6 percent of the cases. Several of the elements of a truly adversarial trial are simply not available in a significant number of cases.[19]

The rights of defendants are also ignored in many courts during the pre-trial stage. Table 3 summarizes the number of courts who have adopted innovations relating to the treatment of defendants in the pre-trial period.

As Table 3 shows, ten percent of the courts still do not allow any suspects to be released on their own recognizance. Less than one-third of the courts have night sessions (28.1 percent) or weekend sessions (29.7 percent) of court. Therefore, someone arrested on Friday night will often have to remain in jail until at least Monday before his case, no matter how petty, is resolved. Another potential threat to the defendant is the finding that 42.5 percent of these courts do not monitor their jail lists; that is, no one is responsible for keeping up-to-date records on who is in jail and how long they have been there. A related problem is that only 49.6 percent of the courts have any limit on the length of time allowed to pass before a defendant must be brought to trial.

The power to decide the social risk a defendant presents and to determine how to deal with him after conviction is frequently exercised haphazardly and with little emphasis on rehabilitating the offender. Table 4 summarizes the number of courts who have adopted innovations relating to defendant rehabilitation services.

Although three-fourths of the courts studied do provide some sort of probation services, the actual probation activities tend to consist of post-sentencing monitoring of defendants rather than pre-sentencing investigations. Only

Table 4. PERCENTAGE OF COURTS WHO ARE AND ARE NOT CHARACTERIZED BY
INNOVATIONS RELATING TO DEFENDANT REHABILITATION

| Innovation | Do You Have This Innovation? | |
| | Yes | No |
(N=128)	N (%)	N (%)
1. Probation services	95 (74.2)	33 (25.8)
2. A youthful offender treatment program which may refer youthful offenders (too old to be classified as juveniles) without trial to another social agency	30 (23.6)	97 (76.4)
3. A work release program either for adult misdemeanants in jail or instead of jail	73 (57.0)	55 (43.0)
4. Volunteer probation officers	32 (25.0)	96 (75.0)
5. Indeterminate sentencing	34 (27.0)	92 (73.0)

23.6 percent of the courts have a youthful offender treatment program, an especially serious weakness when one remembers that "for crimes of violence, the peak years are those from 18 to 20," and that "the 15-to-17-year-old group is the highest for burglaries, larcenies and auto theft."[20] Many careers in crime begin with a history of criminal misdemeanor violations.[21] Also, only about half (57.0 percent) of the courts have work release programs for inmates.

Most previous observers of criminal misdemeanor courts have concluded that these courts suffer overwhelming caseloads which, according to the Crime Commission, lead to "the almost absolute preoccupation in such a court with the movement of cases."[22] Analysis of the data in Table 5 weakens the notion that overload is a universal problem of crisis proportions in criminal misdemeanor courts.

Evidence debunking the overload problem is ample. For instance, 75 percent of the courts surveyed allow defendants the option of a jury trial.[23] Unlike felony trials, juries are neither a universal nor traditional feature of misdemeanor courts. As noted above, fully one-fourth of these courts do not now offer a jury trial option. A look at the date of adoption of juries shows that 39 percent of these courts adopted them since 1950, 20 percent since 1960, and 14 percent since 1965. Also, juries were instituted by many misdemeanor courts during a period of rapid increases in crime rates. It is clear that jury trials take longer than non-jury trials and therefore are an obvious potential source of delay. Thus we could infer that allowing jury trials indicates that delay is not a serious problem.

The finding that about three-fourths of these courts have not found it necessary to institute extra sessions of court at night or on weekends seems to indicate again that overload is not overwhelming. Only half (49.6 percent) of the

Table 5. PERCENTAGE OF COURTS WHO ARE AND ARE NOT CHARACTERIZED BY
INNOVATIONS RELATING TO PROBLEMS OF CASE OVERLOAD

Innovation (N=128)	Do You Have This Innovation?	
	Yes N (%)	No N (%)
1. A criminal justice information system involving regular collection and summary of case volume and disposition	63 (49.2)	65 (50.8)
2. Separate traffic court	86 (67.2)	42 (32.8)
3. Administrative adjudication of traffic cases	33 (27.1)	89 (72.9)
4. Separate housing court that handles both criminal and civil matters	49 (38.9)	77 (61.1)
5. All-purpose-parts calendaring (same judge hears all aspects of a single case	88 (69.3)	39 (30.7)
6. Summonses instead of arrest warrants for use in certain types of misdemeanors such as littering, trespass, loitering, and so on	96 (76.8)	29 (23.2)
7. Separate family court for criminal misdemeanors involving members of the same family	20 (15.6)	108 (84.4)
8. Transferring judges between and/or within courts for crash programs to reduce backlog	66 (51.6)	62 (48.4)

courts have made the decision at some time in the past to transfer judges between and/or within courts for crash programs to reduce backlog.

Also, the fact that 50.8 percent of court bureaucrats do not collect and publish overload statistics suggests that overload is not thought of by bureaucrats as a problem worth exploiting as a political issue and as a way to increase budgetary allotments. Of course the incomplete and undiscriminating data available on actual amounts of cases and backlog make it impossible to prove the argument being made; however, the indirect measures of overload described above do seem to support this point of view.

The data in Table 5 also offer some insights into plausible reasons why overload is not a universal problem. Although exact figures are not available, it is generally agreed that traffic violations do comprise a significant if not dominant proportion of the criminal misdemeanors handled by local courts.[24] About two-thirds (67.2 percent) of the courts studied reported that all of these traffic-related misdemeanors were handled in a separate court. Also, 38.9 percent of the courts stated that in their city a separate housing court handled both criminal and civil cases. Again, no exact figures are available to indicate the numerical importance of housing cases carrying criminal penalties. However, in New York City during 1971, for example, the city's housing and development administration initiated 21,083 criminal misdemeanor cases.[25] This figure represents approximately 12.4 percent of all criminal misdemeanors initiated that year.[26] Thus the removal of criminal misdemeanors related to traffic and housing plus the frequency of plea bargaining and non-jury trials could help explain why overload and backlog do not produce universal crises in urban criminal misdemeanor courts.

Other insights into the operations of criminal misdemeanor courts can be gained from examining Table 6, which summarizes the number of courts who have adopted other kinds of innovations.

One inescapable conclusion from Table 6 is that more and more misdemeanor courts are becoming courts of record, a non-traditional situation. About half (49.2 percent) of the courts do have a criminal justice information system involving the regular collection and summary of case volume and disposition. Increased sophistication in record-keeping is shown by the finding that 25 percent of the courts have computerized their information systems and that 22.7 percent of the courts microfilm their records.

Also, almost half (46.1 percent) of the courts now have at least one full-time court reporter. An intriguing question arises from the discrepancy between the number of courts with an information system and the number of courts with a full-time court administrator. Although half of the courts keep records, only one-third have professional administrators. It would appear that some other group, perhaps the chief clerk or part of the clerical staff or even one of the judges is assuming this additional function.

Table 6. PERCENTAGE OF COURTS WHO ARE AND ARE NOT CHARACTERIZED BY INNOVATIONS RELATING TO ADDITIONAL ASPECTS OF COURT OPERATIONS

Innovation	Do You Have This Innovation?	
	Yes	No
(N=128)	N (%)	N (%)
1. Computerization of criminal court records	32 (25.0)	96 (75.0)
2. Full-time court reporter	59 (46.1)	69 (53.9)
3. A professional court administrator	44 (34.4)	84 (65.6)
4. An installment plan for fine payment instead of jail time for inability to pay	104 (81.3)	24 (18.7)
5. New court facilities or major renovations in last five years	73 (57.0)	55 (43.0)
6. Microfilming of case records	29 (22.7)	99 (77.3)

Many political scientists have investigated the problem of assessing the impact of Supreme Court decisions. One example of impact is found in this study. In a recent case, the Supreme Court ruled that convicted defendants could not be jailed because of inability to pay their fines.[27] By the fall of 1971, 81.3 percent of the courts studied had complied with the Supreme Court's ruling by instituting an installment plan for fine payment. Thus, it took only 7 months for the decision of the highest court in the land to reach and be implemented by most of the lowest criminal courts in the land.

In their 1967 report, the Crime Commission recommended for criminal misdemeanor courts that "As an immediate step . . . their physical facilities should be improved so that these courts will be able to cope with the volume of cases coming before them in a dignified and deliberate way."[28] This recommendation seems to have been taken to heart, since slightly over half (57.0 percent) of the courts surveyed reported that new court facilities or major renovations were completed between 1966 and 1971.

What kind of summary can be made about the universe of innovations which have or have not been adopted by criminal misdemeanor courts in big cities? One trend seems to be that misdemeanor courts are becoming more and more like felony courts. The direction seems to be toward adding more elements of the felony trial court environment: full-time prosecutors, full-time judges, probation services, and a formal system of record-keeping. This transformation is obviously not complete, and some elements are being adopted more quickly than others, often not in any particularly logical progression.[29]

Given the academic and governmental lack of interest generally in criminal misdemeanor courts, it is perhaps not just a little amazing that these courts have innovated as much as they have. As Judge David L. Golden, president in 1971 of the North American Judges Association, pointed out in his endorsement letter of this study:

> We have been the neglected courts for so long even though we have the responsibility of the punishment and the rehabilitation of over 90% of the people involved in criminal complaints. I hope that (this) research will open to public view the innovativeness that we have done to this date especially with our very limited resources.[30]

It is also important to remember that not all of the innovations described are appropriate for all courts. For example, the volume of cases in a misdemeanor court located in a city with just over 100,000 population may not logically warrant an investment of time and money into computerized or microfilmed record-keeping. This same consideration can be applied to many of the innovations included in this survey. Thus, nonadoption does not necessarily indicate that the court administrators are either uninformed or backward or both.

TABLE 7. CORRELATION MATRIX FOR 29 MARKER VARIABLES

Variable	1	2	3	4	5	6	7	8	9	10
1. Population category of city	1.00									
2. Percent foreign stock in city	.19	1.00								
3. Percent income under $3,000 in city	-.08	-.36	1.00							
4. Population of city as percent of state population	(.51)	.12	-.01	1.00						
5. Length of judges' terms in years	.20	.23	-.31	-.04	1.00					
6. Salary category of judges	.28	.35	-.49	-.06	(.62)	1.00				
7. Number of full-time judges	.47	.30	-.18	.40	.33	.32	1.00			
8. Number of full-time prosecutors	.42	.21	-.21	.27	.16	.32	.34	1.00		
9. Are probation officers county-level employees	-.01	.36	-.38	-.17	.34	(.50)	.09	.26	1.00	
10. How many clerical personnel county-level employees	.35	.20	-.12	.28	.08	.26	.14	(.63)	.16	1.00
11. How many law schools in city	(.71)	.18	-.00	.39	.26	.24	(.55)	.38	-.07	.08
12. How many decentralized courts	(.56)	.22	-.05	.39	.11	.14	.49	.46	-.02	(.65)
13. Has court ever contacted cj state planning agency (SPA)	.20	.08	-.14	.23	.19	.23	.18	.06	.02	.18
14. Is LEAA regional headquarters located in city	(.51)	.12	-.05	.35	.06	.13	.37	.18	-.09	.17
15. Court ever applied for grant from LEAA	.20	-.02	-.04	.37	-.05	-.01	.13	.07	-.12	.14
16. Was grant application funded	.22	-.01	-.17	.35	.01	.03	.18	.09	-.03	.13
17. Helpfulness of SPA	.25	.15	-.21	.31	.22	.24	.23	.06	.05	.14
18. Helpfulness of o.j. region	.11	.02	-.23	.10	.30	.18	.22	.04	.16	.10
19. Court contacted region	.10	.08	-.21	.06	.28	.20	.19	.07	.19	.15
20. Percent LEAA grants to state for block action	-.07	-.14	-.01	-.18	-.12	-.04	-.05	.05	.14	.05

Variable	11	12	13	14	15	16	17	18	19	20
21. Percent LEAA grants for technical assistance	.10	.02	-.09	-.11	.41	.28	.10	.01	.04	-.02
22. City in southern state	-.12	(-.58)	(.57)	-.22	-.35	-.43	-.23	-.23	-.39	-.16
23. Revenue of city government	(.75)	.31	-.07	.49	.38	.33	(.79)	.42	-.01	.39
24. Number of police organizations in city	.30	.39	-.09	.23	.26	.24	.41	.12	.02	.27
25. Do police belong to PBA (Police Benevolent Assoc.)	.01	.31	.01	.02	.04	-.01	.26	-.09	-.14	-.02
26. Police organization not affiliated with either state or national group	.18	.44	-.15	.24	.13	.14	.45	.04	-.02	.08
27. Number police strikes	.23	.43	-.09	.19	.20	.22	.41	11	.02	.23
28. Total LEEP personnel (education for law enforcement personnel)	.44	.23	-.06	.24	.37	.26	(.60)	.09	-.05	.08
29. Number participating schools in LEEP program	(.63)	.29	-.06	.44	.24	.26	(.58)	.37	-.03	.34
Variable	*11*	*12*	*13*	*14*	*15*	*16*	*17*	*18*	*19*	*20*
11. How many law schools in city	1.00									
12. Percent decentralized courts	(.58)	1.00								
13. Court ever contacted SPA	.23	.14	1.00							
14. LEAA regional headquarters in city	.42	.44	.29	1.00						
15. Court ever applied for grant from LEAA	.15	.08	.48	.16	1.00					
16. Was grant application funded	.14	.13	.47	.21	(.74)	1.00				
17. Helpfulness of SPA	.25	.15	(.68)	.31	.39	(.52)	1.00			
18. Helpfulness of criminal justice planning region	.14	.10	(.58)	.22	.44	(.51)	(.64)	1.00		
19. Has court ever contacted regional office	.13	.12	(.62)	.20	.43	(.53)	(.53)	(.86)	1.00	
20. Percent LEAA grants to state for block action	-.20	.05	-.11	.04	-.03	-.04	-.20	.11	.11	1.00

TABLE 7 (continued)

Variable	11	12	13	14	15	16	17	18	19	20
21. Percent LEAA grants for technical assistance	.32	-.04	.11	-.05	-.10	-.08	.17	-.03	-.03	(-.64)
22. City in southern state	-.12	-.06	-.20	-.05	-.20	-.13	-.18	-.12	-.17	.13
23. Revenue of city government	(.80)	(.65)	.25	.48	.17	.19	.27	.15	.14	-.21
24. Number of police organizations	.40	.26	.22	.29	.09	.03	.22	.15	.12	-.16
25. Do police belong to PBA	.10	.03	.11	.02	.01	.04	.09	.06	.11	-.08
26. Unaffiliated police organization	.29	.19	.21	.24	.04	.01	.20	-.02	-.06	-.08
27. Number police strikes	.36	.28	.26	.21	.14	.07	.25	.13	.06	-.04
28. Total LEEP personnel	(.57)	.35	.20	.31	.02	.05	.25	.04	.02	(-.50)
29. Number participating schools in LEEP program	(.60)	(.53)	.19	.44	.21	.17	.19	.11	.14	-.03

Variable	21	22	23	24	25	26	27	28	29
21. Percent LEAA grants for technical assistance	1.00								
22. City in southern state	-.15	1.00							
23. Revenue of city government	.32	-.22	1.00						
24. Number of police organizations in city	.07	-.29	.43	1.00					
25. Do police belong to PBA	-.06	-.07	.19	(.50)	1.00				
26. Unaffiliated police organization	-.05	-.22	.39	(.63)	(.51)	1.00			
27. Number police strikes	-.04	-.26	.44	(.50)	.32	(.67)	1.00		
28. Total LEEP personnel	(.65)	-.19	(.76)	.33	.19	.34	.23	1.00	
29. Number participating schools in LEEP program	.10	-.25	(.75)	.33	.13	.27	.24	(.60)	1.00

CHARACTERISTICS OF INNOVATORS:
FACTOR ANALYSIS

As noted earlier, the dependent variable in this part of the study is each court's score on the index of innovativeness. Independent variables include organizational variables, budgetary variables, city-type variables, Law Enforcement Assistance Administration (LEAA) variables, and attitudinal variables. All of the independent variables were factoranalyzed using the principal-components technique (with iterations) and varimax rotation for the purposes of transforming data, delineating interdependencies and patterns, and revealing data structure (Rummel, 1967: 444-480).

Marker variables (above ± .50 factor loadings) on five rotated factors (inclusion of the factor required explaining at least 9 percent of the common variance) were isolated for a total of 29 variables.[31] These 29 variables were standardized by Z-scoring and then were used to calculate factor scores for the courts. The resulting factor scores served as the independent variables in a multiple regression analysis.

Table 7 shows the correlation matrix for the 29 marker variables. Correlations greater than ± .50 are enclosed by parentheses. Table 8 shows the marker variable factor loadings on the rotated factors. The five factors plus one other factor (explaining 7.6 percent of the variance) account for 100 percent of the total variance among the original 45 variables.

The interpretation and naming of factors are the key steps in factor analysis. Computer programs can very quickly and accurately produce the factor matrix and its loadings, but the analytical ability of the researcher determines the usefulness of the technique to the research problem. An attempt has been made to infer the underlying dimensions represented by the marker variables. When appropriate, the areal or geographic distribution of individual courts' factor scores is examined.[32] In the following paragraphs, each factor is interpreted and the underlying dimensions are inferred.

Factor 1: Size of City

Table 9 displays the marker variables for Factor 1, which accounts for 42.6 percent of the variance.

All of the marker variables on Factor 1 reflect the size of the city in which the criminal misdemeanor court is located. The set of smallest cities (those with populations of 100,000 to 250,000) account for all of the Factor 1 factor scores below −1.00, and the set of biggest cities (those with populations over 500,000) account for all of the Factor 1 factor scores above +1.00.

Knowing that city size is a significant dimension of innovativeness, however,

Table 8. MARKER VARIABLE FACTOR LOADINGS ON ROTATED FACTORS

Variable	1	2	3	4	5	(h^2)
1. Population category of city	.74	.16	−.02	.17	.18	.665
2. Percent foreign stock in city	.14	−.03	.47	.50	.03	.548
3. Percent income under $3,000 in city	−.02	−.17	−.59	−.07	.01	.387
4. Population of city as percent of state population	.54	.28	−.13	.18	.07	.503
5. Length of judges' terms in years	.07	.13	.52	.14	.36	.530
6. Salary category of judges	.16	.07	.74	.10	.16	.728
7. Number of full-time judges	.44	.13	.14	.51	.18	.587
8. Number of full-time prosecutors	.65	−.04	.37	−.10	−.13	.594
9. Are probation officers county-level employees	−.05	−.02	.71	.02	−.15	.557
10. How many clerical personnel	.70	.04	.26	−.04	−.15	.593
11. How many law schools in city	.68	.12	−.04	.28	.35	.718
12. How many decentralized courts	.77	.06	.00	.15	−.04	.645
13. Hasc ourt ever contacted SPA	.09	.74	.11	.15	.12	.612
14. Is LEAA regional headquarters located in city	.51	.25	−.08	.21	.01	.384
15. Court ever applied for LEAA grant	.16	.67	−.06	.02	−.03	.524
16. Was grant application funded	.14	.73	−.01	−.01	−.05	.568
17. Helpfulness of SPA	.11	.71	.10	.14	.20	.590
18. Helpfulness of criminal justice region	−.01	.80	.16	.03	−.05	.716
19. Court ever contacted region	.00	.76	.19	.02	−.07	.646
20. Percent LEAA grants to state for block action	.00	.00	−.00	−.05	−.63	.421
21. Percent LEAA grants for technical assistance	−.01	−.04	.21	−.13	.90	.888
22. City located in southern state	−.08	−.15	−.67	−.26	−.12	.687
23. Revenue of city government	.73	.12	.07	.42	.41	.931
24. Number of police organizations in city	.23	.08	.13	.65	.09	.508
25. Do police belong to PBA	−.10	.03	.01	.61	−.02	.385

Table 8 (continued)

Variable	1	2	3	4	5	(h^2)
26. Police organization not affiliated with either state or national group	.11	.01	.03	.84	.03	.723
27. Number police strikes	.21	.13	.11	.63	.00	.476
28. Total LEEP in-service personnel	.33	.04	.05	.36	.76	.826
29. Number participating schools in LEEP in city	.63	.12	.06	.30	.23	.562
Sum of squares of factor loadings	4.53	3.57	2.76	3.18	2.48	17.50*
Percent of total variance	42.6	15.6	14.5	10.3	9.4	100*

*Based on six factors and 45 variables

is like knowing that big businessmen tend to vote Republican. In both cases a relationship has been identified but has not been explained. There are many ways city size could be crucial to the innovativeness of a local criminal misdemeanor court. The environment of a large city could, for example, be important to court innovation because of impact of city size on budgets, organizational slack,[33] and the quality of staff that can be recruited.

For instance, one could hypothesize that being in a very large city implies that a court will have an excessive caseload volume. This large volume could either prevent innovation by eliminating organizational slack or it could foster innovation to insure organizational preservation. Cross-tabulating city population with each court's innovativeness index score does show that 42.9 percent of the cities over one million population score in the top third of the index (that is, between 20 and 30) while only 1.3 percent of the cities between 100,000 and 250,000 population score in the top third.

Table 9. FACTOR 1

Variable	Factor Loading
1. Number of decentralized (geographically) misdemeanor courts in city	.77
2. Population category of city	.74
3. Total governmental revenue of the city in 1971	.73
4. Number of clerical personnel attached to court	.70
5. How many law schools in city	.68
6. Number of full-time prosecutors	.65
7. Number of schools in city participating in LEEP program	.63
8. Population of city as percent of state population	.54
9. Is LEAA regional headquarters located in city	.51

Thus, the relationship between size and innovativeness is positive and large, but more elaborate analysis is necessary before it can be determined what it is about city size that affects innovativeness.

Factor 2: Court Interaction with Agencies
Administering the Law Enforcement Assistance Act

Table 10 contains the marker variables for Factor 2, which accounts for 15.6 percent of the variance.

All of the marker variables on Factor 2 deal with patterns of interaction between local criminal misdemeanor courts and governmental agencies which distribute federal funds allocated under the Law Enforcement Assistance Act.

This interaction first involves communication by letter, phone, and in person with state criminal justice planning agencies and their subordinate regional planning offices. It also consists of the courts applying for LEAA funds from both state and federal agencies. The third element is the quality of interaction as reflected in the success or failure of applicants and in the opinions of misdemeanor court judges regarding regional and state planning offices.

Factor 3: Political Independence of
City Government from State Government

Table 11 displays the marker variables for Factor 3, which accounts for 14.5 percent of the variance.

At first glance, the marker variables on Factor 3 appear to be a rather disparate group. To aid in understanding the underlying dimension, an areal analysis of individual courts' factor scores was done. This analysis revealed that courts located within a particular geographical region tended to have either all positive factor scores or all negative factor scores instead of an even distribution between the two. Thus, courts located in western and mid-Atlantic states predominantly had positive factor scores on Factor 3; courts located in southern, midwestern, southwestern, or New England states predominantly had negative factor scores on Factor 3.

Table 10. FACTOR 2

Variable	Factor Loading
1. Court's opinion about helpfulness of criminal justice planning region	.80
2. Has court ever contacted region	.76
3. Has court ever contacted state planning agency	.74
4. Was court's application for assistance grant funded	.73
5. Court's opinion about helpfulness of state planning agency	.71
6. Has court ever applied for assistance grant	.67

Table 11. FACTOR 3

Variable	Factor Loading
1. Salary category of judges	.74
2. Are probation officers county employees	.71
3. Is court located in a southern state	−.67
4. In city, percent with incomes under $3,000	−.59
5. Length of judges' terms in years	.52

Thus Factor 3 could have been named "region in which misdemeanor court is located." However, it seemed more logical to find out the reasons behind this pattern of regionalism. The underlying dimension seems to be the degree of political independence city governments have from their state governments. Positive factor scores are associated with states and regions where city governments are less independent, while negative factor scores occur in states where cities are more independent.

One indicator of local dependence-independence would be the formal powers of state governors. In his article, "The Politics of the Executive," Joseph Schlesinger (1971: 232) develops an index of gubernatorial power based on a governor's tenure potential, appointive powers, budget powers, and veto powers. Among cities with high positive factor scores on Factor 3, 56 percent are located in states where the governor's combined index score is between 18 and 20 (the highest possible score); for cities with negative factor scores, only 9 percent are in states where governors score between 18 and 20. Forty-six percent of southern governors score 10 or less, while 67 percent of the governors of western states score between 18 and 20. Thus we can conclude that positive factor scores on Factor 3 indicate a court located in a state with a strong governor, while the opposite is true for courts with negative factor scores.

A more direct measure has been developed by Ira Sharkansky and Richard Hofferbert (1971: 336) in their article, "Dimensions of State Policy." They develop a dimension called "professionalism-local reliance," with which they rank states from 1 to 48 (Alaska and Hawaii are excluded); a low rank indicates higher local dependence on state governments. States containing courts with high positive factor scores on Factor 3 have a mean rank of 7.4; those containing courts with high negative factor scores have a mean rank of 20.1. Fifty-six percent of the states with high positive courts have a rank below 10, while 55 percent of the states with high negative courts have a rank above 20. Southern states have a mean rank of 23.5. Again it seems clear that high positive factor scores are associated with strong state governments and high negative scores are associated with weaker state governments.

Another indicator would be whether state reorganizations of court systems have resulted in control over local courts being transferred to the state. Two of the high positive marker variables on Factor 3, salary of judges and length of judges' terms, have correlations of .35 and .22, respectively, with this kind of court reorganization. Being located in a southern state, however, has a −.36 correlation with such a transferral.

The percentage of city revenues which comes from other levels of government also provides evidence about dependence of cities on states. Salary of judges and length of judges' terms are correlated .43 and .42 with percent of revenue from other governments, indicating that these two marker variables are associated with a higher proportion of city funding by other governments. Being southern, on the other hand, has a −.41 correlation with other-government funding.

Finally, having probation officers who are employees of county governments rather than local governments also reveals a lack of political independence of cities. County-supplied probation officers are associated with having other non-city criminal justice personnel. For example, the correlation between having county-level probation officers and city-level prosecutors is −.33. Also, the presence of county-level probation officers is correlated −.29 with data describing the extent of a city's contribution to plan, coordinate, and administer LEAA money.

From the above kinds of analyses, it seems correct to conclude that the marker variables on Factor 3 reflect the degree to which a city government operates as an independent and self-contained political system.

Factor 4: Level of Police Personnel Organization in City

Table 12 contains the marker variables for Factor 4, which accounts for 10.3 percent of the variance.

Naming Factor 4 is rather straightforward. Four of the six marker variables clearly deal with various aspects of police personnel organization, including amount, type, and behavior. The category of "police organization not affiliated

Table 12. FACTOR 4

Variable	Factor Loading
1. Police organization not affiliated with either state or nation group	.84
2. Number of police organizations in city	.65
3. Number of police strikes	.63
4. Do police belong to Policeman's Benevolent Association	.61
5. Number of full-time judges	.51
6. Percent foreign stock in city	.50

with either state or national group" reflects the fact that Policeman's Benevolent Associations are usually characterized by this type of organizational autonomy.[34]

The two remaining marker variables are positively associated with measures of city size, which in turn are positively associated with the presence of police personnel organizations. For example, the correlation between number of full-time judges and population category of city is .47. Number of police personnel organizations is correlated .30 with population category of city. Also, all except one of the marker variables on Factor 4 load second highest on Factor 1, which we have named city size.

Factor 5: LEAA's Evaluation of the Job Skills of Criminal Justice System Personnel

Table 13 displays the marker variables for Factor 5, which accounts for 9.4 percent of the variance.

The three marker variables on Factor 5 all involve funding decisions by the Law Enforcement Assistance Administration. The allocation of federal funds among the different assistance categories would seem to be a reflection of LEAA's evaluation of the particular needs of various criminal justice systems. The specific variables and their loadings on Factor 5 seem to tap LEAA's opinions about local criminal justice personnel job skills.

Technical assistance funds are of three main types: for dissemination of educational materials to criminal justice agencies; for enabling local agencies to hire consultants; and for sponsoring conferences for law enforcement personnel. Three projects funded in 1970 which illustrate this emphasis were a grant of $228,301 to prepare and disseminate technical assistance materials regarding bombs, bomb threats, and related police procedures, a grant of $642 for consultative assistance on correctional problems in Louisiana, and a grant of $1,500 to conduct a conference for parole administrators on decision-making and management.[35] These examples of funding clearly seem to relate to efforts to improve the job skills of various kinds of criminal justice personnel.

The Law Enforcement Education Program (LEEP) finances college studies by

Table 13. FACTOR 5

Variable	Factor Loading
1. Percent of state's grants from LEAA's technical assistance program	.90
2. Total number of LEEP in-service personnel	.76
3. Percent of state's grants from LEAA's block action program	−.63

law enforcement personnel, predominantly police officers. The underlying assumption of the program, namely that sending law enforcement personnel to college will improve their job skills, is made obvious in the following excerpt from a LEAA pamphlet outlining the LEEP program: "The man who goes into our streets in hopes of regulating, directing, or controlling human behavior must be armed with more than a gun and the ability to perform mechanical movements in response to a situation. . . . Their intellectual armament—so long restricted to the minimum—must be no less than their physical prowess and protection."[36] Thus, the number of local criminal justice personnel participating in LEEP programs would seem to be an indicator of the financial commitment LEAA has made to increasing job skills in a particular city through support of higher education programs.

Block action grants, on the other hand, cover the entire spectrum of criminal justice problems, from construction of new buildings to fighting organized crime to criminal code revisions. Awards are based on state population and the approval of annual state plans for "comprehensive state-wide law enforcement improvements."[37] Each state outlines its general program priorities, but it is left up to the state to make sub-grants to local criminal justice agencies. Thus, the negative factor loading on the variable "percent of state grants from LEAA's block action program" is not surprising since these programs are much more diffuse in content and do not represent LEAA's evaluation of problems in the specific area of personnel job skills.

A related point is that grants for LEEP and technical assistance programs involve the exercising of much more discretion by LEAA officials than do block action grants. Therefore, it could be argued that block action grant decisions do not represent the kind of particularistic, localistic evaluations involved in decisions about LEEP and technical assistance funds.

CHARACTERISTICS OF INNOVATORS:
MULTIPLE REGRESSION ANALYSIS

After completing the naming of factors and the calculation of factor scores for individual criminal misdemeanor courts, a multiple regression analysis was done. In the regression, the dependent variable is a court's innovativeness index score and the independent variables are the court's factor scores on the five factors. Table 14 displays the results of a multiple regression analysis for all 128 criminal misdemeanor courts.

Factor scores for five factors explained 39 percent ($R^2 = .39$) of the variance in innovation. The best explanatory variable is the factor score representing the amount and quality of court interaction with agencies administering LEAA. The

Table 14. MULTIPLE REGRESSION ANALYSIS OF DIFFERENCES AMONG
CRIMINAL MISDEMEANOR COURTS WITH RESPECT TO LEVEL
OF INNOVATIVENESS

	Regression I		
Independent Variables	b	(s)	F
1. Factor one score: Size of city	.23	(.61)	7.09***
2. Factor two score: Amount and quality of court interaction with agencies administering the Law Enforcement Assistance Act	.34	(.48)	21.63***
3. Factor three score: Political independence of city government from state government	.10	(.92)	1.83
4. Factor four score: Level of police personnel organization in city	.23	(.57)	8.18***
5. Factor five score: LEAA's evaluation of the job skills of local criminal justice system personnel	.06	(.88)	.63

Dependent Variable: Innovativeness Index Score	
Mean	12.89
Standard deviation	5.21

R^2	.39
F-Ratio	15.68***
Number of cases	128

Notation: b = Beta weight coefficient; (s) = standard error of regression coefficient;
F = F-value of regression coefficient
*** = Significant at the .001 level; ** = significant at the .01 level; * = significant at the
.05 level

positive sign of the interaction beta weight indicates that courts which interact
more with LEAA-related agencies tend to be more innovative than courts which
do not interact.

The next best explanatory variable is the size-of-city factor. The positive sign
of the city-size beta weight indicates, as shown earlier, that courts located in
larger cities tend to be more innovative than courts located in smaller cities.
Third, the level of police personnel organization in a city also explains a
significant portion of the variance in court innovativeness. The positive sign of
this variable shows that cities having more police personnel organization are
more innovative than those in cities where police personnel are not so organized.

The two other factor scores both have positive beta weights, indicating that
greater court innovativeness is related to being in a city which is more politically
dependent on state government and to being in a city where LEAA believes the
job skills of criminal justice personnel are not adequate. However, neither of
these two variables explains a significant portion of the variance in innovativeness.

Now we will examine in more depth the three significant independent variables. First, it is not surprising that the amount and quality of communication between a local court and LEAA-related agencies is the most powerful explanatory variable for innovativeness. After all, the diffusion of innovations is essentially, as Everett M. Rogers (1962: 13) points out, "the human interaction in which one person communicates a new idea to another person." Thus it could be argued that communication is the most basic element of any innovation.

What is interesting here is that it is communication with LEAA-related agencies that is crucial. This would seem to indicate that these agencies function as opinion leaders who furnish information and money to courts contemplating change. It would also seem plausible to assume that the LEAA agencies influence a court's priority of choices among innovations. In fact, LEAA openly admits its desire to direct the path innovation takes in local criminal justice systems by each year publishing a list of "priority" areas that they prefer to fund.[38]

Since we have already discussed in the factor analysis section the possible implications of city size for innovation, we will not elaborate further.

The third most powerful factor score deals with the level of police personnel organization in a city. The positive relationship between police personnel organization and court innovation could be explained in several plausible ways. First, many of the complaints initiated by police organizations relate to their interactions with criminal courts.[39] For example, one frequent gripe is that policemen are forced to sit around courtrooms for long periods of time waiting for their cases to be heard. This waiting is frequently done during the police officer's off-duty hours and thus without pay. Perhaps the pressure from police personnel organizations about these kinds of court-related problems act as a spur to a court's introducing such innovations as full-time prosecutors to replace police or night sessions of court.

Another plausible hypothesis is that heightened activity by one part of the criminal justice system, namely the police, has a psychological spillover effect on other parts of the criminal justice system; for example, the criminal misdemeanor courts. If, for example, the local police department, through innovating, is capturing favorable newspaper headlines and an upsurge of public and political support, it is not inconceivable that the local misdemeanor judges, often elected officials, would want to get into the act with their own innovations.

A third possible explanation is that the organization of police personnel indicates in a city an overall dissatisfaction with the operations of the entire criminal justice system. Thus it would not be surprising to find changes occurring in both police departments and courts at the same time.

Finally, it should be remembered that organization of police personnel is itself an innovation within a police department. So what we are actually seeing is the correlation of one kind of innovation (police) with another kind (court). Perhaps this finding demonstrates that what we call the "criminal justice system" really is a "system" in the sense that changes in one sector have important consequences for other sectors.

CONCLUSION

This paper has examined three major aspects of criminal misdemeanor courts in large American cities. First we have described the organizational characteristics of this universe of courts. The typical criminal misdemeanor court is small but geographically centralized and is staffed by full-time judges who serve for relatively short terms of office, who are either locally elected or appointed by mayors and/or city councils, who are relatively well-paid, and who rotate from civil to criminal cases. Most of the courts simultaneously handle criminal misdemeanor cases and preliminary hearings for felony cases. The other actors in these courts typically include a small number of probation officers with limited responsibilities, and a small number of full-time prosecutors.

Our second major goal was to describe the kinds of innovations which criminal misdemeanor courts have adopted. Analysis of these innovations first reveals that the process of professionalization of judicial personnel in criminal misdemeanor courts has not yet been completed. Second, there is strong evidence that these courts frequently still give inadequate attention to the rights of individual defendants. Third, strong evidence derived from indirect measures indicates that case overload is not a universally significant problem in criminal misdemeanor courts. Fourth, criminal misdemeanor courts are gradually becoming more like felony courts in their organization and activities.

The final aim of this paper was to gain insight into why courts do or do not innovate. A total of 45 independent variables were factor analyzed and produced five significant orthogonal factors: size of city; amount and quality of court interaction with agencies administering the Law Enforcement Assistance Act; political independence of city government from state government; level of police personnel organization in city; LEAA's evaluation of the job skills of local criminal justice system personnel. The three best predictors of variance in innovativeness for the entire sample of courts were amount and quality of court interaction with LEAA-related agencies, city size, and level of police personnel organization.

Two other observations should be made. First, it is striking that the five factors which were isolated from the original 45 independent variables all describe some aspect of the external environment of criminal misdemeanor courts rather than any internal organizational characteristics. This phenomenon is not due to the exclusion of organizational characteristics as variables in the factor analysis.

Several possible explanations exist for the association of the environment with innovations of a criminal misdemeanor court. It could be that the environment socializes misdemeanor court judges to be innovators. Alternatively, it could be that the environment acts primarily as a communicator of ideas about innovation. Or, the environment could function as a source of pressure to innovate. Finally, the environment could be as important as it is simply because courts usually require financial and political support in order to innovate at all. In-depth case studies are obviously needed to flesh out the real significance of an environmental predictor variable such as city size.

Second, we must accept the fact that we are unable to predict innovativeness with any great degree of accuracy. In our multiple regression analysis of the entire group of criminal misdemeanor courts, we were able to account for only 39 percent of the variance in the level of innovativeness. What are some possible explanations for this generally poor predictive ability?

One possibility is that the index of innovativeness used as the dependent variable is inadequate. Innovativeness is obviously not a unidimensional concept, to be operationalized by a single measure. To cope with this contingency, the original 36 innovative items were themselves factor analyzed and five independent orthogonal factors emerged. However, when each court's factor score on each of the five factors was correlated with the index utilized in this paper, all five factors were significantly correlated with the original index. Thus, there seemed to be no advantage in constructing an index made up of factor scores rather than the less exotic index actually used. It does seem clear, however, that additional thought must be given to the question of how to operationalize innovativeness and also how to distinguish between the decision to innovate and the ability to innovate.

Also, it is obvious that studies of criminal misdemeanor courts will continue to be inadequate until more complete and more accurate court records are kept for such key variables as budgets, caseload volume, case disposition, and delay. Exploiting budgetary data, for example, has yielded useful results in the study of state and national decision-making (Sharkansky, 1969). Without knowing how much money courts have available for innovating, or without knowing the size and substance of their caseload, analysis at best can only be suggestive.

APPENDIX

INNOVATIVENESS INDEX SCORES FOR ALL COURTS

Courts by City in Which Located	Innovativeness Index Score
1. Akron, Ohio	12
2. Albuquerque, New Mexico	16
3. Alexandria, Virginia	10
4. Allentown, Pennsylvania	8
5. Amarillo, Texas (Municipal Court)*	7
6. Amarillo, Texas (County Court)	8
7. Amarillo, Texas (Justice of the Peace)	11
8. Arlington, Virginia	13
9. Atlanta, Georgia	11
10. Austin, Texas (Municipal Court)	18
11. Austin, Texas (Justice of the Peace)	3
12. Baltimore, Maryland	16
13. Beaumont, Texas (Municipal Court)	14
14. Beaumont, Texas (County Court)	6
15. Berkeley, California	9
16. Birmingham, Alabama	12
17. Boston, Massachusetts	9
18. Buffalo, New York	24
19. Canton, Ohio	6
20. Cedar Rapids, Iowa	15
21. Charlotte, North Carolina	9
22. Chicago, Illinois	24
23. Cincinnati, Ohio	16
24. Cleveland, Ohio	20
25. Colorado Springs, Colorado	15
26. Columbia, South Carolina	13
27. Columbus, Georgia	6
28. Corpus Christi, Texas (County Court)	7
29. Corpus Christi, Texas (Justice of the Peace)	10
30. Dallas, Texas (Municipal Court)	14
31. Dallas, Texas (County Court)	11
32. Dayton, Ohio	6
33. Dearborn, Michigan	9
34. Denver, Colorado	25
35. Des Moines, Iowa	17
36. Detroit, Michigan	17
37. Elizabeth, New Jersey	10
38. El Paso, Texas (Justice of the Peace)	14
39. Erie, Pennsylvania	13

*In Texas cities, three separate court systems have criminal misdemeanor jurisdiction within each city.

Courts by City in Which Located	Innovativeness Index Score
40. Flint, Michigan	14
41. Fort Lauderdale, Florida	20
42. Fort Worth, Texas (County Court)	11
43. Fresno, California	11
44. Garden Grove, California	11
45. Gary, Indiana	8
46. Glendale, California	14
47. Grand Rapids, Michigan	16
48. Hampton, Virginia	13
49. Hartford, Connecticut	18
50. Hollywood, Florida	12
51. Honolulu, Hawaii	17
52. Houston, Texas (Justice of the Peace A)	6
53. Houston, Texas (Justice of the Peace B)	9
54. Huntington Beach, California	11
55. Huntsville, Alabama	5
56. Independence, Missouri	7
57. Indianapolis, Indiana	19
58. Jackson, Mississippi	3
59. Jersey City, New Jersey	10
60. Kansas City, Kansas	5
61. Kansas City, Missouri	21
62. Knoxville, Tennessee	8
63. Lansing, Michigan	10
64. Las Vegas, Nevada	9
65. Lexington, Kentucky	16
66. Lincoln, Nebraska	15
67. Little Rock, Arkansas	6
68. Livonia, Michigan	15
69. Long Beach, California	16
70. Los Angeles, California	16
71. Lubbock, Texas (Municipal Court)	11
72. Lubbock, Texas (County Court)	5
73. Lubbock, Texas (Justice of the Peace)	11
74. Macon, Georgia	8
75. Madison, Wisconsin	17
76. Memphis, Tennessee	13
77. Miami, Florida	11
78. Milwaukee, Wisconsin	23
79. Minneapolis, Minnesota	23
80. Mobile, Alabama	13
81. Montgomery, Alabama	8
82. Newark, New Jersey	20
83. New Bedford, Massachusetts	13
84. New York, New York	27
85. Norfolk, Virginia	12

Courts by City in Which Located	Innovativeness Index Score
86. Oakland, Virginia	19
87. Oklahoma City, Oklahoma	10
88. Omaha, Nebraska	10
89. Pasadena, California	11
90. Peoria, Illinois	16
91. Philadelphia, Pennsylvania	24
92. Phoenix, Arizona	12
93. Pittsburgh, Pennsylvania	8
94. Portland, Oregon	21
95. Portsmouth, Virginia	6
96. Providence, Rhode Island	3
97. Raleigh, North Carolina	10
98. Richmond, Virginia	9
99. Riverside, California	12
100. Rochester, New York	19
101. Sacramento, California	18
102. Saint Louis, Missouri	7
103. Saint Paul, Minnesota	18
104. Saint Petersburg, Florida	15
105. Salt Lake City, Utah	11
106. San Bernardino, California	14
107. San Jose, California	10
108. Santa Ana, California	22
109. Savannah, Georgia	7
110. Scranton, Pennsylvania	14
111. Seattle, Washington	16
112. Shreveport, Louisiana	6
113. Spokane, Washington	13
114. Springfield, Missouri	11
115. Stamford, Connecticut	15
116. Stockton, California	19
117. Toledo, Ohio	10
118. Topeka, Kansas	8
119. Torrance, California	12
120. Trenton, New Jersey	12
121. Tucson, Arizona	14
122. Tulsa, Oklahoma	18
123. Virginia Beach, Virginia	14
124. Washington, D.C.	24
125. Wichita, Kansas	14
126. Winston-Salem, North Carolina	18
127. Yonkers, New York	20
128. Youngstown, Ohio	8

NOTES

1. President's Commission on Law Enforcement and Administration of Justice (1967: 26).

2. Ibid.

3. The organizational characteristics of American criminal misdemeanor courts have not been systematically or thoroughly studied in the past. The extent of this situation is shown, for example, by the fact that when I began designing this survey in 1971, it took one month of phoning to obtain a complete list of the names, addresses, and phone numbers of these courts and the name of each chief judge. Several publications, however, do contain information about certain aspects of these courts. For example, the U.S. Bureau of the Census compiled in 1970-1971 a list of all American criminal justice agencies, and in the fall of 1971 conducted a national survey of a limited number of organizational characteristics of all non-federal courts. The final report for the two projects can be obtained by writing the Director, Statistics Division, National Institute of Law Enforcement and Criminal Justice, U.S. Department of Justice, Washington, D.C.

4. This factual information concerned the following: court personnel including selection procedure, length of office, and salary category of judges; type of prosecutorial arrangements (that is, primarily by police or by regular prosecutors) and type of probation services; court organization including data on reorganization efforts, jurisdictional scope, and geographical and/or subject-matter decentralization; court caseloads including data on frequency of different kinds of cases, number of cases filed and disposed, number of warrants issued, and amount of criminal fines collected; and finally, court budgets including procedures for drawing up budgets, budgetary track records, and size of budget. All of the survey questionnaires used in this paper were returned by January 1972. The final return rate was 77.6 percent.

5. The inventory of items was constructed after a review of available literature about current trends and discussions with court administration experts. The experts consulted in the summer of 1971 were the following:

(a) Dr. John A. Gardiner, Director of In-House Research, National Institute of Law Enforcement and Criminal Justice, Law Enforcement Assistance Administration, Washington, D.C.

(b) Professor Fannie J. Klein, Associate Director, Institute of Judicial Administration, New York, New York.

(c) Mr. Lester Goodchild, Executive Officer, Criminal Court of the City of New York, New York, New York.

(d) Judge John R. Hargrove, Administrative Judge, District Court of Baltimore City, Baltimore, Maryland.

(e) Judge James A. Belson, Judge, District of Columbia Court of General Sessions, Washington, D.C.

(f) Mr. Neil Lamont, Executive Director, Louisiana Commission on Law Enforcement and Administration of Criminal Justice, Baton Rouge, Louisiana.

(g) Mr. Robert Lipscher, staff member, Institute of Judicial Administration, New York, New York.

(h) Mr. Harold Fait, staff member, National Institute of Law Enforcement and Criminal Justice, Washington, D.C.

(i) Mr. Stan Kalin, staff court specialist, National Institute of Law Enforcement and Criminal Justice, Washington, D.C.

(j) Professor J. Woodford Howard, Department of Political Science, Johns Hopkins University, Baltimore, Maryland.

6. The group was made up of law school professors, political scientists, professional court administrators, misdemeanor court judges, federal law enforcement assistance personnel, and legal research organizations such as the Institute of Judicial Administration. The alternative response categories were extremely innovative, highly innovative, moderately innovative, or slightly innovative.

7. The method used is here described, followed by several alternative weighting methods considered. Three percentages were calculated for each item: the percentage agreeing with either of the top two categories (extremely or highly innovative); the percentage agreeing with either of the middle two categories (highly or moderately innovative); and the percentage agreeing with the bottom two categories (moderately or slightly innovative). Whenever at least 66 percent of the respondents agreed with one category for an item, that category was used; thus 66 percent agreement on the high category gave that item a weight of three; on the middle category, a weight of two; and on the low category, a weight of one. A total of 16 items out of the original 36 fulfilled the 66 percent agreement requirement, for a total of 30 points possible.

The 16 items comprising the innovative index in this paper and their weights are the following:

(a) Full-time prosecutors = 1

(b) Full-time judges = 1

(c) A professional court administrator = 3

(d) Public defender services = 2

(e) Release on suspect's own recognizance as part of bail policy = 1

(f) Computerization of criminal court records = 3

(g) A requirement that judges be lawyers = 1

(h) Weekend sessions of court = 3

(i) A separate traffic court = 1

(j) Administrative adjudication of traffic cases = 3

(k) Summonses instead of arrest warrants for use in certain types of misdemeanors such as littering, trespassing, loitering, etc. = 2

(l) Separate family court for criminal misdemeanors involving members of the same family = 3

(m) Right to a jury trial in misdemeanor cases = 1

(n) Orientation program for new judges = 2

(o) Civil service status for clerical court employees = 1

(p) Indeterminate sentencing = 2

Alternative weighting schemes considered were the following:

(a) Same weighting scheme as original index but item included if more than 50 percent of the respondents agreed on the weight.

(b) The total number of items adopted out of the possible items.

(c) All items included with each item's weight equal to 4 times the number of experts labeling adoption of that item extremely innovative plus 3 times the number labeling adoption as highly innovative plus 2 times the number labeling the adoption as moderately innovative plus 1 times the number labeling the adoption as slightly innovative.

(d) The mean number of item adoptions (calculated for the entire sample) minus the number of items adopted by the specific court in question.

(e) Five separate indexes, each one consisting of a particular court's factor score on one of five factors derived from an orthogonal factor analysis of all 36 items.

8. Examples of these five types of variables include number of full-time judges, use of full-time prosecutors, salary category of judges, budgetary track record, total governmental revenue of city, percent black, median income, population, amount of communication between court and state planning agency, percentage of the members of the state criminal justice planning agency who were judges, whether respondent felt his court was receiving its fair share of assistance funds, and whether respondent felt state planning agency was helpful.

9. Factor scores for each court were computed from the factor loadings of marker variables (loading above ± .50) for each factor. It is important to note that values for the marker variables were standardized by the technique of Z-scoring before these variables were used to calculate factor scores. Outside of these primary methods, other techniques such as computing correlations, constructing frequency distributions, and graphing were used whenever appropriate.

10. Robert K. Merton, quoted in Peterson (1965: 194).

11. President's Commission (1967: 296-297).

12. Chief Justice Warren Berger, report of the Williamsburg Conference on the Administration of Justice, p. 8.

13. For example, the total LEAA budget for fiscal year 1969 was $63 million; for fiscal year 1970 it was $263 million; for fiscal year 1971 it was $480 million; for fiscal year 1972 it was $699 million; for fiscal year 1973 it is $850 million; and for fiscal year 1974, $891 million is proposed.

14. President's Commission (1967: 128).

15. See, for example, Ibid., pp. 296-297; or Advisory Commission on Intergovernmental Relations (1971).

16. President's Commission (1967: 147).

17. Ibid.

18. Ibid., p. 128.

19. Ibid.

20. Ibid., p. 44.

21. Ibid., p. 128.

22. Ibid.

23. It should be noted, however, that some of the limits on maximum time allowed to elapse before trial are a matter of state statute rather than being up to the discretion of local courts. The fact that an innovation may be state-imposed is of significance in this study only because it says that the attitude of the state legislature or upper state courts is important to explain local court innovativeness. In other words, we are interested here in innovativeness of a court system, regardless of the source of that innovativeness.

24. See, for example, Task Force on the Police, President's Commission on Law

Enforcement and Administration of Justice (1967: 17). Also see, for example, Barrett (1965: 92).

25. *Annual Report, 1971,* City of New York Housing and Development.

26. This percentage is calculable from data supplied in the questionnaire returned to the author by the Criminal Court of the City of New York.

27. See Tate v. Short, 401 U.S. 395 (1971).

28. President's Commission (1967: 129).

29. The larger study from which this paper is taken includes an analysis of the diffusion of these innovations among big-city criminal misdemeanor courts.

30. The American Judges Association (formerly known as the North American Judges Association) is a professional organization for judges of courts of first jurisdiction. The association is run by a president, a president-elect, two vice-presidents, a secretary, a treasurer, an executive director, a board of governors made up of representatives from 16 geographical districts, and six members at large. On September 27, 1971, Judge David L. Golden, the association's president, wrote an open letter endorsing this study and urging judges to participate. The headquarters for the organization are located at 188 Chestnut Street, Holyoke, Massachusetts 01040.

31. According to Phillip M. Gregg and Arthur S. Banks (1965), a factor loading value above ± .30 is generally considered to be significant. This paper uses a much higher criterion for significance and thus the validity of the factor names is increased.

32. This technique is used extensively in the factor analysis done by Gregg and Banks (see footnote 31).

33. The definition of "organizational slack" used here was given by Lawrence Mohr (1969: 126). His definition [borrowed from Richard Cyert and James March (1963: 278-279)] was the following: "A great deal of innovation in organizations is 'slack' innovation. After solution of immediate problems, the quest for prestige rather than the quest for organizational effectiveness or corporate profits motivates the adoption of most new programs and technologies."

34. Stephen Halpern, Department of Political Science, State University of New York at Buffalo, provided this information based on research he has done on police personnel organizations in three cities.

35. Law Enforcement Assistance Administration (1970a: 80).

36. Law Enforcement Assistance Administration (1970b: 15).

37. Ibid., p. 3.

38. See, for example, Law Enforcement Assistance Administration (1971: 13-15).

39. This information furnished by Stephen Halpern, Department of Political Science, State University of New York at Buffalo (see footnote 34).

REFERENCES

Advisory Commission on Intergovernmental Relations (1971) Court Reform. Washington, D.C.: U.S. Government Printing Office.

BARRETT, E. L., Jr. (1965) "Criminal Justice: The Problems of Mass Production," in H. W. Jones (ed.) The Courts, the Public and the Law Explosion. Englewood Cliffs, N.J.: Prentice-Hall.

BURNS, T. and G. M. STALKER (1961) The Management of Innovation. London: Tavistock Publications.

City of New York Housing and Development (1971) Annual Report.

CYERT, R. and J. MARCH (1963) A Behavioral Theory of the Firm. Englewood Cliffs, N.J.: Prentice-Hall.

GREGG, P. M. and A. S. BANKS (1965) "Dimensions of political systems: factor analysis of a cross-polity survey." American Political Science Review 59, 3 (September): 602-614.

Law Enforcement Assistance Administration (1970a) LEAA 1970. Washington, D.C.: U.S. Government Printing Office.

――― (1970b) A Program for a Safer, More Just America. Washington, D.C.: U.S. Government Printing Office.

――― (1971) Corrections Program LEAA. Washington, D.C.: U.S. Government Printing Office.

MOHR, L. (1969) "Determinants of innovation in organizations." American Political Science Review 63, 1 (March).

PETERSON, P. G. (1965) "Some Approaches to Innovation in Industry," in G. A. Steiner (ed.) The Creative Organization. Chicago: University of Chicago Press.

President's Commission on Law Enforcement and Administration of Justice (1967) The Challenge of Crime in a Free Society. Washington, D.C.: U.S. Government Printing Office.

ROGERS, E. (1962) Diffusion of Innovations. New York: Free Press.

RUMMEL, R. J. (1967) "Understanding factor analysis." Journal of Conflict Resolution 11, 4: 440-480.

SCHLESINGER, J. A. (1971) "The Politics of the Executive," in H. Jacob and K. Vines (eds.) Politics in the American States. Boston: Little, Brown.

SHARKANSKY, I. (1969) The Politics of Taxing and Spending. New York: Bobbs-Merrill.

――― and R. HOFFERBERT (1971) "Dimensions of State Policy," in H. Jacob and K. Vines (eds.) Politics in the American States. Boston: Little, Brown.

Task Force on the Police, President's Commission on Law Enforcement and Administration of Justice (1967) Task Force Report: Crime and Its Impact—An Assessment. Washington, D.C.: U.S. Government Printing Office.

WIRT, F. et al. (1972) On the City's Rim: Politics and Policy in Suburbia. Lexington, Mass.: D. C. Heath.

Chapter 7

JUDICIAL REFORM: INFORMAL
PROCESSES AND COMPETING EFFECTS

RAYMOND T. NIMMER

The jurisprudential model of criminal justice posits primary reliance on adversary representation and adjudicated dispositions. Under this model, the attorneys represent competing positions of the state and the defendant; these positions are resolved by an impartial judge or jury after presentation of facts and arguments. In practice, however, this model is supplanted by reliance on informal, discretionary decisions. Guilty pleas and dismissals predominate; trials and hearings on legal issues are infrequent.

In discussing both the current practice in criminal courts and the potential of changing that practice, the reference point must, therefore, be the informal process that produces these nonadjudicated results. This informal process consists of an interaction of at least four parties—the defense attorney, the defendant, the prosecutor, and the judge. This interaction leads directly to the dominant, nonadjudicated disposition format. Even in cases where the eventual disposition is a trial or a nonadjudicated disposition preceded by adjudication of one or more issues of law, this interaction controls the timing of the disposition and determines whether an adjudication is necessary.

A variety of objections can be raised to the pattern of outputs produced by this informal process; the rationale underlying the objections varies. For example, one characteristic of the process is that many cases are disposed of speedily and with minimal judicial time. One policy objection to this characteristic is that it fails to test the sufficiency of the evidence supporting criminal charges and does not allow the defendant sufficient time to reflect, analyze, and choose among alternative courses of action. On the other hand, a number of cases take months or years for disposition and a variety of objections have been raised to this phenomenon, which is commonly described as judicial delay. For example, delay leaves a legal cloud over the defendant's head for an extended period and, in certain cases, keeps him in state custody for an extended period without a criminal conviction.

Reforms of judicial practices are recurrently proposed in response to these objections. These reforms often assume the relevance of the adversary-adjudicatory model in criminal justice practice. When implemented, they frequently fail to produce any change in practice and, in fact, may create unexpected, often objectionable results.

The topic of this paper is the process of reform of criminal justice practices at the judicial level. The focus of discussion is a study of the single reform—the omnibus hearing—as implemented in the Federal District Court for the Southern District of California (San Diego). The purpose is not a complete presentation of the results of that study, but the development of a basis for examining and planning judicial reform.

DISCRETIONARY SYSTEM

Criminal court disposition patterns are characterized by a predominance of rapid dispositions involving minimal time input by all concerned parties.[1] Typically, the speedy dispositions are offset by a minority of cases that require both substantial time inputs and lengthy time intervals for disposition. Both of these apparently contradictory results are predictable results of the informal process.

The discussion that follows is a tentative outline of informal processes. It is limited to those criminal justice systems in which plea negotiations, differential sentencing, and similar practices to encourage guilty pleas are common, and to those characteristics of the informal process that are relevant to a discussion of the omnibus hearing.

FACTORS LEADING TO CHOICE OF DISPOSITION

The prevalence of nonadjudicated dispositions is partially explicable in terms of administrative necessity. Courts and prosecutors' offices are characteristically understaffed but must process large caseloads. This imbalance of resources and workload compels an emphasis on efficient disposition. Time-consuming trials and hearings are avoided if such avoidance is consistent with other objectives of the official's perceived role. Guilty pleas, outright dismissals, and diversion, on the other hand, are relatively efficient and are often preferred dispositions.

The prosecutor's desire for efficiency, while persuasive, may be constrained or superseded by other policy considerations. Two of these should be noted. First, in some jurisdictions, there is a perceived necessity to maintain high conviction rates. These rates have potential political importance and, often more importantly, reflect on the prosecutor's self-evaluation of his performance. In connection with this concern, adjudicated dispositions are undesirable because their result is uncertain; that is, they contain a possibility of acquittal. However, dismissals and diversion, both of which do not result in conviction, are also not preferred under this rationale.

Second, the prosecutor makes an evaluation of the "worth" of individual cases in terms of their perceived seriousness; an evaluation that can either enhance the tendency toward a nonadjudicated disposition or override it. In part, this evaluation is a response to resource limitations.[2] Low seriousness (read as "low priority") offenses do not justify substantial prosecutor time and may receive lenient charge or sentence concessions, or even noncriminal disposition, in order to conserve time. On the other hand, serious (high priority) offenses do justify substantial time and may result in trial, if a trial is necessary to obtain conviction. In part, also, the evaluation of cases is a quasi-judicial function. Some defendants are viewed as marginally criminal; a harsh sentence or, perhaps, even a conviction is not warranted. On the other hand, serious criminals "deserve" serious penalties, even if the prosecutor is forced to trial to obtain them.

The position taken by the prosecutor and the extent of his control over actual sentences influences the defense willingness to force an adjudicated disposition. However, in discussing the defense perspective it is necessary to distinguish between the defense attorney and the defendant. Most criminal defense attorneys maintain large caseloads to ensure adequate income levels. As a result, they face time constraints similar to those of the prosecutor, a similarity that is also present in public defenders' offices.[3] They may be unwilling to devote substantial time to each case; and they select among their cases on the basis of an individualized and, to this point, largely unexamined priority scale.

In practice, the defense attorney's role is not solely one of an advocate, but is more accurately described as cooperative advocacy.[4] The defendant's interests are advocated, but most attorneys desire to avoid antagonizing prosecutors and judges with whom they will have future informal dealings. Although the precise limits of cooperation have not been defined, it extends to not forcing a trial without good cause and conforming to informal agreements. The extent of cooperation varies according to the individual's personality, the perceived necessity for cooperation, and the degree of acquired respect for or friendship with individual prosecutors.

As a result, the defense attorney does not seek acquittal at all costs in all cases.[5] In many cases, even in the absence of the constraints noted above, acquittal is not a realistic objective. If the provable guilt of the defendant is apparent, the goal of the defense attorney is the best disposition rather than an acquittal. Negotiation occurs to achieve sentence or charge concessions that would not be available following a trial; it also conforms to the mutual interests of the prosecutor and defense attorney in efficient disposition.

Although negotiation leading to a plea of guilty is most common, informal discussions also may lead to a dismissal of charges. If the prosecution evidence is weak and a trial conviction unlikely, the attorneys' mutual interest in disposition without a time-consuming trial is apparent. On the other hand, if some probability of a trial conviction exists, the defense attorney may be able to persuade the prosecutor that the case is not "worth" the time required for trial. In such cases, either a dismissal or an increased concession in a guilty plea bargain may result.

The defendant is not involved directly in informal discussions but must agree to or reject their results. In part, he defines the positions that the defense attorney takes, but the attorney also influences the defendant through persuasion.

The defendant's desire for a nonadjudicated disposition varies. Some defendants desire to admit guilt on valid charges; others may believe or be persuaded that informal disposition offers sentence or charge concessions not available if a trial occurs. Additionally, informal disposition may appear to be a speedier disposition; a result consistent with the defendant's desire to be released from pretrial custody or to end the uncertainty of pending charges. However, some defendants insist on trial and others require strong persuasion to agree to nonadjudicated dispositions.

Judges are affected by many of the same considerations that influence the prosecutor. However, the decisions made by judges and the policies that they follow tend to be more individualized. Most jurisdictions lack central policy-making processes for judges.

Direct judicial participation in decisions leading to a nonadjudicated disposition is sporadic. In some cities, largely as a result of idiosynccatic tradition, judges control charging or plea bargaining decisions.[6] Also, with respect to minor offenses and during the early stages of the process for felony charges, judges frequently exercise discretion to dismiss cases. These dismissals may be based on an evaluation of apparent evidence, or they may be based on policy considerations reflecting either the pressure of inadequate resources or an evaluation of the seriousness of the offense.[7]

More often, direct judicial involvement in achieving a guilty plea disposition is limited by ethical considerations and legal constraints, which raise the possibility of reversal if a plea is obtained with judicial involvement. The judge's role is also limited by expediency. For the most part, the judge's information concerning informal activities is limited to information obtained during court appearances. He can become directly involved in informal decision-making only with personal effort; this requires additional time involvement and this additional time may not be available. However, direct judicial involvement occurs when the judge perceives sufficient incentive to become involved in the case; the nature of the incentive varies according to the individual judge.

On the other hand, indirect judicial involvement is common. The judge is an integral part of the formal system and cases must intermittently appear before him. Therefore, his attitudes as perceived by the other parties affect informal practices. If, for example, judges control sentence decisions, informal practices may seek to arrange a disposition before a judge whose sentencing policies are appropriate; the defense seeks a lenient sentencing judge and the prosecutor seeks one whose sentencing policies fit the prosecutor's assessment of the case. On the other hand, in many systems, judges routinely follow prosecutor recommendations; this acquiescence gives added leverage to the prosecutor during negotiations.

Although relatively infrequent, adjudicated dispositions occur in all systems. Trials result from a failure of the informal system to agree to a nonadjudicated disposition. This occurs if the concessions offered by the state appear inadequate to the defense, because either its evaluation of likely success in adjudication or its evaluation of the worth of the case differs from that of the prosecutor. On the other hand, a trial might occur when the evidence raises a sufficient possibility of acquittal for the defense to refuse a guilty plea, but insufficient for the prosecution to dismiss charges (for example, the case is serious and warrants adjudication). Again, because this is an informal system, individual attitudes of defense attorneys define the level of probable acquittal that is sufficient to force adjudication.

FACTORS DETERMINING DISPOSITION TIMING

A dominant factor leading to nonadjudicated dispositions is the necessity for efficient use of resources. Efficiency in that context is a concept distinct from disposition speed. Time-consuming appearances could be telescoped into a small number of days. Similarly, long time intervals may involve minimal judge or attorney time.

In practice, however, informal considerations create a predominance of both efficient and speedy dispositions. Long-pending cases may reflect poorly in evaluation of prosecutors' or public defenders' offices.[9] Similarly, in part as a result of contemporary concern over judicial delay, many judges and some court systems regard the speed of disposition as an evaluative index of their performance. For the private defense attorney, speedy dispositions represent a rapid turnover of caseload and fees. For defendants, they shorten the period of anxiety and often reduce the time spend in pretrial custody.

The desire for speedy disposition is, however, less intense and more subject to manipulation than that focus on efficiency. Although the prosecutor desireses rapid disposition of his caseload, he is not likely to seek this objective at the cost of additional trials or of losing convictions in serious cases. An analogous limitation applies to the public defender. Also, defendants faced with the inevitability of conviction may desire to postpone disposition.[10] The private defense attorney, on the other hand, may derive adequate income from the turnover of other cases and, in fact, delaying some cases may permit him to focus attention on cases that, for monetary or other reasons, he grants priority.

In general, the point at which the informal system reaches a mutually acceptable result determines the timing of nonadjudicated disposition. The timing of an adjudicated disposition is determined by the decision that adjudication of some or all issues is necessary, and by the additional time required to schedule and prepare for a mutually acceptable date for adjudication.

Speedy dispositions predominate, but many cases take months or years for disposition. These lengthy dispositions reflect a protracted informal process. The possible explanations for protraction are varied. It often reflects repeated haggling over a nonadjudicated disposition. On the other hand, it might reflect an intent to force adjudication, with a delay in preparation caused by the press of other cases. Additionally, delay may indicate that the defendant does not desire speedy disposition but wishes to defer resolution of the case. Finally, either side may employ delay to weaken the opposition's evidence and the stringency of its demands.

The role of the judge varies. Potentially he can be a decisive actor; he has the authority to schedule the dates of later appearances. While the nature of the formal process provides a strong power base, judicial influence on timing is most often indirect and supervision of the progress of the case toward disposition is minimal. Some judges express a strong interest in speedy disposition of their caseload. In such circumstances, even without direct pressure on the parties, the state interest may shape informal decision-making; given the authoritative position of the judge, attorneys who repeatedly deal with him desire to cooperate with his wishes. Most judges, however, permit the informal process to flow at its own pace. No pressure, indirect or direct, is placed on case flow; continuances are granted pro forma. This passive role avoids time-consuming, repetitive judicial intervention; it permits the defendant to take full advantage of informal discussions; it avoids forcing an unprepared party to premature disposition; and it allows informal discussions, which commonly result in nonadjudicated dispositions, to have a thorough opportunity to achieve this result.

Direct pressure to force a case to disposition occurs where the judge perceives a sufficient motivation to do so. For example, some judges may seek speedy dispositions in order to protect defendants. On the other hand, in Chicago, for example, direct pressure is often applied to avoid a mandatory dismissal under the Illinois speedy trial rule.[11]

The informal interaction of the parties is a process of limited negotiation. While many cases involve actual bartering, others are characterized by coalesence of interests and immediate agreement. To the extent that negotiation occurs, it does so within the policy, pragmatic, and resource constraints discussed above.

In negotiation, the defendant's ability to force adjudication is a strong tool in his favor. On the other hand, the prosecutor's tools include the ability to manipulate charges and sentences and, often, the ability to win an adjudication.

As a result, one point of reference is a prediction of the likely result of adjudication. Since individual assessments of this factor shape the nature of the disposition acceptable to either side, the flow of information concerning the opposition's evidence affects the timing of the disposition.

In all jurisdictions, the defense has a limited, formal right to obtain information concerning the prosecution's evidence; a right that can be invoked on formal motion in court. In most cases, however, knowledge of the prosecution evidence is obtained informally. In many situations it is apparent without an actual exchange of information; in others, prosecutors transfer extensive information as a form of cooperation between attorneys.[12]

Prosecutor discovery of defense evidence is, in statute law, severely limited. In practice, moreover, it is often unimportant because the defense has little affirmative evidence. When it is potentially important, it may be transmitted during informal discussions.

In addition to the flow of information, a variety of other factors determine the timing of the disposition. For example, does the attorney have other business that conflicts with a scheduled appearance or that has delayed his preparation for that appearance? Have the parties reached an agreement, or is there an impass in negotiations? Will delaying the case weaken the evidence of the other side? Does the defendant desire a rapid disposition? Will the judge permit the parties to delay the case or will he attempt to force a speedy disposition?

OMNIBUS HEARING

The omnibus hearing was promulgated in 1967 by the American Bar Association Minimum Standards of Criminal Justice.[13] It proposes a model of criminal justice procedures differing markedly from both the adversary model and the pragmatic model followed in current practice. The omnibus hearing keys a variety of results to the premise that the flow of information between the parties is, or can be made, the key determinant of the flow of the case toward disposition. A forced, early, and complete flow of information, coupled with a thorough discussion of issues, is established. Hypothetically, this sets the stage for an early disposition of all cases and a more efficient use of judge time by avoiding unnecessary appearances and continuances of scheduled appearance dates.

Although commonly described as the omnibus hearing, the subject our discussion includes more than a single appearance in court. It is a three-step process involving substantial reliance on out-of-court interaction between attorneys supplemented by increased judicial supervision of caseflow.

The first phase involves discussion between attorneys without judicial supervision. The focal point is a semi-formal conference of counsel. During this period there is an exchange of information amounting to a virtually complete description of prosecution evidence and a full discussion of the case. A checklist motion form, containing a summary of potential items of disclosure and motions, is used to ensure that full discovery occurs and that all factual and legal issues are discussed. Although plea discussions occur during this phase, the emphasis is on information exchange and issue identification.

The second phase initiates judicial supervision. It begins at the omnibus hearing; under the American Bar Association proposal, the hearing occurs shortly after arraignment on the indictment.

The purposes of the hearing are numerous and interrelated. It provides a forum to enforce the disclosure rules of the new process; immediate rulings on disputed discovery issues are available. Also, the judge discusses the case with the attorneys to ensure that all issues have been identified and raised. Any motions or defenses not identified on the form or discussed during the hearing are waived. The hearing also provides a focal point for the simplification of motion practices. Notation on the checklist form is sufficient to raise an issue; written motions and briefs are unnecessary.

Motions not requiring the presentation of evidence may be decided during the hearing; other hearings, as well as trials, are scheduled for later court appearances that minimize elapsed time to disposition of the case. The assumption is that, since full exchange of information and discussion of issues has occurred, the scheduled appearances will routinely be complied with.

The third stage of the process is devoted solely to trial preparation. It is labeled a pretrial conference and occurs shortly before the case scheduled for trial in those cases in which the trial is likely to be complex. Since few cases proceed to trial, and many of those that do need no final preparation, this element of the process is of little importance.

SAN DIEGO EXPERIENCE

The omnibus hearing was implemented in San Diego during 1967. It achieved the objective of establishing routine disclosure of prosecution files to the defense. However, omnibus apparently increased, rather than decreased, elapsed time to disposition of the cases filed and, further, increased the amount of judge time involvement in individual cases. Rather than compressing informal decision-making into earlier periods in the judicial process, which result might have produced a saving of judge time and a reduction of elapsed time to disposition, the omnibus hearing prolonged informal decision-making in many cases.

Our study was conducted in 1970-71.[14] Briefly, the methodology involved analysis of randomly selected cases filed one year before and after the introduction of the omnibus hearing. The samples were taken for periods that, respectively, ended three months prior to the effective date of the omnibus hearing and began three months following that date. Cases were sampled from three crime types: heroin importation, marijuana importation, and minor drug violations. However, due to changed border enforcement practices, the marijuana samples reflected a large increase in the number of cases filed for the post-omnibus period. Thus, there was a possibility that the post-omnibus marijuana cases differed in substance from those filed prior to the omnibus hearing, and marijuana cases could not be used for comparative analyses. For the purposes of this article, a representative of the American Bar Foundation revisited San Diego to take additional samples of cases involving interstate transportation of stolen vehicles. The analyses in this paper deal solely with cases involving auto theft, heroin importation, and minor drug offenses.

A sample of cases was also taken from 1970. This sample involved a 50 percent sampling of marijuana, heroin, and minor drug offenses filed during calendar year 1970. The analysis of these samples was supplemented by informal interviews, analysis of printed materials (including available transcripts), and observation of 1970 practices. Time series analyses were precluded by administrative and caseload changes occurring during the period from 1966 to 1970.

Discovery

As a result of the omnibus hearing, early disclosure of prosecution evidence became routine practice in San Diego. During 1968, use of the informal disclosure aspects of the omnibus hearing was high; over 75 percent of the cases in the 1968 sample participated in omnibus. In examining this high level of usage, it is necessary to discuss the incentives of each of the three relevant parties: judges, defense attorneys, and prosecutors.

During 1968 there were two judges on the San Diego bench. One had participated in the initial drafting of the omnibus proposal and was a strong advocate of the concept. The other judge was equally committed to the experiment. Thus, implementation was accomplished under a strongly favorable and unified judicial attitude.

Since we are dealing with two individuals, it is unproductive to attempt to explore the reasons for their enthusiasm. Undoubtedly, however, they believed that omnibus would add fairness to the court process and would expedite dispositions.

Prior to omnibus' implementation, the judges held meetings to introduce the omnibus concept to the attorneys. During these discussions the judges expressed strong support for omnibus. Following implementation, they willingly assumed the time commitment necessary to implement the formal stages of the process and to enforce disclosure of prosecution evidence. With the exception of requests for the identity of informants, they routinely granted all defense requests for disclosure.

Omnibus was established by court rule, but participation in individual cases was voluntary at the option of both the prosecutor and the defense attorney. In practice, both attorneys routinely elected to participate. In part, this is attributable to their desire to cooperate with the expressed desires of the judges. However, the attorneys were also influenced by the expectation that benefits would accrue to them during omnibus proceedings.

The expectations of the defense attorneys are not difficult to identify. Although federal discovery rules are broader than state rules, prior to omnibus, formal discovery involved time-consuming motions and did not extend to all elements of the prosecution case. Under omnibus, however, the defense was guaranteed virtually full information; this information was obtained informally and early in the process. Full knowledge of the prosecution case would permit a more accurate assessment of the probabilities of successful adjudication and would serve to verify or contradict the defendant's story.

Omnibus involves three elements that might lead some defense attorneys to decline participation. The first is that, in form, omnibus requires reciprocal disclosure of defense evidence. In practice, however, defense disclosure was seldom important, the defense having no affirmative evidence to present. On the other hand, in cases where affirmative defense evidence was present, if the defense objected, it was not forced to disclose evidence.

The second area of possible difficulty was that the omnibus proposal requires that the defense specify all issues and defenses to be raised in the case; issues not specified on the checklist form or raised during the hearing are waived. The potential objection to being forced into an early commitment to a specific line of defense is apparent. However, in practice, there was little or no pressure on the defense to comply with this element of omnibus. The issue of waiver of an unspecified issue was not raised in any case in our sample. Similarly, an examination of checklist motion forms reveals a pattern of pronounced over-indication of issues. In practice, defense attorneys were permitted to indicate that virtually all issues were possible and to defer decisions concerning defense tactics until later in the process.

These patterns with respect to both defense disclosure and issue specification reveal a key element of the manner in which omnibus was implemented in San Diego. The emphasis of judicial pressure focused on obtaining prosecutor disclosure. Other elements of the process were considered secondary or as the derivative products of increased prosecutor disclosure.

The third area of potential detriment for the defense attorney is that participation required additional time in court and, for cases that would have been disposed of at arraignment, two to five weeks delay to obtain disclosure. In most cases, defense counsel regarded these factors as justified by the additional information received from the prosecution and by their desire to cooperate with the judges. Also, the discussions during the omnibus hearing carried a potential of identifying weak points in prosecution evidence. Significantly, however, in approximately 15 percent of the cases in the sample, participation in omnibus did not occur because the defendant plead guilty at arraignment. In these cases, informal pressures including the nature of the plea offer and, possibly, the clarity of the evidence, made further delay undesirable. Similarly, there are indications that the Federal Defenders Office, which handles a large portion of the cases in San Diego, minimized its time input by assigning one or two attorneys to handle all omnibus hearings.

A more difficult analysis of incentive concerns the prosecutor. The prosecution refused to participate in omnibus in less than 4 percent of the cases in the 1968 sample. In each refusal, the apparent reason was that the defendant was charged with major importation of drugs. (In an additional group of cases, it is unclear from our data whether omnibus disclosure occurred. In these cases the defendant was a fugitive during the early portion of the case and, when he was apprehended, the case proceeded directly to disposition.) Similarly, once the prosecution elected to participate, it voluntarily complied with disclosure in most instances. Seventy-seven percent of these cases were processed with no defense request for judicial enforcement of disclosure. Of the remaining 23 percent, an undetermined number of the requests for enforcement and the court orders granting disclosure were pro forma and did not reflect actual resistance.

In part, the high level of voluntary compliance is tied to the strong advocacy of the judges. Disclosure of prosecution evidence occupied a central position in the literature and in public discussions.[15] Further, the process provided a routine court appearance at which the judicial interests could be restated and enforced. In practice, although most cases did not require an order enforcing disclosure, discovery issues were the most frequently discussed matters at the omnibus hearing. Thus, in part, the voluntary compliance reflects the inevitability of enforcement and the desire to avoid antagonizing the judges.

Also important is the fact that disclosure reflected merely an extension of prior informal practice. Prior to omnibus, the prosecutor's office made its file available in appropriate cases to defense attorneys. The change was not, therefore, from complete nondisclosure to full disclosure, but from discretionary disclosure to routine full disclosure.

Finally, voluntary compliance occurred as a result of a trade-off in which the prosecutor relinquished secrecy in return for potential benefits in other areas. Although, as we discuss later, the expected benefits did not materialize, the increased disclosure was not discontinued because it had little or no apparent impact on the type of disposition of the cases.

The nature of the trade-off is apparent when we examine the manner in which the discovery concept was promoted. The literature distributed by the court sets the theme. Disclosure was promoted only partially as an objective in its own right, and additionally as a tool to achieve other objectives. Many of these objectives appeared desirable to the prosecutor; for example, reduced post-conviction challenges, more frequent guilty pleas, earlier guilty pleas, firmer schedules for court appearances, and early and firm listings of defense issues to be raised.

An article authored by the chief prosecutor at that time raises many specific objections to increased disclosure. However, it is prefaced by the author's admission that the circumstances in the district made the innovation essential.[16] The circumstances referred to were indicated by an assistant prosecutor: "the purpose of the increased discovery was to increase guilty pleas and to facilitate firm scheduling of appearances in court." Faced with a large caseload and small staff, the prosecutor apparently wasted substantial staff time in preparing for scheduled appearances that were never held. The prospect was that the omnibus hearing, and the broad discovery that was part of the concept, would help to alleviate this lost time.

The compliance was facilitated by the fact that the discovery had no observable impact on the rate of trials, as shown in Table 1. At first, this may appear unexpected. However, the explanation lies in the role played by the disclosure in the context of the informal system in San Diego.

The disclosure did not weaken the prosecution's case, but provided other benefits to the defense. One attorney remarked that he could not rely on the prosecution's evidence in preparing his case for trial. Even if the files were complete, they were prepared from a dissimilar viewpoint and would not sufficiently explore issues beneficial to the defense. However, the attorney did indicate that the disclosure provided a tool to examine the accuracy of his client's description of the crime. Similarly, the disclosed evidence often was useful to persuade otherwise reluctant clients to accept favorable plea bargains. Other defense attorneys took a less pessimistic view of the value of the prosecution files, but most emphasized the intra-defense impact of the disclosure. Rather than strengthening their case against the prosecution, the major impact was to test their client's credibility.

Several prosecutors noted this internal use of the disclosed evidence. However, they emphasized a second explanation for the lack of a strong, observable impact on the disposition of cases. It was their suggestion that the discovery produced offsetting effects. Cases that were borderline with respect to a defense decision to plead guilty, but in which the state's evidence was strong, would be pushed toward a guilty plea. When the evidence was weak and there existed some tendency on the part of the defense toward a trial, the case might be pushed away from a guilty plea. For most cases, however, disclosure was

Table 1. PERCENT OF TOTAL CASES DISPOSED OF BY TRIAL,
              BY CHARGE AND YEAR

	1966	*1968*
Heroin	11 (44)*	20 (49)
Minor drug	14 (61)	9 (64)
Auto theft	8 (24)	14 (29)

*Number in parenthesis is total cases in sample.

largely irrelevant since the factual basis for prosecution was simple and understood by all.

The chief prosecutor in 1970, who was previously a defense attorney, also distinguished among the cases within his caseload. However, he preceived no negative effect as a consequence of disclosure with respect to more than a few of the cases. He indicated that, although some assistants felt that disclosure hindered their preparation, they would be hard-pressed to cite a single, specific illustration. For cases in which a protracted series of negotiations or an eventual trial occurred, both sides would be fully prepared before the termination of the case regardless of whether disclosure occurred. For the bulk of the caseload, however, a guilty plea would be the eventual product regardless of the presence of broad disclosure. In these cases, he felt, the disclosure served merely to add an element of fairness.

Effect on Informal Decision-Making

Although increased disclosure did occur, the other anticipated benefits of the omnibus hearing did not. Rather, our data suggest that omnibus proved counterproductive in other areas of concern.

The underlying thesis of omnibus with respect to disposition timing and case scheduling might be restated: benefits in these areas would be achieved if the concentrated, early information flow compressed the informal decision-making into the period immediately prior to and around the omnibus hearing itself. The data, however, suggest that, rather than compressing informal decision-making, the omnibus hearing served to prolong the informal process in some cases.

The elapsed time to disposition increased for cases in each of the three crime types sampled, as shown in Table 2. The significance of this increase is best explicated by a closer examination of three patterns.

A. Informal Decisions in Early Disposition Cases. While omnibus did not affect the frequency of guilty pleas, it did affect the timing of decisions to enter a guilty plea. The defense decision to comply with omnibus practices frequently resulting in a decision to defer a guilty plea until disclosure was completed. One comparative index to measure this shift is the point (measured in terms of the

Table 2. MEAN NUMBER OF DAYS FROM FILING OF CHARGE
            TO DISPOSITION

	1966	*1968*
Heroin	100 (44)*	160 (49)
Minor drug	52 (61)	147 (64)
Auto theft	33 (24)	85 (29)

*Number in parenthesis is total cases in sample.

number of court appearances following arraignment) at which either a guilty plea was entered or a firm indication was stated in court that a plea would be entered. The data are shown in Table 3.

In addition to the obvious shift, two relevant observations derive from this table. The first is that, prior to the omnibus hearing, the informal process produced a large number of early pleas of guilty. The second is that the shifting effect was apparently localized around the omnibus hearing step (second appearance) and the immediately subsequent appearance.

The early disposition pattern reflects a discretionary adjustment to an extremely heavy caseload. In 1966-68, San Diego was the federal district court with the heaviest load of criminal cases per authorized judgeship. Similarly, the district functioned with a small, overworked prosecutors office.

As a result of the imbalance between caseload and resources, the prosecutor engaged in extensive negotiations that began virtually from the point at which the criminal complaint was filed. Also, in part, the ability to terminate cases early must be attributed to the nature of the caseload; border offenses predominate in the district and often present few, if any, issues for negotiation. Also, the negotiating tools used by the prosecutor were highly effective. One tool involved the statutes charged. With respect to heroin cases, the statute most frequently charged involved extremely high minimum and maximum penalties.[18] The purpose in charging this statute was often not to achieve a conviction under the higher statute, but simply to obtain negotiating leverage. All of the guilty plea cases in the 1966 heroin sample produced charge reductions; a lesser charge being substituted for the high-penalty statute. A

Table 3. CUMULATIVE PERCENT OF GUILTY PLEA CASES DISPOSED OF OR INDICATING INTENT TO PLEAD GUILTY BY STEPS OF THE PROCESS

	1966	1968*
Heroin:		
arraignment	16	12
second appearance	47	43
third appearance	61	55
Minor drug:		
arraignment	46	25
second appearance	68	59
third appearance	74	76
Auto theft:		
arraignment	71	22
second appearance	95	59
third appearance	95	91

*For 1968 cases the second appearance is the omnibus hearing.

second negotiating tool was that of offering extremely light sentences. Finally, the judges in the district, recognizing the prevalence of negotiations, regarded them as essential and most often followed prosecutor sentence recommendations.

In addition to extensive plea negotiation, the prosecutor followed a highly selective prosecution policy. Criminal complaints were presented to the office from a variety of sources. A rough estimate suggests that as many as 50 percent of all complaints presented were not prosecuted. The net product of the screening was that prosecutions were concentrated on cases in which the government's case was relatively strong.

The resultant concentration of early guilty pleas was weakened under omnibus, but the data suggest that the shift was dissipated by the court appearance immediately following the omnibus hearing. Two alternative explanations exist to explain this result. The first is that the omnibus process produced off-setting effects—the disposition of some early guilty plea cases was deferred, but other cases that would not have previously plead guilty during this earlier period were moved forward by the increased disclosure. Although this explanation might be applicable to some cases, the comments of attorneys involved in the process suggest that an off-setting effect, if any occurred, was applicable to only a small number of the cases.

The second, more plausible explanation is the continuing existence of informal pressures and interests in pleading guilty early. The desire to participate in omnibus justified a deferral of guilty pleas. However, when the justification ended, the inclination to plead guilty persisted. Deferring the guilty plea until a later appearance in court did not reflect the abandonment of efficiency-oriented procedures. Instead, it reflected a decision by defense attorneys to defer acceptance of a plea until omnibus disclosure occurred; this decision is explicable in the discussion previously presented concerning compliance with disclosure.

B. In-Custody Defendants. Cases involving defendants held in pretrial custody generally involve an increased defense interest in speedy disposition. While such defendants may receive credit for time served in the eventual sentence, speedy disposition tends to minimize length of time that the defendant spends in custody. Similarly, the federal rules of criminal procedure require that defendants in custody be given priority handling. As a result, both the prosecutor and the judge are alerted and react to the need for speedier disposition in such cases.

In San Diego the effect of the omnibus hearing on elapsed time to disposition was minimized or eliminated for cases involving in-custody defendants (see Table 4). Although the number of in-custody cases in our sample was small, two

Table 4. MEAN DAYS FROM FILING OF CHARGE TO DISPOSITION FOR
CASES IN WHICH DEFENDANT WAS IN CUSTODY

	1966	1968
Heroin	50	64
Minor drug	51	59
Auto theft	20	30

observations are suggested by the data. In both samples, in-custody defendants were handled speedily (100 days average difference) regardless of whether their cases were terminated by guilty plea or trial. In the second year, although in-custody cases experienced the early guilty plea shift discussed above, they went through the greater number of steps prior to disposition with no statistically significant elapsed time increase, as shown in Table 4.

The explanation lies in a reduction of the time-lapse intervals for each early step in the court process. In-custody cases were arraigned with more speed than noncustody cases, a phenomenon occurring in both years. Equally important, the interval between arraignment and the omnibus hearing was shortened for in-custody cases. This was accomplished in the scheduling of the omnibus hearing made at arraignment.[19] Finally, the data suggests that there was prompt compliance with omnibus in in-custody cases; only one of the cases in the sample experienced a continuance of the scheduled omnibus hearing, while continuances occurred in 15 percent of the noncustody cases.

C. Informal Decisions in Other Cases. The omnibus hearing anticipates that, following informal disclosure and discussion, cases could be scheduled for firm appearances that promote an orderly flow to disposition. This anticipation was based on the related notions that omnibus would enable attorneys to make early decisions concerning the case and that later scheduled appearances would voluntarily be complied with or, failing that, that the judges could enforce the later schedules.

In practice, these expectations reflect an overly simplistic view of the causes of noncompliance with scheduled appearances. The extent of compliance is determined by a number of factors. Included are the state of plea discussions, the presence of schedule conflicts within the defense attorney's caseload, the defense interest in deferring disposition, and other informal factors. In San Diego, due to these factors, the extent of schedule certainty following the omnibus hearing was similar to that found in cases at comparable points in the court process prior to the implementation of omnibus.

One measure of comparative schedule compliance is to examine the rate of compliance with schedules set at omnibus hearings in relation to the rate of compliance with schedules existing at a similar point in preomnibus cases. In the

1968 sample, only 34 percent of all cases holding an omnibus hearing complied with the later scheduled appearance; 36 percent of the 1966 cases complied with appearances set on the first court appearance following arraignment. Similarly, the rate of continuances of scheduled appearances did not decrease in the 1968 sample, as shown in Table 5.

It is clear that scheduled dates for trials or hearings did not reflect a firm decision to proceed with the scheduled appearance. This result should not be misread as reflecting the court's failure to discuss legal and factual issues during the omnibus hearing. Although discussion of discovery matters predominated, these matters do relate to the facts of the case and the discussion was accompanied by discussion of potential issues. More accurately, this result reflects a failure of omnibus to compress informal decision-making into the preomnibus interval so that the schedules requested would reflect firm decisions to proceed.

One method that might have been used to obtain firm schedules would have been to force compliance; refusing requests for continuances in the absence of extremely good cause and barring or discouraging pleas after trial or hearing schedules had been made. However, the judges were unable to engage in this enforcement in the absence of a pre-existing compression of informal decision-making.

There is an unstated but obvious element of expediency involved. While the judges could afford the time for enforcement of disclosure at the omnibus hearing, they could not afford to hold a trial in anything approaching the number of cases set for trial after omnibus. Such a massive use of adjudicatory mechanisms could not be tolerated for even the short period necessary to accomplish a change in the meanings attached by attorneys to requested schedules.

Another explanation suggested in our interviews is that denying requests for continuances or refusing to accept guilty pleas was viewed as an unfair procedure. The judges were aware of the fact that the negotiated plea was the primary method of disposition for their cases. The continuance request was frequently regarded as a vehicle for permitting negotiations to run their full course. Since negotiation practices had not been compressed, the judges believed that enforcing schedules in the face of a discretionary process that continued to

Table 5. MEAN NUMBER OF CONTINUANCES

	1966	1968
Heroin	1.6	2.6
Minor drug	0.7	2.0
Auto theft	0.5	1.9

rely on judicial willingness to grant extensions would deny the defendant the fruits of a potentially favorable bargain and force unprepared parties into adjudication. This potential unfairness, apparent in individual cases, overcame the generalized judicial interest in enforcing schedules.

D. Judge Time. Omnibus increased the average time spent in court for cases handled in San Diego. In examining comparative time in court, we constructed an estimation of time spent on the various appearances held in each case.[20] The estimates were applied to appearance information for cases in the sample. The before-after comparison revealed an increase during 1968 roughly equivalent to the time estimated for the omnibus hearing appearance.[21] Recomputation of the comparative figures, deleting time estimates for omnibus, indicated that except for added time at omnibus hearings the cases in the two samples were handled similarly (see Table 6).

This result is understandable in light of the performance of the pre-existing informal process. The frequency of early guilty plea dispositions was a part of the generalized thrust toward minimization of judge time in court per case. As a result of this thrust, 65 percent of the 1966 sample cases were handled with estimated in-court time of less than or equal to the equivalent of a 3-step disposition pattern; indictment, arraignment, disposition hearing. For such cases, omnibus frequently functioned as a fourth step. Given the already minimal time input, it could not have achieved any offsetting time decreases.

In other cases including but not limited to cases going to trial, omnibus also apparently served as an additional step. Reductions of continuances and trials did not occur. Also, omnibus was seldom used to dispose of legal motions, except for those relating to discovery; cases requiring adjudication of motions continued to require additional hearings. The hearing's primary function, enforcing disclosure, was not routinely performed in cases prior to 1967.

The additional judge time is best described as a trade-off. The omnibus proposal assumes that, in order to ensure routine disclosure, judicial intervention at the omnibus hearing is necessary. The two judges willingly accepted this additional court appearance in order to achieve disclosure. In so doing, they compromised the efficiency-oriented thrust of the pre-existing process.

Regardless of the method of estimation, the increased expenditure of judge

Table 6. INDEX OF ESTIMATED TIME IN COURT
DELETING OMNIBUS HEARING (median value)

	1966	1968
Heroin	7.0	7.0
Minor drug	6.5	7.0
Auto theft	5.1	5.8

time was substantial. During 1967-68, omnibus hearings lasted approximately 10 to 25 minutes per case. Averaging over 1,700 cases per year (the annual caseload in San Diego), the additional judge time amounts to approximately 425 judge-hours. Viewed from another perspective, the bulk of the cases in the district were handled with a three-step or less process which could not have required more than 40 minutes in court per case. The addition of omnibus in these cases increased judge time by a factor of almost 40 percent.

OMNIBUS IN 1970

The fact that our study began in 1970-71 limited the nature of data available concerning the events surrounding implementation. However, it provided an opportunity to observe an administrative restructuring of a reform concept. The omnibus hearing observed in 1970 resembled neither the theoretical omnibus hearing format nor the actual format followed during 1967-68. This modification occurred without a formal change of policy or purpose, and transformed the omnibus procedure to fit more comfortably into the overriding system rationale of efficiency.

Between 1968 and 1970-71, the San Diego district court underwent a number of changes relevant to omnibus. Both judges present at the inception of omnibus left the court. Second, legislation created the position of magistrate, a quasi-judicial officer with authority to handle minor cases and preliminary matters in more serious criminal cases. Third, as a result of the pattern beginning in late 1968, the caseload of the district increased. Fourth, following three years of working with omnibus, disclosure of prosecution evidence became accepted practice within the district.

In 1970, omnibus was a more efficient mass production process. Whereas in 1967 the hearings required between 10 and 25 minutes and individualized attention to each case, by 1970 the hearings lasted no more than five minutes and most were completed within one minute. A single prosecutor appeared for all omnibus hearing hearing. One or two members of the staff of the federal defender's office handled the omnibus hearing caseload for that office. The judicial officer, no longer a judge, but rather the magistrate, devoted only one day per week to omnibus matters; between 60 and 80 hearings were handled in a single day.

Under this format, the omnibus hearing was transformed from an appearance in which the judicial officer discussed and suggested the proper progression of the case, into an appearance in which all of the substantive discussions were disposed of by stipulation. At each "hearing," the defense attorney filed a stipulated motion form on which he indicated issues to be raised during the case.

However, once these forms were filed with the magistrate, they seldom were a factor in the later progression of the case. During the hearing, the judicial officer inquired into the need for schedules for trials, disposition, or hearings, and ascertained whether the informal discovery had been completed. No effort was made to discuss the facts of the case. Also, informal discussions between attorneys prior to the omnibus hearing were compressed into a mass production model. Typically, these discussions consisted primarily of the prosecutor handing the defense attorney a copy of his file. Discussion of issues was infrequent, and any discussions that occurred related primarily to plea negotiation.

The primary purpose of the hearing was the scheduling of future court appearances. However, examination of a sample of cases for 1970 found that the schedules were seldom followed. Excluding cases that indicated an intent to plea guilty, only 15 percent of the cases in the 1970 sample conformed to the schedule indicated at the omnibus hearing.

During the interval between 1968 and 1970 two devices had been experimented with in an attempt to ameliorate the recurring scheduling problems found in the district. The first was the institution of an intermediate scheduling device for cases, labeled "trial call." This scheduling calls for an appearance by counsel on the data scheduled to indicate whether a trial date should be set. A second device was a formal order of court requiring that, once a case was set for trial, no plea of guilty to a lesser charge than that contained in the complaint should be accepted. Since reduced charges were a primary plea bargain format, this order attempted to minimize bargaining after a case was set for trial.

Despite these two devices, the district continued to experience a major problem with respect to trial dropouts (cases set for trial that either involved a continuance or a plea of guilty on the date set). Substantial time was spent in preparing judicial and prosecutorial resources for trial, only to have the preparation rendered unnecessary. Recognizing this pattern, the magistrate often scheduled as many as eight trials per judge on a given day. He expressed the hope that such scheduling would leave the judge with at least one or two cases for trial.

Quite obviously, the omnibus hearing was intended to meet this problem, but in discussing possible solutions, the personnel in the district no longer referred to the hearing. A frequently stated opinion was that omnibus occurred too early to be effective in establishing firm trial dates. In part, the reference was to the time necessary to prepare for trial. More important, however, was that omnibus came too early in the plea negotiation process. Several judges emphasized that defendants frequently wished to defer inevitable conviction as long as possible, and that the prosecutor continued to negotiate with most defendants until the last moment. These two factors, they believed, created frequent deferral of guilty plea decisions.

Omnibus played only a nominal role in enforcing disclosure. At each hearing the magistrate inquired whether discovery had been accomplished, and if it had not, he delayed the hearing until the files had been reviewed by the defense attorney. However, if disclosure had not occurred, the initial leaning of the magistrate was to regard the failure as a result of defense attorney laxity. Disclosure had become so routine that reluctance on the part of the prosecutor had become virtually nonexistant.

In 1970, cases were initially handled by the complaint section of the prosecutor's office. The members of this unit expressed no reluctance to provide disclosure to the defense. As a result, no enforcement was needed for disclosure while the case was within this suit. However, the complaint unit's jurisdiction terminated when the case was set for trial; most commonly after the omnibus hearing appearance.

Although some of the prosecutors at the trial level freely disclosed evidence obtained during later investigations in the case, many refused to make such disclosures. Since the omnibus hearing had already been held, enforcement of full disclosure with respect to late-developing evidence could occur only during normal court appearances or on formal motion by the defense. The new judges in San Diego treated such late-developing discovery issues as matters of prosecutorial discretion, unless the matter was controlled by a federal statute or procedural rule. As a result, the extent to which the defense received late disclosures was controlled by the attitude of the prosecutor who happened to be handling the trial.

CONCLUSION

The phenomenon of plea negotiation has a direct and substantial impact on disposition patterns in the criminal courts relative to both the type and timing of dispositions. It is, however, only one manifestation of a larger, informal process that controls the performance of cases in court. In any attempt to modify the results produced in court, the reform idea must account for and manipulate these informal processes.

As we have seen, the omnibus hearing's performance in San Diego was characterized by conflicting results. One objective of the process, disclosure of prosecution evidence, was achieved; however, along other variables, the hearing was counter- or non-productive. One explanation for this pattern is that the omnibus proposal proceeded from a misconception of the determinative elements of case flow.

Omnibus proceeds under a rationale strongly shaped by an adversary conception of criminal justice practice. This conception postulates a series of results tied to an underlying focus of the system on disposition of issues by contest and adjudication between competing interests. In practice, however, neither of these characteristics commonly applies. The system functions under an accommodation of often similar interests. The thrust of practices is to avoid adjudication in most cases.

Omnibus achieved increased prosecution disclosure because, despite the inaccuracy of its basic rationale, it offered sufficient incentives to all of the participants to engage in disclosure. It did not alter schedule compliance practices because most of the factors leading to continuances and late guilty pleas were not affected. It increased court time because it placed an additional routine court appearance into the context of a system whose primary thrust had been to minimize court time.

In a broader context, the lesson to be learned from the San Diego experience is that desirable results can be achieved through reforms only if they recognize and take advantage of the underlying rationales and interests exhibited in prevailing practices. Several illustrations suggest the problem.

While omnibus did not function effectively in San Diego, its performance is more likely to fit reform expectations in a jurisdiction in which plea negotiation is minimal. In the absence of plea negotiation, there should be an increased emphasis on issue adjudication. As a result, the forced early information flow promulgated under omnibus is likely to have some significant effect on disposition patterns.

An often-stated objection to current criminal court practices is that there is too much emphasis on negotiated pleas of guilty. It should be apparent that most attempts to restrain the process of plea negotiation have been unsuccessful. For example, there is a requirement that the defendant be asked in court whether his guilty plea is voluntary and not the result of promises or threats. The flaw in this approach is revealed by a rhetorical question. What incentive is there for a defendant who accepts a bargain that he believes is preferable to other modes of disposition to answer the judicial question truthfully, if he believes that his answer will endanger that bargain?

Other methods exist that might lower the frequency of negotiated pleas. To understand these responses, one must ask why are bargains offered and accepted with such frequency?

On a simplistic level, suitable only for general discussion, prosecutors offer concessions because they cannot dispose of their caseload without frequent guilty pleas. An obvious response is indicated. If prosecutors and courts were adequately staffed, they would have less reason to offer concessions. One could increase the number of prosecutors and judges or decrease their caseloads. The decreased caseload could occur by intensifying screening practices, changing arrest policies, or repealing certain statutes.

Why do the defendants accept guilty plea concessions? Again, for the sake of discussion, a simplistic answer: because they believe or are persuaded that the concession offers them the best disposition of the case. A wide range of responses occur in this regard. One could eliminate prosecutor control of charges after a case is filed in court; one could remove prosecutor influence on actual sentences and, perhaps, judicial influence on the same by forcing compliance with probation report recommendations; and one could reduce statute penalty provisions.

Similarly, in connection with a lessening of prosecutor control of sentence and charge decisions, we could build up the defense willingness to resist. Can arrangements be made to lessen defense attorney caseload pressures? Can the actual degree of proof necessary for conviction be increased? Can steps, including appropriate incentives, be taken to establish a functional appellate procedure to contest negotiated plea convictions? The point, obviously, is not that all of these changes are desirable. Rather, it is that to lessen the negotiated plea rate, a rational response is to weaken the bargaining position of one of the sides in the negotiation as well as the nature of the concessions it can offer.

A further illustration may be found in the current drive to establish noncriminal disposition alternatives as part of the criminal justice system. The concept involved is labeled diversion and involves the deferral of criminal charges pending the defendant's entry into treatment or counseling. Successful completion of treatment leads to dismissal of charges.

To illustrate the problem in this context, let us assume that a statute creates the alternative of two years of institutional treatment in lieu of prosecution. Under what circumstances will a prosecutor desire to invoke this statute? Several answers appear. For example, he may invoke the statute if it saves his office time in disposing of cases; if a given defendant's conduct does not justify a criminal penalty; or if two years of institutionalization is a more severe punishment of a "serious" case than that in fact available under prosecution. On the other hand, a defendant is likely to choose the best disposition available to him. What sentence can he anticipate under prosecution and how does it compare in terms of nature and length of supervision to that available under treatment. In practice, such statutes are seldom invoked because neither side has incentive to do so.

It is evident that the required reform is complex. However, in an overall view of the judicial process, a further complication arises. Simply stated, it consists of the fact that implementation of a response to one problem is likely to produce offsetting effects along other variables.

For example, if, by a manipulation of the respective strengths, we minimized plea negotiation, would this affect other variables? Undoubtedly. For example, to what extent would a weakened prosecutor be able to obtain early dispositions of his cases? The question might be reversed: what changes could be adopted to ensure speedy disposition of all cases? One answer would be to impose and enforce penalties (for example, increased sentences) on defendants who delay cases. Obviously, this implies increased, not decreased, negotiating strength.

The problem is, therefore, not only to find an effective mix of incentives and pressures, but a mix that is acceptable on other policy grounds. In discussing court delay, for example, a basic observation is that not all of the participants routinely desire speedy disposition. If they did, lengthy cases would be even less frequent than they now are. Obviously, therefore, any reform must provide incentives to hasten disposition without imposing on the valid interests of the parties. The issue may be, what policy, other than the presumably objectionable punishment scale noted above, will induce a defendant facing inevitable conviction and desiring to postpone it, to reverse that view and seek speedy disposition?

The answers to these and other issues are less than clear. It does appear reasonable, however, to conclude with two observations. First, we must know specifically what the ideal goals and acceptable compromise objectives of reform are. Presumably, an ideal is speedy disposition (however "speed" is defined). But is it acceptable to prompt (or coerce) speed from a defendant or to accomplish that objective by intensified plea negotiation? Second, when these objectives and parameters are fully outlined, we need a thorough understanding of why and how current practices deviate from the ideal; an understanding not cloaked in the idealism of the adversary model or in the jaded view of those who believe that the system always functions corruptly and for corrupt purposes. Given this requisite data, a rational program for reform via a careful reshaping of structure, power, and incentives might proceed with some assurance of success.

NOTES

1. But see L. Katz et al. (1972). In any discussion of judicial delay or similar alleged problems faced by the criminal justice process, the commentator must define the point of reference that he takes in discussing case flow. It is well-documented that a pyramid effect obtains in the processing of criminal cases, with most cases being disposed of at early points in the process (for example, police or prosecutor screening). Obviously, if the commentator focuses only on those few cases which have passed through all prior screening steps, the obvious conclusion is that delay and excessive time in court are rampant. However, if the focus includes some or all of the other parts of the pyramid, different conclusions are suggested. In this article, our reference point is all cases filed in court, including those disposed at early steps. See McIntyre and Lipman (1970).

2. See generally Frank W. Miller (1969); Nimmer (1974).

3. See J. Taylor et al. (1972).

4. See Skolnick (1967); Battle (1971).

5. See Blumberg (1967).

6. See McIntyre (1968).

7. See generally, I. Robertson and P. Teitelbaum (1973: 665).

8. The extent to which a judge may participate in plea negotiations has been the subject of extended and diverse discussion. See generally, American Bar Association (1968).

9. The extent to which the prosecution is concerned about avoiding delayed dispositions varies according to both the specific crime charged and to the nature of the office and the pressures it feels from outside sources. Occasionally, a desire to avoid protracting disposition is cited in explaining prosecution reluctance to engage in treatment or other non-criminal dispositions. See J. Cooper (1971). Obviously, lengthy delays of disposition raise the possibility of weakening the prosecution eidence of guilt. However, they also carry the possibility of weakening defense evidence or, at least, defense stringency in demanding favorable plea bargains.

10. On the surface, the desire of the in-custody defendant for speedy disposition may appear to be uniformly present. Since he is already in-custody, delaying disposition, even if a conviction is virtually inevitable, appears undesirable. However, if delay may appear to be likely to weaken the prosecution case or its plea bargain demands, an in-custody defendant may desire delay on the assumption that he will receive credit for time served in any eventual sentence.

11. See generally, Columbia Law Review (1971: note).

12. See Battle, supra, note 4. The practice of informal disclosure of prosecution evidence flows as part of the cooperative practice of criminal law that many defense attorneys engage in.

13. See American Bar Association (1967).

14. An interim report on this project has previously been published. See Nimmer (1971).

15. The literature in San Diego followed the format described in the original ABA report and emphasized disclosure as a central feature of the new process. (See American Bar Association Report, supra, note 13.)

16. See Miller (1963).

17. See Ad. Off. U.S. Courts, Annual Rep., Table XI (1969).

18. See 21 USC 174 (1964). The penalty provisions of this statute and other respects of the federal drug legislation have subsequently been modified. See 21 USC 840 et. seq. (1972).

19. For in-custody cases, the interval for cases in our sample measured in terms of mean value was 13 days, while for defendants released on bail, the interval was 25 days. Also, interview data suggests that both attorneys in in-custody cases exerted every effort to complete disclosure within the minimized interval, while in other cases, disclosure often did not reach completion until after the original, scheduled date.

20. In estimating time in court, we applied a weighting scale which approximated relative time in court for the various appearances noted in the data. The specifics of the scale are discussed in Nimmer, supra, note 14.

Weighted Number	Appearance Type
1	Indictment, all continuances other than continuances for trials, and evidentiary hearings
2	Arraignment, bail hearings, habeas corpus hearings, trial and evidentiary hearing continuances
4	Omnibus hearings and legal issue hearings not requiring the presentation of evidence, including plea-acceptance hearings
6	Evidentiary hearings
16	Court trial day
48	Jury trial day

21.

INDEX OF ESTIMATED COURT TIME (mean value)

	1966	1968
Heroin cases		
non-trial	7.6 (39 cases)	13.2 (36 cases)
trial (pre-trial time only)	6.0 (5 cases)	7.2 (11 cases)
All heroin	7.4 (44 cases)	11.0 (49 cases)
Minor drug		
non-trial	7.0 (52 cases)	10.5 (59 cases)
trial	3.6 (9 cases)	7.0 (5 cases)
All minor	6.5 (61 cases)	10.2 (64 cases)
Auto theft		
non-trial	5.8 (22 cases)	9.4 (25 cases)
trial	3.5 (2 cases)	7.4 (4 cases)
All auto	5.6 (24 cases)	9.1 (29 cases)

This result is further suggested by the comments of one of the original judges on the court.

The US Attorneys and defense counsel have been saved much paperwork on motions, offset by the time used for the additional appearance in court at the omnibus hearing.

Memorandum from Judge Carter to serve as discussion material for a seminar for new federal judges (1968).

REFERENCES

American Bar Association (1968) Project on Minimum Standards for Criminal Justice, Standards Relating to Pleas of Guilty. Approved draft.

——— (1967) Project on Minimum Standards for Criminal Justice, Standards Relating to Discovery and Procedure Prior to Trial.

BATTLE (1971) "In search of the adversary system—the cooperative practices of private defense attorneys." Texas Law Review 50, 60.

BLUMBERG, A. (1967) "The practice of law as a confidence game: organizational cooption of a profession." Law and Sociology Review 1, 15.

Columbia Law Review (1971) "Speedy Trials and the Second Circuit Rules Regarding Prompt Disposition of Criminal Cases." Volume 71.

COOPER, J. (1971) "The Heroin Addict in the New Haven Criminal Justice System." Unpublished manuscript. New Haven, Conn.

KATZ, L. R. et al. (1972) Justice is the Crime. Cleveland: The Press of Case Western Reserve University.

McINTYRE, D. (1968) "A study of judicial dominance of the charging process." Journal of Criminology and Political Science 59, 463.

——— and LIPMAN (1970) "Prosecutors and early disposition of felony cases." American Bar Association Journal 56, 1154.

MILLER, F. (1969) Prosecution: The Decision to Charge a Suspect With a Crime. New York: Little, Brown.

——— (1963) "The omnibus hearing—an experiment in federal criminal discovery." South Dakota Law Review 5, 293.

NIMMER, R. (1974) Alternate Forms of Prosecution: Diversion from the Criminal Justice Process. Chicago: American Bar Foundation Press.

——— (1971) Omnibus Hearing—An Experiment in Relieving Judicial Delay, Inefficiency and Unfairness. Chicago: American Bar Foundation.

ROBERTSON, J. and P. TEITELBAUM (1973) "Optimizing legal impact: a case study in search of a theory." Wisconsin Law Review 3.

SKOLNICK, J. (1967) "Social control in the adversary system." Journal of Conflict Resolution 11, 52.

TAYLOR, J. et al. (1972) "Defense Attorney Status and the Processing of Criminal Cases." Unpublished manuscript. Washington, D.C.: Institute for Defense Research.

Chapter 8

CHANNELING LAWYERS:
THE CAREERS OF PUBLIC DEFENDERS

ANTHONY PLATT and
RANDI POLLOCK

Overview

This paper concerns the careers and ideology of lawyers who have worked in the Public Defender's Office in Alameda County—a highly populated and industrial community on the West Coast. While partly building on a variety of studies on occupational careers inside and outside the criminal justice system (Hughes, 1959; Carr-Saunders and Wilson, 1933; Janowitz, 1964; Slocum, 1966; Grosman, 1969), this study also attempts to place the concept of "career" in a larger social and political context by borrowing from recent contributions to theories of the state and the "new" working class (Miliband, 1969; Mallet, 1963; Gorz, 1972: 27-41; Manifesto, 1972: 65-84).

In general, there are very few appreciative studies of the working conditions and attitudes of persons who staff the criminal justice bureaucracies. They are

AUTHORS' NOTE: The research for this paper is based on a pilot study in Chicago, sponsored by the Center for Studies in Criminal Justice, University of Chicago, and a research project supported by the Center for the Study of Law and Society, University of California at Berkeley. Sharon Dunkle Marks in Chicago and Suzi Tanguay and Jay Adams in Berkeley provided essential help in collecting and interpreting data. Herman Schwendinger gave supportive criticism of a first draft. We are especially grateful to the many present and past members of the Public Defender's Office who gave us their time and confidence.

[235]

popularly characterized as "faceless bureaucrats," "public servants," or "insidious technocrats," depending on the author's political perspective. Public defenders, like other sectors of the law enforcement labor force, have been victimized by this kind of stereotyping. They are either uncritically celebrated by government and professional authorities as indispensible public servants[1] or they are depicted by critics and muckrakers as lackeys of prosecutors or, at best, dangerous do-gooders (Sudnow, 1965: 265-276; Platt et al., 1968; Casper, 1971: 4-9).

This case-study is designed to present a more accurate and sympathetic portrait of people who work as public defenders; why they enter public defender offices, how they are recruited, who remain to make a career as public defenders, who leave and why, and how their subsequent careers develop. It is also about what the job of public defender does to people's aspirations, identities, values, and human potentialities. Hopefully, this analysis has larger implications for understanding some of the problems and dilemmas faced by a growing and important sector of the labor force who work as "servants of the state" (Miliband, 1969: ch. 5).

Methodology

A list of all 64 attorneys who worked in Alameda County Public Defender Office (PDO) between 1927 and 1969 was compiled and chronologically ordered. Minimal background and career information was collected through public and official records. Extensive interviews—partly structured and partly open-ended—were conducted with 75 percent (48) of the former PDO attorneys and a small number of important or helpful informants were reinterviewed. Two of the interviewees, as friends of the authors, helped to evaluate the reliability and accuracy of data collected through interviews.

In addition, minimal background and career information was collected on the 58 attorneys who were employed in the PDO as of May 1971. Through interviews and questionnaires, more extensive data were gathered on 64 percent (37) of these attorneys. Additional data were derived from annual budget reports, local newspapers, published articles, and office memoranda. In summary, this study is based primarily on data concerning 122 attorneys in the PDO, 85 (70 percent) of whom were researched in considerable depth. Comparative references in this paper are derived from a larger project on the legal careers of public defenders in Cook County, Illinois, and prosecutors in Alameda County, California.[2]

Development of Public Defender System

The public defender system, as distinguished from other kinds of legal aid, was first implemented in Los Angeles in 1914, though it had been discussed since the early 1890s (see Silverstein, 1965). Typically, it involves salaried lawyers who devote all or most of their time to the specialized practice of representing poor defendants charged with criminal offenses. Defender systems vary considerably in the kinds of cases they handle, in the quality of legal service, and in their territorial jurisdiction (Silverstein, 1965: ch. 3). According to the National Legal Aid and Defender Association, there are approximately over 1,000 public defenders in the United States, of whom about half are full-time (The President's Commission, 1967: 57). While the assigned counsel system is used in most counties (approximately 2,750 of the 3,100 counties in the country), the public defender system is presently in operation in about 270 counties (including many large cities) and handles approximately one-third of all felony defendants in the county (The President's Commission, 1967: 57; Silverstein, 1965: 40-45; James, 1972: 129).

Public defender systems were adopted in most large urban jurisdictions because they offer a more efficient and centralized method of processing a high volume of cases (The President's Commission, 1967: 59). Since the majority of criminal defendants are poor and incapable of retaining a private attorney,[3] there is an ever-increasing need for free legal services. The public defender system has grown considerably in recent years, partly as a general reflection of the expansion of state bureaucracies and more specifically as a result of efforts to centralize and rationalize the criminal justice system.

Alameda County Public Defender Office

Alameda County, located on the coast of northern California, includes a large industrial city (Oakland) and a college town (Berkeley). The Public Defender's Office has its central office in Oakland, a sprawling and ugly metropolis which suffers, like many American cities, from chronic unemployment, deteriorating public services, and an economy reminiscent of the depression. Its unemployment rate is about twice the national average and its welfare caseload is the second largest in California. One-quarter of all families in Oakland live in extreme poverty (at less than $4,000 per annum) and almost half of all families in the city live in deprivation or worse. In the flatlands area of the city, where Blacks, Chicanos, and poor whites live, almost half of the eligible work force is either unemployed or subemployed (Hayes, 1972: 45-46). Although Oakland's total population has been declining slightly in the last ten years, its proportion of Black residents has been gradually increasing. Over 90,000 Blacks, approximately one-quarter of the city's population, live in Oakland (Lunch, 1970).

Though Oakland is typical of many moderate-sized American cities confronted by profound economic and political problems, it has a national reputation among professionals and policy makers for an above-average system of criminal justice. The Oakland Police Department is reputed to have high professional standards and is governed by a reform-minded chief; the District Attorney's Office has trained several well-known professional and politicians, and has a reputation for honesty and high standards; and the Public Defender's Office is locally and nationally recognized for its technical competence, high ethical standards, excellent training program, and freedom from political interference. This study, therefore, is about a public defender system which, comparatively speaking, ranks very high and sets standards which other offices try to emulate.

Alameda County's PDO was created by a county charter passed in 1926, in accord with provisions of a statute passed by the California legislature in 1921, permitting the extension of the public defender system in Los Angeles to other more populous counties of the state (see Ivens, 1939). Alameda's PDO was supported by many notables and leaders in the community, including the local district attorney and grand jury (Ivens, 1939: 66). On January 18, 1927, Alameda County's Board of Supervisors unanimously ratified the state law and appointed a prominent Oakland attorney as public defender for the county. A few years later, the Alameda County Grand Jury reported that the PDO not only provides "experienced counsel for accused persons unable to pay fees, but it brings the public interest into a closer bearing on the problems of dealing with the offenders. Trials under this system are more expeditious, sufficient court time being saved to pay the cost of the public defender and possibly even result in economy. The cost per case handled is only about $18.00." In short, the PDO was suggested and supported by elite members of the judiciary and political system. In this respect, it was no different from many welfare reforms which accompanied the rise of corporate capitalism at the turn of the century (see, for example, Kolko, 1967; Weinstein, 1969).

When the first public defender took office in 1927, his total budget was less than $7,500 and he supplemented his income by maintaining a civil practice. During his 24-year office as chief public defender, from 1927 to 1951, his staff increased to four lawyers and his budget to $27,000. The PDO continued to slowly grow during the 1950s, adding more lawyers and becoming a full-time operation. During the late 1960s it suddenly expanded into a complex organization requiring a division of labor and specialization of skills. When the fourth chief public defender entered office in 1963, there were five lawyers handling 1,964 cases; by 1968, there were 38 lawyers handling 16,500 cases. As of May 1971, the PDO consisted of 58 lawyers (of whom 6 were in supervisory positions) and 10 investigators processing almost 20,000 cases annually.

ENTERING THE PUBLIC DEFENDER OFFICE

Recruitment: The Employer's Perspective

While Alameda County's District Attorney's Office is elective, the public defender is appointed by the Board of Supervisors, to whom he is legally and politically responsible. Assistant public defenders, however, are governed by the Civil Service Commission, which is designed, in theory at least, to protect them from political interference. Since the public defender plays a key role in the recruitment and selection of assistants, it is important to understand some basic political features of his office.

Between 1927 and 1971, there have been five chief public defenders. Public Defender One, who held office from 1927 to 1951, was previously a deputy clerk in the district court of appeal. He was appointed as first public defender with the support of a federal judge, who "put in a good word for me," and the local district attorney, whom he later supported in his successful bid for attorney general. In the early days of the PDO, the staff was very small and the public defender had difficulty recruiting young attorneys because salaries were inadequate and assistants were required to supplement their income through private practice.

Public Defender Two, who held office from 1951 to 1959, was a senior trial attorney in Alameda's District Attorney Office before his appointment as public defender. His political connections on the Board of Supervisors and the power of the local district attorney combined to defeat his competitors in the PDO. Public Defender Three, 1959-1963, came from the ranks and was groomed for the job by his predecessor. After his appointment as judge in 1963, he was succeeded by Public Defender Four, who also had been a life-long civil servant working as a probation officer and assistant public defender for many years. The present Public Defender Five, appointed in 1970, was the personal choice of his predecessor and had worked in the office for about 15 years, except for a brief and unsuccessful episode in private practice. His selection as chief public defender was helped by his long friendship with the present district attorney, whom he has known since college.

Thus, in 44 years there have been only five public defenders, indicating the remarkable stability and continuity of Alameda's PDO. The leadership selection process has been exclusive and ingrown, dominated by a powerful District Attorney's Office and conservative Board of Supervisors. Since the public defender and his budget are almost totally dependent on the support of these two organizations, it is not suprising that all five public defenders are men of diplomatic restraint and caution, ideologically and bureaucratically conservative, avoiding publicity and controversy.

In the earlier days of the office, the civil service exam was a formality incidental to the main problem of finding lawyers willing to work as assistants. Public Defender One personally recruited a couple of acquaintances and other recruits were referred to him by judges and local law schools. As the office became larger and more formalized in the 1950s, more systematic efforts were made to recruit young law school graduates. The public defender gave talks at local law schools and the office developed a summer internship program to attract law students.

The public defender has always had a great deal of control over the civil service exam. Civil service regulations require that a prospective assistant pass a written and oral exam[4] and place in the top three on the overall test. The written exam is superficial and counts much less than the oral exam, which is typically administered by Alameda County's public defender together with a public defender from another county and a local private attorney.[5] The oral exam is open-ended and covers a range of formal and informal topics. The whole process is sufficiently flexible for the public defender to select any candidate, with the exception of outrageous failures:

> When I took the test, they had a written and an oral test, which supposedly gave some objectivity to it because you had to get a certain grade on the written and a certain grade on the oral. But as a practical matter it was a joke because one of the guys who took the test with me failed the written but the boss wanted him. . . . They wanted him because they liked him. He was a kind of healthy jock-like fellow who they figured wouldn't make any worries. So they wired it up so that he would do very well on the orals so he would just barely get over the line on the civil service exam. They just arranged it. You see, they control the civil service panel [Interview No. 25].

While minimum standards of educational and technical competence are required, the public defender still has many opportunities to select candidates whom he personally or ideologically approves. For example, he hires assistants provisionally before taking the exam, thus giving them priority even over other applicants who score better on the tests:

> I didn't take the tests [originally] . . . They had a system where they could hire you provisionally subject to review and when the test came up you took it and of course by that time you couldn't help but pass it [Interview No. 53].

The public defender can also control the selection process by waiting until his choice becomes eligible through encouraging the top three candidates to take other jobs.

Until the mid-1960s, the PDO always had a problem in finding young lawyers who met their formal and informal standards of eligibility. The postwar boom in the legal profession made it difficult for the PDO to compete with private firms and businesses which offered more money and better career opportunities. For those with political and governmental ambitions, the District Attorney's Office was a much more effective vehicle of upward mobility (Tanguay, 1967: ch. 4). Throughout the 1950s and into the early 1960s, a determined law school graduate could get into the PDO if he or she exhibited proper demeanor and had character references from reputable professionals:

> For hiring at that time [1964], you could pretty much, if you were really interested in it, . . . get a job there because there weren't that many people interested. If you were kind of interested and aggressive, you could probably work there. . . . That's not true any more because it's highly competitive now. It wasn't very competitive at the time I went in [Interview No. 9].

When the PDO was smaller and not characterized by a division of labor and responsibilities, there was a "tremendous esprit de corps and feeling of loyalty to the office," according to an ex-public defender. New assistants were personally recruited and smooth functioning of the office was maintained on an ad hoc and informal basis. In the last ten years, the character of the PDO and legal marketplace have significantly changed. Prior to 1968, the PDO had at most 17 attorneys on the staff; four years later, over 60 were employed in the same office. Whereas previously the PDO had difficulty recruiting assistants, it now has too many applicants and law school graduates vigorously compete for every opening. The expansion of the PDO is consistent with the increasing centralization of power and management of social life by the state (Miliband, 1969; Kolko, 1967; Weinstein, 1969), as well as with the disproportionate growth of professional and technical workers within the labor force (see, for example, Gintis, 1970). In addition, the PDO is one of the few places where young attorneys can get paid while gaining extensive trial experience and working with poor clients.

The increased size and popularity of the PDO was accompanied by the development of more regulated methods of recruitment and an internal system of hierarchical controls. This is characterized by organizational distinctions between administrators and staff attorneys, the development of technical specializations (juvenile law, appelate work, felony trials, and so on), and a division of labor based on experience and seniority. The era of "esprit de corps" was formally concluded when the majority of assistants recently joined the union which represents state and county employees and demanded better working conditions.

Antagonisms within the office between assistants and administrators are not solely "bread and butter" disputes over pay and fringe benefits. They also involve different concepts of the appropriate role of public defenders. This was dramatically illustrated in 1967 when a small group of assistants signed a "Lawyers Against the War in Vietnam" petition which appeared in local newspapers. The public defender criticized the signers for "unprofessional conduct" and accused them of disloyalty to the office. He argued that public demonstrations of militancy or involvement in controversial political issues weakened the office by attracting bad publicity, annoying an already conservative Board of Supervisors, hurting clients by prejudicing judges and juries, and complicating their working relationship with the District Attorney's Office.[6] The controversy was quickly ended when several assistants either resigned or were "encouraged to leave." "Up to that point," says an ex-assistant, "everybody thought that the public defender (and his chief assistant) were just the greatest people in the world. Everybody loved his job. It was just really rosy and this thing blew the lid off everything. And ever since then this Office has been really shaky" (Interview No. 9). According to another ex-assistant, "that one incident was the turning point in a lot of people's attitudes in the Office and in fact it began the great departure of the group that I was part of, which was about ten lawyers" (Interview No. 55).

So long as there was no apparent conflict within the office, its regulating principles remained hidden behind the rhetoric of professionalism and political neutrality:

> Another thing I had as a policy as Public Defender—no individual self-aggrandizement and hunting for headlines and courting the newspapers and grandstand stunts. . . . I told everybody who came to work for me: "If you're riding some hobby-horse and some kick, then you're not going to work for me." I wanted no zealots, no person who had a philosophy of this, that and the other thing. I was not on the side of crime, I was not on the side of criminal and anti-social behavior. Nobody who worked for me was going to be either [Interview No. 29].

> We feel that the more obscurely we live the more likely it is that we will be permitted to do what we think we ought to do. Basically, I think the public and the Board of Supervisors do not look on us with favor because, to be oversimplified about it, I think they have a kind of gut reaction that we are employed to raise impediments in the way of the conviction of bad people. . . . So we have always felt that we will stay out of the press. We have never called, to my knowledge, in all my years in the office, a press conference. . . . We have tried to avoid letting causes swamp cases. . . . I think in terms of representing a person in court on a criminal charge if you, as a lawyer, permit yourself to be swept up in causes, you're likely to blow your case [Interview No. 26].

When political contradiction in the society directly affected the PDO, as exemplified in the "Vietnam incident," the mask of legitimation was suddenly ripped off and the administrative staff temporarily lost control. This was caused not by any change in policy but through the realization by several assistants that the neutrality and independence of the PDO is a fiction, that it in fact depends for its existence on continued good relationships with and loyalty to local political elites and the District Attorney's Office.

While this incident revealed a certain naivete on the part of some assistants, it also served as a warning to PDO administrators to pay closer attention to the ideology and moral character of new applicants. Public Defender Five rejects applicants who "have been involved in political activities to the extent where I think they can no longer view the situation or our situation rationally" (Interview No. 19). Persons who are too "idealistic" or "scholastic" are also discouraged. "I think a good deal of idealism is helpful if it's channeled properly," commented another administrator. "You have to temper your idealism with a practical sense of reality" (Interview No. 53).

Background of Public Defenders

The PDO, like the criminal bar and other unglamorous forms of legal practice, is a route of upward mobility for the children of the skilled and semi-skilled working class, of minor entrepreneurs, salaried professionals, and middle-management personnel (Ladinsky, 1963; Wood, 1967; Carlin, 1962). About 90 percent of the grandparents of PDO lawyers were born in Europe; their parents, as children of immigrants, were modestly successful in economic terms, though less than one-third of their fathers completed college education. With one or two exceptions, their parents did not accumulate any significant wealth and the PDO lawyers were required to either work their way through college or support themselves with the help of the GI bill and other kinds of loans.

In terms of religious, educational, and political background, PDO lawyers are comparable to lawyers in other public defender offices but differ in many important respects from their adversaries in the District Attorney's Office. A minority of public defenders was brought up as Protestants or related religions (41 percent), while the remainder came from Catholic (20 percent), Jewish (20 percent), and agnostic (19 percent) families. About 37 percent of the PDO attorneys were educated in high-ranking state university law schools and the rest were distributed through a variety of modest and low-ranking state and city law schools. Close to 50 percent finished in the top third of their law school classes, while over 10 percent finished in the lower third.

In terms of political affiliation, PDO lawyers are for the most part liberals. Until 1969, only 20 percent of the PDO lawyers were registered as Republicans;

between 1969 and 1971, this declined to approximately 11 percent. Democrats presently account for about 68 percent (an increase of about 12 percent since 1969) and 16 percent identify themselves as Independents and to the political left of the Democratic Party. The left-liberal ideology of PDO lawyers is further reflected in their membership in organizations like the ACLU, the Lawyers Guild, and various antiwar groups. A small group of assistants also worked in the Peace and Freedom Party, supporting Robert Scheer's senate campaign.

Between 1927 and 1971, there were one Black and seven women lawyers in the PDO. This is a reflection of institutionalized racism and sexism in the legal profession (one percent of the national bar is Black and 3 percent women), as well as in the specific programs of government and industry in Alameda County.[7] As of 1971, there was no affirmative action policy in the PDO and the legal problems of the white and Third World poor continued to be handled for the most part by white men who received their training in an educational system based on class and caste privileges.[8] The present Chief Public Defender Five intends to continue these policies:

> My own personal prejudices are opposed to the selection of anyone on the basis of race. I neither favor it or am against it. . . . I would like to have about 3 or 4 women on the staff. . . . There are cases where it is better balanced and better theory and actually more realistic practice to use a woman. They have defects too—they can't get into jails, they can't be locked up in interview room with some of the people. . . . So if we had too great a percentage of them, we would lose flexibility in some of these areas [Interview No. 19].

The Alameda County PDO recruits its lawyers from persons with varied working and middle-class white backgrounds, more typically from non-Protestant families, with liberal political affiliations, and an education in state or city law schools. A comparable study of 45 lawyers who worked in Cook County's PDO between 1930 and 1967 revealed a similar profile: 41 whites, 5 Blacks; 25 Catholics, 12 Jews; attended local law schools; and the overwhelming majority were registered Democrats and came from working-class backgrounds (Platt, 1968).

Lawyers in the Alameda County District Attorney's Office, however, differ from attorneys in the PDO In several important ways. A study of over 150 attorneys who worked in the District Attorney's Office between 1926 and 1969 indicated that they are predominantly Republicans (at least 64 percent, more likely to have Catholic backgrounds (36 percent), 71 percent came from middle- and upper-middle-class families, and many were active in athletics or social clubs while in college. During this 43-year period, there were only 4 Jews, 5 women, and 3 Blacks in the District Attorney's Office (Tanguay, 1967: ch. 1).

These differences in social-economic background confirm the well-established fact that organizations regularly use informal criteria, such as class background and political affiliation, in addition to technical competence when assessing the reliability of potential recruits (Becker and Strauss, 1956). The distinctions between the two offices also indicate that the PDO does not try to compete with corporate law firms or the District Attorney's Office in trying to recruit more conservative lawyers trained in elite law schools who are potential partners in business law firms or career politicians. Rather, the PDO seeks lawyers interested in civil service careers or preparing for extensive trial work. In this respect, it plays an important role in channeling lawyers into careers consistent with their class background and with the demands of the legal marketplace.

Although there are significant differences in the social upbringing of public defenders and prosecutors, there are also several similarities which suggest that recruitment is based on more complex factors than simply economic or religious background. Ralph Miliband (1967: 123) has pointed out that the recruitment of civil servants in advanced capitalist countries is "no longer in the main determined on the basis of social provenance or religious affiliation." And Gabriel Kolko (1969: 14-15) similarly concluded in a study of federal executives that "there is no evidence whatsoever to prove that social and educational origins determine policies of state." Social background is an important indicator of potential performance, but it is certainly not an assurance of reliability and ideological soundness, as the "Vietnam incident" clearly demonstrated. For this reason, PDO administrators make every effort to recruit assistants who are ideologically prepared to follow their leadership, to accept existing regulations in the office, and to subordinate any personal idiosyncracies to the prevailing administrative consensus. During their interviews for jobs in the PDO, applicants are clearly told what is expected of them:

> When I came into the Office, [the Public Defender] indicated that this was not an ACLU office. . . . He said we were here to make the system work in the best way possible. . . . We were not necessarily engaged in the process of advocating major social change through the processes of the Office itself [Interview No. 45].

> It was the only interview I ever had in my life where it took 20 minutes to tell me what was *wrong* with the job. [The Public Defender] had the view that he didn't want people coming in naively and he made it a point to tell me what was wrong with the Office [Interview No. 57].

> The people in the Office who interviewed me were very explicit in telling me that, "We represent cases not causes." . . . They sort of hold their breath and hire you and try to caution you and hope that you turn out not to be a troublemaker [Interview No. 52].

Motivation and Aspiration

Recruitment is a process of interaction. While the employer holds the power of evaluating various formal and informal criteria of assessment, the potential employee is also a participant in the recruitment process and his demeanor, intentions, and credentials influence the chances of employment. For the overwhelming majority of recruits, the PDO serves as the initial step in a consciously selected career. For most it is the first job involving criminal trial work, a specialized form of practice which prepares lawyers not only for general practice but for most specialties involving extensive trial work. Lawyers entering the PDO typically understand that this choice is the beginning of a specialized legal career.

This is a fairly recent phenomenon, dating back to the expansion of the legal profession in the 1950s. Previously, lawyers entering the PDO were glad to get a job, any job, because it was a matter of "making a living in those days" (Interview No. 38). Career lines and long-range planning were not entertained because the legal marketplace was unstable and unpredictable. As one lawyer who left the PDO in 1946 commented, "I am a child of the great depression and it's only in the last few years that I've really been able to feel that when one loses one's job this is not necessarily the end of the world" (Interview No. 15).

During the last 15 to 20 years, ideological preference has played an important role in the selection of legal careers. Before 1960, a considerable number of lawyers applied for jobs in both district attorney and public defender offices, regarding them as equally capable of providing technical training. The two offices were not regarded as morally or politically antagonistic. This attitude started to change in the late 1950s, and by the early 1960s young attorneys expressed an ideological preference for the PDO:

> I don't have a DA personality. I am, for example, diametrically opposed to the death penalty, and if you're going to be a DA that's a built-in limitation [Interview No. 39].

> I wanted to do trial work and I wanted to help people whom I considered to be deprived and underprivileged, and it seemed to me that the P.D.'s Office was the avenue to go into [Interview No. 29].

> I did not wish to work for a D.A.'s Office particularly because at that time I identified very strongly with the oppressed and downtrodden [Interview No. 15].

> I think my whole inclination at that point was connected to my theological background and I was just upset, I think, with the law and I didn't think that people should pay for legal services [Interview No. 44].

These attitudes are typically held by most potential assistants in the PDO on the grounds that they are "not inclined to prosecution," "not prosecution-minded," or are "opposed to the death penalty."

But ideology is *not* the essential issue in job preference. The majority of applicants seek out a job in the PDO in order to get trial experience in preparation for a future career in private practice. This aspiration can be expressed crudely—"I was there just to sort of rape the Office of experience and to go out and become a criminal law attorney" (Interview No. 24)—or in more professional terms:

> I think this [PDO] is a good training ground for a reservoir of skilled criminal lawyers who can go out and practice and participate as members of the private bar in the practice of criminal law [Interview No. 36].

Most applicants want a technical and professional apprenticeship in an office which does not violate their moral and political beliefs:

> I don't like prosecuting. I'd much rather defend . . . I don't think you get very good training as a prosecutor. You don't really learn how to try a case as a prosecutor because you never learn how to cross-examine. Prosecutors don't have as much opportunity to cross-examine [Interview No. 25].

Prosecution is regarded as a comparatively simple job, given the high number of guilty pleas, the investigative and political support of the police, and the anti-defendant perspective of most judges and juries. Aspiring trial lawyers argue that the PDO is a better place to sharpen one's wits and master informal strategies as well as develop technical competence. This view is reflected in the comments of two assistants who worked in both a PD and DA Office:

> It's easy to be a DA—and I was one for a few short months—because you've got all the facts on your side and generally all you have to do is ask a few simple questions and let the witnesses answer and you've got the case won. The only way you ever won a case on the defense side is through some generally very imaginative work because all the cards are stacked against you. The type of odds you have as PD breeds more imaginative thinking and more confidence as a trial lawyer [Interview No. 28].

> I don't enjoy [prosecution] work as much; it's not as challenging. It's more cut and dried. You don't have to use your imagination. You're served your case on a silver platter literally and all you have to do is serve it up. What the PD has to do is take an extraordinary weak case and fabricate out a whole cloth, as it were, to give himself a reasonable defense. Not "fabricating," mind you, but using imagination to take weak points and trying to deal with them [Interview No. 36].

Prior to 1960, some lawyers entering the PDO were not certain about their career plans and regarded the office as a place to evaluate different possibilities, including a civil service career in a PDO. "I didn't enter the Office," said one ex-assistant, "with the specific expectation of staying there two years and then leaving. That was not clear in my mind as I think it was clear in other people's minds. I came in with the idea if I liked the work I would have no reason to leave and might stay a considerable period of time" (Interview No. 52). Those who are uncertain about their careers quickly learn from their colleagues that opportunities for promotion and success within the PDO are limited and that most intend to leave after they have accumulated sufficient experience, contacts, and technical expertise. The official policy of the PDO recognizes and legitimizes the temporary commitment of its recruits. According to the present chief PD:

> If they want to learn all there is to learn about the practical application of trial work or the rules of evidence and then they want to go out and progress into the other fields of trial work, I have no objection to it. . . . I would ask that they [assistants] give me at least two years of their time. But apart from that I assume we're lucky to keep them and I assume that they're free to go. . . . Once you become a trial lawyer in this Office, you're probably as good after two years as about 85-90% of the trial attorneys in the area. You will have had as many trials as the average practitioner has in his lifetime [Interview No. 19].

The majority of lawyers entering the PDO view their experience as a form of technical and professional apprenticeship, a means for developing informal contacts in the private bar and exploring various job possibilities. In this sense, the PDO is not unlike other public organizations (hospitals and welfare agencies, for example) which perform training services for the private sector and are faced with a constant turnover of personnel (For an overview of related studies, see Becker and Strauss, 1956). PDO lawyers are, to use Alvin Gouldner's distinction, typically "cosmopolitans" rather than "locals," because their commitment to a professional career transcends their loyalty to the organization (Gouldner, 1957: 446-467). While the PDO is *formally* concerned about recruiting lawyers interested in and committed to a lifetime of public service, it is informally and openly recognized that the office cannot expect to keep most of its assistants beyond two or three years. There are obvious organizational disadvantages with this policy: the need for an ongoing training program, the loss of specially skilled personnel, and the inability to develop esprit de corps. But there are also considerable advantages: the rapid turnover prevents assistants from developing an effective organization vis-a-vis administrators; recruits are more dependent and more easily managed; and the PDO achieves some legitimacy with the Board of Supervisors and Bar Associations as a service and training center for the private bar.

While most assistants regard their commitment to the PDO as temporary and instrumental, we do not intend to imply that these lawyers are merely opportunists who use the office as a vehicle to advance their own careers and narrow self-interests. Many assistants are motivated by a genuine concern for the lives and problems of poor defendants; many attempt to reconcile their professional aspirations with their moral and political beliefs; and others are unclear about their career plans and regard the PDO as an opportunity to explore different job possibilities. This is strikingly different from public defenders in Cook County, many of whom regard a job in the PDO as second-best to a job in the District Attorney's Office and as an instrumentality for advancing their careers.[9]

Lawyers who begin their legal careers in Alameda County District Attorney's Office do it for comparable reasons to their counterparts in the PDO. For the majority, it is regarded as an opportunity to learn technical skills, to gain extensive trial practice, to become visible and accessible to the job market, and to develop contacts which might be useful to their careers. Their choice of the District Attorney's Office as opposed to the PDO is motivated partly by ideological reasons but more importantly by aspirations for a political career or a job in an elite law firm (Tanguay, 1967: ch. 2). But lawyers in both offices are in basic agreement on one point: despite variations in motivations and aspirations, very few plan to pursue careers as civil servants.

STAYING AND LEAVING

Career Public Defenders

Very few lawyers in the PDO become career public servants. Of the 64 attorneys in the office between 1927 and 1969, only 8 made a career out of the job; 4 as chief public defenders in Alameda County and 4 in public defender offices in other counties. Of the 58 attorneys employed in the PDO as of May 1971, only 5 claimed that they seriously intended to remain in the office as a career. Similar findings were reported in studies of the District Attorney's Office and Cook County's PDO (see Tanguay, 1967; Platt, 1968).

To develop a successful career in the PDO requires a great deal of patience, persistence, and luck. The pyramid structure of the PDO bureaucracy makes it almost impossible for a recruit to reasonably anticipate promotion to chief public defender. In the last 44 years, there have only been five chief public defenders in Alameda, and one of these was recruited from the District Attorney's Office. Appointment as chief public defender requires the support of the Board of Supervisors and the District Attorney's Office, as well as several years of trial and administrative experience. Some assistants hope to achieve the position of chief PD in other counties, but this also requires informal sponsorship from judges or district attorneys, and the competition for these positions is intense and often unpredictable. Many assistants who enter the office with the intention of making it their career quickly change their minds when they assess their chances of promotion. "I didn't think," said one ex-assistant, "that I wanted to spend the rest of my life as 'the number three man in the Public Defender Office' " (Interview No. 23).

Those who stay in the PDO do so for a variety of reasons. Some claim that the job is more secure and exciting than private practice. "What I think keeps me here," says an assistant, "is the sense of great challenge and the sense of ingenuity that's able to be used" (Interview No. 53). Some prefer a salaried job to the unpredictable income and demeaning aspects of fee collecting in private practice; others enjoy constant trial work and argue that "private lawyers do not have as much of a need to be in court" (Interview No. 47).

Becoming a career public defender is not so much a positive choice as it is a process of attrition and inevitability. For the assistant who neither wants nor is capable of successful private practice in criminal or general practice, there are very few options. The cautious civil servant is not likely to be attracted to the economically precarious existence of solo practice (see Carlin, 1962), and established law firms are not usually interested in recruiting older assistants who have forsaken trial work for administrative duties. Upward mobility in the PDO, therefore, may be a consequence of failing to leave the office "at the right time" or to be recruited into a law firm.[10]

Failure to leave the office, however, does not guarantee successful promotion. Organizational success, as C. Wright Mills (1956: 263) observed, is a "series of small calculations, stretched over the working lifetime of the individual: a bureaucracy is no testing field for heroes." Promotion depends on "agility rather than ability, on 'getting along' in a context of associates, superiors, and rules," and "on loyalty to, or even identity with, one's own firm, rather than entrepreneurial virtuosity." It is not surprising, then, that chief public defenders are not charismatic leaders, but rather cautious bureaucrats who "don't make waves" and will "do anything to keep people from being mad, which means doing nothing" (Interview No. 25). The career public defender rejects the entrepreneurial ethos of private practice and pursues the gradual accumulation of power and responsibility through hard work, patience, and diplomacy. Most assistants, however, regard the "occupational climb" as psychologically draining and economically limited, preferring instead to take their chances in the "open market" of private practice.

Burning Out

Most assistants only stay in the PDO long enough to complete their apprenticeship and become qualified for private practice. Prior to 1960, the median length of stay in the office was 4.75 years; from 1960 to 1968, the median dropped to 2.5 years. Similarly, lawyers in Cook County's PDO (1930-67) stayed for a median of 3.0 years and in the District Attorney's Office (1926-70) for about 4.0 years. Fluctuations in the length of stay are primarily determined by the availability of jobs in the legal marketplace.[11]

There are several reasons for leaving the PDO: some are fired or "cooled out" for inefficiency or unprofessional conduct; some are recruited into better paying jobs in private law firms; some seek the independence and challenge of solo practice; and some become disillusioned and jaded. Most assistants leave for more than one reason, typically a combination of an opportunity in private practice and disenchantment with the PDO. Assistants refer to the latter process as "burning out."

Many young lawyers enter the PDO with confused liberal commitments, rather broad notions about how they can contribute to changing the world, and enormous amounts of energy and optimism. By the time they leave the office, their idealism has developed into cynical pragmatism resulting from the realities of professional practice.[12] The following comments typify the attitudes of the majority of assistants:

> The public defenders are steeped in a tradition where you don't win things, where you lose everything, where you're constantly demoralized and where the DA's always on top [Interview No. 9].

> I was becoming callous. . . . I tried I don't know how many death penalty cases in the last two years. Well, a fellow just can't keep trying that kind of case without either losing his mind or becoming somewhat callous. . . . When I found that happening I became dissatisfied with the business and decided to get out of it [Interview No. 13].

> In about two and a half years I felt a certain routine setting in. . . . There's just so many ways you can commit a burglary and just so many ways you can commit a robbery. And these things boil down to the same cross-examination for the purpose of shaking an identification witness. . . . I felt that I was getting too hardened and I wasn't going to be able to do the kind of job that I should be able to do. . . . You're burned out, you know, you've done it. You give an awful lot and you get damn little, except pretty good pay and at some point you just poop out [Interview No. 44].

The realities of the PDO differ dramatically from formal descriptions of criminal courts portrayed in law school. Law students do not expect to be "bucking a stacked deck all the time" (Interview No. 12), nor do they view themselves as potential "salesmen" required to "get along with people you don't like" (Interview No. 56). After a short time in the PDO, however, assistants learn to "never become personally involved in cases," to "build a shield around yourself," and to develop "professional detachment" (Interviews No. 7, 12, and 56).

The duties of lawyers in the PDO are time-consuming, technical, and specialized. They include determining the economic eligibility of clients, conducting pretrial investigations, interviewing witnesses, negotiating pleas and sentences with prosecutors, defending persons charged with everything from traffic offenses to murder, preparing sentencing reports, writing appeal briefs, and doing public relations and community speaking. These tasks have become bureaucratically organized and specialized according to function so that assistants rarely handle a client's case from beginning to end. In addition, the cooperative ethic of the criminal courts requires an attitude of accommodation and willingness to work harmoniously with different actors in the system (Skolnick, 1967). According to a former chief district attorney, the ideal temperament required of persons working in the criminal courts is stability:

> I didn't want any oddballs or queers or eccentrics, you see. I wanted somebody that's well-rounded. That's why I didn't pay too much attention whether they were phi betas or Coif or law review because sometimes these brilliant guys can be awfully odd. They can be oddballs and give you trouble. . . . Stability was very important—yes, stability, working with others, and getting along with other people.

This view is reciprocated by an ex-chief public defender who characterized his assistants by their "ability to be practical and to compromise."

The realities of the job-mechanical processing of cases, lack of adequate resources and time for proper research and pretrial investigation, the availability of extensive resources (for example, the police) to the District Attorney's Office, and the prosecutorial bias of judges—not only cultivate an attitude of cynicism to the job but also to clients. Occasionally, this cynicism develops into explicit animosity and prejudice:

> What makes the job difficult for public defenders is the clients. . . . The fact of the matter is that you're dealing with the scum of the earth and they'll stab you in the back at the first opportunity. They'll walk over you and anybody else to get what they want. They're one cut above the animal—in fact, they're by and large worse. . . . They're just the lowest of the low. . . . Oddly enough, I wasn't bothered by the clients any more than a scientist in a lab dealing with extremely dangerous virus is bothered by virulents. He's careful because he recognizes that if you're dealing with bubonic plague, you're very careful how you handle it [Interview No. 21].

An ex-public defender similarly described his experience in the office as a "voyage through a sewer in a glass-bottomed boat," while an ex-assistant classified some of his clients as the "great unwashed" and observed that "most colored people just scream and yell" (Interviews No. 27 and 42).

This kind of explicit prejudice is rare among ex-assistants; typically, their hostility is implicit and ambivalent, reflecting feelings of guilt about the betrayal of their original liberal idealism:

> About the time I was getting ready to leave, I'd almost figured I was as eager to prosecute my client as I was to defend him. I think that's psychologically the time when you've got to get out of that sort of situation. . . . I got disillusioned [Interview No. 15].

> I started out with some kind of avenging zeal to protect these people who'd been ensnared in the clutches of the law. And I grew progressively sourer and had progressively less patience with them as I stayed there, and it finally got so that my animosities for them were very thinly disguised. I just didn't like them by and large. Nobody else liked them either really, but some of them were a little more patient finally than I became [Interview No. 20].

Various assistants claim that their clients lie, are sullen and distrustful, and are ungrateful. As one assistant reflected, "in all the cases I handled in the Public Defender's Office, even if I won a fantastic victory, the defendant never said 'thank you' " (Interview No. 40). Given their inaccurate expectations of the job, it is not surprising that assistants become "less sympathetic the longer they've been on the job. They've seen more; they've been burned more times" (Interview No. 52).

Most assistants report that they develop an immunity to the job and become somewhat callous. "The job is like a doctor's job. After a while a doctor gets tired of seeing forty people a day with colds. He tells them to take aspirins, drink juice and go to bed. What else can you do?" (Interview No. 52). An ex-assistant, now working in another PDO, also found the medical analogy appropriate:

> Public Defender work is an ordinary mundane thing. It's patching up people in the first-aid sense. . . . It's something like being in an emergency ward all the time. There's nothing but emergencies. You try to help a lot of people who come in that front door and patch up the big gaping holes that they all have in them, but you don't really . . . make a great medical finding [Interview No. 48].

By the time assistants are ready to leave the PDO, many are embittered, cynical, and burned out. This process partly derives from the failure of law schools to properly prepare students for professional realities; and this is reinforced on the job when assistants learn that "success" is characterized by an ability to be accommodating, manipulative, and pragmatic. The emphasis on mass processing of cases, technical virtuosity, and salesmanship which characterizes the PDO is interpreted by most assistants as an indication of the hopelessness and inevitability of the situation. The experience in the PDO is generally an embittering rather than radicalizing process, for assistants leave the office with an attitude of futility and defeatism about the possibility of making major changes in society.[13]

Leaving

While most assistants voluntarily leave the PDO because they are burned out and have better opportunities in private practice, a small minority is "forced to resign" or "cooled out." This group ranges from persons accused of immoral behavior (drug use, alcoholism, and so on) to those considered inefficient or technically incompetent. The former is considered a liability to the PDO because they are likely to generate public scandals or incur charges of professional misconduct. Given the vulnerability of the PDO to criticism from the local Board of Supervisors and the media, the "heavy drinker" and "known drug user" are encouraged to leave the office rather than risk exposure or prosecution.

"Inefficiency" is broadly defined to include inappropriate etiquette (too long hair, an untrimmed moustache, flashy clothes, and so on), poor judgment and demeanor (overly aggressive behavior in court, abrasive relationships with judges and prosecutors, and so on), and even sentimentality (one lawyer was encouraged to leave because she "handled every case like it was Leopold and Loeb"). Assistants who are unable to remain personable and cooperative while processing large numbers of cases are liable to the charge of "inefficiency":

> She wasn't a good PD in the sense that she couldn't handle volume. She just wasn't willing to handle cases on a volume basis. She wanted to act like a private lawyer and the Office couldn't afford to give her that much time. . . . [Assistant C.] didn't make a very good appearance in court. He was a nice-looking guy but he looked slow and talked rather hesitantly, and he wasn't aggressive enough to make him sound good. He got a couple of bad reviews from judges and they just very summarily got rid of him [Interview No. 25].

There are several options open to an organization that wants to remove or neutralize an employee who is considered inefficient or "unsuitable." He can be fired, or moved laterally within the organization, or demoted, or even promoted to an honorific but essentially powerless position (Levenson, 1961). In the PDO, as in most formal organizations, employees are rarely fired but rather "encouraged to leave":

I can never remember a person being outwardly fired. A couple of people were told they wouldn't be suitable for PD's. Saying "You're fired"—they don't do that. It's too dangerous, there may be a hearing later or something [Interview No. 52].

The Office said, "You're never going to be happy here because you believe in justice for everyone and we can't do that." . . . He [Public Defender] told me five months before I left that he thought I wasn't going to be happy there, that it wasn't suited for my personality and that I should think about looking elsewhere for a job [Interview No. 16].

He wasn't told to leave the day after tomorrow or anything like that. He was given to understand that it would be in everybody's best interests if he looked elsewhere for a job [Interview No. 39].

This pressure to leave is invariably successful because assistants cannot risk getting bad references for future jobs. Moreover, if they refuse to resign, office administrators can informally punish them by, for example, holding up pay increases or assigning them to less interesting duties in municipal or juvenile court. The reluctance of the office to explicitly fire wayward employees stems from a desire to maintain organizational integrity and avoid bad publicity. As Edwin Lemert (1967: 204) has observed in more general terms:

Even when the person is almost totally excluded and informally isolated within an organization, he may have power outside. This weighs heavily when the external power can be invoked in some way, or when it automatically leads to raising questions as to the internal workings of the organization. This touches upon the more salient reason for reluctance to eject an uncooperative and retaliatory person, even when he is relatively unimportant to the organization. We refer to a kind of negative power derived from the vulnerability of organizations to unfavorable publicity and exposure of their private lives that are likely if the crisis proceeds to formal hearings, case review, or litigation.

The majority of assistants, however, leave voluntarily and with the reluctant approval of administrators who have become used to seeing trained personnel leave for more lucrative jobs in private practice.

The Careers of Ex-Assistants

With the exception of a small group of tired and disillusioned "drop-outs" who turned to art, poetry, teaching, missionary work, yoga, and travel, the majority of assistants was recruited into small- to medium-sized general practice firms in the local area. After two or three years, most assistants are ready to leave the PDO in search of greater professional autonomy and more money. "The thing is," said an ex-assistant now specializing in criminal practice, "that it gets to a point where you get so competent that you really want to be your own man" (Interview No. 9). Another typical ex-assistant said that he left the PDO because "I felt I'd had enough of it. I wanted to try private practice. My wife was going to have a baby and I was afraid that if I got locked in on a civil service salary after having a child, it would be harder to get out" (Interview No. 34).

The "criminal bar" in Alameda, as in most counties, is small and its participants know each other and maintain informal ties through contact in the courts, client referrals, and occasional social activities (Skolnick, 1967). General practice lawyers do a considerable amount of criminal work and they are able to do first-hand evaluations of assistants when they are defending a "crime partner" of a client of the PDO. They also have many opportunities to observe assistants while waiting for their own cases to be called. It is within this informal context that assistants become familiar with the legal marketplace and are eventually recruited into private practice.

About one-third of the ex-assistants entered specialized practices; usually criminal or personal injury work. The remainder, with a few exceptions, entered general practices involving criminal, family, personal injury, probate, and other routine kinds of law. The kind of law practice in which ex-assistants work ranges from solo practice (about 28 percent) to medium-sized partnerships or associateships (about 45 percent). Ex-assistants are not to be found in large firms practicing business or corporate law. Their annual incomes, which are typical of general practitioners involved in volume business and "small fee" cases, range from under $20,000 (about 35 percent) to over $30,000 (about 8 percent). In this respect, ex-assistants in Alameda County are very similar to criminal lawyers and general practitioners in Detroit and New York who went directly into private practice from law school (see, for example, the studies of Ladinsky, 1963; Carlin, 1962).

By contrast, ex-prosecutors from Alameda County are less likely to go into criminal law practice (13 percent) and more likely to go into personal injury (26 percent) and corporate law practice (26 percent). Forty percent of ex-prosecutors (compared with 13 percent of all attorneys nationally) became partners in law firms, while only 14 percent (compared with 80 percent of all attorneys nationally) are in solo practice or salaried associates. Differences between ex-public defenders and ex-prosecutors are most clearly demonstrated in income levels: 39 percent of ex-prosecutors earn between $20,000 and $40,000 annually, while another 15 percent earn between $40,000 and $60,000.

Very few ex-assistants from the PDO participated in local politics. One became a member of the Oakland City Council and four were eventually rewarded with judgeships (three in municipal and one in superior court). The PDO, unlike the District Attorney's Office, is not a route into local or state politics. It even may count against lawyers with political aspirations because of its negative associations with "charity" law and "defense of criminals." On the other hand, most assistants are not interested in political careers and prefer, as Jack Ladinsky (1962) has observed of solo lawyers in Detroit, to test their entrepreneurial and technical skills in the highly competitive marketplace of general practice.

Ex-prosecutors, who are generally more interested in pursuing political careers, discover that the District Attorney's Office is not only a good place to make contacts but also serves as a certifier of their technical competence and ideological reliability. Twenty-two percent of ex-prosecutors moved on to jobs in state and federal prosecuting agencies, federal legislation, and state legislative and executive bodies. In addition, another 10 percent became judges in courts ranging from local municipal court to the United States Supreme Court (Tanguay, 1967: ch. 4).

While ex-prosecutors leave the District Attorney's Office to become the functionaries of economic and political elites, ex-assistants usually remain in general practice and discover that they have exchanged old problems—excessive caseloads, limited resources, bureaucratic inflexibility, ungrateful clients, and so on—for new burdens and crises, such as competing for clients with lay organizations (accountants, insurance agencies, real estate companies, savings and loan associations, and so on), collecting fees, rising overhead costs, and long hours of work. The only way out of this channel is to try to cross over into another profession, like teaching, or to drop out of professional work completely. The former requires enormous discipline and conviction, while the latter demands the total reversal of some thirty years of socialization.

SUMMARY AND CONCLUSIONS

In this essay, we have followed the careers of lawyers who spent some time in a Public Defender's Office in the years between 1927 and 1971. The office has considerably changed and grown during this period, beginning as a very small and part-time operation in the 1920s, gradually becoming more stable and respectable during the 1950s, and emerging in the late 1960s as a medium-sized bureaucracy characterized by an hierarchical division of labor and a formal apparatus of recruitment, training, and promotion.

During the 1950s, the background, motivation, and careers of ex-assistants began to follow a general pattern. Most recruits were male, white, from working and lower-middle-class origins, and with non-Protestant and liberal political backgrounds. The typical new assistant regarded the PDO as a place to develop technical skills and professional values in an atmosphere which would not violate their liberal political principles. Very few assistants planned to make a career in the PDO and only a small minority remained as career civil servants. Their decision to remain was typically motivated by either an unwillingness or inability to successfully compete in the marketplace of private practice rather than by a positive commitment to a public service career. Most lawyers, however, left the PDO after an average of two and a half years, feeling "burned out" and often embittered by the realities of professional practice in a public office. While a few assistants were "cooled out" and encouraged to leave, the majority left voluntarily to continue their legal careers locally in solo to medium-sized private firms.

While this study provides a clearer understanding of specific legal careers, it also raised more general questions about the relationship between the state, the legal profession, and public service. The PDO is an example of how the state subsidizes the apprenticeship and training of professionals who in the final analysis devote themselves to the practice of law for profit. It is through the PDO that young lawyers are professionally socialized and introduced to the legal marketplace. As in other public institutions—notably county hospitals, welfare departments and ghetto high schools—the clients of the PDO are poor, powerless, and disproportionately Third World. After lawyers in the PDO have completed their apprenticeship and refined their technical skills, they generally leave the PDO to enter private practice and defend predominantly middle-class clients.

This analysis, however, does not imply that lawyers join the PDO with the intention of instrumentally exploiting poor clients in order to develop profitable skills. On the contrary, most recruits are ideologically liberal, conceive of their work in humanitarian terms, and initially undertake their work with enthusiasm and optimism. Pragmatism and cynicism are not motivating factors for joining the PDO but instead gradually develop as a consequence of working there. The PDO is generally a disillusioning experience for young lawyers who at one time considered devoting themselves to public service careers.

Rather than becoming radicalized by their experience in the PDO, most assistants became embittered and alienated from political action. Malaise rather than rebellion characterized their frustrations. (For more general comments on this process, see Manifesto, 1972: 78-81.) This occurs for several reasons. First, the lack of a proper education about the nature and role of legal institutions in society lays the grounds for the development of cynicism. With the exception of the National Lawyers Guild, law students are not exposed to an analysis of the political economy of law or to other models of professional practice which might allow them to combine a reasonable salary with public service. Secondly, by the time they leave the PDO, they are usually married, have children, and have become accustomed to a comfortable life style. Their life style and financial responsibilities make it difficult to take risks in a different kind of occupation or even to make radical changes within the legal profession. And finally, the emphasis on technical virtuosity and professionalism, which characterizes the socialization process in the PDO, serves to reduce political consciousness and increase social distance from oppressed groups (Miliband, 1969: 119-145). This last point needs further elaboration.

Lawyers in the PDO occupy an ambiguous position in the labor force and society comparable to scientists, technicians, engineers, and other professionals. While they are an occupationally privileged group by virtue of their education, training, and income, at the same time they have no independent access to productive property and minimum control over the conditions of their work. Though their life styles are "middle class," they are also part of a "new working class of educated labor necessitated by the increasingly technological and scientific character of the process of production" (Marcuse, 1971-72: 3). As state workers performing unglamorous and professionally unrewarding work, public defenders are subject to additional exploitation and indignity.

Compared with most workers, assistants possess a relative degree of control over their work. But their autonomy is tolerated only so long as it does not violate the operating conditions of the PDO. The illusion of autonomy is maintained through constant reference to "professional discretion" (Manifesto, 1972: 71). Control of assistants, however, is maintained by the hierarchy of bureaucratic power and by the division of labor into technically disconnected roles. The former provides a mechanism for maintaining compliance with organizational goals, while the latter assures that assistants are "inserted into a microcosm that allows them no overall view" (Manifesto, 1972: 73).

Public defenders have not begun to examine the source and conditions of their own exploitation as workers. Rather, they see themselves as enlightened and privileged professionals who, as James Weinstein (1972: 49) has similarly observed of the student movement, tend to neglect their own grievances and "relate to the under-classes only through feelings of guilt and liberal missionary politics." The relationship of public defenders to their clients is, at its best, one of benevolent service, sustained by an ideology which emphasizes political neutrality, efficiency, and technocratic rationality (see, generally, Gorz, 1964: 120-125). Many assistants become aware that their work primarily consists of ameliorism and band-aid reform. They even acknowledge that the solution to "crime" lies in the economic and political transformation of society. But these are seen as "problems" to be solved in another context and by other persons, while assistants adapt to their role as inevitable and "realistic." They come to justify their role as mediators between the poor and the courts, resigned to seeking occasional loopholes in the system, softening its more explicitly repressive features and attempting to rescue the victims of blatant injustices. But even this makeshift effort to link everyday work with liberal humanitarianism proves inadequate, since most assistants are regarded with resentment, ingratitude, or indifference by their clients. When they leave the PDO, they have become cynical and embittered, alienated from politics, and preoccupied with problems of survival and success in the legal marketplace.

The process we have described is not, of course, unique to public defenders. Neal Shover (1972) has reported on the routine development of cynicism in correctional workers, Arthur Niederhoffer (1967) on comparable traits in police officers, and Abraham Blumberg's (1967: 158) study of probation officers concluded that "frustrated as professionals, stripped of real decision-making power, lacking a genuine career motif, and assigned relatively low status by the community, it is not surprising that [they] often develop a high degree of cynicism."

The basic solution to these problems does not lie in more training, better facilities, more money,[14] or even recruitment of more women and Third World professionals. As recent studies have indicated, the recruitment of Black probation officers and police officers makes little difference to the treatment received by oppressed groups and even tends to increase the marginality, isolation, and cynicism of Third World professionals (see, for example, Blumberg, 1967: ch. 7; Alex, 1969). So long as the criminal justice system is used as an instrument of class and racial exploitation, its employees cannot expect to resolve the contradictions inherent in their role as servants of the state. The solution to the cynicism and disillusionment of public defenders lies not only in devising new ways of offering their service to the victims of oppression, but also in contesting the fragmentation, meaninglessness, and exploitation of their own work.

NOTES

1. According to the American Bar Foundation (1955: 90), for example, "the public defender's office is one of the most valuable contributions in modern times to the administration of criminal justice." Similarly uncritical comments can be found in the President's Commission on Law Enforcement and Administration of Justice (1967: ch. 5).

2. The results of the Cook County study have not been published. The other study is partially reported by Suzi Tanguay (1967).

3. The President's Commission conservatively estimated that approximately 60 percent of all felony defendants and close to 50 percent of all misdemeanor defendants are unable to retain a private attorney.

4. The written exam is no longer required.

5. The local private attorney is often an ex-assistant from Alameda's PDO, thus ensuring a cooperative relationship between the PDO and the private bar.

6. The chief district attorney at that time was a strong anti-communist and had organized a powerful "red squad" within his Office.

7. As of 1966, there were 4,164 judges and lawyers in Oakland, of which only 1.3 percent were Blacks. See Hayes (1972: 51).

8. As a major study of legal careers concluded, "in its attraction and appeal to young people the law seems to do its fishing in restricted waters stocked largely with the product of professional families, private schools, and the upper social strata" (S. Warkov and J. Zelan, 1965).

9. Between 1930 and 1967, 16 out of a total of 46 public defenders left Cook County's PDO to join the District Attorney's Office.

10. For similar observations about the mobility of teachers and lawyers, see Howard S. Becker (1952: 470-477) and Erwin O. Smigel (1964: 74-85).

11. For example, the present economic crisis has increased the length of stay in Alameda County's PDO, though most assistants are ready to move on after two years.

12. For a comparable study of medical students, see Howard S. Becker and Blanche Geer (1958: 50-56).

13. By contrast, ex-prosecutors in Alameda County generally report that their experiences in the District Attorney's Office conform to their expectations and ideology.

14. As suggested, for example, by the President's Commission and Howard James (1972: 129).

REFERENCES

ALEX, N. (1969) Black in Blue: A Study of Negro Policemen. New York: Appleton.

American Bar Foundation (1955) The Administration of Criminal Justice in the United States. Chicago.

BECKER, H. S. (1952) "The career of the Chicago public schoolteacher." American Journal of Sociology 57 (March): 470-477.

——— and B. GEER (1958) "The fate of idealism in medical school." American Sociological Review 23 (February): 50-56.

——— and A. L. STRAUSS (1956) "Careers, personality, and adult socialization." American Journal of Sociology 62 (November): 253-263.

BLUMBERG, A. (1967) Behind the Shield. New York: Doubleday.

——— (1967) Criminal Justice. Chicago: Quadrangle.

CARLIN, J. (1962) Lawyers on Their Own. New Brunswick, N.J.: Rutgers University Press.

CARR-SAUNDERS, A. M. and P. A. WILSON (1933) The Professions. Oxford: Clarendon Press.

CASPER, J. D. (1971) "Did you have a lawyer when you went to court? No, I had a public defender." Law and Social Action 1, 4 (Spring): 4-9.

GINTIS, H. (1970) "The new working class and revolutionary youth." Socialist Revolution 3 (May/June): 13-43.

GORZ, A. (1964) Strategy for Labor. Boston: Beacon Press.

——— (1972) "Technical intelligence and the capitalist division of labor." Telos 12 (Summer): 27-41.

GOULDNER, A. W. (1957) "Cosmopolitans and locals." Administrative Science Quarterly 2 (December): 446-467.

GROSMAN, B. A. (1969) The Prosecutor. Toronto: University of Toronto Press.

HAYES, E. C. (1972) Power Structure and Urban Policy: Who Rules in Oakland? New York: McGraw-Hill.

HUGHES, E. C. (1959) Men and Their Work. New York: Free Press.

IVENS, C. P. (1939) Office of the Public Defender in California With Special Reference to Alameda, Los Angeles, and San Francisco Counties. Unpublished Masters thesis. Berkeley: University of California School of Criminology.

JAMES, H. (1972) Crises in the Courts. New York: David McKay.

JANOWITZ, M. (1964) The Professional Soldier. New York: Free Press.

KOLKO, G. (1967) The Triumph of Conservatism: A Reinterpretation of American History, 1900-1916. Chicago: Quadrangle.

––– (1969) The Roots of American Foreign Policy. Boston: Beacon Press.

LADINSKY, J. (1963) "Careers of lawyers, law practice and legal institutions." American Sociological Review 28: 47-54.

LEMERT, E. M. (1967) Human Deviance, Social Problems and Social Control. New York: Prentice-Hall.

LEVENSON, B. (1961) "Bureaucratic Succession," pp. 362-375 in A. Etzioni (ed.) Complex Organizations. New York: Holt, Rinehart & Winston.

LUNCH, W. M. (1970) "Oakland Revisited: Stability and Change in an American City." Unpublished manuscript. Berkeley: University of California, Oakland Project.

MALLET, S. (1963) La Nouvelle Classe Ouvriere. Paris: Editions du Sevil.

MANIFESTO, I. (1972) "Technicians and the capitalist division of labor." Socialist Revolution 9 (May/June): 65-84.

MARCUSE, H. (1971-72) "The movement in a new era of repression: an assessment." Berkeley Journal of Sociology 16: 3.

MILIBAND, R. (1969) The State in Capitalist Society. New York: Basic Books.

MILLS, C. W. (1956) White Collar. New York: Oxford University Press.

NIEDERHOFFER, A. (1967) Behind the Shield. New York: Doubleday.

PLATT, A. (1968) "Notes on the Careers of Public Defenders in Cook County." Unpublished manuscript. Berkeley: University of California School of Criminology.

––– H. SCHECHTER and P. TIFFANY (1968) "In defense of youth: a case study of the public defender in juvenile court." Indiana Law Journal 43, 3 (Spring).

President's Commission on Law Enforcement and Administration of Justice (1967) The Courts. Washington, D.C.: U.S. Government Printing Office.

SHOVER, H. (1972) "Experts and Diagnosis in Correctional Agencies." Paper presented at annual meeting of the Society for the Study of Social Problems, New Orleans.

SILVERSTEIN, L. (1965) Defense of the Poor. Chicago: American Bar Foundation.

SKOLNICK, J. (1967) "Social control in the adversary system." Journal of Conflict Resolution 11: 52-70.

SLOCUM, W. L. (1966) Occupational Careers. Chicago: Aldine.

SMIGEL, E. O. (1964) The Wall Street Lawyer. New York: Free Press.

SUDNOW, D. (1965) "Normal crimes: sociological features of the penal code in a public defender's office." Social Problems 12, 3: 255-276.

TANGUAY, S. (1967) Role of the Prosecutor's Office in Legal Careers. Unpublished Masters thesis. Berkeley: University of California School of Criminology.

WARKOV, S. and J. ZELAN (1965) Lawyers in the Making. Chicago: Aldine.

WEINSTEIN, J. (1969) The Corporate Ideal in the Liberal State, 1900-1918. Boston: Beacon Press.

––– (1972) "The left, old and new." Socialist Revolution 10 (July/August): 49.

WOOD, A. (1967) Criminal Lawyer. New Haven, Conn.: College and University Press.

Chapter 9

THE OUTSIDER IN THE COURTROOM:
AN ALTERNATIVE ROLE FOR DEFENSE

LYNN M. MATHER

Recent research on criminal courts has emphasized how an informal set of norms prescribing cooperation, exchange, and compromise for prosecutors and defense attorneys has replaced the formal norm of adversary conflict (Newman, 1966; Skolnick, 1967; Blumberg, 1967a, 1967b; Alschuler, 1968; Cole, 1970). Yet it is not entirely clear what the incentives are for defense counsel to discard their Perry Mason role of trial lawyer in favor of the negotiator who deals for guilty pleas. Financial incentives are paramount for private defense attorneys, according to Blumberg (1967b) and Cole (1970), since attorneys are generally paid a flat fee for each case. But as Feeley (1973: 419) points out, Blumberg's (1967b) discussion of fee motivation somewhat contradicts his earlier argument that defense attorneys are "forced" to abandon their adversary role because of court demands for expeditious processing of cases due to heavy caseloads. Skolnick (1967), in finding similarities in the cooperative posture of both private

AUTHOR'S NOTE: This title is adapted from Huitt (1961), whose article, "The Outsider in the Senate: An Alternative Role," provided a helpful framework for the organization of the data reported here. I am grateful to Martin Shapiro for referring me to Huitt's article and for offering many helpful suggestions on the original draft of this chapter.

attorneys and public defenders, suggests that the role is chosen not only for administrative and personal (long-term interaction with prosecutors) reasons, but also because cooperation instead of adversary conflict is seen to be in the best interests of their clients. This theory of defense is common to public defenders and most private defense attorneys, he argues (1967: 62):

> It is a theory that stresses administrative regularity over challenge, and emphasizes decisions most likely to maximize gain and minimize loss in the negatively valued commodity of penal "time."

Perhaps because the cooperative role of defense has been so frequently described in the literature, it is time to consider an alternative role—that is, the more traditional adversary role—which does appear, albeit infrequently, in the criminal court. This article then will describe: first, the situations in which even the most cooperative attorneys choose a full-fledged adversary trial; secondly, those defense attorneys who prefer not to plea bargain and are more oriented to trial dispositions; and finally, defendants who, after all, are not socialized into the court bureaucracy and its norms of cooperation, and who may reject the plea bargains recommended by their counsel. The decision-making process for defense which results in either a guilty plea or a trial is the focus of this study. Notwithstanding the frequency of guilty pleas, some criminal cases do go to trial. And thus, investigation into the factors determining the method of disposition may clarify the differences between a cooperative and an adversary role for defense.

SETTING AND METHOD

The data presented here come from a study of a felony court: the Central District of the Los Angeles Superior Court. The Los Angeles Superior Court is divided into eight districts, the largest being the Central District, located in downtown Los Angeles. In 1970, over 12,000 felony defendants had their cases heard in the Central District. The majority of defendants were black or Mexican-American. Roughly 70 percent of the defendants were represented by attorneys in the Public Defender's Office.

After a preliminary hearing in the Municipal Courts, defendants were arraigned in the master calendar department of the Superior Court. Almost all the defendants pled not guilty at this arraignment, and the presiding judge assigned each a date and courtroom for trial. There were 26 trial departments. Associated with each one was a judge, two or three deputy district attorneys (hereafter, DAs), a clerk, reporter, and bailiff. Also, several deputy public defenders (hereafter, PDs) usually had settings for cases in the same courtroom. Thus, each courtroom took on its own character with the daily interaction of a small group of people. Defense and prosecuting attorneys did not tend to socialize with each other outside of court, however. For example, at the noon recess, the attorneys generally went to their respective offices (DA or PD) to meet colleagues for lunch. Attorneys shared a great deal of information and folk wisdom this way on the actions of other attorneys and on the behavior of judges in other trial departments.

Research for this study began in July 1970 with almost daily observation in court, listening to and talking with attorneys, judges, and court staff. In each trial department, I would observe the court proceedings (and frequently the discussions in hallways and in judges' chambers), and then question participants on particular dispositions that had occurred. Later, in interviews, I asked attorneys and judges about more general patterns and strategies involved in settling cases. Field work continued through June 1971, with a total of five months of observation in court, interviews with numerous participants, analysis of case files, and the collection of some statistical data.

GENERAL PATTERN OF CASE DISPOSITION

For most defendants, about two months elapsed between arraignment in the master calendar department and the date set for trial. During that period, pretrial motions would be heard (for example, motions to quash the information or to suppress evidence). These motions occurred in an estimated 20 percent of the cases and were generally independent of any plea negotiations. If successful, the case would be dismissed; if not, the defense attorney would discuss with his client the alternatives for disposition. The frequency of different methods of disposition in 1970 is summarized below (Bureau of Criminal Statistics, 1970: 12):

47.6%	Guilty plea
32.3%	Trial by "submission on the transcript"
8.0%	Court trial
3.6%	Jury trial
8.5%	Dismissal (following a pretrial motion or "in the interests of justice")
100.0%	(31,571 defendants in Los Angeles County)[1]

Only the full court or jury trial can really be considered adversary proceedings. Trial by "submission on the transcript" (SOT) frequently operates as a slow plea of guilty. The SOT proceeding, while authorized for all of California, rarely occurs outside of Los Angeles. By this method of disposition, the defendant submits the transcript of his preliminary hearing (with additional evidence or argument if desired) to the trial judge for final adjudication. Some SOT trials are used in place of a dismissal, as it is known to all parties beforehand that the judge will find the defendant not guilty. In other cases, SOT is a semi-adversary proceeding where the defendant concedes certain points but wishes to contest others, thus argument is focused only on the issues in conflict. But in general, SOT substitutes for a plea of guilty and often involves the same kinds of bargains as to charge and sentence as in a guilty plea. For example, the defendant may be found guilty of a lesser offense, or of only one of several offenses charged against him. Or, the judge may commit himself, formally or informally, on what the sentence is likely to be.

There appeared to be a significant relationship between the method of disposition and certain characteristics of the case; in particular, the type of offense and the defendant's prior record. Cases involving severe crimes were more likely to be resolved by adversary processes; cases with less serious offenses were more likely to be settled by guilty plea or SOT. Thus, while 11.6 percent of the *total* felony dispositions were by adversary trial, 36.1 percent of the homicides, 28 percent of the kidnappings, 27.1 percent of the forcible rapes, and 22.2 percent of the robberies were resolved by full court or jury trial. But only 8.6 percent of the drunk driving cases, 8.2 percent of the marijuana and the dangerous drug (pills, not opiates) cases, 6.2 percent of the forgeries, and 5.0 percent of the bookmaking cases were settled by trial.[2]

In addition, the longer the defendant's record, the more likely that his case would be resolved by adversary trial. The Bureau of Criminal Statistics (1969: 111) distinguishes among four categories of prior criminal record: no record; minor record (e.g., convictions of less than 90 days in jail); major record (e.g., convictions with 90 days or more in jail); and prison record (prior prison commitment). Comparing prior record of defendants to methods of disposition, Greenwood et al. (1973: 42), found that while 14.1 percent of the defendants with prison records took their cases to trial, only 11.8 percent of the defendants with major records, 10.9 percent of defendants with minor records, and 9.5 percent of defendants with no record had trial dispositions; again this is in comparison to 11.6 percent of all dispositions which were by trial. That the defendant's record and the type of offense would be related to the method of case disposition is explained in part by the fact that these two factors are crucial for sentencing. As will be discussed in the next section, a defense attorney's prediction of the likely sentence is a key element in the choice of disposition method.

There are various possible sentences for convicted defendants. If a defendant is sent to state prison, then the actual length of his prison term is determined by the Adult Authority, within a range set by law. But most of the other options are set entirely by the trial judge. For defendants convicted in 1970, the distribution of sentences was as follows (Bureau of Criminal Statistics, 1970: 5):

6%	State prison
70%	Probation (about one-third of these also with jail time)
15%	County jail
9%	Other commitments (fine, California Youth Authority, California Rehabilitation Center and Department of Mental Hygiene)
100%	(25,642 convicted defendants in Los Angeles County)

Much of the information for the sentencing decision comes from the "probation report," a presentence investigation prepared by an officer of the probation department. The report includes a summary of the defendant's record, background, and the circumstances of the offense, along with a recommendation on the advisability of probation. Most judges tended to follow these recommendations and, to the extent that they did not, it was generally the judges (often as a result of a plea bargain) who were more lenient than the probation officers.

One final aspect of case disposition is the level of conviction, which is determined by the type of sentence imposed, not by the charge. Of all defendants convicted in 1970, 59.3 percent received misdemeanor sentences (and thus were convicted at the misdemeanor level) and 40.7 percent received felony sentences. But while 59.3 percent of the defendants were convicted at the misdemeanor *level*, only 9 percent were actually convicted of misdemeanor *charges* (Bureau of Criminal Statistics, 1970: 18). The DAs were reluctant to reduce charges to misdemeanors in exchange for a guilty plea. They preferred instead to let the judges use their discretion in sentencing to set the conviction at the misdemeanor level. The fact that such a large percentage of defendants charged with felonies eventually were convicted at the misdemeanor level is attributed less to leniency on the part of Los Angeles judges than to inadequate screening in the earlier stages of the process. Relatively minor cases which might be prosecuted as misdemeanors in other California counties are more likely to be handled as felonies in Los Angeles because of the split jurisdiction for prosecuting agencies between city and county; in Los Angeles, the District Attorney is responsible for felony prosecution and city prosecutors handle misdemeanor prosecution, thus cases tend to be prosecuted as felonies in Superior Court if they contain any elements of a felony (see Judicial Council of California, 1971: 123-124; but see also Greenwood et al., 1973: 25).

PUBLIC DEFENDERS

The Norm

There was a consensus among most PDs as to which cases "ought" to be tried and which "ought" to be settled without trial. This view was based upon predictions of case outcomes, in terms of the chances of acquittal and the probable sentence if convicted. In making these predictions, PDs investigated their client's version of what happened, the arrest report made by police, the transcript of the preliminary hearing, testimony of possible witnesses, any physical evidence and other pertinent information. There was a staff of investigators for attorneys in the Public Defender's Office to help check out evidence and interview witnesses, and the PDs themselves had one day a week with no cases assigned to allow them time for investigation in the field. The PDs then evaluated all of the strengths and weaknesses in each case against perceived judge and jury behavior on the issue of reasonable doubt. PDs referred to cases with a very high chance of conviction as "dead bang" cases; that is, cases with very strong evidence against the defendant and no credible or consistent explanation by the defendant for innocence. "Reasonable doubt" cases, on the other hand, were those with limited or conflicting evidence and some plausible defense. They were essentially of two kinds. In one type of "reasonable doubt" case, the doubt centered on the degree of the defendant's involvement in the crime or on the gravity of the offense; defense attorneys considered these cases to be "overfiled," and while there was a chance of acquittal on the original charge, there was a high likelihood of conviction on a lesser offense. In the other type of "reasonable doubt" case, the doubt arose from insufficient evidence either to clearly connect the defendant with the crime or to prove that any crime had been committed; in these cases, there was a good chance of complete acquittal.

Few cases in court were perceived as this latter type of "reasonable doubt" case (with a good chance of complete acquittal). The majority were "dead bang" or overfiled "reasonable doubt" cases. As one PD commented:

> The fact is that the doctrine of reasonable doubt is not useful anymore. In most cases, there's hardly any doubt at all. In fact, most of the cases we win at trial are because of sloppy prosecution.

And another PD explained:

> Most of the cases we get are pretty hopeless—really not much chance of acquittal. But often the defendant realizes that too. The important thing to understand is that a "win" for the defense does not necessarily mean that the defendant walks home free. Instead a "win" to a burglary accused may mean petty theft with six months suspended. Or a "win" to a

defendant with a long prior record may mean a year in county jail—which
is the maximum time for a misdemeanor but could be a terrific break for
that particular defendant.

Thus, not only did PDs evaluate cases for the legal sufficiency of the evidence,
but they also evaluated cases according to the sentencing alternatives. In view of
current patterns of sentencing, PDs considered the alleged offense as well as their
client's background and prior record in order to determine how "serious" the
case was.

A "serious" case was one with a high probability of a harsh sentence, such as
state prison. Either a bad criminal record for a defendant or a severe offense
identified a case as "serious." To determine whether a case was "serious" or
"light," PDs considered all of the criteria used in sentencing, such as the
defendant's background (age, family, employment, and so on) and the
circumstances of the offense. "Light" cases were those with no real possibility of
a state prison sentence, and a good chance of a sentence of probation and a
misdemeanor level of conviction.

The most important features of a case for constructing a disposition strategy
were the strength of the prosecution's case and the seriousness of the case, in
terms of the likely sentence on conviction. The terms presented above, "dead
bang" vs. "reasonable doubt" and "serious" vs. "light" cases, are described each
as dichotomous categories, but clearly strength and seriousness are continua and
some cases fall in between the extremes. Nevertheless, these categories were used
by the PDs as they talked about their cases, and they are useful analytical
devices for explaining the processes of case disposition. Figure 1 illustrates how
the categories of strength and seriousness interacted to produce trial or non-trial
dispositions.

In "light" cases which were either "dead bang" or with "reasonable doubt"
of the degree of the defendant's involvement in the crime, generally a non-trial
disposition was chosen, either a guilty plea or SOT. There was little explicit
bargaining accompanying most of these dispositions as specific outcomes were
fairly well-known and predictable. That is, it was known that the DA would get
some type of conviction (whether on the original charge or on a lesser charge),
and since the cases were "light," the defendant would get a lenient sentence.
Further, both parties knew the kinds of charge reductions and dismissals
routinely permitted according to DA office policies. If the judge hearing the case
would not "chamberize" (indicate to defense counsel in chambers what the
likely sentence would be), then the PD (with the approval of the DA) could have
the case transferred to a "short cause" court. There were two short cause courts
among the 26 trial departments; they were designed to handle only guilty pleas
or SOT trials which would last less than an hour. Judges who would chamberize

STRENGTH OF PROSECUTION'S CASE (Prediction of Conviction or Acquittal)			SERIOUSNESS OF CASE (Prediction of Severity of Sentence)		
			"Light" case	"Serious" case	
				If good offer from D.A.	If bad offer from D.A.
		"Dead Bang" case	Negotiated disposition (Implicit bargaining)	Negotiated disposition (Explicit bargaining)	Trial
	"Reasonable Doubt" case	Chance of conviction on lesser charge	Negotiated disposition (Implicit bargaining)	Negotiated disposition (Explicit bargaining– easier to obtain good offer here than above)	Trial
		Chance of complete acquittal	Indeterminate	Negotiated disposition (Explicit bargaining	Indeterminate

Figure 1: RECOMMENDATIONS BY DEFENSE ATTORNEYS ON METHOD OF DISPOSITION AS A FUNCTION OF STRENGTH OF PROSECUTION'S CASE, SERIOUSNESS OF CASE, AND DEFENSE ATTORNEY'S PERCEPTION OF D.A.'S OFFER

and who were known to be lenient sentencers were generally assigned to the short cause departments, thus facilitating non-trial dispositions. Typical "light, dead bang" cases would include bookmaking, forgery and bad check cases, and possession of marijuana or pills. A typical "light" case which was seen as overfiled might be a minor burglary (which would be reduced to petty theft) or auto theft (which would be reduced to joyriding).

In "light" cases which were weak because there was reasonable doubt that the defendant was guilty of *any* offense, PDs would seek a complete acquittal, either by explicit bargaining or by trial. Depending upon his perception of the DA handling the case, the PD might try to persuade the DA to dismiss the charge or to talk with the judge to arrange a SOT trial for not guilty. But many DAs were not perceived as very receptive to such a suggestion for acquittal, and so the PD would go directly for adversary trial disposition. He would choose between court and jury trial depending on the type of case and the judge in the court where the case was set. There were few or no sentencing risks involved in a trial disposition on a "light" case, as the sentence even after trial would probably be quite lenient. An example of this type of case would be a defendant with little or no record charged with possession of marijuana, auto theft, or drunk driving, who had a credible explanation in his defense.

"Serious" cases presented more problems for constructing a defense strategy because both DAs and judges hesitated to exercise discretion in cases involving grave offenses or defendants with bad records. In cases of this type where there was a good chance of conviction on the original charge ("dead bang") or on a lesser charge, PDs would bargain for leniency and try to settle the case by guilty plea or SOT. After explicit bargaining, the PDs would recommend a negotiated disposition or a trial disposition depending upon their perception of the final offer. In the overfiled "reasonable doubt" cases, the PDs were frequently successful in their bargaining because they could point to the weak points in the prosecution's case. In the "dead bang" cases the bargaining was more difficult; here, any mitigating factors in the offense or in the defendant's background were emphasized to show that this was "not really a state prison case." But where a favorable bargain could not be obtained, the case would be settled by trial since "the defendant's got nothing to lose—he'd go to the joint anyway." One judge commented:

> If the defendant did what he did and he's going to prison for it anyway—particularly if it's a heinous offense—then he's not going to get any consideration from me or the probation department. In that case, his lawyer will tell him that he can't do anything for him, so he might as well go to trial, and take his chances on an acquittal.

Typical cases which are likely to go to trial because "there is no room for negotiation" included (the judge continued):

> Armed robbery—that gets five to life. Forcible rape. First degree burglary with maybe some injuries involved. Murder cases. Some child molestation cases.

In "serious" cases where there was "reasonable doubt" that the defendant was guilty of any offense, the disposition choice was difficult. Here the sentencing risks were high but the possible gain, complete acquittal, was considerable. The sentencing risks were high since, if the defendant was convicted as charged, the judge might be statutorily restricted from granting a misdemeanor sentence or probation (because of the gravity of the offense or the defendant's prior record). In a bargained disposition to a lesser charge (or if the DA agreed to offer no evidence on any prior felony convictions), then the judge would be able (and was perceived to be more willing) to use his discretion for a lenient sentence. The PD's perception of the value of a DA's offer in cases of this type depended not only on considerations of sentence and charge, but also on whether he believed his client was in fact guilty of the offense. If the defendant admitted his guilt to his attorney, then the PD would probably recommend a negotiated disposition because of the high sentencing risks of trial. But what if the defendant solidly maintained his innocence, in addition to having a chance of acquittal based on the evidence? Then any offer of a lenient sentence was bad, and yet the sentencing risks of trial were high, and a negotiated dismissal or SOT for not guilty was nearly impossible to obtain because of the seriousness of the case. The PD's final recommendation on disposition method was indeterminate because it depended so heavily on the attorney/client interaction and specific characteristics of the case. Frequently the PDs would recommend trial in spite of the risks, but they were also likely to leave the decision more to their clients with no recommendation. Interestingly, very few cases in this category (of "serious" with a chance of complete acquittal) were observed. Perhaps because they did present the most serious questions on the propriety of plea bargaining, there was a tendency for attorneys to redefine cases of this type; that is, to describe them as "dead bang" instead of "reasonable doubt," or to minimize the seriousness of the case. Or, perhaps earlier pretrial screening had diverted these cases so that they didn't reach the trial stage.

These patterns of case disposition correspond roughly to the ways in which most PDs routinely recommended trial or non-trial disposition. Certainly PDs varied in their judgments and their predictions, so that one attorney might evaluate his client's chances differently than another would have. Or, what is a "good" bargain to one PD might not be to his colleague. But, in general there was a consensus on how to evaluate cases and choose the best method for disposition. Most PDs then strongly encouraged their clients to accept the recommended disposition method. However, a significant sub-group of PDs (described in the next section on "The Mavericks") felt that they should do "just what their client wants to do" rather than "what's best for their client." Obviously *all* PDs tried to do both in theory, but the reality of disposition choice forced them to lean to one role or another. Thus, most PDs would urge a negotiated disposition if it appeared to be in their client's best interest. Three different PDs expressed this view as follows (italics added in each comment):

> There's too much risk involved to take [some of] these cases to trial. It makes whores out of us. *We'd like to do jury trials. But that's not what's best for our clients.*

> I try to tell them [clients] what all the possibilities are, the different alternatives for disposition. I try to avoid telling clients what to do. I don't overrule them. . . . *Well, sometimes I go down on them a little harder. You've got to for their own good.*

> Yeah, I'll twist arms. They [some other PDs] kid that it's because I'm lazy. The others in the office, they'll say "Fuck him. Give him his jury trial if he wants it." But I won't do that. I think *it's in my clients' interests for me to get them the best deal that I can. . . . That's what I'm here for.*

I've had some nasty, arrogant people that I've defended. "Society" hasn't been helped by what I've done. But I fugure that's not my problem. *My job is to do what I can for my client. If you've got a bad case and it's a loser, then it's not worth the risks of trial. You've gotta come down hard on a client sometimes.*

The Mavericks

Skolnick (1967: 65) distinguished between two normative meanings of the notion that an attorney "represents" a client: first, "that he accepts his client's view of the strategy of the case" and offers advice on how to implement that strategy; and second, "that the attorney is responsible both for strategy and tactics."[3] Skolnick found that defense attorneys typically accepted the latter definition. As indicated above, most PDs in this study also accepted that view of the proper role of defense attorney. However, between four and seven PDs (out of the 50 in felony trials) were designated by their fellow PDs and by DAs as being "mavericks." These PDs were generally more trial-minded and more willing to accept their client's view on the strategy for case disposition.

For example, one PD described a rape case for trial that he had had transferred from department 64 to department 107, since department 64 was too congested to handle a jury trial. This was an unusual move, because Judge O'Neill[4] (in department 64) was considered to be the best judge (from defense point of view) on issues of reasonable doubt. When asked why he didn't waive jury and have a court trial before Judge O'Neill, the PD replied:

I would have. And O'Neill is probably the only judge that I would have waived jury before, judging by what the other PDs say about him. But my client wouldn't waive jury. . . . You see, the defendants don't understand the finesse of court-shopping, or the risks there are with different judges, etc. They just get some bullheaded notion and stick to it.

I then asked the PD, "Don't you try to explain the situation to them and talk them into what you think is best for them?" He answered:

No. *And I'm kind of a maverick that way.* Among the people in our office, I'm certainly different. I can't talk to these clients—it's frustrating and you never really do get through to them. So if they want their jury trial, then O.K., I'll give it to them. I prefer to deal with the people of the court—*I'd rather talk and argue my case with reasonable people in court, instead of arguing with my clients.* Particularly with a state prison case. . . . Remember in talking to me that I'm a maverick. I take probably more cases to jury trial than any of the other deputies. Well, except maybe for George Birch, Ted Peterson and Mark Rothenberg. They do a lot of jury trials too. . . .

My position is, *"I don't insist that a defendant do anything other than what he wants to do."* It's just like if a patient goes to a doctor and the doctor thinks maybe he should operate, but the patient doesn't want him to. Then the doctor should not operate. If the patient were to die from that operation, it should be the result of the patient's choice, not the doctor's. It's the same thing with lawyers. The client must ultimately be the one to consent to a disposition or to trial. *With many cases, I cannot say with absolute certainty that it would go one way or the other.* And since I cannot, I don't want to try to convince my client that one way is definitely preferable. I don't want a guy in state prison thinking that he was copped out by his attorney. [Emphasis added]

Most of the other PDs could not say "with absolute certainty" what the outcome of a case would be at trial. But they were more willing than the "mavericks" to play the game of predicting the costs and benefits of trial and to impress upon their clients the importance of those predictions. The "maverick" PDs also settled cases through bargaining, but handled a much larger proportion of their cases at full trial than did their colleagues. It did not appear that the bargains arranged by "maverick" PDs were any better or worse than deals arranged by others. Several of the "mavericks" were among the more senior members of the PD's office. This meant they often were assigned tougher, more "serious" cases than their junior colleagues, and hence bargains were harder to obtain. For example, one DA described plea discussions in his court between two PDs, Bill Hirsch and Mark Rothenberg, and the other DA:

Rothenberg makes such a big deal out of everything. He's so different from Bill. Bill comes in and sits down with Herb (the other DA) and in ten minutes, they're all disposed of—all four cases. Rothenberg had just *one* case this morning and he's still yelling about it. *Although, Bill does get the more dealable cases. He doesn't have as much seniority as Rothenberg.* [Emphasis added]

The only real sanction against the "mavericks" is that their clients may be hurt on sentencing because of the risks taken at trial. In one case, the defendant was charged with grand theft auto and receiving stolen property. The offenses were considered very minor, but the defendant (age 26, in custody, Mexican-American) had a record which included, among other charges, two misdemeanor convictions for burglary, one for forgery, and a prior felony conviction for robbery (for which he did two years in prison). Riley, a "maverick" PD, took the case to jury trial and the defendant was convicted of grand theft auto, the more serious of the two counts.[5] The main defense raised was the defendant's denial of knowledge that the car was stolen, but his prior convictions were brought out on cross-examination to somewhat discredit his testimony. After the trial, the DA complained:

That Riley is incompetent. He doesn't know how to evaluate a case realistically. . . . And his client will suffer.

I asked the DA, "Will he be sentenced more severely?" The DA answered:

Sure, he probably will. He got on the stand and perjured himself by making up that story. So the judge isn't going to think much of him . . . Riley's so bad. We offered to let him plead to Receiving Stolen Property as a misdemeanor . . . and to strike the prior. He'd probably be out of custody by now. Well, not exactly. He'd have to wait the three weeks for the probation report. And then he'd get time served [which was four months] or maybe ten days more. But now he'll be sentenced on GTA [Grand Theft Auto] with a prior. He's going to face a lot more.

But actually in the above case it is difficult to say if the defendant really was hurt by having an attorney who was "not realistic." The probation report included a statement from the defendant's parole officer which said that the defendant's behavior on parole was "marginal to fair," and that he would probably be returned to prison on *any* new conviction as a violation of parole. In this light, the PD's behavior was more "realistic" and the DA's offer was not so attractive. The problem is that, especially with "serious" cases, one cannot ever say for certain "what the punishment would have been if . . . " Outcomes are shaped by predictions and interactions of many participants, some of whom may not be directly involved in the case at hand (such as the parole officer in this case). What does emerge, however, is that the "mavericks," in comparison to the other PDs, seemed to care much less about sentence predictions, preferring to concentrate on argument over the facts and their legal implications. One of the maverick PDs said, at the end of his interview:

I can't get emotional about these guys [clients]. They're nuts. They've got to be to do the things that they do. *It doesn't matter really what you do for them. They keep coming back.* There are only a very few that you can really help.

When asked, "Doesn't that depress you? How can you keep going?" The PD replied:

I enjoy my work. It's fun. We've got a great office here with a good competitive spirit.

And thus, the "mavericks" defined themselves more as "real lawyers" engaged in the adversary process, instead of being client advocates in the business of sentencing.

COMPARISON OF PRIVATE ATTORNEYS WITH
PUBLIC DEFENDERS

Several studies have found that private defense attorneys settle fewer of their cases by guilty plea than do public defenders (see, for example, Silverstein (1965); Sudnow (1965); Oaks and Lehman (1968). This finding has variously been explained by differences in the quality and motivation of the attorneys and by differences in the characteristics of their clients. Skolnick (1967), on the other hand, found that most private attorneys were just as likely to bargain for guilty pleas as the public defenders, and further, that five of the six leading private defenders in the county he studied reported that they settled a greater percentage of their cases by pleas of guilty than did the public defenders. Skolnick also warned of the impossibility of making any systematic comparison between the private attorney and the public defender because of the fact that clients are *assigned* to the public defender, rather than personally selected by him. This leads to the problem of "client-control," which "is experienced by all defense attorneys, but is exaggerated in relations between the public defender and his client" (Skolnick, 1967: 65).

In this section, data on the choices of disposition method by private attorneys (in the central district of Los Angeles) will be presented, with particular reference to the pattern for PDs described earlier. First, the differences in the caseloads of the attorneys will be summarized as they have been found in other studies. Smith and Wendel (1968) analyzed all felonies in Los Angeles in 1966 and found several statistically significant differences between the caseloads of private attorneys and PDs. In terms of the offense charged, the PD handled proportionately more burglary and auto theft offenses in their caseloads, while private attorneys had proportionately more drug law violations and bookmaking offenses. Also, the PD represented proportionately more defendants with prior prison records and more defendants under existing criminal status (such as probation or parole). No difference was found in the racial makeup of defendants in the two caseloads. Finally, Greenwood et al. (1973: 52), based on analysis of a sample of burglary and robbery defendants in 1970, found that less than one-fifth of private attorney clients were in custody pending their trial, while over one-half of the PD clients were in custody during this period.

Unfortunately I was unable to obtain complete statistical data to determine whether the method of case disposition varied according to the type of defense attorney. Greenwood et al. (1973: 52-56), did such an analysis for a sample of 2,617 burglary and robbery cases for all of Los Angeles County in 1970. They found no difference between the percentage of cases settled by trial by PDs and private attorneys. But they did find a slightly higher percentage of cases at trial for those handled by court-appointed private attorneys.[6] Private attorneys were appointed in a small number of cases to represent indigent defendants who could not be represented by the public defender; these court appointments are described in more detail later in this section. The data of Greenwood et al., however, are not conclusive for several reasons. First, their analysis is limited to two offense types; they examined 712 robbery cases and 1,905 burglary cases. Since PDs handle proportionately more burglary cases, a broader range of offense types should be examined in order to hold constant the variation in type of representation by offense. For example, drug or bookmaking cases should be included, since private attorneys represent proportionately more of these offenses. Secondly, Greenwood et al. (1973: 48), excluded all defendants with prior prison records from their sample. Defendants with prison records present "serious" cases which PDs often take to trial where a good bargain cannot be obtained. Since PDs represent proportionately more defendants with prison records, these defendants should be included in any analysis of method of disposition according to type of attorney. Finally, the data of Greenwood et al., are for the entire County, while the interview and observational data presented below on differences between private defenders and public defenders are only for the Central District.

There was a group of private attorneys who handled a high volume of criminal cases and who were regularly seen in the Central District of the Superior Court. And then there were the "non-regulars"; attorneys who handled primarily civil cases, or a general practice, or who were just beginning their law practice. Informal relationships and mutual trust were important to working out case dispositions, and so, as one DA put it,

> The best thing for a defense attorney is that he mix well with the criminal law community. He shouldn't be a lone wolf or a shyster. He should be able to walk into the DA's office or the City Attorney's office and he'd have some friends there. He should be able to walk into courtrooms and the clerks would know him by first name. He's got to be willing to become a part of the community he's working in. Then he can do a lot for his client.

A comment heard several times was, "the best private attorneys are the ex-DAs and ex-PDs." Naturally, those were the attorneys who had been part of that crucial "criminal law communtiy," as well as having had extensive experience with criminal law.

In general, the regular private defense attorneys used the same factors as the PDs to recommend the best method for case disposition. Thus, trial or non-trial disposition depended upon predictions of case outcomes, according to the strength of the prosecution's case and the seriousness of the case (Figure 1, presented earlier). One very old, experienced private attorney described these two factors used in settling cases:

> Let me put it to you this way: What is our job as a criminal lawyer in most instances? Number one is . . . no kidding, we know the man's done it, or we feel he's done it, he may deny it, but the question is: *Can they prove it?* The next thing is: *Can we mitigate it?* Of course you can always find something good to say about the guy—to mitigate it. Those are the two things that are important, and that's what you do. [Emphasis added]

But while these same factors were relevant to determining case disposition for private attorneys, the frequency of cases settled by full trial was estimated by prosecuting and defense attorneys to be *less* for private attorneys than for PDs. Court participants suggested two reasons for this: financial considerations for private attorneys and the problem of client-control for PDs.

Many private attorneys set the same fee for handling a case, whether it was settled by trial or by guilty plea or SOT. So, because of the time involved with a trial, especially a jury trial, there was a financial incentive for private attorneys to settle cases by non-trial means. The following comments illustrate this view:

> PD: Private attorneys have much fewer trials than the PDs, because they must wait for Witness Green.

> DA: PDs take many more cases to jury trial than do private attorneys, because they're the only ones who can afford to. A private attorney can usually only lose money because of the time involved.

Said one private attorney who had been practicing criminal law for four years (the first two years in association with a high-volume criminal attorney):

> The problem is private attorneys can't afford to go to trial too much really. Like I set two fees—one for [non-trial] disposition and the other for trial. And I tell my client the risks of trial. But most attorneys won't do that. Like the other guy I used to work with. He'd ask a flat fee. . . . That wasn't right.

Some attorneys did set separate fees according to the method of disposition, and then cases might be settled by trial for clients who could afford the high fee. But it should be noted that most of the private attorney clients in this downtown court could not afford these trial fees. One probation officer (with fourteen years experience) noted that PDs took more cases to trial than private attorneys, then added:

> When some of these private attorneys do go to trial, it's just for the money they'll get. They know their client doesn't have a chance.

Hence, while private attorneys (as did the PDs) examined the strength and seriousness of a case to determine the best method for disposition, the final choice of the private attorneys was usually determined, in addition, by financial considerations.

Defense and prosecuting attorneys suggested a second reason for the greater frequency of trial dispositions by PDs than by private attorneys. This reason was expressed by one DA as follows:

> When a man pays money to hire an attorney, he's more likely to listen to his advice. After all, this is what he's paying for. While the PD's clients won't even listen to them sometimes. So if the private attorney thinks a [non-trial] disposition would be better, he can talk to his client like a Dutch uncle. He can do a little arm twisting. But the PDs can't do that. They have to do what the defendant wants even if they don't think it's in his best interest.

As noted earlier, the PDs may "twist arms," but only to a point. Some cases went to trial as a result of disagreement between a PD and his client (examples of this will be presented in the following section on "Defendants"). But a private attorney had sanctions available to make his client accept his advice on case disposition; he could threaten to withdraw from the case, or he could set an extremely high fee for trial disposition. Note that most private attorneys (like most PDs) believed that their role as defense attorney meant that *they* should suggest the proper strategy for settling a case, rather than implementing the strategy suggested by their client. A private attorney described this aspect of the lawyer/client relationship using an analogy to the doctor/patient relationship. Interestingly, this is the same analogy used by a "maverick" PD quoted earlier, but with an opposite conclusion:

> I think this way . . . If I go to my doctor, first of all I go to him because I have faith in him. If he tells me to take the blue pill, I guess I'll take that blue pill. It might kill me, but I'm gonna take that blue pill. . . . So when a client starts telling you what to do, he's a dummy. The poor PDs, they get most of these wise guys—it never dawns on them that if they were so smart, maybe they wouldn't have to have a PD. Not that there's anything wrong with the PD. . . . I'll say on record, the PD office does a good job.

While most of the regular criminal attorneys settled a very high percentage of their cases without trial, some of them, like the "maverick" PDs, were more trial-minded. These few lawyers were characterized as either respected, capable trial lawyers or incompetent obstructions. It was not clear whether these more trial-oriented lawyers were sanctioned in any way by DAs or judges, because of the large number of different courtrooms involved and the infrequency with which I encountered them. In addition, there were the "non-regular" attorneys who appeared only occasionally in court and were inexperienced with criminal law, often coming from primarily civil law practices. One DA described "the non-regulars—some just bumble around. Often they cooperate and we help them out. Some you trust and others you don't." Unfortunately, again because of the size of the court system studied, these attorneys cannot be systematically described with respect to their attitudes and behavior on choosing disposition methods.

Finally, some defendants were represented by private attorneys who were appointed and paid on an hourly basis by the court. These court appointments were authorized by Section 987a of the Penal Code for indigent defendants who, for one reason or other, could not be represented by the PD. Usually this occurred in multi-defendant cases, where there was a conflict of interest if the PD were to represent both defendants in the case. In 1966, approximately two percent of the defendants in the County were represented by court-appointed attorneys (Smith and Wendel, 1968). The figure has increased slightly since then, and it would be somewhat higher for the Central District since there were more indigent defendants there than in the County as a whole. One PD characterized these 987a attorneys as follows:

> 987a attorneys run the gamut completely from new guys just starting out in practice to ex-PDs or DAs with a great deal of expertise who are just starting to build a criminal practice of their own. Court appointments don't pay as well as fees for most private attorneys with big practices. So it's often for guys just starting out. The balance are known to the judge and he chooses them. . . . You don't see the most common criminal lawyers seeking 987a appointments. . . . They have a big criminal practice already. So they wouldn't need the 987a work—unless they're right there in court and do it as a favor to the judge.

While some attorneys saw no particular difference in the choice of disposition method by court-appointed attorneys, a few indicated that these attorneys were more likely to take cases to trial. For example, one DA commented:

> Some 987a attorneys will take cases to trial because they are getting paid by the court for their time. But the cases don't warrant a trial. Some attorneys don't do this, but others do. Even where their client wants to plead, they'll go to trial. Or, where it is a case that clearly should be disposed of, they'll go to trial for the money.

However, court-appointed attorneys who blatantly took cases to trial just "for the money" could risk not being appointed in the future. The presiding judge who made the appointments had a list of attorneys eligible for 987a work, and he said that he crossed off the names of people he knew to be "incompetent, dishonest, or just bad attorneys."

DEFENDANTS

The preceding discussion indicates factors determining the method of case disposition according to defense attorneys' recommendations, either for public defenders or for private attorneys. But the final decision to plead guilty or go to trial belongs to the defendant, not to his attorney. As one PD said:

> You know, the DAs can holler all they want about what fools we are sometimes to turn down their deals. But you gotta remember that we've got our clients to answer to. We're not free agents in this thing, like the DAs are.

And another PD was discussing characteristics of a "triable case" and then added:

> But look, for defense, if a guy wants to go to trial, you've got to go to trial.

However, as indicated earlier, this last comment is somewhat more applicable to the PDs than to private attorneys. It appeared that clients of private attorneys were more likely than PD clients to accept their attorney's advice on disposition.

Some cases went to trial because of disagreement between the defendant and his attorney, not because of disagreement between the defense attorney and the DA. For example, a PD described such a case:

> The defendant was black and had been living in Hollywood, trying to make that scene up there, but not completely in it. He had no record at all. He was charged with kidnapping and two counts . . . forcible rape and forcible oral copulation. The charges looked bad but by the circumstances it wasn't really a bad case. I talked to the DA about it and he agreed. So we went in to talk to Judge Jones. The DA explained that there really wasn't much of a case here, and agreed to let him plead to one count, and the judge would sentence him to 10 months County Jail. That's really a break and I went into the jail elated with it to explain it to my client. But he wouldn't take it. He was a real hard head, saying, "I ain't going to plead to no fucking white man. I didn't do it and I want a trial." The guy was crazy but I had no choice. We took it to trial. . . . And the judge found him guilty and sentenced him to three concurrent terms of one to 25 years in state prison. I was angry and talked to the judge. I said, "Look, before you were willing to give him 10 months in County Jail. Nothing has changed now. Why can't you still do that? Don't you realize that this man

is being penalized just because his attorney fell short and couldn't communicate with him? He would have listened to a private attorney, but he wouldn't listen to me," I argued. But no, the judge said that he's a hard head and is going to have to be punished.

I asked the PD:

Was the defendant penalized then because he pled not guilty? Do judges penalize defendants who demand trial?

He answered:

No, it isn't a club that they hold over you that the sentence will be worse if you don't cop out. It's just that the judges get angry at the man because he's so foolish. He still wasn't a bad man, but he was penalized for being stupid.

The PD did not explain this further, but it appeared that he felt somewhat responsible for the sentence because of his perceived inability to communicate effectively with his client. This PD, Vinson, was especially concerned with rehabilitative possibilities in sentencing, and added that:

I've got a bad reputation around here . . . because I'm always such a bleeding heart. The judges get so they don't listen anymore. You know, "It's just old Vinson again with another sob story."

The following case was taken to jury trial by a PD at his client's insistence. The defendant, a legal secretary, was accused of stealing about $1,000 from her employer. The charges included two counts of grand theft and five counts of forgery. After the second day of trial, the DA complained privately, "this case shouldn't be at trial. It's a waste of time." When asked why it hadn't been settled by negotiation, the DA replied:

It should have been, but the PD wouldn't do it. He's on salary. He doesn't care. We would have been glad to accept a guilty plea to just one count and dismiss the other six. But he wouldn't do it.

At the end of the five-day trial, the jury found the defendant not guilty of one count of grand theft, but guilty as charged of the remaining six counts. I asked the PD why this case had gone to trial and he said, "she maintained the entire time that she was innocent." I asked if the defendant could have pled to just one count and the PD said:

Of course . . . We knew she'd lose before a court. But maybe she had a chance before a jury. It doesn't make any difference in sentencing before this judge. The woman will get probation probably anyway whether by plea to one count or by conviction of six counts—it doesn't matter. Remember that Jordan [the judge hearing the case] is a woman judge.

And so's my client and she's married with three kids. She's never been arrested before. No record at all. Besides, she didn't take much. She's not a real thief.

About ten months later I examined the file on this case and was surprised to find that the defendant had been sentenced to state prison. A probation officer had found on presentence investigation that the defendant had a five-year history of forgery and larceny convictions on the East Coast and that her performance on probation for those offenses had been poor. Thus, the report recommended that probation be denied in this case. The judge had the defendant sent to the Department of Corrections for a three-month diagnostic study, and then followed their recommendation on commitment to prison. I returned to the PD on this case and he explained that the defendant had "fooled everyone" about her record ("including the DAs—she was released OR [on her own recognizance] the whole time"), except the probation officer who had conducted a very thorough check. I asked the PD:

> Had you known about her record, would you have still gone for the jury trial, or would you have tried to dispose of it?

He answered:

> Oh, I would have tried to negotiate it. In fact, I tried that anyway, but she wouldn't hear of it. She was so adamant that she was innocent. But it was a dead-bang case. . . . I did get the judge to consolidate the counts, so she was only being sentenced on one count. She got less that way then.

This case illustrates some of the difficulties involved for a defense attorney whose client had not been completely candid with him. In taking the case to trial, the PD did not think that there were any risks involved, because he knew nothing of his client's record. On the other hand, the defendant probably thought she had nothing to lose by trial, since her record had not been discovered during the six months before the trial, and she might escape any penalty with an acquittal.

The final decision on disposition does rest with defendants, and so it is important to consider on what basis their decision is made. Obviously guilt or innocence affects a defendant's decision to plead guilty or go to trial, but that cannot be independently ascertained by a researcher. Past studies have suggested that certain characteristics of defendants are related to the choice of disposition method; characteristics such as pretrial custody status, race, and prior record. For example, pretrial detention limits a defendant's ability to aid in his defense at trial and also pressures him to cop out to avoid the uncertainty and dead time of waiting in jail. Thus, it is likely that defendants in custody pending trial are more likely to plead guilty than defendants who are released on bail. Also, Mileski (1971), in a study of lower court dispositions, found that white defendants pled guilty more often than black defendants, holding constant the nature of the offense charged. It was unclear, she said (1971: 495), whether the race difference in guilty pleas was due to:

> More numerous instances of innocence among black defendants, fewer opportunities for them to engage in plea bargaining, greater willingness to undertake the risks of "going for broke," an unwillingness to submit to "white man's justice," a higher level of combativeness, or even ignorance of the fact that in the long run they might be better off pleading guilty.

Finally, Newman (1956), in an early study of plea bargaining, suggested that defendants with prior records were less likely than first offenders to assume an adversary posture against the prosecutor because recidivists knew of the advantages which they could obtain through bargaining.

Defendants were not interviewed for this study, nor was a complete analysis made to compare the method of disposition with these characteristics of defendants. However, interview data here plus some statistical data from Greenwood et al. (1973), allow a few observations to be made on defendants' choice of disposition. For instance, the likelihood of an adversary trial disposition increased with a defendant's prior record: 14.1 percent of all defendants in Los Angeles County with prior prison records chose adversary trial, while only 9.5 percent of defendants with no record chose trial in 1970 (Greenwood et al., 1973: 42). This relationship is most likely explained by the fact that prior record was crucial for sentencing, and, as indicated earlier, defense attorneys tended to recommend trial disposition for defendants with bad records in many cases where a lenient sentence could not be arranged by bargaining. But the relationship between prior record and trial could also be due to unwillingness by defendants with records to accept their attorney's bargained dispositions because of suspicion about the actual value of the bargain. This occurred in some instances where a defendant knew that probation officers and parole boards could consider the original charges filed rather than just the charge on which the defendant was convicted. A private attorney described such a case:

> First degree armed robbery—five counts of it. There were fingerprints, physical evidence, and positive identification. They offered a plea to one count. That's a good deal, but my client refused to plead. It was based on his personal knowledge that the parole board was going to consider the other four counts. His view was, "I won't serve any less time if I'm convicted on one or five." . . . So I had to go to trial.[7]

Defense attorneys said that their clients usually accepted their recommendation on the method of disposition. Thus, where a relationship is found between a personal characteristic of defendants (such as prior record) and frequency of trial disposition, it is not clear whether the explanation lies more with the attorney's recommendations or with the defendant's refusal to accept those recommendations. The data of Greenwood et al. (1973), on the relationship between pretrial custody status and disposition method pertains only to the sample of 2,617 burglary and robbery defendants described earlier. Within that total sample, 16.9 percent were released on their own recognizance (OR), 38.3 percent were released on bail, and 44.9 percent remained in jail. With regard to the frequency of adversary trial, 11.7 percent of defendants out on their own recognizance chose jury or court trial, compared with 11.2 percent of defendants released on bail and 11.1 percent of defendants who remained in custody (Greenwood et al., 1973: 48-49). For this sample of defendants, then, there was little difference in the frequency of trial dispositions for defendants in custody and defendants who were released pending trial.

Using the same sample of defendants described above, Greenwood et al. (1973: 56-59), analyzed the relationship between ethnic group and disposition method. Within their sample, 48 percent of defendants were Anglo-American, 40 percent black, and 12 percent Mexican-American. They found a very large difference in the guilty plea rates: 62.4 percent of Anglo-American defendants and 56.7 percent of Mexican-American defendants pled guilty, while only 39.9 percent of black defendants did so. They note that:

> Of course, the salient question, which remains unanswered, is whether the lower rate of guilty pleas among black defendants reflects a distrust of the judicial system independent of the defendant's guilt, or a greater willingness to fight their cases because of a higher proportion of unwarranted prosecutions.

Unfortunately the authors did not report the rates for SOT, court, and jury trial according to ethnic groups. It could be that black defendants used SOT much more frequently, thus minimizing the implied differences in adversary trial rates. On the basis of observations and interviews for this study, no difference appeared in the recommendations by defense attorneys for disposition method according ethnic group. But there were occasional indications of a relationship between race and a defendant's refusal to accept his attorney's recommended disposition, as for example in the first case described in this section. And a probation officer described "a racial block" that he had observed with defendants who would not admit their guilt: "among blacks, it's strongly felt for some that you don't cop out to the Man." Such a "racial block" was not necessarily irrational from the black defendant's point of view, since the overall acquittal rate for blacks in the sample above was *higher* than the rate for Anglo-American or Mexican-American defendants (Greenwood et al., 1973: 56).

Decision-making by defendants should be investigated much further and in a systematic way. These comments are meant only to indicate some of the factors which may or may not be operating in defendants' choice of guilty plea or adversary trial.

CONCLUSION

The cooperative role for defense was clearly the dominant one in the court studied. While financial incentives helped to dictate this role for private defense attorneys, for them and certainly for most of the public defenders this role was seen to be in the best interests of their clients. And most defendants tended to accept, at least formally, their attorney's view on the best strategy for case disposition. But the cooperative role did not prescribe plea bargaining for every case. Adversary trial proceedings were chosen in principally two situations. A DA summarized these situations as follows:

> Cases for full trial . . . let's see . . . The weaker a case is from our standpoint, the more likely it will be tried. There the defendant thinks he can walk away from it. Rather than take a disposition, he'll try to beat it altogether. Another kind of case that's often tried is the really hopeless case. There we have an overwhelmingly strong case and it's a bad, very serious case where the defendant has a long record. So he'll go to state prison anyway. He's got nothing to lose by trying it.

In terms of the framework presented earlier, these cases which called for full trial were the "reasonable doubt" cases with a chance of complete acquittal, and the "serious, dead bang" case where a lenient sentence bargain could not be obtained. According to this prevailing defense role, the most effective way a defense attorney could represent his client was to seek an acquittal where there was a predictable chance of it, but where there was not (and these were most of the cases), then the attorney should seek the disposition which minimizes the sentence for his client. Further, this defense role prescribed that the attorney should represent his client by doing what was best for him, rather than simply implementing what the client wanted.

But there were also "outsiders" in the courtroom: defense attorneys and defendants who followed more closely the traditional adversary role.[8] The "maverick" public defenders, their few counterparts among private attorneys, and some of the court-appointed attorneys (who had financial incentives to go to trial) represented clients by settling cases more the way their clients wanted, which frequently called for full trial. The negative consequences of this adversarial posture occurred primarily with sentencing, particularly for "serious" cases which were taken to trial. But these attorneys accepted the consequences because, within the adversary tradition, "effectiveness" was evaluated according to how well the attorney argued on behalf of his client's innocence, not according to how well he argued his client's potential for rehabilitation. "Winning" a case for the adversary role meant working vigorously for an acquittal; "winning" a case for the cooperative role meant obtaining the most lenient sentence for clients who were factually guilty.

Finally, some defendants were "outsiders" because they were more interested in fighting for an acquittal than they were interested in minimizing their penal "time," regardless of how good their chances looked for an acquittal. Defendants who were more experienced with probation officers and parole boards may have distrusted how those authorities would exercise their discretion after the plea bargaining process was over. And there was some evidence to indicate that black defendants were more likely to choose this adversarial role.

While the cooperative defense posture may secure more lenient treatment for offenders, the adversary posture may secure a higher proportion of acquittals but with harsher treatment for those convicted. With increasing emphasis on the importance of defense counsel in criminal proceedings it is necessary to consider by what criteria the quality of defense representation should be evaluated. Any attempt to prescribe these criteria leads ultimately to questions about the function of the criminal courts. For, if defense counsel are necessary to protect the rights of accused persons in court, it must be made clear what the tasks of the court are.

Traditionally the primary task of the criminal court was to ascertain facts in dispute and to determine their legal significance, thus deciding the guilt or innocence of accused persons. Theoretical models of the criminal process, such as Packer's (1968) Crime Control model (which views the process as an assembly line) or the Due Process model (which depicts an obstacle course), essentially end their concern with defendants at the point of conviction or acquittal. But these models are not adequate to explain the dynamics of what actually is occurring in court, nor are they useful to guide defense attorneys who sincerely want to improve the quality of representation for criminal defendants. For, in the vast majority of cases, the conflict between the accused and the state is not over the question of guilt or innocence, but it is over the question of what punishment will be imposed on them.

The question of punishment has assumed much larger proportions with the emphasis upon individual rehabilitation as a guide to sentencing. Courts are not only supposed to "sort" defendants into categories of convicted and acquitted, but they are also charged with "sorting" convicted offenders according to their prospects for rehabilitation. Thus one convicted burglar goes to state prison, another to county jail, and a third walks home free on probation. And this decision is expressly made according to individual personal characteristics of offenders, characteristics which are irrelevant to the decision on guilt or innocence. The dilemma for the defense attorney is how can he best defend his client when both of these sorting processes occur simultaneously, as they may in the decision on whether to plead guilty or go to trial. And the dilemma is intensified by the fact that frequently defendants, as part of the general public, are unaware of dimensions of the sentencing decision and its interactions with the issue of guilt or innocence.

In order to improve the quality of defense representation, we must decide what that job means, and that calls for a thorough reevaluation of the functions of criminal courts. The public, not the individual interactions within the court community, ought to decide what should be done with the task of sentencing. As Wilson (1973: 9) has recently written:

> Indeed, there has been very little serious public discussion of what we even mean by a "good" or a "bad" sentence. And only be deciding that question can we begin to think seriously about what other reforms are necessary in the criminal courts.

NOTES

1. These figures and those to be cited henceforth are for felony dispositions in the entire County, although descriptions given here are for the processes of the Central District only. Complete statistical data was not available for the Central District, but where it was available, it indicated that patterns in Countywide figures accurately reflected patterns in figures for the Central District. Almost 40 percent of the cases in the County were handled in the Central District.

2. I am grateful to the Bureau of Criminal Statistics, Sacramento, California, for providing me with this data. For a complete table showing type of disposition for felony defendants in Los Angeles by offense charged, see Mather (1972: 26-27).

3. Note that these two roles for representation by attorney are parallel to the delegate vs. trustee orientations found in the representational roles of legislators (Wahlke et al., 1962: 272-280).

4. The names and the numbers of departments in this and all other quotes have been changed to protect the anonymity of the participants.

5. The counts were alternatives for the jury in that the defendant could not legally have been convicted of both. Appellate courts have held that a person cannot be both a receiver of stolen property and a thief of that same property.

6. Greenwood et al. (1973: 53) report that, within their sample, 8 percent of defendants represented by PDs went to trial, as did 8 percent of defendants with private attorneys and 11 percent of defendants with court-appointed attorneys. However, on the next page of their report (p. 54) they report that a total of 11 percent of the cases in the sample were disposed of by trial. Unfortunately, their raw figures were not shown to enable the reader to figure out the discrepancy in their percentages.

7. Many PDs said that they would not recommend a plea bargain which would send a defendant to prison because they were aware of these parole board practices.

8. The concept of "outsiders" in the criminal court could be applied as well to other participants besides defense. For example, among judges and DAs, some preferred the traditional adversary role and were disinclined to participate in plea bargaining.

REFERENCES

ALSCHULER, A. (1968) "The prosecutor's role in plea bargaining." University of Chicago Law Review 36: 50.

BLUMBERG, A. S. (1967a) Criminal Justice. Chicago: Quadrangle.

——— (1967b) "The practice of law as a confidence game: organizational cooptation of a profession." Law and Society Review 1: 15.

Bureau of Criminal Statistics (1969) Crime and Delinquency in California. Sacramento: State of California, Department of Justice, Division of Law Enforcement.

——— (1970) Felony Defendants Disposed of in California Courts: Reference Tables. Sacramento: State of California, Department of Justice, Division of Law Enforcement.

COLE, G. (1970) "The decision to prosecute." Law and Society Review 7: 331.

FEELEY, M. M. (1973) "Two models of the criminal justice system: an organizational perspective." Law and Society Review 7: 407.

GREENWOOD, P. W. et al. (1973) Prosecution of Adult Felony Defendants in Los Angeles County: A Policy Perspective. Santa Monica, Calif.: Rand Corporation.

HUITT, R. K. (1961) "The outsider in the Senate: an alternative role." American Political Science Review 55: 566.

MATHER, L. M. (1972) "To Plead Guilty or Go to Trial?" Paper presented at the Annual Meeting of the American Political Science Association, Washington, D.C.

MILESKI, M. (1971) "Courtroom encounters: an observation study of a lower criminal court." Law and Society Review 5: 473.

NEWMAN, D. J. (1956) "Pleading guilty for considerations: a study of bargain justice." Journal of Criminal Law, Criminology and Police Science 46: 780.

——— (1966) Conviction: The Determination of Guilt or Innocence Without Trial. Boston: Little, Brown.

OAKS, D. H. and W. LEHMAN (1968) A Criminal Justice System and the Indigent. Chicago: University of Chicago Press.

PACKER, H. (1968) The Limits of the Criminal Sanction. Stanford, Calif.: Stanford University Press.

SILVERSTEIN, L. (1965) Defense of the Poor in Criminal Cases in American State Courts. Chicago: American Bar Foundation.

SKOLNICK, J. (1967) "Social control in the adversary system." Journal of Conflict Resolution 11: 51.

SMITH, G. W. and M. A. WENDELL (1968) "Public defenders and private attorneys: a comparison of cases." The Legal Aid Briefcase 27: 95.

SUDNOW, D. (1965) "Normal crimes: sociological features of the Penal Code in a Public Defender Office." Social Problems 12: 255.

WAHLKE, J. C., H. EULAU, W. BUCHANAN, and L. C. FERGUSON (1962) The Legislative System: Explorations in Legislative Behavior. New York: John Wiley.

WILSON, J. Q. (1973) "If every criminal knew he would be punished if caught . . . " New York Times Magazine 9 (January 28).

Chapter 10

BLACK POLITICAL CONSCIOUSNESS IN
NORTHERN STATE PRISONS

FRANK L. MORRIS

> Black men born in the United States and fortunate enough to live past the
> age of eighteen are conditioned to accept the inevitability of prison. For
> most of us it simply looms as the next phase in a sequence of humiliations.

Among other things, the above excerpt from the writings of the late George
Jackson reflects the fact that throughout the U.S. Black men and women are
imprisoned greatly disporportionate to the percentage of Blacks in the U.S.
population.[1] There is good reason to believe that this imbalance will be worse
in the future. First, it is well-known that a disproportionate number of crimes
for which there are arrests, convictions, and imprisonment are committed by
poor, Black, urban males between the ages of 14 to 24. The number of young
Blacks aged 14 to 24 in central cities will rise about 63 percent from 1966 to
1976 compared to a 32 percent increase in the central city Black population as a
whole (National Advisory Commission, 1968: 269).

Using data based on a special 1960 U.S. Census report, Wright (1973: 32)
notes that one out of every 26 Black men between the ages of 25 and 34 was either
in jail or in prison on an average day in 1960, compared to one out of every 163
white men in the same age group. For Black men aged 20 to 24, the figures are
one out of 27 Blacks behind bars compared to one out of 116 whites of the

*AUTHOR'S NOTE: This research was sponsored by a dissertation fellowship from
the Russell Sage Foundation. The Foundation is not responsible for the views
expressed here.*

same age groups. It was especially interesting to note that the disproportion of Blacks to whites in jails and prisons was greater in the northern states than it was in the southern states. The imprisonment rate for Black men 20 to 24 was one out of 41 in Alabama compared to one out of 130 whites; for Mississippi the figures were one out of 62 Blacks and one out of 180 whites; in New York the figures were one out of 20 Blacks compared to one out of 123 whites; in California the figures were one out of 22 Blacks behind bars compared to one out of 83 whites. The New York rate of imprisonment of Blacks was six times that of whites, whereas in Alabama and Mississippi the rate of Blacks times whites was three times (Weight, 1973). Using data based on July 1968 figures from the U.S. Bureau of Labor Statistics and the U.S. Census, Gordon (1971: 279) notes that as of July 1968 there were 140,000 Blacks serving time in penal institutions at the federal, state, and local levels. If the percentage of Black males in prison had been as low as the proportion of white men, the number of Black men in jail would not have been 140,000, but instead it would have been 25,000!

While considering the disproportionate number of Black men in jail, we should keep in mind the following: first, as well as being disproportionately imprisoned, Blacks are also disproportionately victimized by urban street crimes. This is especially so in the case of the most feared crimes; namely, crimes against a person. A Black male in Chicago is six times as likely to be a victim of a crime against the person as a white male and eleven times as likely as a white female. A Black woman is eight times as likely to be a victim of a crime against the person as a white woman and four times more likely to be victim of a crime against the person than a white male. According to Reiss (1967: 44):

> A rank order of victimization exists in Chicago then such that Negro males should have the highest expectation that they will be victims of a major crime against the person, followed in order of risk by Negro females, white males, and white females.

> This same rank order holds for offenses of forcible rape and assaults with intent to rape. Negro women are far more likely to be victims of forcible rape or an assault with intent to rape than white women. Indeed the probability that a Negro woman will be a victim of forcible rape is about 18 times greater than the probability for white women.

Second, it is important to remember that the process of law enforcement involves great discretion and selectivity. A number of leading criminologists have noted that numerous national surveys have demonstrated that many citizens presumed to be law-abiding have at one time or another been engaged in some behavior for which they could have gone to prison (Schur, 1969: 12). Goldfarb (1971: 311) points out that a national survey of 1,700 people without criminal records found that 99 percent had committed offenses for which they could have ended up in prison.

> Businessmen and lawyers were highest in tax evasion, perjury, falsification and fraud; teachers and social workers in malicious mischief; writers and artists in indecency, criminal libel, and gambling; military and government employees in simple larceny; mechanics and technicians in simple disorderly conduct; farmers in illegal possession of weapons; laborers in grand larceny, burglary and robbery; students in auto misdemeanors.

Third, it is also important to remember that the punishment for crimes, especially imprisonment, is basically a political act. First, the form and the severity of punishments for specific offenses is most often either heavily influenced or determined by official policy or legislatures. Also, punishment as a deterrent is an essential tool of social control by a political system.[2]

Fourth, when analyzing the plight of Black prisoners in the United States it is important to remember that the probability of winding up in prison bears little or no relationship to the total volume of crime in U.S. society. This is strongly influenced by the fact that the wealthy do not have to commit crimes of economic necessity and, unlike the poor, are likely to get other options such as probation, training, fines, restitution, medical attention, or other options. The author was surprised to find that even the President's Commission on Law Enforcement and the Administration of Justice (1966: 48) could not adequately estimate the extent of so-called white-collar crime.

The overrepresentation of Blacks in prison, the fact that it has become rather widely known that a number of Black heroes have gotten themselves together in prison, the fact that many of the crimes that most of the Black inmates were imprisoned for were economic crimes, and finally the possible widespread feeling that Blacks were discriminated against both in sentences and within the prisons have clearly demonstrated the need for research on these topics. It is likely that these factors have influenced increasing political consciousness in state prisons. Clear evidence of this is in the writings of Fleeta Drumgo (1971: 131), another of the Soledad Brothers:

> I am constantly thinking about unemployment, underemployment, poverty and malnutrition that are the basic facts of our existence; it is this which sends persons to these concentration camps; it is this which causes so called crime in general.

> I'd like to express that there is a growing awareness behind the walls; we're seeing throughout the madness of capitalism, class interest, surplus value and imperialism, which this gestapo system perpetrates. It's this which we have to look at and understand in order to recognize the inhumanity inflicted upon the masses of people here in America and abroad. As

Brother Malcolm X once said, "We as people, as human beings have the basic human right to eliminate the conditions that have and are continuously destroying us.

A number of articles and books by Black prisoners and others have documented numerous acts of oppression against Black prisoners who hold certain political views, especially the militant or revolutionary views spelled out above ("Martin Sostre vs. Nelson Rockefeller . . . ," 1971; Al Aswodu, 1971; Wade, 1971; Chrisman, 1971). Many of these political views and levels of political indoctrination or consciousness have been associated with Black political and religious-political groups both within and outside of the prisons. I have found no study that addresses the following key questions: Are Blacks who hold certain political views or who are members of certain religious-political groups singled out collectively for oppression more than other Black brothers who do not hold these views? Is any oppression against Blacks who hold certain political views greater than prison oppression against Blacks who may not hold these views but who may be looked upon as undesirable by the prison staff? Does political group membership affect support by friends, relatives, and others for Black inmates? What Black inmates see themselves as political prisoners and why? Is this affected by political group membership? How has the development of Black political-religious groups affected institutional interactions within prisons and what effect does this have on incarceration in the future?

This article will address itself to these questions. I am focusing upon Black political consciousness and Black political-religious groups in prisons for two fundamental reasons. First, the writings of many Black prisoners contend that the reactions of most prison officials to Black political organizations seems to be emotional and irrational. Prison officials supposedly see all Black political organizations either as aimed against all whites in authority (like them) or as organizations aimed against the rest of American society. Thus they may see either holding certain political views or membership in certain political organizations as evidence of an anti-rehabilitation tendency per se. They fail to see or understand that just as the rise of Black political organizations and activity in the non-prison Black community has had many positive effects associated with increases in self-esteem, identity, consciousness (Banks, 1972), and awareness outside the walls, it may also have similar benefits inside the walls.

A second reason for examining Black political organizations and consciousness was my hypothesis (or more properly, belief) that there has often been ignorance, skepticism, division, and even fear among Black inmates themselves over the roles of Black political organizations in prisons and the question of whether Black inmates in these organizations receive differential treatment.

The fact is that we do not know whether and in what way contemporary developments such as the rise of Black political organizations and consciousness affect Black inmate attitudes or behavior. Major prison scholars, such as Daniel Glaser (1969) and Erving Goffman (1961), have stressed that the staffs of prisons are quite concerned with prisoner attitudes. Thus it is very important to see whether the hustle is being rewarded. Under the hustle, a Black inmate decides that saying what the prison officials want to hear or doing what they want him to do is the best way to become a "rehabilitative" success. It is the converse of this that is more devastating. Specifically, Black men who say what the prison may not want to hear, that is, revolutionary rhetoric that is often associated with Black political group membership and Black political consciousness, are likely to be perceived as non-rehabilitated and thus may receive negative sanctions.

Irwin (1970), among a number of prison scholars, stresses that the concept and action of "doing one's own time" is highly valued by prison authorities and some inmates. I will point out later how this helps in the attempt to maximize social control by the prison authorities. The point that I want to make is that any political consciousness-raising and political group recruitment often requires and values social interaction that is not consistent with the "do you own time" value. Note that this activity, which may not have anything to do with probability of an inmate becoming a recidivist, could bring on him negative sanctions. Irwin (1970), in his California study, noted that some of the convicted felons *with the most likely potential of being recidivists, such as thieves, burglars, and junkies, were likely to have some of the best records in prison and thus look better to the parole board than the other, less recidivistic-prone inmates because of their greater propensity to do time* (emphasis added).

In summing up many studies, Wolfgang and Radzinowicz (1971) believe that few who are incarcerated for any length of time escape the dependence and the loss of self-respectability which are both common adaptations yet common dangers of institutional life. They write that imprisonment can be both dehabilitating and corrupting. They stress that criminal learning, when it occurs, often affects prisoners in different ways, at different speeds, and at different stages of their criminal careers. The nature of a man's links with the outside world, his own record and attitudes, as well as the position he occupies and the contacts he makes in prison will affect his response to criminal learning. It should be clear that most Black political organizations in prison will affect the inmate's contacts in prison and in some cases may well affect the status and position he occupies within the prison. Among other things, a major focus of this paper will be to examine the extent to which Black political organizations in two maximum security state prisons in Massachusetts have affected inmates' attitudes, their records (especially in terms of conduct violations), and finally their links with the outside world, that is, visits or letters from non-relatives.

Much of the pioneering work on inmate adjustment in a total institution was done more than 10 years ago, and none of the research noted whether there were any differences in the way Black and white inmates adjusted to prison life. It is also important to point out that there hardly has been any research done by Black scholars. There is a great need to analyze and examine how Black inmates are currently adjusting to prisons and some of the key factors that affect those adjustments. This article attempts to fill the research and community needs and gaps by looking at both repression against Black inmates and political consciousness among Black inmates in two maximum security state prisons in the State of Massachusetts.

THE DATA COLLECTION AND THE PRISONS STUDIED

The data for this paper is part of a larger study and was gathered from March through October 1972.[3] The prisons involved are Concord Reformatory and Walpole State Prison in the State of Massachusetts. These are two of the three main adult prisons for males for the whole state. At the time, both were maximum security institutions. Both of these prisons are located within the suburbs of Boston, the largest city in the state, the state capital, and also the city with the largest number of Black people in the state. Concord is located about 23 miles from Boston and Walpole is about 30 miles away.

Walpole houses the state electric chair, death row, and more than one-half the prisoners there are serving sentences of seven years or more. In my sample of Black prisoners at Walpole more than one-half of them were serving sentences of 10 years or more; this included 20 percent who had either life imprisonment or death sentences before the death sentence was temporarily suspended by the U.S. Supreme Court. The average age at Walpole is 32.

Walpole, which was opened in 1956, has relatively good physical plant and facilities such as an auditorium, library, three chapels, an avocation area, a gymnasium, school rooms, barber shop, a tv-radio repair shop, an infirmary, a counseling and meeting and visiting area, a sizeable industrial area, and a 27-acre outdoor prison yard for recreation. These two prisons provide interesting contrasts because none of the inmates, Black or white, complained about the physical facilities at Walpole. We shall see below that this was not the case at Concord.

During the period of this study, Walpole housed an average of approximately 585 to 610 men, of which anywhere from 150 to 180 were Black. The Black population has to be an estimate because Walpole was the prime receiving prison for men before they were either permanently assigned there or transferred to other institutions. The number of Black prisoners in the institution is therefore constantly changing. This may be made clearer by seeing what the Corrections Department itself says about Walpole.[4]

> Walpole is also a receiving and classification institution for the Massachu-setts Department of Corrections. A steady inflow of commitments from the courts are constantly being screened and classified and those qualified are transferred to other Massachusetts Correctional Institutions through-out the state. . . . The most rehabilitative cases are usually sent to one of the two correctional Forestry Camps. The younger inmates are usually sent to MCI-Concord. The better type, but older inmates are sent to MCI-Norfolk. Serious mental cases and chronic medical cases are sent to MCI-Bridgewater. This screening, classification and transferring process is a continuing operation which is carried on throughout the year.

Note carefully what the above says about the department's opinion of most of the men who are permanently assigned to Walpole. They are not considered to be the "most rehabilitative," nor are they expected to be the younger inmate, nor are they expected to be the "better type but older inmate." Although not true for every case, generally those prisoners whom the Corrections Department sees as the most difficult, hardened criminals are sent to Walpole.

The courts commit most men to Walpole directly, but the commissioner of corrections can and does transfer men there from other institutions in the state. The Corrections Department reports that the crime for which most men are sent to Walpole is armed robbery, and most are in the 25 to 29 age group at the time of commitment. The majority of the Black inmates in my Walpole sample were also in this age group.

Walpole has a segregation unit and an isolation unit that provides one meal a day. In September and October of 1972, each time the author had access to the segregation and isolation units at Walpole they were full.

Concord was opened in 1878 as the state prison. From 1884 to 1955 it was primarily reserved for younger offenders, and for those years nobody over the age of 30 could be sent there. Today, although there is no rigidly enforced age limitation, it is still used mainly for younger offenders. The average age of those committed there by the courts is 22 years.[5] More than one-half of my Concord sample of Black inmates (53 percent) were from 21 to 24, 8 percent were under 18 (compared to one percent at Walpole), and a cumulative total of 86 percent were under 25 years old. The average sentence for both the overall Concord population and for my Black sample was a 2 to 5 year indefinite sentence.

During the decade of the 1960s more than $5 million worth of new construction was built at Concord. The first priority items completed under this new building project were facilities that primarily benefited the staff, such as new gun towers, hospital, conference room, visiting room, staff dining room, a two-story office building for the social service, and a two-story building for receiving and segregation. A 208-room housing unit, and an inmate kitchen and dining room was completed in a second phase. Nevertheless, at the time of this study, an old residential cell-block wing built in 1878 was still in use and housed a majority of the prisoners. The general run-down condition of this unit in general and especially of the plumbing, heating, and cooling systems was a major source of inmate tension and agitation.

One unusual aspect of Concord is the fact that 20 to 25 percent of the inmates are assigned to the prison farm on a sort of trustee basis. The farm is outside the walls, but the inmates are still under surveillance 100 percent of the time and under lock and key when they return from their various chores. Concord has the usual amount of prison industries and counseling and support services. The institution appeared to be making a major attempt to provide a wide array of counseling and other programs aimed at drug abuse. During this study the average daily population of Concord was around 640, of which approximately 170 were Black.

The Data Collection and Analysis

Most of the data for this study came from a 100-plus item questionnaire that the author attempted to administer to all Black prisoners who had been at the prison for more than one month. These questionnaires were administered to small groups of from 5 to 10 prisoners at a time in a counseling room of Walpole and at the old dining room at Concord.

The questionnaires were taken from April to June at Concord and from July to October at Walpole. It took quite a while to get the questionnaires completed because the prison officials, especially at Walpole, would only permit them to be given at times when there were no other activities scheduled for any prisoner. Concord permitted some exceptions to the rule, but it was rigidly enforced at Walpole. Before the questionnaires were given, a letter was sent to Black inmate leaders (those considered leaders by the administration) at Concord and a meeting was arranged. At the meeting the purposes of the study were explained and the questionnaire was pretested. After this successful meeting, letters were sent to each Black prisoner, first at Concord and later at Walpole.

Great effort was expended to be sure that every Black prisoner had an opportunity to take the questionnaire. It was explained to each prisoner that nobody at the prison would see their responses, that their participation was entirely voluntary, and that they did not have to sign their names to the questionnaire. Nevertheless I was quite surprised to find that more than one-half of the prisoners at each prison signed their names to the questionnaires. This provided an excellent opportunity for matching some questionnaire data to data in the official Corrections Department files.

The questionnaire took from one-half hour to 50 minutes for each prisoner to complete. There were no guards or prison staff in the rooms while the questionnaires were administered. Because the majority of Black Muslim inmates at Walpole were in segregation and to be sure that I got the men who had been kept in segregation for a long time, I was able to administer questionnaires to men in the segregation and isolation units at Walpole. I was not able to do this at Concord, but that did not bias the results because an extensive analysis of the Department of Correction records (and the in-depth interviews concurred) led me to conclude that all of the cases of isolation and segregation at Concord were for relatively short times (no longer than five days). At Walpole, in contrast, some highly selected prisoners spent months or years, in some cases, in segregation.[6]

At Concord about 135 of approximately 150 men who were eligible (Black men who had been at the prison more than a month) took the questionnaire and 123 completed it. Of these 123, 112 or about 75 percent of the total eligible respondents were included in the data. At Walpole I received 110 questionnaires out of approximately 135 to 150 eligible Black prisoners. Of these 110, 95 are included in the data analysis.[7]

The relatively high response rate can be attributed to a number of factors. Most important was the help that I received from other Black inmates, some of whom were inmate leaders. This help included canvassing cell blocks at both prisons and encouraging other prisoners to take the questionnaire. Another asset was the fact that I had received personal permission from the then new Black commissioner of corrections, but some of the Black inmates noticed that many on the prison staff did not seem to be making any effort to cooperate with me. The strong support of the commissioner was an asset in this phase of the study.

The decision was made to offer every Black inmate the chance to take the questionnaire so that the study would not raise the suspicions that a random sample might raise; it was also to give every Black prisoner who wanted to a chance to express himself on the data; and finally it was a chance for the author to personally talk to as many Black prisoners in person as possible. Since the result was (as expected) a relatively representative sample, it is important to know which Black prisoners are underrepresented and how much this might bias the conclusions. The only organized body of Black prisoners who did not take the questionnaire was about three-quarters of the Black Muslim body at

Concord. This was not the case in Walpole, where almost all members of the Nation of Islam took the questionnaire, even though almost all of them were in the segregation block when they took it.[8]

Other Black inmates who were underrepresented included some who were illiterate, some who were extreme loners, some who were anxious to do their own time and did not want to get involved with anything they might not fully understand, and finally there were a few Black prisoners who simply did not believe that anybody who was not a Corrections Department spy could gain admittance to the prison.

I was able to compensate for the above in the following ways. First, I was able to make personal contact and talk to some of the Concord refusals in their cells. Some of the prisoners who refused to take the questionnaire did agree to an in-depth personal interview. At least 10 percent of the in-depth interviews represent Black prisoners who refused to take the questionnaire.

Second, I had full access to the files of the prisoners at the central headquarters of the Department of Corrections. This permitted me to compare the data on some of the questionnaires with the records of the Corrections Department; it also permitted me to gather statistical data on my non-responses. The conclusion was that the non-respondents did not greatly differ from those who took the questionnaire save for the points mentioned above.

Although most of the data comes from questionnaires, considerable data was also elicited from in-depth interviews. Twenty Black in-depth interviews were obtained at each prison for comparison with 20 white in-depth interviews with randomly selected white inmates. Attempts to interview 15 to 20 guards at each prison proved less successful.

It is very important to recognize that the conclusions of this article have to be tentative because of the following fundamental sampling and data problems of this limited study. First, one must be careful not to generalize because maximum security prisons in Massachusetts may not be representative of maximum security prisons in other states or regions of the United States.[9]

Second, it is regrettable that this is not a longitudinal study. The lack of longitudinal and time series data keeps me from having a baseline for comparisons that would show either political group consciousness or political group membership at different stages of incarceration or even prior to incarceration.

Third, I could not find any adequate application of organizational theory to prisons. This plus the absence of theory about how political influences affect the prison system make any quantitative, predictive, or explanatory models of the prison system virtually impossible at this time. Furthermore, for quantitative models to be useful and valid the quantitative measures should be relatively precise and representative. Burnham (1968: 8-9) has pointed out that for quantitative measures of a prison system to be effective, it is necessary that there be a high level of stability in the system while the measurements are being done.[10] If this is not done or possible, then the techniques now known can only cope with a certain degree of chance, variation, and flexibility *provided* certain parameters of outside interference are known. If these outside parameters are not known, then the validity of the more sophisticated measuring devices are in doubt.

Anybody who knows anything about the Massachusetts prison system during the time period under study knows that it was tremendously unstable and subject to numerous attempts at political manipulation and control. The main actors were the new commissioner, the governor, the guards' union, and the state legislature among others. The main point is that this tremendous system instability must make quantitative measurements during this time relatively unstable.

I am pointing out these sampling limitations not to downgrade the importance of the data, but rather to advise caution in extrapolation. The advice of Glaser (1969: 184) was taken in the data analysis:

> It is a statistical maxim, in most behavioral science problems, that with strong data you can use weak methods; the strong methods . . . are useful primarily to squeeze a suggestion of relationship out of weak data. Strong relationships can be demonstrated adequately with simple tables of percentages. Perhaps the high intelligence and dedicated effort invested in research into statistical methods would be more fruitful to the correctional system if they were not employed so much in seeking new methods of analysis for old types of data (that can be left to mathematical statisticians in the universities who can be hired as consultants), but preferably in obtaining new types of data, derived from closer study and greater involvement in correctional operations. Furthermore, greater confidence in the reliability of correctional research results generally is gained by obtaining a redundancy of data, by procuring similar findings independently from several alternative indices of the key variables, than by mere statistical tests which assume the absence of bias in sampling or measurement.

Because the key dependent variable (Black political group membership) was a nominal variable, the one tailed chi-square test was used to test relationships.[11] It should be carefully noted that in terms of the chi-square test, both the Concord sample and the Walpole sample are relatively small. Blalock (1972: 294) among others has pointed out that when the chi-square is used, statistical significance can be obtained with a very strong relationship and small samples or a very weak relationship and large samples.[12] It is crucial to keep in mind that the use of this test in this article is a relatively conservative measure. Stated more specifically, this analysis is not likely to be guilty of a type one or alpha statistical error, but there may be an increased probability of a type two error.

THE MASSACHUSETTS STATE PRISON
ENVIRONMENT AND SETTING

Massachusetts, and Concord and Walpole in particular, experienced considerable prison unrest after the Attica revolt in September of 1971.[13] On September 24, 1971, about 400 inmates stages a peaceful protest and presented a list of grievances to prison officials at Concord. These grievances dealt primarily with food, medical care, and living conditions, especially the living conditions in the almost 100-year-old east wing. Unrest based primarily on these issues continued to arise periodically at Concord in February, May, and July. None of these protests were accompanied by damage to either people or property.

There was property damage at Concord in early October of 1972 when the prisoners protested broken windows and freezing temperatures in the old wing. Unlike the earlier ones, this protest had to be broken by heavily armed state police going through the prison. This October protest was after the data collection had been completed.

At Walpole unrest also accelerated immediately after Attica in 1971. The prisoners in September of 1971 stopped working and discussed with prison officials such grievances as better living conditions, better medical care, and liberalized parole policies. These discussions continued without violence until mid-November 1971, when Walpole prisoners caused $30,000 damage by setting fires and smashing machinery. This resulted in a two-week lock-up (at that point the longest in the state's history), charges and counter-charges, and finally, on November 10, 1971, the resignation of Prison Commissioner John Fitzpatrick.

John Boone, the new Black commissioner of corrections, was appointed in early January while there was still extensive unrest at Walpole. Some of Boone's early moves, such as closing down the Corrections Department's "special" segregation unit at Bridgewater State Hospital and replacing the Warden at Walpole with one of his appointees from out of state, poured fuel upon Boone's rift with the prison guards that was to last throughout his term as commissioner.

On March 17 and 19, 1972, Walpole had one of the most severe riots in the state's history. Although many correctional officers contended that it was a race riot, there were very few personal injuries compared to the extent of property damage. There were minor injuries to two guards and six prisoners, but more than one million dollars in property damage was done as prisoners destroyed the prison library, auditorium stage, smashed windows, television sets, plumbing fixtures, and ruined some 200 cell-door locks.

The key point to keep in mind is that there was extensive protest and activity before and after the data collection but not during the April to June period at Concord or the July to October 1972 period at Walpole. There was, however, extensive political activity that involved prisons. Between April and October of 1972 the superintendents at both Concord and Walpole had resigned;[14] the Prison Guard Union had filed suit in court contending that Boone had not had the required five years of prison administrative experience to qualify for the commissioner's job;[15] about 200 prison guards' wives had demonstrated before the governor and the state legislature and had demanded that Boone be fired because he had permitted the prisons to become so dangerous that the safety of their husbands was threatened; and finally the legislature, under Boone's urging, passed an extensive prison reform bill which stressed communtiy treatment and even included furloughs. This was a period of rather extensive publicity, legislation, and discussion about prisons in the state.

Some portion of the tension at Walpole and especially at Concord was probably influenced by relatively overcrowded conditions. The prison populations at each institution seems to have increased considerably since 1969 and especially since the decade of the 1960s.[16]

In Massachusetts as in other states, some of the tension in prisons could be attributed to differential sentencing. Although one of the reasons for differential sentencing is wide discretion by judges, there are other reasons as well. A prestigious Committee for Economic Development (1972) report on nationwide conditions notes:

> Sentences imposed on conviction are highly variable, ranging for the same crime between extremes in leniency and severity not only from state to state but from judge to judge within the same court system. Two felons convicted of identical offenses with comparable case histories may receive prison terms differing in length by three or four to one, and most court systems lack means to minimize such discrepancies. Judges have little guidance by statute or education on sentencing philosophy or alternatives; many even lack personal knowledge of prison conditions.

Any area where an official has wide discretion (such as in passing sentence) is especially suspect as an area of racial discrimination. I was therefore rather surprised to find that there were not major differences in the overall percentages of Black and white inmates in either institution who saw themselves as having sentences heavier than other inmates. A majority of inmates of both races at Walpole saw themselves as having sentences "heavier than most other inmates," and in each institution a greater percentage of Black inmates than white felt that their sentences were heavier.[17]

In the in-depth interviews many of the white inmates who felt that their sentence was "heavier than most of the others" attributed that to the fact that they felt they may have had longer records than many of the other prisoners. But many of the Black prisoners who felt that their sentences were heavier than most seemed especially bitter about it and almost all attributed it to racism. Most of the Black prisoners at both Concord and Walpole could name numerous white (but not Black) prisoners who had received better sentences. I am including some examples below of prisoners who did not contest that they had committed the acts in question. Many other Black prisoners contended that they were innocent. Black prisoners put it this way:

I got 6 to 12 for unarmed robbery. White guys get 3-5. I got 5-7 for an attempt to sell narcotics. White guys go to narcotics houses (halfway houses). The DA was asking for up to 40 years so I had to take the 6-12. [Walpole, mid-twenties in age]

No, it [sentence] wasn't fair cause when I got in here and read the papers [white] dudes got 5 years. I got 12-15 years and got to do 10 more—2 on an old bit and 8 additional for this before I finished. In the time I've been in here white dudes have been paroled 3 times and come back for armed robbery with lesser sentences. [Walpole, late 30s in age, spent more than 18 months in segregation and in segregation at the time of interview, considered a militant and troublemaker in Corrections Department files]

My sentence was not fair compared to whites. I've seen other people come in here who haven't gotten the same time. There are at least 10 guys, white, who have come in here for murder and have got 18-20 year sentences and I got life or 90 years. These guys have done several bits and they say that they "got a break in court" and they have lesser sentences. [Brilliant and highly thought of by other Black prisoners, mid-twenties, served almost 6 years at Walpole]

Black first offenders especially felt that they got discriminatory sentences:

I'm a first offender doing 20 years. I feel that I'm a political prisoner. I've seen white guys who are second and third offenders get 5-7 years. [Concord, Muslim, early thirties, in prison 5 years, U.S. armed forces veteran]

I was a first offender and got 10-15 year sentence. Whites charges with the same and other offenses received 5-7 and 6-9 years. Two white guys charged the same day got 5-7 and 7-10 year sentences and this was not their first offense. [Concord, mid-twenties, veteran of the "special" segregation unit]

I got a 5 year sentence for larceny when on drugs, I had some juvenile offenses. Others, mostly white have probation, six month sentences and other things like that. [Concord, late teens, in prison about 6 months]

Resentment over discriminatory sentencing is only one aspect of the Black prisoner's environment. Equally prevalent is racism and discrimination within the prison. The racism documented in the report of the New York State Commission on Attica (1972: xi, 4, 39, 40, 79-82) is similar to the racism that Black inmates described at both Concord and Walpole.

Much of the racism in prison arises out of areas where the staff and especially the guards have rather wide discretion. Some racism involved discretion in providing basic services. One Black prisoner stressed that white guards make much greater efforts to find white prisoners when they have visitors then they do for Black prisoners:

They'll [guards] call and call white dudes for visits—the white dudes [both inmates and visitors] don't get hasseled but the Blacks do. A white dude don't get shipped out when he attacks others but Blacks do. Banquets[18] are delayed for the Blacks but not for the whites. [Concord, young Black leader in his early twenties, in prison past 3 years].

The discretion is especially noted in punishments:

A white inmate who took sugar to his room was given a suspended sentence and my [Black] friend got three days loss time for doing the same thing. Whites get courses that Blacks ask for but don't get. Whites get jobs that they ask for, Blacks don't. Blacks whom they fear get more play than Brothers who don't speak out. Disciplinary cases for Blacks is more severe—looking at the screw in the wrong way has led Black men to be isolated and receive loss time. A Black guy asked for a certain cereal and the screw[19] said they didn't have it—move on down the line. A white group came in and asked for the same kind and got it. It almost started a riot. [Concord, mid-twenties, Correction Department records say transferred from another prison as a "revolutionary leader"] [20]

I lost 45 good days for being out of bounds and going into somebody's room. I got 3 days [Norfolk prison] for "silent insolence"—giving a guard a dirty look.[21] [Walpole, mid-twenties, sentenced for armed robbery]

Even as far as parole is concerned, percentage wise there's always more whites paroled than Brothers. Plus punishment—they're more harder on Brothers than they are on their own. [Walpole, Black Muslim, early twenties in age]

It is in job discrimination that Black prisoners really note the racism. This was especially the complaint at Walpole:

This is one of the most open racist places in Massachusetts. The administration is openly racist. No Blacks work in the hospital, canteen, etc. so the white inmates benefit from these things not the Blacks. The superintendent has done nothing about it and when I approached him and told him that Blacks were qualified for these jobs he gave me 15 days in the hole. [Walpole, aged in the 30s, has been in Walpole at least 5 years]

The white guys have better jobs or if not better jobs they're lying around in their rooms smoking, etc. The brothers get the sloppy jobs—sweeping, washing walls and the like. [Walpole, early twenties, quoted once before above]

They're discriminated against (Blacks). In the woodworking shop there's not one Black. . . . To date not one Black man has been in that shop. Whites who are paroled and who have worked in that shop leave with 10 or 15 thousand—no Black can do this.

There are 10 people working on outside jobs—4 are lifers who are not supposed to leave the institution—they are all white. The superintendent told us that in the whole time only one Black has ever worked on the outside! . . . Most of the computer training is all white—it's Honeywell's equipment. The classrooms are small so the percentage of Blacks is very minimal. The course takes 2 years and is only given to men with 2 years to go. This automatically excludes most Blacks because their sentences are longer.

Certain types of razors (electric), tape recorders, TVs are required[22] but the whites have any type they want and they are visibly displayed and are not confiscated as contraband. Some white boys don't get shaken down and as a result don't get their stuff confiscated. [Walpole, mid-twenties, trying to organize an all-Black group]

One Black Walpole prisoner summed up the job problem:

Avocations[23] have mostly whites in them. There are more Blacks than whites in the metal shop. There are more whites in the print shop—the easier the work, the more whites. [Walpole, mid-forties, loner]

Possibly because of the above, many Black prisoners at both Concord and Walpole felt that they could not become a prison trustee. At Concord, 41 percent of the Black prisoners felt that they did not have a chance to become a trustee. When the evidence from the questionnaire of Black prisoners and the in-depth interviews with white prisoners is combined, it supports Black prisoners' claims of racial discrimination in job assignments at both Concord and Walpole.[24] In Concord, 78 percent of my Black sample answered that they had job assignments compared to only 48 percent of my Black Walpole sample. Blacks at Concord were also working at a wider range of jobs, some of which were semi-skilled such as the tailor shop, furniture shop, and the paint shop. About 80 percent of the Black brothers at Concord were working compared to only about one-third at Walpole. The most interesting comparison at Concord was between Black and white inmates in the desirable jobs. More than 36 percent of my white inmate random sample had desirable jobs such as clerical or counseling service jobs and jobs in the kitchen or staff dining rooms. Only about 5 percent of the Blacks in my Concord sample had jobs that were in this most desirable category. Black inmates were also overrepresented in the undesirable cement-making shop.

At Walpole the job discrimination was worse. Fifty-seven percent of the Black inmates at Walpole who were working were working in the worst places to work, namely the kitchen, the auto-plate or metal shop, and janitorial or custodial work. Less than 30 percent of the white inmates interviewed worked in these job categories. Also whereas almost 30 percent of the white inmates interviewed were in desirable jobs such as clerical and working for the counseling service, less than 10 percent of the Black prisoners had these desirable jobs.

In light of the above, it is not surprising that many Black prisoners at both Concord and Walpole believed that they did not have a chance to become a trustee. At Concord the percentage of Black prisoners who felt this way did not differ significantly from the percentage of white prisoners who felt this way, and in fact a slightly higher percentage of white prisoners felt they did not have a chance to become a trustee. Forty-six percent of both white and Black Concord prisoners felt that they had a chance to become a trustee, while 41 percent of the Blacks and 53 percent of the white prisoners felt that they did not. The answer to this question may have been slightly misinterpreted because it was not clear whether all Concord prisoners considered the farm as trustee status.

At Walpole a majority of the white prisoners (53 percent) felt that they had a chance to become a trustee while only 28 percent of the Black prisoners felt that way. While 40 percent of the white prisoners felt that they did not have a chance to become a trustee, 60 percent of the Black prisoners felt that way. Furthermore, more Blacks listed racial and religious discrimination than any other factor as the reason why they could not become a trustee. Once we get an understanding of the extensive racism in northern Black prison environments, we can then understand the factors that affect Black prisoner political consciousness.

BLACK POLITICAL CONSCIOUSNESS IN NORTHERN PRISONS

Before we go further it is necessary to define what is meant by high Black political consciousness. For the purposes of this study, a Black prisoner with high political consciousness is in one of the following categories: (1) he believes that he has been the recipient of punishment in prison either because of believing in or acting on a political belief; (2) the Black prisoner sees himself and defines himself as a political prisoner; (3) the Black prisoner is a member of a political group. Political group inmates are considered to be members of the Nation of Islam, the Black Panther Party, the Republic of New Africa, the Congress of African Peoples, the Organization of Afro-American Unity, other Muslim organizations, and the Peaceful Movement Committee at Concord.[25]

A number of items on the questionnaires dealt with political questions. Respondents were asked what they thought was the major purpose of the prison; they were asked whether they felt there were political prisoners in the U.S.; whether they felt that there were political prisoners at the institution and, if so, to name them; they were asked whether they saw themselves as political prisoners; whether they were members of political organizations; whether they felt that they or others had to hide organizational membership from prison officials; whether they were members of political organizations before they came to prison; and whether they believed that brothers who were in political organizations were treated the same, better, or worse than other brothers who were not members of political organizations.

Although most prisons, including the two in this study, contend that they are greatly concerned with rehabilitation, they are in reality primarily, and in some cases almost totally, concerned with custody and social control. Fifty-one percent of the Black inmates at Concord saw the major purpose of the institution as either to punish people or to serve as a warning; only 6.3 percent saw the purpose of Concord as to provide treatment. At Walpole a similar percent (52 percent) saw the purpose of the institution as either to punish people or serve as a warning. Almost all major prison scholars agree that social control and custody, not treatment, is the prime concern of American corrections (Cressey, 1965; Irwin, 1970; Wright, 1973).

The fact that most prisons are more concerned with custody rather than preventing recidivism has great ramifications for Black prisoners who may be involved in political groups. The fact is that groups and especially Black political groups can easily be seen or perceived as a major threat to custody, the prime concern of the prison. A major prison scholar (Cloward, 1960) has noted that prisons gear their rewards only to those who "do their own time" outside of group activity. The rewards are not focused upon the likelihood of the person becoming a recidivist:

> In other words keeping out of trouble was defined as "keeping away from other inmates"; the two phrases may be interchanged without doing appreciable violence to the meaning of either. And the warning implicit in official statements was inescapable: formal rewards (parole, time off for good conduct, etc.) would presumably be granted only to those who assiduously abstain from participating in primary group activities.

> Custodial exhortations to "go it alone" are one facet of a systematic attempt to restrain solidary relations among prisoners by reducing the frequency and saliency of their interaction. By definition the model prisoner is the isolated prisoner.

Thus the politically conscious Black prisoner, especially one who may be a member of a political consciousness-raising group, is far from the ideal inmate in the minds of control- and custody-minded prison officials, almost all of whom are of a different race and from a different life-style than the Black prisoner.

I do not want to leave the impression that only the clearly custody-oriented prisons are not pleased with the prospect of coexisting with increasing Black political consciousness or Black political groups. It is an accepted behavioral axiom that the behavior of many individuals is strongly influenced by group membership and various group interplay. Thus, if the groups are congruent with the goals, values, and perspectives of the treatment officials, they are perceived as an asset; when they are not, they are considered a problem. Some sociologists and psychiatrists have noted that some groups can be and are anti-treatment because of their strong cohesive nature. Basically, the more stable the frame of reference of the individual, the more resistant the individual is to a contradictory frame of reference; the frame of reference stability depends not so much on the individual's own experience and reality testing as much as it does on *group consensus and reinforcement* (Crosser, 1958). Furthermore, it is important to note that treatment philosophy, with its emphasis upon rehabilitating and treating the individual prisoner, differs completely from the philosophy of Black political groups who emphasize the sickness, racism, and inequality of American society.[26]

The point of the above is that many or most prison officials who are attempting to maximize social control and custody, or "treatment," will not see the rise of either increased Black political consciousness or, especially, Black political groups as being in their interests. Thus the extent that Black prisoners see themselves as either political prisoners or join political organizations can be perceived as a breakdown in social control or, worse, could be seen as a threat to the stability of the institution.

Let us first look at Black inmates who see themselves as political prisoners. Glaser (1969) has written that as a prisoner gets older he gets more concerned with doing his own time; he begins to see other inmates as potential sources of trouble. Thus, since the prisoners at Concord are younger than the prisoners at Walpole, I expected to find more of them who saw themselves as political prisoners and members of political groups. A lot of the general publicity in the mass media and even documents such as the Attica Commission (1972) report had stressed that most young Black prisoners from ghetto streets "would or very

Table 1. PERCEPTION OF POLITICAL PRISONER BY AGE: CONCORD

Political Prisoner	Under 18	18-20	21-24	25-29	30-39	Row Total
No	6	16	30	4	0	56
Yes	1	7	23	10	2	43
$x_2 = 05$						

soon would" see themselves as political prisoners, victims and not criminals. I therefore expected to find that a majority of the Black inmates at both institutions and especially at Concord would consider themselves political prisoners.

At Concord 51 percent of the Black prisoners did *not* see themselves as political prisoners while 39 percent did. At Concord, age was an important variable in the perception of oneself as a political prisoner, as shown in Table 1. Thus at Concord, more than three-quarters of those who saw themselves as political prisoners were 21 or older (especially 21 to 25), while 40 percent of those who did not see themselves as political prisoners were less than 21 years old. The fact that at an institution with a large proportion of younger prisoners I did not find that the younger Black prisoners were more likely to see themselves as political prisoners was counter to my prior hypothesis. Black perceptions of oneself as a political prisoner in prison may thus require some maturity.

At Walpole, in contrast to Concord, a majority of the Black prisoners in the sample saw themselves as political prisoners. Fifty point five percent of the brothers at Walpole saw themselves as political prisoners while 44.2 percent did not. The percentage of Black prisoners at Walpole who did not see themselves as political prisoners was still rather high. Unfortunately, the lack of longitudinal or trend data does not permit any conclusion on the key question of whether political consciousness is rising or the rate of the increase.

In both prisons in the study, members of political groups were significantly more likely to see themselves as political prisoners. Tables 2 and 3 should help to demonstrate that both Black political consciousness and political group membership are part of a similar underlying factor.

Table 2. POLITICAL GROUP MEMBERSHIP BY INMATE SELF-PERCEPTION OF POLITICAL PRISONER: CONCORD

Member of Political Group	Sees Self as Political Prisoner		
	No	Yes	Total
No	40	20	60
Yes	17	24	41
	57	44	101
$x_2 = 05$			

Table 3. POLITICAL GROUP MEMBERSHIP BY INMATE SELF-PERCEPTION OF
POLITICAL PRISONER: WALPOLE

| | Sees Self as Political Prisoner | | |
Member of Political Group	No	Yes	Total
No	33	24	57
Yes	9	24	33
	42	48	90

$x_2 = 01$

Now let us examine political consciousness by looking at Black prisoners who are members of political groups. Table 4 reflects the organizations that the 112 Black prisoners at Concord and the 95 Black prisoners at Walpole checked on the questionnaire. These are raw numbers and percentages. The extremely high total at Concord reflects the fact that members of the Peaceful Movement Committee (PMC) are also members of other organizations. Multiple memberships varied from organization to organization. Members of the Nation of Islam, especially at Walpole, tended not to be members of other organizations. Members of the Black Panther Party also tended to be members of at least one of the other organizations.

When overlapping group memberships were controlled, approximately 45 percent of the Concord sample were members of one or more political groups and about 35 percent of the Walpole inmates were members of one or more political groups. A substantial portion of the differences in group membership participation in Concord in contrast to Walpole can be attributed to the fact that the PMC exists at Concord but not at Walpole.

One of the major concerns of this study was to determine whether Black prisoners who were members of political groups were collectively singled out for

Table 4. GROUP MEMBERSHIP

| | Concord | | Walpole | |
	Frequency	Percent	Frequency	Percent
Nation of Islam	11	10	19	20
Black Panthers	11	10	7	7
Republic of New Africa	6	5	5	5
Congress of African Peoples	6	5	5	5
Organization for Afro- American Units	5	4	4	4
Other Muslim organizations	4	4	2	2
Peaceful Movement Committee	30	27	–	–
Total Black Respondents	112		95	

repression because of their political views. At Concord 46 percent of the Black prisoners said that they believed that Black inmates in political organizations were treated differently from Black brothers not in political organizations. About one-third of these brothers said that Blacks in these organizations were treated worse than other Blacks. When asked about the ways in which they believed that they were treated worse, most mentioned harassment of these brothers by the prison staff. About 22 percent of the Concord inmates felt that Black members of political groups had a worse chance for parole than non-group Blacks. Yet 60 percent of the members of political groups at Concord felt that they did not have to hide their organizational membership from the staff of the institution.

At Walpole there were similar patterns. Forty-four percent of the Walpole sample said that they believed that brothers in political organizations were treated worse or very much worse than Black brothers who were not in political organizations. At Walpole also, 62 percent of the members of political groups felt that they did not have to hide their organizational membership from prison officials, but 14 percent said that they did.

The above makes clear that for both institutions there were a considerable portion of Black prisoners who felt that there were major costs that they must pay if they joined political organizations. This should be a matter of concern for the entire Black community. There are a number of possible effects of a sizable number of Black inmates perceiving sanctions for group membership. One possibility is that this keeps down the number of Black group members as a means of social control. This possibility will be discussed in detail later. Another possibility is that much political group membership activity would have to operate underground in the prison. The fact that this has not been done more extensively attests to the strength of the Black political institutions at this time and the ability of the institutions to get information from spies or stool pigeons within the prisons. More about Black political organization strength will be discussed later when I discuss the concept of "threshold."

Another possible reaction to the expectation of sanctions for joining political groups could be that a disproportionate number of brothers with very long sentences would be the likely ones to join political organizations. The work of sociologist Stanton Wheeler (1969) especially suggests this possibility. This possibility was not the reality, at least for the Black inmates at Concord and Walpole. Further analysis revealed that there was no significant difference in either release date or length of sentence between Black prisoners who were members of political groups and Black prisoners who were not members of political groups at either Concord or Walpole. Thus the tentative hypothesis that only or mostly those prisoners with long sentences or release dates far into the future join political groups is not confirmed, at least not for Black political groups at these prisons.

One of the major purposes of this study was to get a more precise estimate of the probability of a Black prisoner who is a member of a political group receiving negative prison sanctions compared to a Black non-group member. We will first look at Concord and then Walpole.

Concord

Although the differences are not statistically significant, what the figures below will show is that for Concord, *in all cases of negative sanctions by prison officials, the Blacks who were in political groups were more likely to receive the negative sanction than Blacks who were not members of political groups.*

When or if they are ever required to explain negative differential sanctions to members of Black political groups, prison officials would probably respond that prisoners in Black political groups are more likely to engage in acts for which they would likely be punished. Much more research on this question is needed, but elsewhere (Morris, 1973) I have noted that Black prisoners in political groups do not differ from Black prisoners not in political groups on an extensive number of psychological, social, economic, educational, and other key independent variables. If political organization Blacks are in fact quite different from non-group Blacks as the prison officials contend, then it should show up under rigorous examination.

Table 5 examines the likelihood of whether members of political groups were more likely to be punished by isolation. Note that in Table 5 the percentage of political group members to have faced isolation was 10 percent higher than the percentage of non-political group members. Black prisoners in the Concord in-depth interviews did not contend that the Concord administration was likely to use isolation or segregation against political activity per se.

At Concord a similar pattern persists when examining whether Black political group members are more likely to be hit or beaten by the staff. Even though the overall numbers and percentages are relatively small, Table 6 shows that almost

Table 5. CONCORD

| | Punished by Isolation | | |
Political Group Membership	No	Yes	Row Total
No	44	18	62
	(71%)	(29%)	
Yes	27	18	45
	(60%)	(40%)	

Corrected x_2 = 0.95662 with 1df—ns

Table 6. CONCORD

Political Group Membership	Hit or Beaten by Staff		Row Total
	No	Yes	
No	63	3	66
	(95.5%)	(4.5%)	
Yes	42	4	46
	(91.3%)	(8.7%)	

Corrected x_2 = 0.24594 with 1df—ns

twice the percentage of political group members had been hit or beaten by the Concord staff compared to non-group Blacks. The questionnaire was not precise enough to pick up what I would call "perception of the prison staff as a militant or bad Nigger." I noticed that at least two of the three Blacks who were beaten, but who were not members of political groups, could likely have been highlighted if the instrument were more precise. So there are two important points to keep in mind. First, physical abuse of prisoners by guards or the staffs in Massachusetts is now relatively rare. Second, it is associated with a perceived aggressive, militant, or "bad Nigger" attitude.

A less marked but similar negative pattern is evident when one examines Black political group membership and the likelihood of being "written-up" receiving disciplinary reports, as shown in Table 7. Note that two-thirds of the non-group Black inmates never received a written-up disciplinary report while less than one-half the Black prisoners in political groups were so lucky. Because of the small numbers in many of the cells, one must interpret it with care. Nevertheless, note that almost twice the number of prisoners in political groups had been written-up for disciplinary violations compared to Black prisoners not in political groups. There was no change in the relationships even when length of time in prison was controlled. In the in-depth interviews, a number of Black prisoners stated that members of Black political groups at Concord (save for some of the leaders) were watched more closely, were required to show passes

Table 7. POLITICAL GROUP MEMBERSHIP BY WRITTEN-UP
DISCIPLINARY ACTIONS: CONCORD

Group Member	Number of Written-Up Violations				Row Total
	Never	1 or 2	3 or 4	5 or more	
No	44	14	5	3	66
	(67%)	(21%)	(8%)	(5%)	
Yes	20	15	5	5	45
	(44%)	(33%)	(11%)	(11%)	

Corrected x_2 = 5.76795 with 3 df—ns

within the institution more often, and were generally harassed more by the guards.

The data above suggests that for Concord, negative institutional sanctions were only slightly more likely to have been taken against Black members of political groups compared to Black prisoners who were not members of political groups. In none of the key independent variables—punishment by isolation, hit or beaten by the staff, or number of written-up disciplinary reports—were the relationships statistically significant at Concord for members of Black political organizations. The non-statistically significant relationships among these key variables may help account for the fact that, at Concord, a sizeable percentage of Black prisoners did not feel that Black prisoners in political organizations were treated differently from other Blacks not in political organizations. There were more Black prisoners (37 percent) who felt Black prisoners in political organizations were treated the same or better than other Blacks than there were Black prisoners who felt that Blacks in political organizations were treated worse or very much worse (33 percent).[27] We shall see below that this differs considerably from Walpole.

Walpole

All but one of the prisoners who had spent time at both Concord and Walpole felt that Walpole was a more oppressive institution. This was especially the case for Blacks who were members of political groups. In contrast to Concord, when Black prisoners were asked how Blacks in political organizations were treated differently from other Blacks not in political organizations, more than twice the percentage of prisoners stated that they felt Blacks in political organizations were treated worse or very much worse (44 percent) than those who said the same or better (22 percent). Other evidence bears this out. Whereas the data from Concord strongly suggest certain patterns, the data from Walpole show statistically significant relationships.

Table 8 looks at the relationship between political group membership and punishment by isolation. It is quite clear that members of political groups had a

Table 8. WALPOLE

Political Group Membership	Punished by Isolation		Row Total
	No	Yes	
No	39 (70%)	17 (30%)	56
Yes	12 (37.5)	20 (62.5)	32

x_2 = 8.87813 with 1df—.01 $>$

considerably greater risk of having to spend time in isolation than Black prisoners who were not in political groups. Black prisoners at Walpole felt that the prison administration had looked for any opportunity to put the Muslims in isolation.

> In the past the Administration put the word out that the Muslims were going to kill Blacks or other inmates. They would name the individuals to try to separate and divide us [Blacks].

> The Black Panthers and Muslims are definitely treated differently. When they gas the Muslims they gas them until they get tired. One guard from Texas said, "Come on down here and watch the fun. They had a murder down here, Black on Black and they're going to lock up all the Muslims."

> They don't lock up all Catholics, Protestants, etc. when whites get killed. [Black inmate considered a militant who had spent more than one year in isolation and who was in isolation at the time of the data collection]

Table 9 examines the relationship of Black prisoners in political groups to the likelihood of being hit or beaten by the staff. It is important to notice that the number of Black prisoners hit or beaten by the prison staff at Walpole, like Concord, is relatively small. Ninety-four percent of the Black prisoners at Walpole had never been hit or beaten by the staff. This was consistent with their contention that psychological, verbal, and social status harassment was much more prevalent than physical abuse by the prison staff. The significant thing about the beatings of Black prisoners was not the number of Black prisoners who said that they had been beaten by the staff; the key factor was that Black prisoners who were members of political groups were significantly more likely than non-group members to have been hit or beaten by the staff. Also, most of the beatings occurred either going to or while at the department's Special Segregation Unit at Bridgewater, the mental hospital and prison. Almost all of these prisoners had been very active or leaders in the political organizations within the prison. Most had also been very articulate organizers:

> The reason they put me in isolation was when I had just started a Mosque. . . . At DSU Bridgewater, 40 guards, the Warden and others tried

Table 9. WALPOLE

Political Group Membership	Hit or Beaten by Staff		Row Total
	No	Yes	
No	60 (98.4)	1 (1.6)	61
Yes	28 (84.8)	5 (15.2)	33

x_2 corrected = 4.47728 with 1df−.05 $>$

to move me and some got busted up, so I got another 7 years for that. I had become angry in isolation because I couldn't get medicine when I was sick so I tore up the room. At that time, if you got sick, you waited 2 months to get to the hospital unless you were white. [Walpole, active in a number of political groups with different intensity over a period of years, Black, considered one of the toughest men in the prison]

One of the interesting items in the official prison file of a Black Panther leader was a news clipping of his activities at a demonstration in the community where he lived.

No I haven't been treated fairly and that's been since November of 1970. They sent me to Bridgewater without a hearing for being a militant and a Black Panther and for threatening officers lives. I did 6 months in DSU–6 months of the hardest years of my life.

The food at Bridgewater contained spit, urine and roaches. Dinner call was for 3:45 but often the food was not served until 5:45 when it was cold. I lost 40 pounds in 6 months and wrote to the Governor and the Commissioner about the conditions. Inmates were let out of their rooms for only 20 minutes each day, the rooms were small and little reading material was available. [Black Panther, sentenced to 5 years and served 3 at time of interview]

The consistent pattern of negative sanctions associated with Black political group membership continues in Table 10. The evidence in the in-depth interviews strongly suggests that a good part of the difference in the likelihood of getting written-up disciplinary violations could be due to the fact that the Walpole guards were particularly anxious to keep members of the Nation of Islam in their place. The Black prisoners in the in-depth interviews stressed that the prime means of official oppression against either Blacks who were in or out of political groups was not by force or physical means but rather by lack of respect and especially harassment. Note in the following excerpts the possibility of abuse of discretion by the staff:

There's harassment from the prison guards—they hold back on our mail; throw away our newspaper. Any laws they have they pick on us for

Table 10. WALPOLE

Political Group Membership	Number of Disciplinary Actions				Row Total
	Never	1 or 2	3 or 4	5 or more	
No	40	13	3	4	60
	(67)	(22)	(5)	(6.7)	
Yes	13	8	3	8	32
	(40.6)	(25)	(9.4)	(25)	

x_2 = 8.54862 with 3 df–.05 >

infractions that we are unaware of. When meeting with others and a "rule" is broken they pick us out; reprimand us and not the others. [Black Muslim prisoner, age 24, on isolation at the time of the interview]

There are petty harassments and they shake down my room quite a few times. They recognize us as a militant group and they treat us as such. There's no militant group here but they treat us as such. His nature is to treat us unfair and he won't change. [Black Muslim, age 29, on isolation at the time of the interview]

Even the non-Muslim Black prisoners are just as ready to acknowledge that Muslims seemed targets for special harassment.

They were forced to go out in the yard and hold their Islam services when there was a room available and others had room for their meetings. They are now being held in a disaster area, and they have been gassed and made to stay there for disturbance other inmates had created. [non-Muslim, mid-forties, sentenced to life in prison]

For instance the doors of the chapel—they [guards] take their time to open them. There are little harassing things. The administration will receive equipment and then hold it. The Panthers sent packages at Christmas for all of us and they held them for 5 weeks [investigating] before they gave them to us. [About 40-year-old prisoner who does not join political organizations, who keeps to himself trying to do his own time]

One of the most important but still tentative findings about differential sanctions to Black political groups involves what I call the "threshold effect." The Black prisoners who were organizers and leaders and even the majority of members in Black political groups all seemed to experience the greatest hassles when the groups were just beginning and thus were at their weakest and most vulnerable point. When Black groups got to be a certain strength, they became more accepted and more of a force to be dealt with. I am not sure at what point this threshold level is; whether it is strongly dependent upon variables such as size of prison, region, or other institutional factors. I am not as yet sure whether the threshold itself is dependent more upon the number and proportion of the Black prison population that is on the Black political organization, or whether the threshold effect is more dependent upon the proportion of Blacks in the total prison population. The lack of longitudinal, trend, or time series data in this study precludes a definitive answer at this time. Nevertheless, the experiences of Black prisoners who have been at Walpole over time and who have been members of political groups give me confidence in this threshold concept. Let me now cite two examples. A Nation of Islam leader talks of the change over time in institutional approaches even while the majority of the membership was under the burden of segregation and isolation in the prison:

Up until recently, the guards discouraged Blacks from coming together for constructive purposes. There was a rule created that no more than 4 brothers could congregate at one time. The Nation of Islam only got started here in 1971. During the 50s and 60s, there were some brothers who were attracted to Islam but were not able to practice.

The administration was at first totally negative—we couldn't get a place to worship and practice our religion. They finally gave us the visitors room but the guards tried to discourage other inmates from joining e.g., they told the men that they would not receive parole if they joined up and it was known that Muslims did not receive paroles. The guards now recognize us as one of the strong Black groups. Through the [Black] Commissioner, we can now write for the paper.

In the past we were considered incorrigible and trouble makers who got long sentences. Now because of our example, they have to give us respect. We're more visible in this enclosed environment. Other Black groups in this penitentiary have mostly been short lived cause they are not organized and structured as well as Islam. . . . We pursue constantly higher education, unlike other groups here and this is not liked by the guards.

There was a contest in the past to give us space to hold our classes every night. For 6 months we brought tables and chairs to meet in the halls. They wouldn't let us meet in the classroom so we congregated in the hall and this they couldn't stop. Other brothers were attracted to this powerful force. [Currently one of the most articulate members of the Nation of Islam]

Black prisoners who were members of political groups in their beginning at Walpole tell stories (most confirmed in their official files) of extreme harassment when their numbers were much smaller. For them, the larger number of Blacks in the institution was crucial.

When I first came in here and started the Black Panther Party, I was busted and locked up at least every 2 months. I spent most of my time in isolation. I later became a Muslim and was busted for that. At the time I got locked up I was one of 5 Muslims. They busted me for trying to start a Black library when there were only 100 Black inmates at the time.

The arrival of more Black prisoners and the test of strength that resulted in the March 17 institution riot made a big difference for this influential, active inmate.

Before the riot this was a white institution—we got the feedback. People who got cut were Black. A firebomb was thrown in my room—a deputy [superintendent] had warned me that this would happen if I didn't stop my activities. I have this case in federal court now. Now after the riot the guards tried to get another one started by locking Blacks and whites together. Instead I served on a negotiating committee where we talked about conditions here. . . . Now Blacks are consulted all the time. Whites are the ones getting cut. [Veteran of the U.S. Army and the DSU, not currently practicing Muslim]

These same sentiments were felt by the Black prisoner who was considered a militant and who had spent the most time in segregation and isolation.

[Black and white contacts] are getting better, much better than I have ever seen them. The population is changing—more Blacks than ever before and the number will get higher so the man feels he had better change his ways. I don't feel there's anything good about the man and I'm glad to see another brother when he comes—he's sort of like another God to me.

The implications of this and other trends will be discussed in the following section.

BLACK POLITICAL GROUP MEMBERSHIP, CONSCIOUSNESS, AND PRISON SOCIAL CONTROL

I have pointed out earlier that the prime concern of most prisons is custody and control. It is perhaps remarkable that Black political consciousness and Black political groups are able to survive at all in prison environments in light of the major efforts to crush them in order to maximize social control, or maybe even because of the extensive racism in American prisons. It is important to keep in mind that the majority of these efforts at social control do not involve overt physical punishment. This is because long ago sharp prison officials learned that it was in their interests to come to some other accommodation than force with prisoners (Cloward, 1960). Prison officials are learning these lessons slower in the cases of certain politically active Black men.

A first defense in authorities' maximizing of social control has been the attempt to keep prisoners out of groups. Sykes (1967) has described these efforts:

Both by accident and design the inmate works with one group and is locked in a cellblock with another. His associations in the mess hall are apt to differ from those of the recreation yard. And all the incipient bonds of solidarity are likely to be disrupted by transfers from one institution to another, paroles, completion of sentence, or confinement in a segregation cell.

Massachusetts prison officials have tried to control or crush inmates who showed high political consciousness, who attempted to organize, or who were members of political groups. These attempts have been unsuccessful.

Other efforts by the prison authorities to maximize control (in contrast to non-recidivism) is through the use of the divide-and-conquer strategy. Sykes (1967) has pointed out that this often involves reducing prisoners' trust in each other by rewarding informers; a strategy of going slow in policing the prison community (neither stop fights and stabbings nor investigate them thoroughly), which would be likely to keep the inmates fighting each other rather than the prison staff; and finally a strategy of permitting the inmates to exploit other inmates by such things as rackets.[28]

These divide-and-conquer strategies posed the most difficulty for Black political organizations and active individuals. General inmate unity and Black prisoner political organization unity was hindered by the fact that many prisoners felt that some of the Black prisoners in leadership positions in the political organizations were too closely identified with a particular clique. Another similar problem that tended to reduce the participation in Black political organizations was the tendency of some Black prisoners to extensively ridicule other Black prisoners at any points where they were vulnerable. This phenomenon has also been noticed in low-income Black children in the schools, among other places (Rist, 1970). It is important to note that these difficulties did not restrict Black political group participation to any great degree, and they were especially insignificant where participation in the Nation of Islam was concerned.

Another method of control that has been attempted, after the "threshold effect" that I discussed above, has been the effort to maximize control by having Black political group leaders have a stake in keeping peace or "keeping the joint cool." Some of the most powerful Black prisoner leaders, many of whom the authorities had attempted to break in the years of 1968-70 in the feared DSU, were in many cases being oppressed less in 1972. Many were less likely to be asked to show passes when moving about in the institution, many had illegal hotplates in their rooms, more access to making phone calls, less hasseling over reporting to work, and such things as better sound equipment in their rooms. This was a clear example of an attempt to control through cooptation.

These extra privileges did not seem to make these leaders more susceptible to prison administration control. Most saw these privileges as something which they had earned by paying some dues in the DSU. They also felt that the privileges which were now granted informally to some Blacks were basically the same that white inmate leaders and especially white Mafia leaders at Walpole had been getting for years. The Black leaders also said that they were "aware of the Administration's game" and would never sell out the other brothers. There was never any evidence of charges that they did.

The fact that some of the most political Black prisoners got some privileges that some other prisoners did not get was both an asset and liability to other Black prisoners in their considerations of whether they should or should not join Black political groups. While some would not join the organizations because they thought that the organization was used by the leaders for personal goals, others were willing to join to hopefully get privileges themselves. The fact that the privileges were noticed helps account for the fact that about 10 percent of the brothers at Concord and about 10 percent of the brothers at Walpole stated in their questionnaires that they felt that Black prisoners in political organizations were treated better or very much better when compared to other Black inmates. It is my opinion, although I have no evidence to back it up, that differential privileges helped Black political organizations at one of the prisons and hurt them (in terms of recruitment) at the other.

It must be stressed that one of the Black organizations, the Nation of Islam, did not have leaders who received differential privileges. This is undoubtedly because the Nation of Islam is a religion, and they have and enforce rather strict and difficult standards. Since the Muslims were not subject to attempts at social control by the above type of manipulation, they may have received special attention through other methods of divide and conquer. Black prisoners contend that the way that this was done at both Concord and Walpole was that the administration told other Blacks that the Muslims were "troublemakers."

> They [Muslims] are discriminated against because of their beliefs. They are not given space for their meetings. Different things were done to prevent them from meeting or existing including not giving the men the type of food they want or their religion requires. The main thing is that they try to convince other Blacks that they are troublemakers and stay away. [Concord, Black political group leader]

None of these attempts at social control of the Muslims by cutting off their access to recruiting other Blacks has worked.

By far one of the best and most powerful tools that has been used against Black political organizations was the indeterminate sentence. The indeterminate sentence was originally a "reform" that was to bring flexibility to sentencing and give an inmate an opportunity and incentive to get out of prison earlier if his conduct demonstrated that he was either rehabilitated or ready to return to society without leading a life of crime. It is virtually impossible to determine whether the states that extensively use indeterminate sentences actually produce shorter sentences in the end than those who don't.[29] But another, more important result of the indeterminate sentence is to increase the discretion and ability of prison officials to control the release date of prisoners and to increase the psychological tension and uncertainty over release in many cases.[30]

Uncertainty about parole was much more of a problem for Black prisoners at

Walpole than at Concord. At Concord the degree of uncertainty for Black prisoners was almost the same for Black as for white prisoners. Thirty-eight percent of Black prisoners and 33 percent of white Concord prisoners either did not know about their parole prospects or they thought their parole prospects were poor; 61 percent of the Black and 67 percent of the white Concord prisoners felt that their parole chances were fair or good.

In contrast to Concord, 58 percent of the white prisoners but only 32 percent of the Black prisoners at Walpole felt that their chances for parole were either fair or good; 41 percent of the white prisoners but 67 percent of the Black prisoners at Walpole felt that their chances for parole were either poor or uncertain. At Walpole there was evidence that the threat of a denial of parole was a factor that kept some Black prisoners from joining Black political organizations.

Two Black Walpole prisoners put it like this:

A lot of Blacks don't want to jump into groups, like I don't want to. There's a lot of Blacks in groups, but they ain't getting out that door. [Walpole, early thirties, doing 7-10 years]

If a person were a Panther it would hurt his chances for parole since the Parole Board thinks they're violent and would endanger others on the street. [Walpole, mid-twenties, been at Walpole two years]

The threat of withholding parole for participating in Black political organizations is not as much a barrier to the growth of the organizations as it might be in other states because of a number of local reasons. First, Massachusetts has a law that says that an inmate who is convicted of a violent crime must serve two-thirds of his minimum sentence before he is eligible for parole. This affects most Black prisoners. After serving two-thirds of their time, many would rather serve the remainder and be free without the restrictions of parole. Furthermore, Black prisoners have found through experience that the most important factors that affect one's parole are: first, whether the prisons are overcrowded; second, whether one has pull or influence with the parole board; and finally, whether it is possible to find a job in the community when finding a job is sometimes a precondition of release.

None of the methods of social control used by prison authorities to suppress Black prisoners have been successful because Black political organizations are filling and addressing certain fundamental needs of Black prisoners. One of these needs is fighting racism in prison. It is clearly racism that must account for possible disproportionate disciplining of members of the Nation of Islam on the grounds of security. Muslim brothers are always disproportionately well-behaved because, as one Walpole Muslim brother put it: "Our spiritual leader teaches us to obey those in authority as long as their rules do not conflict with our laws." I also saw disturbing signs to indicate that members of the Nation of Islam are or may soon be the most *conservative,* as well as the most disciplined, Black prison organization.

Black political groups were also a very important means of both protection and survival. This is especially the case in prisons where Blacks constitute less than a majority of prisoners. The political groups were as much a protection against other prisoners as they were protection against the prison staff.[31] The Black Muslims were especially praised and noted for their ability to protect each other and other Blacks.

> I believe that the Muslims have a togetherness thing going and the other brothers recognize this and help each other. Muslims stay near the shower when another takes a shower; they go places together and protect themselves. The other brothers notice and respect this. [Walpole, late thirties, quoted above]

Respect was a third major need that Black political organizations helped to provide to many prisoners in the organizations. Many prisoners stressed that even the guards had been forced to respect many of the Blacks who were in political organizations.

With the data presented here it is surprising that Black political groups have been able to survive in a hostile and oppressive prison environment. I have concluded that the greatest asset toward continuation of the organizations is the extensive racism; first in American society at large, and secondarily in the prisons. As long as this extensive racism persists, Black political organizations will not be destroyed by the efforts of prison officials, who are primarily concerned with social control rather than truly being concerned with reducing recidivism.

There has not been any research that can give us definitive answers as to whether membership in Black political organizations can, will be, or has been a major factor in helping to keep a Black prisoner from becoming a recidivist. Glaser (1969) has reported in an Illinois study that one of the ways that nonrecidivists differed from recidivists was that nonrecidivists belonged to organizations more than recidivists. When American prisons truly become concerned with reducing recidivism, they may then realize that both high Black political consciousness and Black politcal organizations are major assets to Black prisoners and the Black community.

NOTES

1. For complete statistics on this point see U.S. Department of Justice, Bureau of Prisons (1972); U.S. Department of Commerce (1970). These statistics cover state and federal penal institutions and *not* city or county jails. The focus of this paper is upon state penal institutions.

2. Elaboration on these points is beyond the scope of this article. For an excellent analysis see Wright (1973: 22-41).

3. For a description of the full study see Frank L. Morris, Sr., (1974).

4. Publication by the Massachusetts Department of Corrections, "Massachusetts Correctional Institution: Walpole" (n.d.), p. 3.

5. For some of the background data on Concord, I used a publication by the Corrections Department primarily intended for prospective prison guards preparing to take the civil service exam. This publication is commonly known as the "Green Book." It discusses Concord on pages 120-122 and it was last updated in 1969.

6. At Concord, of those in the sample who had spent time in isolation, 70 percent said that the longest time they had spent in isolation was 3 to 5 days. In contrast, at Walpole 75 percent said they had spent *more* than 8 days in isolation and 14 percent said the longest they had been in isolation was from more than one year to more than 2 years. Nobody had spent this long in isolation or segregation at Concord.

7. Most of the questionnaires that had to be discarded were from Black inmates who had been in the institution less and a month and had not been in the institution before. A number of the Walpole questionnaires had to be discarded because although the prisoner sat through the questionnaire, he did not answer some of the key questions about group membership.

Because the data collection was over a period of 3 months and done on a cellblock by cellblock basis, the total number of Black prisoners eligible to take the questionnaire fluctuated over time at both prisons.

8. I found out through later interviews that most of the members of the Nation of Islam at Walpole had been kept in the segregation unit for about 9 months at the time of the administration of the questionnaire. Supposedly they were put there "for their own protection" after a Muslim allegedly stabbed another Black prisoner on orders from the Walpole Muslim leader. This Muslim leader was later forcibly transferred to a prison out of state.

In months of talking informally with Black inmates at Walpole there was unanimous agreement that the wholesale segregation of the majority of the Muslim population was basically an attempt at repression and social control, not humanitarian protection. This was especially the case after the transfer of the Muslim leaders. I later found out that this main body of the Nation of Islam was finally moved back to the main prison population by December 1, 1972.

9. Remember it is possible, however, that conditions for Black inmates could be worse in other states than in Massachusetts. The fact that permission was granted to carry the study out in Massachusetts with the conditions I requested leads me to believe that the situation could be worse in other states. Some of the most eminent criminologists and sociologists in the U.S. had doubts that I would be able to carry it out in any state during 1971 and 1972.

10. This is especially the case for the more complex measurement methods.

11. The chi-square test has the further advantages of not requiring assumptions of all error being random; it did not require assumption that all exogenous variables were excluded; and it finally did not require an assumption of linearity.

12. Blalock denotes a large sample as 10,000. Rai and Blydenburgh (1973: 156) stress that a sample size of 50 is sufficiently large for chi-square purposes.

13. The best written record of these prisons from mid-1971 to October 1972 is found in numerous issues of *The Boston Globe,* and the prison newspaper of the Peaceful Movement Committee at Concord, especially Vol. 1, no. 5 (March 1972); Vol. 1, no. 6 (April); and Vol. 1, no. 8 (June/July). See also "A Chronology of Recent Events in Massachusetts State Prisons," compiled by John Hough, Massachusetts Counsel on Crime and Corrections in Appendix H of House of Representatives Committee on the Judiciary, 92nd Cong., First session on Corrections, Part III, "Prisons, Prison Reform, and Prisoner's Rights: Massachusetts" (December 18, 1971), pp. 355-370, hereinafter cited as *Hearings.*

14. John O'Shea, the Concord superintendent, was on sick leave during most of the data collection; he later retired. William Donnelly, who was hired by Boone as the Walpole superintendent, resigned after less than 6 months on the job, charging "political interference." This resignation occurred during the Walpole data collection.

15. See *The Boston Globe* and *Boston Herald-American* (August 10, 1972): 10. The suit was later dismissed.

16. According to the "Statistical Report of the Commissioner of Corrections" (Table 14, p. 14) for the year ending in December of 1969, the average daily population for 1959-69 at Walpole was 558 men. During my study it ranged from 585-610. At Concord from 1959-69 the average daily population was 403. During the period of data collection the Concord average population was around 640.

17. It is of course a statistical impossibility for a majority to have a heavier sentence than "most of the others" if the comparison group in context is the other Walpole inmates. The perception is felt by 62 percent of the Black prisoners and 53 percent of the white prisoners at Walpole, and 45 percent of my Black sample and 40 percent of my white sample at Concord. The perception can be real and probably is real for Black prisoners who understood the question to mean if their sentences were heavier than the majority of other (mostly white) prisoners.

The question read: "Compare yourself with others who have been sentenced for the same thing as you. Do you think your sentence was: 1. lighter than most of the others; 2. about the same; 3. heavier than most of the others."

18. Banquets were events in which selected prisoners prepared special foods and guests were admitted into the dining room for a party after or sometimes during visiting hours. Banquets were usually held to celebrate class graduations from the prison school or for an organizational event that had the approval of prison authorities.

19. The term screw is derogatory prison slang or jargon for guard or corrections officer.

20. A prisoner gets one good day or day off his sentence for each month he does not get a disciplinary report while in prison.

21. Corrections Department files confirm that he was in fact sentenced to 3 days isolation for "silent insolence" or giving a guard a dirty look.

22. By required the prisoner really means what types of appliances, razors and other items that prisoners are permitted to keep in their rooms. For example, there are limits on the amplifying capability of recording or sound appliances.

23. Avocations are crafts such as leather-working, cabinet-making, lamp-making, jewelry-making, and so on. These items are sold to the public in a store in the front of the

institution. The number of inmates who can participate in these avocations is limited by the institution, supposedly because of the limited amount of workspace available and supposedly because of the limited number of guards available to supervise the area. The end result of this is to reduce the supply of the goods available and thus keep up the price (the prices are still very low compared to the outside market, however). The end result is also that these "avocations" are looked upon as, and are in fact, businesses. When a prisoner leaves the institution he "sells" the avocation to another prisoner with the concurrence of the administration. The going price for avocations at Concord and Walpole ranged to amounts more than $1,400. This is an enormous sum for a prisoner making 50 cents a day. Needless to say, avocations were much more profitable than other prison activities and Black prisoners were greatly underrepresented at each institution.

24. One has to be extremely careful about making job comparisons across institutions. For example, the kitchen is looked upon as one of the best places to work by inmates of both races at Concord, and one of the worst places to work at Walpole. From extensive in-depth probling, it appears that the Concord kitchen is more modern (less lousy jobs) and it is supervised less thoroughly (more opportunity to steal food) than is the case at Walpole. It also came out that of the third of my Black sample (counting only those who were actually working on jobs) who worked in the Walpole kitchen, most of them had the unskilled and unprestigious kitchen jobs; that is, maintenance or cleaning up, and not food preparation or serving.

25. The Peaceful Movement Committee was organized at Concord after Attica and the September 24, 1971 demonstration at Concord. It is the only group that has white members.

The PMC, as it is called, developed quite a bit of local community support (Concord prison is located in Concord, Mass., one of the most liberal communities in the state). It later developed an office outside the walls and even later got the funds to operate a halfway house.

During the period of this study, however, it acted for all practical purposes as a Black political group inside the prison and was considered as such by prison staff and officials and the overwhelming majority of white inmates.

26. One of the best empirical documentations and expositions of the treatment philosophy in action in prisons is found in Irwin (1970: 37-52).

27. Question 88 asked: "Are Brothers in the above (Political) Organizations treated differently from other Brothers by prison officials?" Twenty-four percent answered no, 46 percent answered yes, and 21 percent did not know. When asked if different, how, 33 percent said worse or very much worse, 31 percent said about the same, and 10 percent said better or very much better. Thirty-four percent did not know.

28. It is beyond the scope of this article to point out numerous instances and evidence that Massachusetts prison officials used all of these control options during the time of this study.

29. Massachusetts sentences are not entirely indeterminate because they have specified minimum and maximum terms. For further elaboration see Glaser (1973).

30. Even though the final decision on release rests with the parole board, the factor which usually has the greatest influence is the prison's evaluation of the prisoner's in-prison behavior.

31. The percentage of Black prisoners at Concord and Walpole who said that they had been hit or beaten by fellow prisoners was about the same percent (but not the same prisoners) as the percent that said that they had been hit or beaten by the staff; around 6 percent in all of these cases.

The need for protection at Walpole was especially great during this time frame because of a rash of stabbings. A disproportionately *low* number of these stabbing victims were Black, and there was no case of the stabbing of a Black by a white at Walpole during the data collection.

REFERENCES

AL ASWODU, S. (1971) "The politics of prisons." Black Scholar II, No. 8 & 9: 28-32.
BANKS, J. A. and J. GROMBS [eds.] (1972) Black Self Concept: Implications for Education and Social Science. New York: McGraw-Hill.
BLALOCK, H. M. (1972) Social Statistics (2nd ed.). New York: McGraw-Hill.
BURNHAM, R. W. (1968) Political Influences on a Correctional System. Berkeley: University of California School of Criminology.
CHRISMAN, R. (1971) "Black prisoners white law." Black Scholar II, 8 and 9 (April/May): 44-47.
CLOWARD, R. S. (1960) "Social control in the prison," in Theoretical Studies in Social Organization of the Prison. Pamphlet No. 15. New York: Social Science Research Council. (Reprinted in L. Hazelrigg [ed.] (1969) Prison Within Society. Garden City, N.Y.: Doubleday.
Committee For Economic Development (1972) Reducing Crime and Assuring Justice. New York.
CRESSEY, D. (1965) "Prison organizations," pp. 1023-1067 in J. G. March (ed.) Handbook of Organizations. New York: Rand-McNally.
CROSSER, G. H. (1958) "The role of the informal inmate groups in change of values." Children V (January/February). (Reprinted in L. Hazelrigg [ed.] (1969) Prison Within Society. Garden City, N.Y.: Doubleday.)
DRUMGO, F. (1971) "A letter from Fleeta," in A. Y. Davis (ed.) If They Come In the Morning. New York: Signet.
GLASER, D. (1965) "Correctional research: an elusive paradise." Journal of Research in Crime and Delinquency II: 1 (January). (Reprinted in Wolfgang and Radzinowitz [eds.] (1971) The Criminal in Society. New York: Basic Books.)
––– (1969) The Effectiveness of a Prison and Parole System. Indianapolis: Bobbs-Merrill.
––– (1973) "Correction of adult offenders in the community," in L. E. Ohlin (ed.) Prisoners in America. Englewood Cliffs, N.J.: Prentice-Hall.
GOFFMAN, E. (1961) Asylums. Garden City, N.Y.: Doubleday.
GOLDFARB, R. (1971) "Prison: the national poorhouse," pp. 310-314 in D. M. Gordon (ed.) Problems in Political Economy: An Urban Perspective. Lexington, Mass.: D.C. Heath.
GORDON, D. M. (1971) Problems in Political Economy: An Urban Perspective. Lexington, Mass.: D.C. Heath.
HAZELRIGG, L. [ed] (1969) Prison Within Society. Garden City, N.Y.: Doubleday.
House of Representatives Committee on the Judiciary, 92nd Congress, First session on Corrections (1971) Prisons, Prison Reform and Prisoner's Rights: Massachusetts. Part III (December 18): 355-370.
IRWIN, J. (1970) The Felon. Englewood Cliffs, N.J.: Prentice-Hall.
JACKSON, G. (1970) Soledad Brother: The Prison Letters of George Jackson. New York: Bantam.

"Martin Sostre vs. Nelson Rockefeller, Paul McGinnis, Vincent Mancusi, and Harold Fallete" (1971) pp. 153-157 in T. Becker and V. Murray (eds.) Governmental Lawlessness in America. New York: Oxford University Press.

Massachusetts Department of Corrections (n.d.) "Massachusetts Correctional Institution: Walpole."

MORRIS, F. L., Sr. (1973) "The Advantages and Disadvantages of Black Political Activity in Two Northern State Prisons." Unpublished Ph.D. dissertation. Cambridge, Mass.: Massachusetts Institute of Technology.

National Advisory Commission on Civil Disorders (1968) Report of the National Advisory Commission on Civil Disorders. New York: Bantam Books.

New York State Commission on Attica (1972) Attica: Report of the Special New York State Commission on Attica. New York: Bantam Books.

OHLIN, L. E. [ed.] (1973) Prisoners in America. Englewood Cliffs, N.J.: Prentice-Hall.

President's Commission on Law Enforcement and the Administration of Justice (1966) The Challenge of Crime in a Free Society. Washington, D.C.: Government Printing Office.

RAI, K. B. and J. C. BLYDENBURGH (1973) Political Science Statistics. Boston: Holbrook.

REISS, A. J., Jr. (1967) Studies in Crime and Law Enforcement in Major Metropolitan Areas. Field Studies III. Vol. 1, Sec. 1, Measurement of the Nature and Amount of Crime. Washington, D.C.: Government Printing Office.

RIST, R. C. (1970) "Student social class and teacher expectations: the self-fulfilling prophecy in ghetto education." Harvard Educational Review XL, 3 (August): 411-451.

SCHUR, E. M. (1969) Our Criminal Society: The Societal and Legal Sources of Crime in America. Englewood Cliffs, N.J.: Prentice-Hall.

SYKES, G. M. (1967) Crime and Society. New York: Random House.

WADE, W. (1971) "The politics of prisons." Black Scholar II, 8 and 9 (April/May): 12-19.

WHEELER, S. (1969) "Socialization in correctional institutions," pp. 1005-1025 in D. Goslin (ed.) Handbook of Socialization Theory and Research. New York: Rand McNally.

U.S. Department of Justice, Bureau of Prisons (1972) National Prisoner Statistics. Washington, D.C.: Government Printing Office.

U.S. Department of Commerce (1970) Prisoners in State and Federal Prisons and Reformatories. Washington, D.C.: Government Printing Office.

WRIGHT, E. O. (1973) The Politics of Punishment: A Critical Analysis of Prisons in America. New York: Harper & Row.

WOLFGANG, M. and L. RADZINOWICZ [eds.] (1971) Crime and Justice: The Criminal in Confinement Vol. III. New York: Basic Books.

Chapter 11

WILL URBAN TRIAL COURTS SURVIVE
THE WAR ON CRIME?

CARL BAAR

The conceptual apparatus of American political science is geared to the research problems suggested by the traditional operation of the American political system. Thus, for example, we can study decision-making in a political system; the influences brought to bear, the process by which choice is made, and the impact of alternative choices. But we have not considered questions centering on the persistence of the political system itself. David Easton (1965) is alone among contemporary political theorists in his emphasis on the importance of making the persistence of a political system problematic (see, especially Easton, 1965: ch. 6). Easton's primary concern, however, is the development of concepts for the analysis of whole political systems; he does not apply the concept of persistence to the study of subsystems of a political system. In turn, Sheldon Goldman and Thomas P. Jahnige (1971: 276-277) have applied Easton's systems

AUTHOR'S NOTE: This article is a revised version of a paper prepared for the urban courts workshop at the 1973 Annual Meeting of the American Political Science Association in New Orleans. It is based in part on ideas developed while I was a Russell Sage Fellow at Yale Law School. Ellen Baar provided extensive and essential criticism of the first draft, and H. Paul Haynes, Sr., Arnold M. Malech, George F. Cole and J. Woodford Howard, Jr., provided helpful suggestions for the present draft.

model to the federal courts, organizing the diverse literature on judicial organization, process, and behavior in terms of a number of systems concepts. But they do not make the persistence of courts problematic. For them, "the fundamental question remains, what enables a judicial system to maintain stress below the critical point and thus persist?"[1] Persistence is seen as a constant: we have always had courts, and the job of American political scientists is to explain why. However, contemporary developments in American politics and in the study of judicial behavior have combined to suggest the need to make problematic the persistence of courts in the United States.

This paper will focus on the role of urban trial courts in the criminal justice system.[2] That role is changing as a result of both institutional changes in the field of law enforcement and organizational changes in courts themselves. Three models of urban trial courts will be proposed: (1) the symbolic trial court, which ratifies decisions made by other actors in the criminal process and thus fails to persist because of disintegration; (2) the service trial court, which uses administrative techniques to serve other elements of the criminal justice system and fails to persist because of absorption; and (3) the change-agent trial court, which performs a leadership function in the criminal process and persists in a new form subject to different conditions of stress.

PERSISTENCE AND SIGNIFICANCE

While the persistence of courts has not been an object of study, stress on the courts from their environment has been a major theme in the popular literature. Demand input overload has produced support stress; that is, rising crime rates, overcriminalization, and increased civil litigation have clogged urban trial courts (and, in turn, appellate courts) so that extensive delays provoke public bitterness about the ineffectiveness of the judiciary.[3] However, the persistence of urban trial courts is threatened not by demand input overload but by the reorganization of the criminal process which has occurred in response to demand input overload. Other institutions in the criminal process have changed their relationships to the courts, and new institutions have developed. As a result, the boundaries of urban trial courts have eroded, so that differentiation between those courts and other institutions in the criminal process has become increasingly difficult. The distinctiveness of urban trial courts has declined. If the stress to which courts are subject from these other institutions in the criminal process affects the "fundamental life processes" of the courts, it may drive the "essential variables"—the distinctive characteristics—of courts beyond the critical limits of their normal range of variation. Under such circumstances, the persistence of courts is threatened.

In attempting to delineate the distinctive characteristics of a court, Theodore L. Becker (1970: 13) states that courts are entities which have the authority to apply, and do apply, "primary normative principles" to the parties in a dispute in a manner characterized by a minimum degree of independence and impartiality.[4] Urban trial courts can be differentiated from other courts on the basis of their jurisdiction. In assessing whether urban trial courts persist, one is therefore concerned with whether they do in fact apply principles to parties in a dispute in an independent and impartial manner.

A political system or sub-system that fails to persist may disintegrate, or may be absorbed (Easton, 1965: 96). An urban trial court which no longer applies legal principles to the parties in cases before it, and/or no longer handles those cases impartially, has failed to persist because the legal system in which it operates has disintegrated. And an urban trial court which is no longer independent but is a component in a larger criminal justice system (like quasi-judicial officers in a regulatory agency) has failed to persist because of absorption.[5]

The persistence of courts is not the same as the significance of courts. A court may lose significance; its jurisdiction may be reduced, or it may be called upon less frequently to resolve disputes and apply legal principles. But it remains a court—it persists—as long as it continues to operate with independence and impartiality in those matters which do come before it. Thus, a court is different than a political system, which is threatened by the development of alternative paths for the authoritative allocation of values for a society.[6] A court is not threatened by the development of alternative paths for dispute resolution (such as out-of-court settlements and administrative adjudication), as long as these developments do not alter the distinctive ways in which courts operate. Therefore input overload reduces the significance of courts if they are unable to develop coping mechanisms that allow an increased number of disputes to be resolved in court. Input overload threatens the persistence of courts only if the mechanisms used to cope with overload substantially alter the distinctive characteristics of those courts.

SYMBOLIC TRIAL COURTS

A symbolic trial court legitimates the actions of other segments of the criminal process.[7] Because its principal function is ratifying the decisions made elsewhere, the symbolic trial court does not apply primary normative principles to the cases brought before it. As a result, the connection between trial and appellate courts is attenuated and the connection between trial courts and other segments of the local criminal process is reinforced. In addition, a symbolic trial court does not actively seek to maintain or increase its significance within the local criminal process. It represents a court which has failed to persist as a result of the disintegration of the legal system in which it operates.

The model of a symbolic trial court provides an avenue for making studies of plea bargaining relevant to a political theory of trial court operation.[8] The use of plea bargaining by prosecution and defense in criminal cases has come to include what Casper (1972: 136) terms the "cop-out ceremony," in which a perfunctory judicial imprimatur has been placed upon previous arrangements between the parties. To the extent that the judge only does "what the prosecutor tells him to do," the essential impartiality of the court may be driven past its critical limits. Furthermore, the ratification of an explicit or implicit bargain prevents the court from applying any legal principles to the case. The trial court acts to maintain its complex set of local relationships with the police, prosecution, and defense; as a result, the connection between trial and appellate decision-makers becomes so attenuated that the production ethic of the surrounding criminal justice organizations directs the trial courts (see, for example, Ban, 1973). The trial courts are no longer directed by a set of legal principles; nor do the trial courts use those legal principles to guide and direct litigants.[9]

Plea bargaining alters the relationship between trial court and other segments of the local criminal process. In an adversarial conception of the court-prosecution-defense relationship, the court's function is to judge. In a bargaining situation, the court most commonly ratifies.[10] Changing from judge to ratifier deprives the trial court of an opportunity to apply appellate court precedents and establish a decision-making role independent from that of the prosecutor. It cannot exhibit any essential distinctive characteristics.

In this argument, plea bargaining has not been considered a way of coping with increased criminal caseloads. Plea bargaining may be a way in which prosecutors cope with overload, but not a way in which courts do so. Thus guilty plea rates may be more closely related to variations in workload per prosecutor than to variations in workload per trial judge. While no contemporary writer has attempted to determine when or how plea bargaining originated or assumed its present form, an empirical study of federal court business (American Law Institute, 1934) concluded that the development of the "guilty plea technique" in the federal courts was not related to an increase in criminal litigation.[11] The key variable associated with different levels of guilty pleas across jurisdictions may be the willingness of the prosecution to accept a guilty plea in exchange for consideration of leniency in charge and/or sentence.[12] In turn, the persistence of trial courts is threatened by growth in the frequency of guilty pleas; that is, by the changes in prosecutorial practice which affect the distinctiveness of trial courts.

The disintegration of the legal system in which trial courts operate would be expected by a student of organizations and management. Such a student would examine the work flow of urban trial courts in the criminal process and note that appellate courts are outside the work flow. Furthermore, appellate courts can only review what occurs in the work flow when called upon (appealed to) by someone who is not satisfied with how his own case was processed. A plea bargaining system is not likely to generate many such appeals, and as the plea bargaining system improves its operation, appeal becomes even less likely. Thus the link between trial and appellate courts is weakened not only because trial courts do not apply appellate precedents, but also because appellate review is so infrequent and irregular. Most large-scale organizations have officials who are outside the work flow and whose purpose is to evaluate that work flow. But in contrast to appellate courts, those officials—ranging from planners to auditors—need not wait until participants request their services. When the student of legal process studies the authority structure of court systems, examining the path of precedents through the judicial hierarchy, he must realize that court systems lack even the most rudimentary management controls characteristic of modern organizations (Amsterdam, 1972: 402-410). As a result, the work flow in the criminal process is governed not by the commands of the judicial authority structure, but by a dynamic of its own.[13]

Within this work flow, the symbolic trial court represents, in its pure form,[14] a formal structure without a significant role in the urban criminal justice process and without certain essential characteristics of a court. The symbolic trial court is premised on a traditional mode of organization in which the courts only participate in the work flow when called upon by the parties in a case, and input overload is not handled by internal organizational alterations which seek to maintain or increase the court's significance. As a result, overload is handled by other agencies extending their authority. Police are encouraged to use techniques which they can administer themselves and which they interpret as producing outcomes similar to those of the judicial process (for example, overnight detention, seizure of contraband, physical "roughing up").[15] Prosecutors are encouraged to develop alternative techniques such as pretrial diversion for processing accused individuals. Involvement of the symbolic trial court is avoided in favor of direct bargaining among the parties. The court's participation becomes peripheral, and the court itself disintegrates.

But how is it possible to say when a court has failed to persist if it disintegrates but does not disappear? If an official in appropriate dress is addressed as the judge and directs the courtroom activity before him, is he not really a judge because he ratifies prosecutorial arrangements rather than applying legal principles to a dispute resolved by his actions? An answer to these questions of whether a given trial court does or does not persist rests in part upon conceptual and operational definitions used by the researcher. For example, if impartiality is a norm, a court exists as long as that norm is observed; that is, given deference. In a symbolic court, exemplified by the court whose major role in the criminal process is the willing acceptance of guilty pleas arranged in advance, the norm of impartiality will be given deference by the judge in his ceremonial role and by the prosecutor in his effort to legitimize the previous bargain. Both the prestige of the court and the power of the court's clientele are increased by the maintenance of the judicial symbols. Thus if a political scientist were to study criminal trial court persistence in American cities by interviewing judges, he would conclude that the courts do persist because the norm of impartiality is alive and well.[16] However, if impartiality is an organizational characteristic measured by the outputs and outcomes of the organization, other research techniques become appropriate,[17] because courts would have failed to persist long before the judicial authorities would have abandoned ceremonial and verbal derference to the norm of impartiality.[18] The lag between the perceptions of an institution held by its officials and the impact of its day-to-day practices may be so great that our methodology will determine our results. Overemphasis on an individual/psychological approach may preclude effective consideration of issues which require analysis through an organizational/behavioral approach.[19] Since the latter approach has charac-terized the empirical study of urban trial courts in the criminal process,[20] the symbolic trial court may serve as a useful ideal type for organizing findings about trial court behavior.

SERVICE TRIAL COURTS AND THE WAR ON CRIME

A service trial court develops internal administrative techniques both to increase the efficiency with which it processes its caseload and to facilitate the work of other elements of the criminal process. These administrative techniques are developed under at least partial direction of other institutions in the criminal justice system.

Differences in calendar management may provide a useful indicator to distinguish service from symbolic trial courts. A symbolic trial court would allow litigants to determine when cases are heard: the prosecutor places the case on the calendar, the defense requests and is granted continuances(s). A service trial court would consider calendaring the responsibility of the court. It may employ professional court administrators to manage the court calendar, and may harness computer technology for gathering, recording, and storing information so that calendaring can be done more efficiently. The calendar would be managed to serve other actors in the criminal process: cases would be set to minimize police time spent in court, and to enable prosecution to move while evidence is fresh. And its operation could be integrated into a criminal justice information system directed jointly by the court and other institutions in the system.[21]

The administrative development of urban trial courts is a method of maintaining or increasing their significance in the criminal process. But it is not a method of increasing the probability that urban trial courts will persist. When the boundaries between courts and other segments of the criminal justice system are no longer distinct because courts share with those segments common goals, common management, and a common language, the courts have been absorbed into a larger system and have failed to persist. Becker (1970: 144) writes that courts require a degree of independence, which he defines as the authority to decide contrary to other government officials and the willingness to do so.[22] In the context of American politics, where courts are not only forums for adjudication but part of a separate branch of federal or state governments, independence has also come to mean that judicial branches as well as individual adjudicators require the authority and the ability to reach judgments contrary to other branches. To place trial courts into increasingly integrated and coordinated criminal justice systems is to convert them into the quasi-judicial arms of a regulatory agency.[23]

The service trial court has been given impetus and direction from the institutions and ideology of our contemporary war on crime. The current war against crime is not an unprecedented phenomenon. The 1920s and early 1930s saw a similar struggle—including a presidential commission, extensive empirical research, and widespread calls for modernization and reform—before the domestic economy generated overriding issues.[24] What is different about the current war on crime is that it has taken permanent institutional form in the federal Law Enforcement Assistance Administration, the second largest (following the FBI) unit in the Department of Justice. Created in 1968 and renewed in 1973, it is the first grant-making agency within the Justice Department. While its major expenditures are in block grants distributed to state and local governments by formula, those grants are conditioned on the creation of a criminal justice planning agency (itself financed by LEAA planning grants) which must produce an annual criminal justice plan.

It is still difficult to discuss the effects of the LEAA and its constituent SPAs. Most discussion of their work has focused on the lack of adequate planning, overemphasis on expenditures for police hardware, mismanagement of funds, and so forth (U.S. Congress House Committee on Government Operations, 1972). A general consensus seems to have developed that more planning and better management of the law enforcement apparatus is a good thing, and that the way to achieve that is through the development of actual functioning criminal justice systems in which police, prosecution, courts, and corrections will work in an integrated fashion so that the system works effectively to serve the public and guard the rights of the defendant. The goal of an integrated criminal justice system was first articulated by political liberals,[25] and has since been made an element of conservative policy as well. The profession of criminal justice planner has emerged from the creation of a grant distribution network for LEAA funds. Planning may be new, untried, and inadequate; but if it is a central goal of the institutionalized war on crime, it is appropriate to articulate the ideology in which it operates and analyze one of its unanticipated consequences: the absorption and non-persistence of urban trial courts through the development of service trial courts.

We are now moving to a no-fault system of criminal justice. The war on crime has its moral overtones, but the "crime problem" is seen as so serious that a pragmatic approach to what works has replaced a traditional notion of punishment for the guilty. The guilt or innocence of an accused individual is peripheral to the operation of the system, because an accused individual enters the system and is processed by it long before the issue of guilt is dealt with. Under a no-fault system, two goals remain: once an individual enters the system, he must be removed as soon as possible; and he must be kept out of the system in the future. That is, his frequency of entry into the system must be reduced. What Griffiths (1970) calls the Family Model replaces the Battle Model of the traditional adversary system.[26]

In pursuit of its objectives, LEAA has funded a number of programs affecting and/or involving courts. While courts and court-related programs receive only a modest percentage of the LEAA dollar, the agency has already become not only a regular source of court financing, but also the primary source of funds for administrative innovation in urban trial courts and state court systems.[27] This situation, as explained by one prominent state court administrator, should come as no surprise to students of the budgetary process:

> Yet one of the problems is that in the normal appropriating process . . . you get money for the routine, you get the money to do this year what you did last year, and you can even get money to expand your system by a certain percentage, but propose a new untried program and you get nothing.[28]

To obtain financial support for administrative development, trial courts may be required to articulate the common goals of the criminal justice system. Thus one court administrator reported in 1972 that a trial court was offered "Impact Cities" money by the local planning organization if it could show how its use of the funds would help reduce armed robbery by a stated percentage in a fixed nmber of years.[29] A $1.1 million grant to double the number of arraignment courts in New York City handling night and weekend arrest cases was justified not on due process grounds, but because it would "allow preliminary hearings to occur at arraignment in substantially more cases, thereby eliminating much of the delay and many of the wasted appearances, and subsequently easing case congestion" (LEAA, 1972: 328). In the development of information systems, trial courts must not only articulate the common goals to win LEAA support, but must also share their information system with executive agencies. One court administrator, who is also a member of a state planning agency, wrote about the pressure to merge judicial and police/prosecutorial information systems:

> More than two years ago, when I applied for a discretionary grant of $3000 from the Regional Office of the LEAA in order to perform a statistical standardization project to provide a universal set of definitions which would relate to our own computer system, I was turned down on the grounds that there were other computer systems in the area and that we should dovetail somehow or other with them. I could not really see tying the judiciary's computer in with the prosecutor's, and we are getting flak right now on that point from the appropriating authorities in [the legislature] as well as from other agencies in the Executive Branch to make our information systems available to the rest of the "criminal justice system."[30]

To assure that they will have a significant role in the criminal justice system, trial courts generate programs that perform a service function for the larger system. As a result, calendaring begins emphasizing techniques such as front-loading (enlarging the number of cases set for hearing at pretrial stages to increase the level of judicial output and encourage early disposition) without providing judges with the tools to enforce a strict continuance policy. Professional administrators are brought in to improve court operations but are kept subservient to fiscal limitations imposed by county executive officers. Court administrators are called upon to make arrangements which facilitate the processing of mass arrests, ensuring in advance that courts will be available if police choose such a strategy.[31] An official in a court which obtains urinanalyses from defendants at the time of arraignment reports that aggregate data from those tests were used to provide information to local prosecutors on the patterns of drug traffic in the area.[32] In each of these cases, trial courts use modern administrative mechanisms to serve the goals of the larger criminal justice system.[33]

Data on the distribution of discretionary grants by LEAA in fiscal year 1971 indicate that trial courts orient program requests toward the service function. In all four instances in which trial courts were subgrantees, the project summaries emphasized a service orientation (LEAA, 1972: 293-295, 300). Such language may indicate only that courts are playing the game by using current phrases favored by federal and state granting agencies. But the process by which discretionary grants are distributed facilitates the integration of courts into larger criminal justice systems. Of 644 different grants totaling $70 million awarded in fiscal 1971, 89 went to court and court-related programs.[34] In every case a state planning agency served as the grantee, and in a majority of cases executive agencies and private groups rather than courts served as subgrantees. Of the 21 programs directed entirely at trial courts, subgrantees included local executive agencies (14), a state executive agency (1), a private association (1), a state court system (1), and the local trial courts themselves (4).[35] This process for distributing grant funds to courts raises interesting questions about the limits of executive discretion over court administration. In the present context, it indicates the extent to which service trial courts are subject to executive branch direction, a necessary step in the integration of courts into criminal justice systems.

A related thrust of LEAA program planning is toward funding non-judicial projects which threaten judicial system boundaries by reducing the distinctiveness of courts. Screening programs within prosecutors' offices are one example. Courts usually applaud such programs because they reduce the trial court caseload, but they also sharpen the decision point of prosecution so that external oversight by courts becomes increasingly less important than internal oversight within the prosecutor's office. Pretrial diversion programs are another example. They are designed to allow community-based corrections programs to begin prior to conviction, so that successful diverted defendants can leave the system without a record of conviction.[36] There is no requirement that such programs be located within a court or under the direction of a court. Thus diversion programs tend to be directed by social agencies or prosecutors' offices and tend to allow broad discretion to the officials making the decision on whom to divert.[37]

In summary, LEAA policies are premised on the development of an overall system of criminal justice in which police, prosecution, courts, and corrections play less sharply differentiated roles. Both task differentiation and specialization are reduced so that the integrated system will have a large number of interchangeable roles. Mechanical solidarity (integration through the performance of interchangeable activities) is sought instead of organic solidarity (integration through the meshing of clearly differentiated activities).[38] Thus in fiscal 1971 LEAA awarded 45 discretionary grants for police legal officers "to interpret laws for members of the police force."[39] Rather than funding programs to make courts better able to do the job of communicating legal standards to policemen (organic solidarity), LEAA funds programs to give police departments an internal legal capability so that certain law-interpreting functions take place within police departments (mechanical solidarity).

While an integrated criminal justice system with interchangeable parts is still in its earliest stages, the outlines of such a system are taking shape: innovation by justice system participants now derives in large part from a common fiscal source; a corps of criminal justice professionals oversees justice system innovations; organizational linkages such as common information systems are planned; system participants increasingly are urged to focus on a common goal (usually stated as the reduction of violent crime). To the extent that such developments occur without sufficient consideration of the conditions for the structural and behavioral independence of urban trial courts, the service trial court faces the prospect of absorption and non-persistence. A formal structure called a court may remain and play a significant role. As long as it is doing a good job—according to the goals of the criminal justice system as applied by system planners—such a court can even be given more responsibilities. Under such conditions, however, every new responsibility drives the independence of the court further beyond its critical limits.

CHANGE-AGENT TRIAL COURTS

The symbolic trial court was identified by its failure to respond to stress from its environment which threatened both its significance and its persistence. The service trial court responded to the stress which demand input overload placed on its ability to play a significant role in the criminal justice system. But its responses failed to deal with the possibility of non-persistence, which was magnified by the service trial court's reliance on LEAA funding and direction for administrative innovations. How can an urban trial court play a significant role in the criminal justice system without yielding to pressures from other actors in that system? One way may be through the use of modern administrative techniques to exercise leadership in the local criminal process.

Thus, the change-agent trial court develops and uses administrative techniques as a way of coping with stress caused by the increased activity of other actors in the criminal justice system. Rather than being directed or dominated by others, the change-agent trial court seeks ways of exerting leadership in the local criminal process. Administrative techniques are designed to enable the trial court to control (that is, set goals for and measure performance of) all participants in the criminal justice system. Since new roles and increased levels of activity are necessary, stress is seen as a catalyst for change; conflict is considered healthy. Thus the change-agent trial court persists by generating changes in its internal operation so that it can more effectively deal with the changes in its environment. Easton (1965: 88) discusses such a response to stress. "The idea of systems persistence extends far beyond that of systems maintenance," he writes:

> Maintenance is weighted with the notion of salvaging the existing pattern of relationships and directs attention to their preservation. Persistence signalizes the importance of considering, not any particular structure or pattern, but rather the very life processes of a system themselves. In this sense a system may persist even though everything else associated with it changes continuously and radically.

Administrative techniques can be used to reorganize the judicial process so that trial judges can intervene at additional stages of the criminal process. Such changes will move certain functions usually performed by other actors in the criminal process into the adjudication process. As a result, judges might participate in the charging process,[40] they might enforce a "ready rule" by dismissing cases after a defendant has waited longer than a fixed period of time,[41] or they might review their own sentences on a regular basis some time after defendants have begun to serve time.[42]

Administrative techniques can be used to increase the level of involvement of trial judges in the criminal process. For example, extending the hours of arraignment might be used to facilitate oversight of police by judges. Thus the Detroit Recorder's Court has before it a proposal for 24-hour arraignment, put forward as a way of cutting down police use of overnight detention and release without charge as a form of non-judicial punishment in that city.[43] Twenty-four-hour arraignment cannot be instituted until the judges of that court amend their local rules by majority vote[44] and reallocate available resources. Administrative changes in the court must therefore precede an increase in the involvement of judges in the local criminal process.

The change-agent trial court can also develop administrative techniques that allow court supporting personnel to oversee the criminal process, so that the court becomes central rather than peripheral to the administration of criminal justice. One of the most important examples of the use of supporting personnel to facilitate trial court leadership of a local criminal justice system is the monitoring procedure created in July 1972 by the Superior Court of the District of Columbia (District of Columbia Courts, 1973: 26). The series of events culminating in the creation of two full-time positions as monitors began in January 1972 when Washington area newspapers, at the instigation of court personnel, reported "two instances of persons being unduly incarcerated"; that is, the jail was not notified that prosecution had dropped charges against defendants, who then remained in jail for as long as six months.[45] In response to the resulting publicity,

Chief Judge Harold H. Greene convened a meeting in his chambers to discuss these events and their causes and prevention. The meeting was attended not only by several employees of the Superior Court, but also by representatives from the major segments of the criminal justice system.

It was determined that a *Narrative* outlining the flow of paper and persons through the local criminal justice system would be drafted by an assistant court executie and used as "an in-house, working document."

The *Narrative* was drafted and submitted to the Chief Judge on February 4, 1972, and distributed to all Associate Judges of the Superior Court and to major segments of the criminal justice system . . .

A second meeting of representatives from the major segments of the criminal justice system was convened by Chief Judge Greene, and he determined that the ills in the system which resulted in certain "injustices of Justice," such as lost defendants and undue incarceration, would be discussed by several Task Forces with the intent of advancing remedial solutions and preventions.

Task Force membership included six clerks and administrators from the Superior Court, four officials from the United States Attorney's Office, three deputy United States marshals, two corrections officials, and three police officers.

The Task Force reported on June 15: Its "most vital recommendation . . . related to a method, *monitoring,* which would lessen these 'human costs' by providing a device which would quickly note and respond to inconsistencies."[46] The report traced losses to failures in system communication and "concluded that a central monitoring function is needed and should be exercised by the court with the authority of the Chief Judge." The Task Force recommended that the chief judge require a number of daily and weekly reports from the U.S. Attorney's Office, the Corporation Counsel of the District of Columbia, the U.S. Marshal, the D.C. Department of Corrections, the D.C. Bail Agency, and the Superior Court. Authority to require such reports was derived from statutory language in the District of Columbia Code requiring officials, agencies, and departments in the District to furnish information to the chief judge or executive officer of the courts which is "necessary to the efficient administration of the courts."[47] Particular emphasis was placed upon improved reporting of dismissals by the prosecutor's office:

Post-preliminary hearing dismissals seem to be the most frequently recurring problem which ultimately result in defendants being unduly incarcerated. This problem will be alleviated by implementation of the monitoring mechanism described previously. By forwarding a daily report to the monitor of the dismissals, a control will be achieved. The present system is a report from the Felony Branch of a list of those awaiting grand jury action. It is issued every thirty (30) days and a defendant could conceivably spend almost a full month incarcerated without being discovered. The recommended monitoring would detect and correct the error within 24 hours.[48]

Following receipt of the Task Force report, Chief Judge Greene ordered that the appropriate court rules be drafted to effect the proposals. Rules were drafted and approved by the Superior Court. In the District's Annual Report (1972: 26), the Superior Court noted that monitors handled an average of "approximately 2,000 cases per week."

Since its inception, the monitors have uncovered numerous instances which could have resulted in undue incarceration in the absence of a monitoring system.

The Task Force produced other recommendations which illustrated the exercise of leadership by an urban trial court. As one example, the group

discussed several instances where a defendant was released in a court only to be required to return to the cellblock in order that his identity be verified. [The Task Force] recommends that the verification of identity be accomplished in the cellblock prior to the prisoner being transported to the courtroom.[49]

The technique that was adopted required changing procedures of the Department of Corrections (which operated the jail) and the Deputy U.S. Marshal, an official of the Justice Department (who transports the prisoners to court).

What do these examples of the exercise of criminal justice system leadership by change-agent trial courts tell us about how urban trial courts can persist? First, the examples suggest that a court is more likely to persist if it adopts a due process rather than a crime control orientation. Each of the programs—monitoring, 24-hour arraignment, ready rules—focuses on the court's role in ensuring that the system provides fair treatment for the accused. When the court's orientation differs from the orientation of other actors in the system, it is possible for the court to use its administrative techniques for its own purposes, not simply to serve the other actors. Thus normative convergence of courts and other criminal justice system participants makes persistence less likely; normative divergence increases the likelihood of persistence. The need for normative divergence does not necessarily mean that courts must be more liberal or civil libertarian to persist, but only that they must be different in orientation. For example, liberals often favor placing sentencing discretion with professionals, while conservatives favor placing sentencing discretion with prosecutors (Wilson, 1973: 9, 44, 52-56); judges would oppose both proposals.[50]

Second, the examples of the exercise of leadership by change-agent trial courts indicates that persistence is a question of power. Change-agent trial courts act to maintain or increase judicial power within the criminal justice system. Playing a significant role in the system is not enough if the price for such a role is the non-persistence of the court. If the chief threat to trial courts, as argued throughout this paper, is the growing power of other actors in the criminal justice system (police, prosecutors, and the LEAA and its constituent planning agencies), a trial court must preserve and perhaps extend its own power to persist under the stress of such competition. When the concept of persistence is applied to subsystems of a political system, it thus redirects research from managerial questions (how efficient?) to political questions (how powerful?). It allows political scientists to ask political questions about urban trial courts.

Third, the examples show how administrative development of trial courts is essential for their exercise of system leadership. Consider how the establishment and operation of the Task Force in the District of Columbia relied on pre-existing administrative apparatus in the Superior Court. The court's rule-making power was used to institute the monitoring program proposed by the Task Force. The position of the chief judge as administrative head of the court permitted him to take initiatives in calling participants together. While the chief judge circulated material to and consulted with associate judges, their relationship to the chief on administrative matters was not that of colleague-to-colleague, but that of chairman to advisory committee. Finally, the existence of a large professional staff within the Superior Court facilitated the judicial initiative. Had the court had but one professional administrator (instead of an executive officer and two high-salaried assistants) the time necessary to coordinate such a special project would have been sharply limited. The availability of a professional judicial administrator who could devote a major protion of his time to the project in a concentrated period enhanced the ability of the court to carry it through.

These characteristics of change-agent trial courts—normative divergence, power orientation, and developed administration—suggest that what happens to urban trial courts facing stress from their environment is not unlike what happens to other public organizations. In particular, the three characteristics of change-agent trial courts all illustrate what S. N. Eisenstadt (1959) has called bureaucratization: "the extension of [an organization's] spheres of activities and power either in its own interest or those of some of its elite." Bureaucratization, Eisenstadt (1959: 312) writes, "tends toward growing regimentation of different areas of social life and some extent of displacement of its service goals in favor of various power interests and orientations."

Eisenstadt uses his concept of bureaucratization differently than political scientists who study courts. They discuss the change from unsupervised and uncoordinated exchange relationships to increasing emphasis on supervision and conformity to group norms (Cook, 1972a and b; Feeley, 1973; Baar, 1972). This use of the concept "bureaucratization" discusses bureaucracy in organizational rather than political terms, as a reflection of increased emphasis on hierarchy and formal rules rather than a reflection of changes in the relative power of courts vis-a-vis other institutions. Eisenstadt's concept of bureaucratization focuses on organizational power. It is one of three outcomes of the interaction of an organization and its environment. In the first, the organization "maintains its autonomy and distinctiveness" because its environment is stable. The second outcome, bureaucratization, is one response to environmental change. But another response (Eisenstadt, 1959: 311-312) is debureaucratization, which is characterized by:

> subversion of the goals and activities of the [organization] in the interests of different groups with which it is in close interaction (clients, patrons, interested parties). In debureaucratization the specific characteristics of the [organization] in terms both of its autonomy and its specific rules and goals are minimized, even up to the point where its very functions and activities are taken over by other groups or organizations.

The service trial court is thus a clear case of debureaucratization.

"The tendencies toward bureaucratization and debureaucratization," writes Eisenstadt,

> may, in fact, develop side by side. . . . [T]he possibility of these tendencies occurring in the same case may be explained by the fact that a stable service-oriented [organization such as a court] . . . is based on the existence of some equilibrium or *modus vivendi* between professional autonomy and societal (or political) control. Once this equilibrium is severely disrupted, the outcome . . . may be the simultaneous development of bureaucratization and debureaucratization in different spheres of its activities, although usually one of these tendencies is more pronounced.

Thus tendencies toward a service function and a leadership function may both occur in an urban trial court. To the extent that one tendency predominates, a service trial court or a change-agent trial court may emerge. In one case, the trial court persists; in the other, it does not. The two ideal types provide a basis for evaluating organizational changes in urban trial courts and analyzing the extent to which administrative techniques contribute to persistence or non-persistence of those institutions.[51]

Are there limits to how bureaucratized a court can become and still persist? Debureaucratization can lead to non-persistence by the absorption of courts into larger criminal justice systems, driving the variation in the organizational independence of courts beyond its normal range. Bureaucratization avoids the prospect of absorption but raises another question: since a court is defined in part by its role in resolving disputes between opposing parties, will a court which does less and less judging and more and more managing not remain a court? Can courts concerned with maintaining their power persist if they use administrative techniques whose relationship to adjudication is increasingly remote?

A clue to the likelihood that change-agent trial courts will persist comes by drawing an analogy to the persistence of the legislative branch of the federal government. The purpose of Congress is to make laws; to enunciate general policy. Yet that textbook maxim is rivalled by the competing maxim that the president is the nation's primary policy maker. In fact, Congress has maintained its power not by the exercise of its legislative functions, but by the exercise of such essentially administrative functions as the oversight of executive agencies by members and committees of Congress. To the extent that Congress persists,[52] it does so by developing cross-cutting ties with executive branch departments and agencies in order to cope with stress from the presidency. Similarly, trial courts may persist not by maintaining the primacy of judging, but by developing alternative means (the performance of administrative functions) for directing other actors in the criminal justice system.

NOTES

1. See Goldman and Jahnige (1971: 131) for another use of the term persistence. Jean Laponce has argued that the tendency to focus on persistence rather than non-persistence illustrates a general tendency of social science research to avoid the negative. See his presidential address before the Canadian Political Science Association, August 1973.

2. Thus the role of the urban trial court in civil justice issues will not be analyzed here. Such an analysis, touching on the development of administrative adjudication and the use of courts as collection agencies and social welfare agencies, would also be appropriate.

3. The systems language is drawn from Easton. For critiques of the courts, see Leonard Downie, Jr. (1972); Howard James (1971); and The American Assembly (1965).

4. Becker's (1970) definition has been somewhat modified for use here. He uses his definition to develop criteria for determining whether or not courts exist in a given society, but not for determining whether they have persisted. Thus his discussion of political trials (pp. 372-379) deals with the use and abuse of judicial structure but not its persistence.

5. A third separate possibility is that the sub-system could be abolished. See the U.S. Commerce Court (1910-13). State court reorganization often involves the merger of courts (absorption). These examples involve statutory changes which are more noticeable and more easily measurable than the changes discussed in the pages that follow.

6. However, the development and use of private judiciaries "might provide major clues to the political order." See Matthew Holden, Jr. (1963: 778-779).

7. A similar notion could be applied to the granting of uncontested divorces on the civil side.

8. Plea bargaining has usually been related to organizational theory. See Abraham S. Blumberg (1967), and Malcolm M. Feeley (1973).

9. Edward H. Levi has argued that "the uses of position" by government officials has produced a "half-law, fitting no model of authorized command." See Levi (1970: 128).

10. It may also arbitrate, pressuring the parties to bargain.

11. The study showed that plea rates remained at 50 to 60 percent from the 1890s to 1915, went over 80 percent by 1917, and persisted at 80 to 90 percent thereafter. The change occurred prior to Prohibition, leading the authors (Charles E. Clark, Thurman Arnold, and William O. Douglas) to conclude that repeal of prohibition would not alter the rates.

12. Thus when the National Advisory Commission for Criminal Justice Standards and Goals called for abolition of plea bargaining by 1978 it did "not condemn entry of guilty pleas," only the system in which pleas "are the result of an agreement in which the prosecution makes some concessions." See National Advisory Commission on Criminal Justice Standards and Goals (1973).

13. The bureaucratic principles which govern the process would not be considered primary normative principles. Becker (1970: 15) excludes from his definition of courts trial by ordeal, trial by combat, and the Eskimo song duel ("in which victory is the result of singing skill").

14. All three types presented in this paper are ideal types in the Weberian sense. For the best-known use of ideal types in the study of the criminal process, see Herbert L. Packer (1968).

15. As a result, abuses of discretion by police may be more extensive in petty offenses than in serious crimes on which further action is seen by police as more likely.

16. Becker's measures are interview and perception-based. See Becker (1970: 46): If the judges "believe it to be important to tell the interviewer that precedent adherence (objectivity) is significant, this tends to support the view that there is a judicial structure in that society."

17. Such as *observational studies:* Maureen Mileski (1971), and Marek Debicki's unpublished research on the Winnipeg Magistrate's Court; *defendant interviews:* Casper (1972); and *the combination of systematic observation and interviewing:* James Eisenstein and Herbert Jacob's comparative study of criminal court processes (forthcoming).

18. This does not mean judges will knowingly say one thing and do another, but that their perceptions of what they do fail to reflect an analysis of the actual impact of their behavior.

19. Thus explanation of individual behavior has been developed using psychological independent variables; however, explanations of organizational outputs and outcomes use behavioral independent variables.

20. For a sample of such work, see George F. Cole (1972: ch. 8-16, 18). The approach contrasts with that of judicial behavioral analyses of the U.S. Supreme Court.

21. For a report stressing calendar management, see U.S. Congress, Senate Committee on the District of Columbia (1970). Other indicators of the degree of administrative development of trial courts can be obtained from the court census completed by the U.S. Bureau of the Census in 1972 under the sponsorship of the Law Enforcement Assistance Administration.

22. Note, however, that Becker emphasizes the judge's belief in his own independence.

23. Gary Dubin of Los Angeles, formerly associated with the Rand Corporation and National Institute of Law Enforcement and Criminal Justice, has advocated adoption of a regulatory model in a series of unpublished papers.

24. See Thurman W. Arnold (1935: ch. VII) for a commentary on "the sacredness of law enforcement" in that period.

25. For example, Daniel J. Freed (1970: ch. 13, pp. 263-284). As an official in the Justice Department during the Kennedy and Johnson Administrations, Freed was a major force behind the Bail Reform Act of 1966 and other criminal justice programs.

26. Griffiths (1970) collapses Packer's (1968) two models (crime control and due process) into a single "Battle Model." Regarding the goals of a no-fault system of criminal justice, note that the effort in the police and prosecution phase to get accused individuals out of the system contrasts with developments in the corrections phase. Community corrections can be seen as an effort to reduce the weight of punishment while extending the duration of government supervision.

27. In a 1972 national survey of state court budgetary processes, state court administrators (or state chief justices) were asked whether they sought funding from sources other than state appropriations when such appropriations were not forthcoming. Twenty-six of 32 responding state court systems reported seeking non-appropriated funds: eight from additional court fees, 25 from LEAA, six from other federal agencies, and three from private sources. Twenty-one of the 25 court systems which sought LEAA funds received them. Similar findings emerge from responses of county-funded courts in urban areas. (Study conducted by Carl Baar under auspices of the National Center for State Courts.) While LEAA's role is important in state courts, it makes no grants to federal courts. Thus federal trial courts are less subject to pressures toward absorption. At the same time, administrative development is so centralized in the federal system that federal trial courts may be more likely to perform a symbolic function than either a service or a leadership function.

28. Quoting testimony of Edward B. McConnell, Administrative Director of the New Jersey Courts, in U.S. Congress, House, Subcommittee No. 5 of the Committee on the Judiciary (1973: 424).

29. Interview sources, 1972.

30. Quoting correspondence with the author, 1973. In 1972, the Missouri court system was under pressure to participate in an information system directed by the state police. The LEAA saw the system as a prototype for other states. However, the Missouri Supreme Court refused to participate after advice from a court systems consultant that court records would be freely accessible to police and prosecution under the proposal.

31. Between 1970 and 1972, interview sources in Colorado, Illinois, Michigan, and the District of Columbia made references to the emergency planning activities of their courts.

32. Interview sources, 1972.

33. But consider the following statement by U.S. Supreme Court Justice William J. Brennan, Jr., in a 1963 address: At the 1962 "meeting of the American Bar Association a symposium was held on the question whether direct participation of judges in the training of police officers in the rules of the game was feasible. No conclusions were reached, although if there was a consensus it seemed to me to be that the approach involved too large a risk of public suspicion of unseemly cooperation between judges and law enforcement agencies, and so might create doubts of the impartiality of judges as between the government and the accused. Nevertheless this may be an area well worth the thought and study of judges and their organizations . . . " (page 229).

34. Abstracts of all 644 grants are contained in Table 2 of Appendix, Third Annual Report of LEAA, pp. 269-377. Appropriations total is in Table 20, ibid., p. 444.

35. These 21 programs do not include 20 grants for juvenile courts and three grants for Indian courts.

36. Even so, conceptions of guilt remain. Note this statement from the summary of a Texas diversion project: "This program will afford the alleged transgressors an opportunity to redeem themselves without the stigma of criminal conviction" (Third Annual Report of LEAA: 328).

37. In 1972, Senators Quentin Burdick (Dem-No. Dak.), Philip Hart (Dem-Mich.) and Edward Kennedy (Dem-Mass.) co-sponsored Senate Bill 3309 authorizing federal diversion programs within the Department of Justice. No guidelines were included in the legislation for determining how divertees would be selected from among eligible defendants. For two recent monographs supporting diversion programs, see E. Harlow et al. (1971) and Edwin M. Lemert (1971).

38. The two terms are drawn from Emile Durkheim (1947).

39. Third Annual Report of LEAA, Appendix, Table 2. The quote is from discretionary grant 71-DF-812 and is similar to other project summaries for police legal officers. The PLOs have a number of functions, including lecturing at the police academy, a task considered inappropriate for judges (see footnote 33 above).

40. For a discussion of this practice in Chicago, see Donald M. McIntyre (1968).

41. Such prompt trial rules may be within the rule-making power of many trial courts or state court systems, although judicial rules could be superceded by legislative action, as in New York. See W. David Curtiss (1972).

42. Following his election to the bench in 1972, Judge Justin Ravitz of the Detroit Recorder's Court expressed interest in such a proposal. For a criticism of the proliferating number of times judges must intervene in a single criminal case, see Judge William J. Campbell (1972: 231): "We now have eight trials to replace the original one!"

43. An unpublished report on 24-hour arraignment which included legal analysis, empirical data from New York City, and interviews and observation in Detroit was prepared by five University of Michigan students (Mark Goldstein, Dave Goodman, Barbara McLeod, Patty Vidmar, and Ben Wallach) for submission to Judge Justin Ravitz in May 1973.

44. And any amendments to local court rules in Michigan are subject to approval by the Michigan Supreme Court.

45. The quotation and other material quoted in this paragraph are from Task Force on the Criminal Justice System (1972). Hereafter cited: Task Force Report. Later correspondence indicated that information on the lost defendants was leaked to the press by court officials to bring pressure on judges and other system participants to accept change.

46. Task Force Report, recommendation A.6; italics in original.

47. District of Columbia Code Sec. 11-1731 (Supp. IV, 1971).

48. Task Force Report, recommendation D.1.

49. Task Force Report, recommendation B.3.

50. As a result, a major function of probation departments is the preparation of presentence reports for judges. Probation departments are often but not consistently located within trial courts.

51. The three models of urban trial courts proposed in this paper can also be related to the three models of local legal subsystems developed by James R. Klonoski and Robert I. Mendelsohn (1966). While Klonoski and Mendelsohn focus on equality of treatment and level of community satisfaction, the present paper focuses on persistence and significance. In practice, the symbolic trial court would be more closely associated with the exchange or communal models; the service trial court with the elite-bar model. More precise connections would require further study of the relationships between local legal subsystems and criminal justice policy makers at the state, regional, and national levels.

52. An analysis of Congress which makes its persistence problematic might also be useful.

REFERENCES

American Assembly (1965) The Courts, the Public and the Law Explosion. Englewood Cliffs, N.J.: Prentice-Hall.

American Law Institute (1934) A Study of the Business of the Federal Courts. Philadelphia.

AMSTERDAM, A. G. (1972) "The rights of suspects," pp. 402-410 in N. Dorsen (ed.) The Rights of Americans. New York: Random House.

ARNOLD, T. W. (1935) The Symbols of Government. New Haven, Conn.: Yale University Press.

BAN, M. (1973) "Local Courts vs. the Supreme Court: The Impact of Mapp v. Ohio." Paper presented at the Annual Meeting of the American Political Science Association.

BAAR, C. (1972) "The politics of federal judicial independence: the administrative side." Unpublished.

BECKER, T. L. (1970) Comparative Judicial Politics. New York: Rand McNally.

BLUMBERG, A. S. (1967) Criminal Justice. Chicago: Quadrangle.

BRENNAN, W. J., Jr. (1963) "Judicial supervision of criminal law administration." Crime and Delinquency 9 (July), 227.

CAMPBELL, W. J. (1972) "Delays in Criminal Cases." Federal Rules Decision 56, 229.

CASPER, J. D. (1972) American Criminal Justice: The Defendant's Perspective. Englewood Cliffs, N.J.: Prentice-Hall.

COLE, G. F. [ed.] (1972) Criminal Justice: Law and Politics. Belmont, Calif.: Duxbury Press.

COOK, B. B. (1972a) "Perceptions of the independent trial judge role in the seventh circuit." Law and Society Review 6, 615 (May).

——— (1972b) "Role lag in urban trial courts." Western Political Quarterly 25, 234 (June).

CURTISS, W. D. (1972) "Achieving prompt criminal trials in New York." New York State Bar Journal 517 (December).

District of Columbia Courts (1973) District of Columbia Courts 1972 Annual Report.

DOWNIE, L., Jr. (1972) Justice Denied. New York: Penguin.

DURKHEIM, E. (1947) The Division of Labor in Society. New York: Free Press.

EASTON, D. (1965) A Framework for Political Analysis. Englewood Cliffs, N.J.: Prentice-Hall.

EISENSTADT, S. N. (1959) "Bureaucracy, bureaucratization, and debureaucratization." Administrative Science Quarterly 4, 302 (December).

FEELEY, M. M. (1973) "Two models of the criminal justice system: an organizational perspective." Law and Society Review 7, 407 (Spring).

FREED, D. J. (1970) "The nonsystem of criminal justice," pp. 263-284 in J. S. Campbell, J. R. Sahid, and D. P. Stang (eds.) Law and Order Reconsidered. New York: Bantam.

GOLDMAN, S. and T. JAHNIGE (1971) The Federal Courts as a Political System. New York: Harper & Row.

GRIFFITHS, J. (1970) "Ideology in criminal procedure." Yale Law Journal 7, 359 (January).

HARLOW, E., J. R. WEBER and F. COHEN (1971) Diversion From the Criminal Justice System. Rockville, Md.: National Institute of Mental Health, Center for Studies of Crime and Delinquency.

HOLDEN, M., Jr. (1963) "Litigation and the political order." Western Political Quarterly 16, 771.

JAMES, H. (1971) Crisis in the Courts. Rev. ed. New York: David McKay.

KLONOSKI, J. R. and R. I. MENDELSOHN (1966) "The allocation of justice: a political approach." Journal of Public Law 14, 323.

Law Enforcement Assistance Administration (1972) Third Annual Report of the Law Enforcement Assistance Administration, Fiscal Year 1971. Washington, D.C.: Government Printing Office.

LEMERT, E. M. (1971) Instead of Court. Chevy Chase: National Institute of Mental Health, Center for Studies of Crime and Delinquency.

LEVI, E. H. (1970) "The crisis in the nature of law." The Record of the Bar of the City of New York 25, 121 (March).

National Advisory Commission on Criminal Justice Standards and Goals (1973) "Advisory commission overrules courts task force in call to eliminate plea bargaining." Criminal Justice Newsletter 4 (January 22).

McINTYRE, D. M. (1968) "A study of judicial dominance of the charging process. The Journal of Criminal Law, Criminology and Police Science 59, 463 (December).

MERRILL, W. J., M. N. MILKS and M. SENDROW (1973) Case Screening and Selected Case Processing in Prosecutors' Offices. Washington, D.C.: National Institute of Law Enforcement and Criminal Justice.

MILESKI, M. (1971) "Courtroom encounters." Law and Society Review 5, 471 (May).

PACKER, H. L. (1968) The Limits of the Criminal Sanction. Stanford, Calif.: Stanford University Press.

Task Force on the Criminal Justice System (1972) Report of the Chief Judge's Task Force on the Criminal Justice System in the Superior Court of the District of Columbia. (Submitted by H. Paul Haynes, assistant executive officer.)

U.S. Congress, House Committee on Government Operations (1972) Block Grant Programs of the Law Enforcement Assistance Administration. 92d Cong., 2d Sess. (H. Rpt. 92-1072).

U.S. Congress, House Subcommittee No. 5 of the Committee on the Judiciary (1973) Hearings, Law Enforcement Assistance Administration. 93d Cong., 1st Sess.

U.S. Congress, Senate Committee on the District of Columbia (1970) Court Management Study. Part I, Summary. 91st Cong., 2d Sess.

WILSON, J. Q. (1973) "If every criminal knew he would be punished if caught . . . " New York Times Magazine (January 28).

DATE DUE